0 1197 0603882 3

INSIDERS' GUIDE® SERIES

INSIDERS' GUIDE® TO
RICHMOND, VA

FIRST EDITION

MAUREEN EGAN

D0002855

INSIDERS' GUIDE

GUILFORD, CONNECTICUT
AN IMPRINT OF GLOBE PEQUOT PRESS

All the information in this guidebook is subject to change. We recommend that you call ahead to obtain current information before traveling.

To buy books in quantity for corporate use or incentives, call **(800) 962–0973** or e-mail **premiums@GlobePequot.com.**

INSIDERS' GUIDE ®

Copyright © 2010 Morris Book Publishing, LLC

ALL RIGHTS RESERVED. No part of this book may be reproduced or transmitted in any form by any means, electronic or mechanical, including photocopying and recording, or by any information storage and retrieval system, except as may be expressly permitted in writing from the publisher. Requests for permission should be addressed to Globe Pequot Press, Attn: Rights and Permissions Department, P.O. Box 480, Guilford, CT 06437.

Insiders' Guide is a registered trademark of Morris Book Publishing, LLC.

Editor: Kevin Sirois
Project Editor: Kristen Mellitt
Layout Artist: Kevin Mak
Text Design: Sheryl Kober
Maps: Sue Murray © Morris Book Publishing, LLC

Library of Congress Cataloging-in-Publication Data is available on file.

ISBN 978-0-7627-6020-6

Printed in the United States of America
10 9 8 7 6 5 4 3 2 1

CONTENTS

Directory of Maps

ABOUT THE AUTHOR

Maureen Egan is a freelance writer who has lived in and loved Richmond since 1992. Her essays, features, and travel pieces have appeared in the *Christian Science Monitor, Virginia Living, Troika, Richmond Magazine,* and other publications. Her quirky "At Home" column has been featured in the regional home and garden publication *R•Home* since 2003. Get the inside scoop on Richmond at Nothing Ever Happens on My Blog, www.maureenegan.word press.com. See Maureen's essays and travel writing at www.maureenegan.com.

ACKNOWLEDGMENTS

It's said that writing is a solitary profession. Not when you're writing a guidebook.

In the course of researching and writing this book, I've spoken to and met hundreds of people. From antiques shop owners to Realtors to drag racers to park rangers to a GRTC bus driver, everyone I've asked for help has·been so gracious. For some, being nice to the travel writer was just good business, but for others, responding to my calls, e-mails, and increasingly desperate requests was just plain generous. I wish I could thank everyone who has helped with suggestions, expertise, and comments here, but you know I can't. The folks at the Future of Richmond's Past, Venture Richmond, the Richmond Association of Realtors, and the Richmond Metropolitan Convention and Visitors Bureau were especially helpful. To my esteemed tour guides at Monumental Church, the State Capitol, the Virginia Museum of Fine Arts, and so many other wonderful attractions, it was my pleasure to see how much pleasure you take in sharing your knowledge. I am happy to acknowledge my debt to Edward D. Ragan, historian at the Valentine Richmond History Center, for reviewing the Richmond history chapter.

To my pals at *Richmond Magazine* and *R·Home*, who gave me my start in travel writing many years ago, thanks for that and more in the years since. I must also thank the *Richmond Times-Dispatch*. Reading the paper every day as I've done for years built up my store of Richmond lore, and pointed me in the right direction for many events and interesting tidbits that I would have otherwise missed. To everyone who provided suggestions and must-dos, thanks so much. I am especially grateful to those who read certain chapters—Mimi, Carolyn, Carol, Ed, George, Susan, and Peter.

My family and writer friends have been especially put upon during the past few months, yet still offered great tips when I needed them. From the bottom of my heart and the tips of my tapped out typing fingers, thank you Leigh Ann, Erin, Ed, and Deirdre for the excruciating amounts of reading, editing, and enduring you did. You were always right! I'm grateful that such smart people were looking over my shoulder. Thanks, too, to my editors, Kevin Sirois and Kristen Mellitt, at Globe Pequot Press for good humor and even better assistance all the way through. Special thanks go to my city-loving children, Luke and Deirdre, with whom I've discovered many of Richmond's treasures. Finally, heartfelt thanks to my husband, Ed, for his patience, love, and support all along, and for keeping me in chocolate (and occasional other food) these past few months.

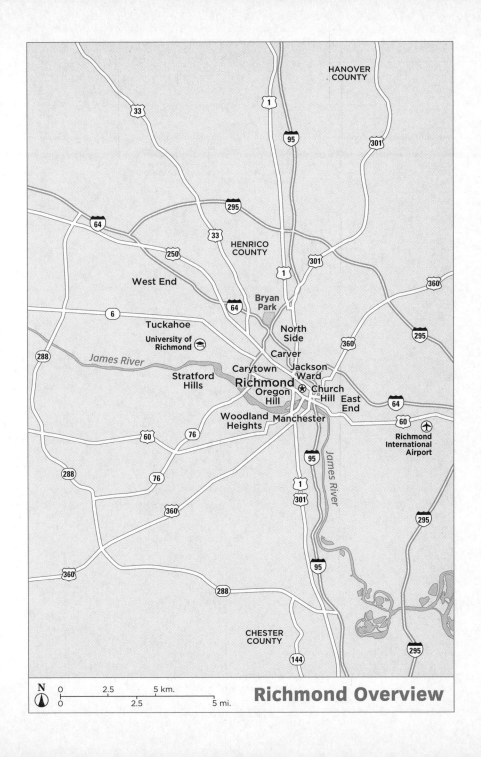

Richmond Overview

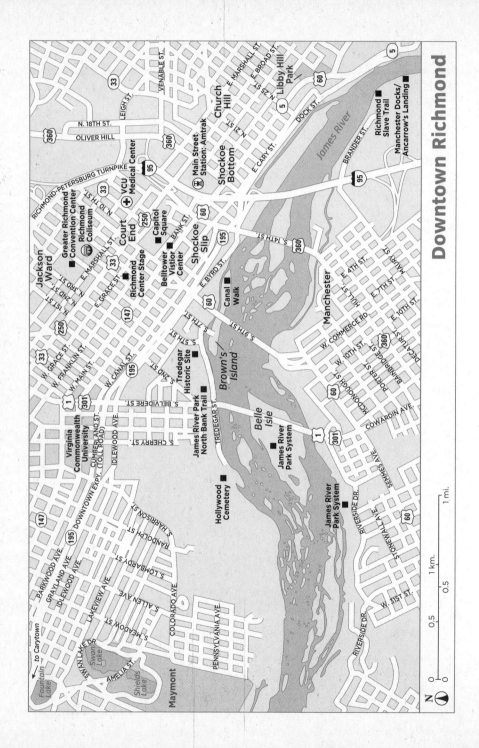

Downtown Richmond

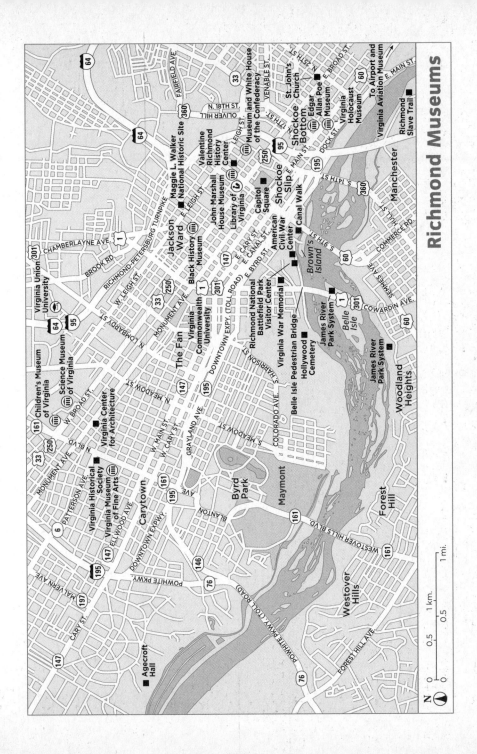

Richmond Museums

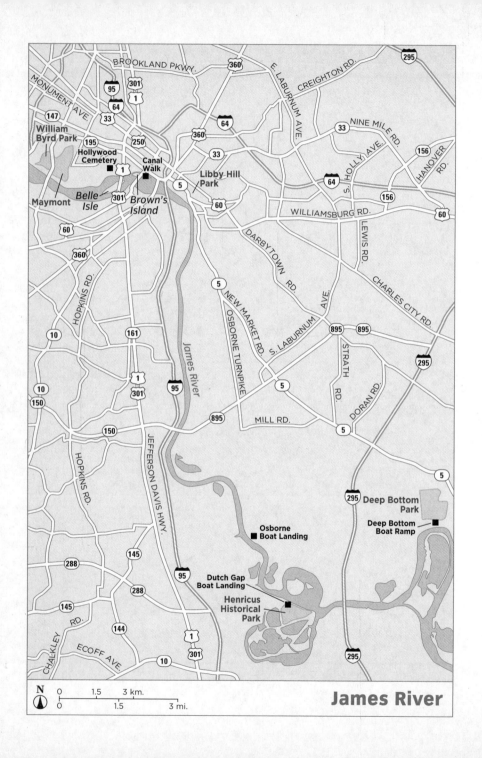

James River

PREFACE

The guy who coined the phrase "pursuit of happiness" spent several years of his life in Richmond. Coincidence? I think not.

I've lived up and down the East Coast, in small towns, big cities, and suburbs, and while I admit there are other fine places to live and visit, I wouldn't want to live anywhere else. Richmond has the advantages of a cosmopolitan city—top-notch museums, historic sites, beautiful and varied architecture, engaged universities, vibrant arts, music, and culinary scenes—and a spectacular setting along the James River that gives the area a natural rush that's not rushed. Go white-water rafting through downtown in the morning and check out the exquisite Virginia Museum of Fine Arts in the afternoon. Dine on everything from barbecue to ethnic specialties to gourmet cuisine in beautifully renovated buildings, trendy hot spots, and beloved dives. The combination of how much there is to do and how easy it is to do it never ceases to amaze me.

Gridlock doesn't exist here. Getting around to where you want to go is a piece of cake—which reminds me, the bakeries are wonderful, too. And the farmers' markets, and the live music, and the unique urban wilderness of the James River Park System. When the Folk Festival takes over downtown every fall, it's magic. For those with high blood pressure, the Rx is to come to Richmond and watch the river run—or run and bike alongside it.

In the 18 years I've lived here, my children have grown into adults, studied Richmond history and architecture, and toured the city by bike, foot, raft, car, and kayak. We've eaten our way all over town, enjoyed the explosion of ethnicity, and visited churches, synagogues, and a mosque.

When my sister moved here with her family a few years ago, I introduced them to some of our favorite haunts. Sometimes I tagged along in their car to see my nephew's reaction to baby goats at Maymont or trains at the Old Dominion Railway Museum. Lucky for you, I won't be in your car—you have this book instead. You can shut it anytime you want me to shut up, then open it back up when you'd like a bit of advice. Everybody's pursuing happiness—Richmond's a great place to grab hold of it.

HOW TO USE THIS BOOK

Well, you've opened it, so that's a start. If I can convince you to keep reading rather than use it as a paperweight, then you're heading in the right direction.

I think Richmond is a wonderful place to live and play and work. I couldn't have written this if I thought otherwise. It's my goal to make you feel welcome and comfortable in Richmond. On my first trip here many years ago, I got lost roaming around with my two small children asleep in the car. I wanted to stop somewhere to buy a map, but we'd had such a rough night I didn't dare stop the car and risk waking them. It wasn't a good feeling wandering around aimlessly relying only on the view out my car windshield to guide me. It eventually worked out fine, but I'd rather you have more to go on when you arrive here for a visit or a move.

Though this is by no means an exhaustive guide to everything you need or want to know about the metropolitan Richmond area, it exhausted me to write it, so I think you should read every word. Some of my best lines are near the end, I swear. Seriously, though, jump around to your heart's content. The "Area Overview" is an introduction to our many separate areas and localities. Read "Getting Here, Getting Around" to learn about traveling here and around town unless you're being chauffeured your entire visit—our roads are quirky. The "History" chapter will give you an appreciation for the good, the bad, and the ugly that has transpired here. The "Accommodations" chapter notes some lovely bed-and-breakfasts in town that offer something different from the hotels listed. If you're staying for a while, you'll find plenty of suggestions as to how to fill your days and nights in the "Attractions" and "Nightlife" chapters, and if kids are involved, there's an entire "Kidstuff" chapter with them in mind. Many of the events listed chronologically in the "Annual Events" chapter are family-friendly; some are even pet-friendly.

If you are in Richmond on business or pleasure, you'll find great restaurants all over the area in the "Restaurants" chapter, including several that are cool nightspots as well, and the "Performing Arts" chapter will point you to many entertaining venues.

I lobbied to include the "A River Runs Through It" chapter because I think it's the key to enjoying and understanding Richmond. I've included multiple suggestions for getting out to enjoy the outdoors in the "Parks," "Recreation," and "A River Runs Through It" chapters. And the "Commemorating the Civil War and Emancipation" chapter highlights the long-overdue and mature approach Richmond is taking to understand and acknowledge its complicated history. It's not all black or white, blue or gray, North or South. You'll see in the "Museums and Art Galleries" chapter just how much a capital of the arts the city is. If you're worried you didn't see your favorite house museum there, don't fret; those are listed in the "Attractions" chapter under Historic Houses. Speaking of those houses, the "Architecture" chapter is an introduction to Richmond's varied and impressive built environment. "Day Trips" will get you out in the mountains to the west, plantations and Williamsburg to the east, or to wineries all over.

Listings include Web sites whenever possible, but to get the latest updates consider checking out the attractions, restaurants, and nightlife spots on Facebook, Twitter, and whatever new social networking site has taken over the world since I wrote this.

Moving to Richmond or already live here? Be sure to check out the blue-tabbed pages at the back of the book, where you will find the **Living Here** appendix with sections on relocation, real estate, education, and health care. Combing through the "Relocation" chapter in conjunction with the "Area Overview" chapter ought to give you the lay of the land.

If you find any errors as you go along, I'm sorry about that. It would help the next edition if you would inform us of any errors or omissions. Please drop us a line at Insiders Guide to Richmond, GPP, P.O. Box 480, Guilford, CT 06437-0480 or at editorial@globepequot.com.

AREA OVERVIEW

Richmond sits in central Virginia, at the fall line of the James River, which means Class IV (and sometimes V) white-water rushes right through downtown. But the vibe of the area is anything but rushed. It's sophisticated yet friendly, and an uncomplicated place to navigate.

The city of Richmond, the capital of the Commonwealth of Virginia, is 62.5 square miles and has a population just over 200,000—small for a big city (and part of our charm, no doubt)—because Virginia's peculiar laws mandate that cities are separate entities from the counties that surround them. So there's Richmond, the actual city, and then there's Richmond the region, which is much larger—2,000 square miles with 975,000 people—and includes the big three counties of Chesterfield, Henrico, and Hanover and the much less populated rural counties of Goochland, Powhatan, and New Kent. The even larger (5,700 square miles) Richmond Metropolitan Statistical Area (MSA), which contains several other localities, including the city of Petersburg to the south, bumps the population to 1.2 million. The region's population surged 12.3 percent from the year 2000 through the first half of June 2009. That growth will likely continue as, among other factors, the expansion of the U.S. Army's Fort Lee base near Petersburg brings in new residents to the southern part of the Richmond region.

Richmond, Chesterfield, and Henrico are among the most populous localities in Virginia, with both counties outnumbering the city's population. The region's ethnic diversity continues to grow as rising numbers of Asians, Hispanics, and Latinos move to the area. The area as a whole is approximately 65 percent white, 30 percent black, and 5 percent Hispanic, Asian, and Native American. Richmond's population is more balanced with 44 percent white, 52 percent black, and 6 percent Hispanic, Native American, Asian-American, and Pacific Islander. The median age of residents is 37.

OVERVIEW

Much of what distinguishes Richmond from other parts of the country sits within the city limits. There's the James River, for one thing, and parks and trails that led *Trail Runner* magazine to rank Richmond one of the country's top seven cities for trail runners in 2009. And there's the varied architecture; historic sites spanning four centuries; world-class museums, art galleries, and theaters; excellent local restaurants; unique shopping districts; and three dynamic universities. We pack a lot into 62 square miles, but you won't feel crowded here. Beyond the city limits, suburbia, farmland, rivers, and lakes are all within reach, so just about any kind of lifestyle is possible in our region, and the 24-minute average commute leaves residents time to enjoy the area. Richmond founder William Byrd II had it right back in 1737 when he boasted that his newly laid-out town just below the falls featured "a pleasant and healthy situation . . . well-supplied with springs and good water." That remains true today.

Most of the attractions and activities highlighted in this book are within the city limits of Richmond because that is where most of the action is. Having said that, more people in the region live in the surrounding counties than within the city, so the most populous counties of Chesterfield, Henrico, and Hanover deserve a fair share of attention, too, with occasional shout-outs to our friends in Goochland, Powhatan, New Kent, and Charles City counties as well as Petersburg. Though our boundaries are plentiful, it can be hard to tell exactly which locality you are in at any given moment, so the organization of the book will try to keep things simple by using the James River as a geographical marker. This and some other chapters will begin north of the river, downtown, and circle around many of the city's distinct areas, and then head to city neighborhoods south of the river. Then we'll head back to the counties north of the river, Henrico and Hanover—first with Henrico because it borders the city to the west, north, and east. We'll zero in on specific regions within these large localities, and then head south of the James River to look at Chesterfield. Finally, we'll take a gander at the outlying rural counties of Goochland and New Kent, both

north of the James, and Powhatan, south of the river.

A few tips before you get in the car. Postal addresses in Richmond are notoriously unhelpful in terms of decoding where a place actually is. Many residences and businesses are officially listed with Richmond addresses but aren't actually within city limits. A Glen Allen address could mean a place in Henrico or Hanover County. Bon Air straddles both Richmond and Chesterfield. You could probably get a speeding ticket in three localities within a mile if you tried hard enough—not that I'm recommending that. There's the Near West End, the West End, and the Far West End, but no official rules for what that means. Luckily, the area is not so large that you can't figure it out as well as we ever have.

CLIMATE

With an average high temperature of 45 degrees Fahrenheit in January, winter doesn't usually drag on so long here, though try telling that to anyone during the unusually snowy winter of 2009–10. The climate is classified as modified continental with an average rainfall of 43.16 inches and snowfall of 14 inches. Honestly, our typically mild winters are usually interspersed with warm days that bring out the runners. Spring, summer, and fall give us plenty of opportunities to dine al fresco at our great array of restaurants. The good news is that four months, June through September, have an average high of 80 or above, but the bad news is that the high humidity, especially in July and August, might just curl your hair. Still, our region revels in each of our four distinct seasons.

RICHMOND

Downtown

As the seat of city government, the state capital of Virginia, the site of the Federal Court of Appeals for the Fourth Circuit, and the headquarters for the Fifth District of the Federal Reserve Bank, Richmond has a few things going on downtown. Federal, state, and city governments are major players in the local economy. City Hall is within spitting distance of Capitol Square (not that I'm trying to start any trouble), where the governor lives and the legislature is supposed to be working to improve Virginians' lives, and of course many state and city workers do the heavy lifting in nearby office buildings. Lawyers, lobbyists, and financial folk fill the many office towers downtown. Not far from Capitol Square, Virginia Commonwealth University Medical Center, made up of several hospitals, clinics, and five health-profession schools, spreads north, east, and west for several blocks until it meets up with the Virginia Biotechnology Research Park, which is exactly the point. Collaboration among more than 50 different entities working at the park—VCU researchers, nonprofits such as United Network for Organ Sharing (UNOS), government labs such as the Virginia Division of Forensic Science, early-stage companies and established ones such as Philip Morris—is spurring development of scientific breakthroughs, products, and jobs. In this area of downtown, 12,000 people work in the life sciences, engaged in research, teaching, education, and patient care.

But downtown is not all work and no play. The arts are evident here with Richmond CenterStage, home of the stunning Carpenter Theatre and the smaller Gottwald Playhouse, the nearby Richmond Coliseum, and the hipper, more intimate music venue the National, which draw artists such as Tyler Perry and Elvis Costello. New and renovated hotels have opened to keep up with the nearby Greater Richmond Convention Center's schedule. The visual arts have their day every first Friday of the month when the popular Art Walk livens up Broad Street and neighboring streets at night. And down toward the James River, the historic Tredegar Civil War site intertwines history and nature. Brown's Island and the Canal Walk connect with Shockoe Bottom, and a pedestrian bridge offers easy access to Belle Isle and the many-splendored James River Park System. The Federal Reserve Bank, Dominion Resources, NewMarket, and MeadWestvaco are all well positioned with buildings overlooking the falls of the James.

Shockoe Bottom and Shockoe Slip

Shockoe Slip and Shockoe Bottom, the old commercial districts of the city, are sometimes referred to as the Slip and the Bottom. With proximity to downtown offices, government buildings, hotels, and restaurants, this cobblestoned area is popular with business folk and visitors. It's also the headquarters of the Martin Agency. You likely know its Geico gecko; you might not know that industry magazine *Adweek* named it the No. 1 advertising agency in the U.S. for 2009. Both the Slip and Bottom retain many late 19th-century brick warehouses now renovated into luxury apartments, restaurants, and stores. The Bottom, below Shockoe Slip, includes other historic buildings as well, including Main Street Station, the 17th Street Farmers' Market, and the Edgar Allan Poe Museum. The Bottom doesn't live in the past, however, and features new high-rise condos, bustling shops and restaurants, and a happening nightclub scene

Richmond Vital Statistics

Founded: 1737 (incorporated 1742)

Area code: 804

Population (in 2009 est.): 204,451 inside the city limits; 907,469 adding in Chesterfield, Hanover, and Henrico counties; 1.2 million in the Richmond MSA, which includes suburbs and other cities such as Petersburg.

Nicknames: RVA, River City

Average temperatures: Jan: 45° Fahrenheit (high), 28° (low); July: 88° (high), 68° (low)

Average annual rainfall: 43.16 inches rainfall; 14 inches snowfall

Major commercial airport: Richmond International Airport (RIC)

Cities and counties in the Richmond Metropolitan Statistical Area: City of Richmond; counties of Chesterfield, Henrico, Hanover, Goochland, Powhatan, New Kent, Louisa, Amelia, Caroline, Charles City, Cumberland, Dinwiddie, King and Queen, King William, Prince George, and Sussex; and cities of Petersburg, Colonial Heights, and Hopewell.

Major colleges and universities: Virginia Commonwealth University, University of Richmond, Virginia Union University, Randolph-Macon College, Virginia State University, J. Sargeant Reynolds Community College, John Tyler Community College, Union Presbyterian Seminary, Baptist Theological Seminary.

Major area businesses: Virginia Commonwealth University Health System, Capital One, Car-Max, HCA Virginia Health System, Bon Secours Richmond Health System, Altria Group, Mead-Westvaco Corp., The Martin Agency, Dominion Resources Inc., Brink's Co., SunTrust Banks Inc., DuPont, Genworth Financial Inc., Massey Energy, Owens & Minor, WellPoint, Federal Reserve Bank of Richmond, NewMarket Corp., Wells Fargo and Co., Honeywell International Inc., Pfizer Inc., SuperValu Inc., Markel Corporation, Hunton & Williams LLP, Universal Corporation.

at various music venues. Heading south lands you on the 1¼-mile Canal Walk, where the six-acre Reynolds site is about to be turned into apartments and mixed-use facilities. Here's hoping that will add some life to the scenic but often empty Canal Walk. East of the Canal Walk is Tobacco Row, old brick warehouses that have been renovated into apartments, offices, and restaurants. The Capital to Capital Bike Trail begins here and follows the river east a bit. Eventually it will wind by the mixed-use riverside development of Rockett's Landing and mirror VA 5 all the way to Williamsburg, which was the colonial capital of Virginia.

Church Hill

Home of the view that led William Byrd II to name our town Richmond and capped by St. John's Church, Church Hill is steeped in history. East of downtown, reached by East Broad Street primarily, it once was the center of residential Richmond. Walking the streets here transports you to another time, thanks

Daily newspaper: *Richmond Times-Dispatch,* www.timesdispatch.com

Alternative newsweekly: *Style Weekly,* www.styleweekly.com

Sales tax: 5 percent

Hotel tax: 8 percent

Famous sons and daughters: Historical figures Henry Clay, Patrick Henry, Thomas Jefferson, Oliver Hill, Maggie L. Walker; dancer/entertainer Bill "Bojangles" Robinson; politicians Eric Cantor and L. Douglas Wilder; tennis champion and activist Arthur Ashe; actors Warren Beatty and Shirley MacLaine; musicians Jason Mraz, Elliott Yamin, and Aimee Mann; writers Tom Wolfe, Tom Robbins, Edgar Allan Poe, James Branch Cabell, Ellen Glasgow, Douglas Southall Freeman; Skull-A-Day artist Noah Scalin; athletes Darren Sharper, Fran Tarkenton, Denny Hamlin, Justin Verlander; designer Charlotte Moss.

Famous residents: First elected African-American governor in the U.S., L. Douglas Wilder; Democratic national chairman Tim Kaine; musician D'Angelo (Michael Archer); actors/producers Tim Reid and Daphne Maxwell Reid; writers David Baldacci and Phyllis Theroux; NFL Hall of Famer Willie Lanier; fictional medical examiner Kay Scarpetta.

Fifteen minutes of YouTube fame:
"River City Richmond." An amusing rap video introducing you to River City: "Yo, this is Richmond."
"YouTube—Elliott Yamin—Richmond." His *American Idol* homecoming and a performance.
"Exploring the James River Park." A video from University of Richmond students.
"Miss Virginia Crowned 2010 Miss America." Caressa Cameron, a junior at Virginia Commonwealth University, wins the crown.

to the concentration of 19th-century homes and devoted rehabbers. Coffee shops, restaurants, parks (for people and dogs), and the Chimborazo Medical Museum—part of Richmond National Battlefield Park—add to the ambience, and proximity to downtown's offerings makes it an ideal place to buy a condo or single-family home.

Jackson Ward and Carver

Jackson Ward, just north of Broad Street downtown, bounded by 3rd Street to the east, was known as the Harlem of the South in the mid-20th century. Though it was split in two by I-95 in the early 1960s, it still is a center of African-American culture with the Black History Museum and Cultural Center and the Maggie L. Walker National Historic Site here. Its concentration of ornate cast iron is second only to New Orleans. Row houses from the 19th- and 20-centuries are being renovated, and the historic Hippodrome Theater will get a new lease on life as a music venue when its renovations are

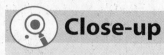 **Close-up**

Virginia Commonwealth University's Transformation of Downtown

During the nearly 20-year tenure of recently retired VCU president Eugene P. Trani, Virginia Commonwealth University built $1.2 billion of projects in the city, contributing mightily to the university's continuing growth in numbers and stature, as well as to the city's. Now the largest university in the commonwealth, with more than 32,000 students and 18,000-plus employees, more than a few things have changed since VCU was created in 1968 by merging Richmond Professional Institute (with its already successful art program founded by Theresa Pollak and its renowned social work program) and the respected Medical College of Virginia (which dates back to 1838). It didn't hurt that in 2002 VCU professor John B. Fenn shared a Nobel Prize for chemistry, or that men's basketball star Eric Maynor sunk that shot to beat Duke in the 2007 NCAA tournament. Such accomplishments do wonders for a university's ego.

People who live in Richmond's suburbs aren't as likely to appreciate what VCU has done for the city until they drive down streets that weren't part of the urban university at all back when it was almost entirely a commuter school. See the transformation of West Broad Street by the Sports Medicine building, the School of the Arts building, the Siegel Center, and the new dorms. Those are just some of the effects of VCU's $105 million of development in the Broad Street corridor, which in turn led to another $100 million in private development, including apartments, condos, retail, and restaurants. Turn right on Belvidere and see the School of Engineering, then left on Cary to see the new School of Business building, which includes engineering's East Hall, and then there's the Brandcenter building. Continue to the MCV campus to see the enormous

completed. This area's proximity to downtown and the convention center makes it that much more attractive to those wanting a piece of the action. Carver, just west of Jackson Ward, is becoming a neighborhood where VCU students live alongside longtime residents. Here industrial buildings mix with Romanesque and Queen Anne homes.

The Fan and Oregon Hill

The tree-lined streets of the Fan, with a tremendous concentration of Victorian architecture, fan out (hence the name) from Monroe Park as they head westward to the Boulevard. In this area, the home of

VCU's Monroe Park Campus—where undergraduate and graduate students enroll in programs such as engineering, business, and the humanities as well as the university's renowned School of the Arts—the energy is palpable throughout the retail stores along West Grace Street and West Broad, and when there's a big game at VCU's Stuart C. Siegel Center. The dynamism fuels the Fan's art scene, performing arts venues, and restaurants and bars. The Uptown section, adjacent to VCU on West Main Street, is home to numerous brightly painted businesses, restaurants, and art galleries. With stores sprinkled throughout this diverse neighborhood, walkable living is just

Critical Care Hospital that is just the latest state-of-the-art building down there. More is coming, on both campuses, under the leadership of current president Michael Rao, including a new English/social work building in the works on Floyd Avenue and a new medical school building downtown.

There are some residents, especially in the Carver and Oregon Hill communities, who think of VCU as an 800-pound gorilla in their midst, but no one would want to see Broad Street return to what it was 10 years ago. The attendant apartments, shops, restaurants, and coffeehouses have brought life to an area that needed it. VCU, caretaker of 40 19th-century buildings, has also poured $9.64 million into renovating and improving them.

The life sciences have been a strong suit for decades, and VCU's graduates have enriched our area by staying and starting their careers here, making Richmond a top-notch place for health care. Creating VCU's engineering school played off Richmond's strength in the life sciences, and in concert with the Virginia BioTechnology Research Park, was built in response to Richmond's business community saying, "We need this here." In time it's expected that the engineers will have a transformative effect on the area, much as VCU's other graduates have in the arts and sciences. Certainly, the area's physical and mental well-being owes much to the thousands of local health-care providers educated at VCU's Medical College of Virginia campus. The graduate programs in the School of the Arts rank fourth overall in the country behind Rhode Island School of Design, Yale, and the School of the Art Institute of Chicago, and No. 1 among public graduate schools. The school has a positive effect on Richmond's health, too, by making us enjoy the arty side of life. The art students and faculty are a main factor in Richmond's emergence as an arts town, as a place where creativity thrives. Just go to First Fridays downtown and you'll see a region that loves its art scene.

one of the advantages of the area; porch sitting is another. The Fan is a popular spot for families living in row houses, who enjoy the numerous pocket parks and acclaimed restaurants. Monument Avenue is a world unto itself, grand and gracious, lined with a mélange of architectural styles from Tudor Revival to Italianate to Arts and Crafts, and on and on. Though mostly residential, some of the mansions house businesses. One is the Virginia Center for Architecture, which will get a nod in the "Museums" chapter. The famous (or infamous) portion of Monument Avenue sports the biggest second-place trophies you'll ever see. See more about it in the "Attractions" chapter.

Back toward the Downtown Expressway, Oregon Hill is a mostly working-class neighborhood that has become popular with VCU students. Its wooden frame houses once housed factory workers, but new housing has taken advantage of the neighborhood's proximity to the river. The area has a couple of interesting restaurants and beautiful Hollywood Cemetery, where U.S. presidents James Monroe and John Tyler are buried.

North Side

North of Broad Street, from North Boulevard and Hermitage Road to a little bit past the Henrico County line, North Side neighborhoods sport early-20th-century architecture that provides character and quirky stores and restaurants that add a lively vibe. The historic trolley-car suburb Ginter Park is a charming mix of early architectural styles on half-acre lots, as is idyllic Laburnum Park. Bellevue, just off Hermitage Road, has some of the loveliest Arts and Crafts homes in the city, and to the east Highland Park has an astounding array of Queen Anne–style homes, many of which are being renovated. More modest homes in Battery Park take advantage of the recently renovated park, which has the courts where Arthur Ashe learned to play tennis. With two seminaries in the area, Union Presbyterian and Baptist Theological, and Virginia Union University, students add all kinds of spirit to the area. North Side gets lots of visitors because the Diamond is where you'll find the baseball-playing Richmond Flying Squirrels and Movieland at Boulevard Square opened a brand new movie theater. Picturesque Bryan Park, Pine Camp Arts Center, and the Arthur Ashe Center are also draws. Some sections of North Side, especially along Chamberlayne Avenue, are a bit downtrodden, but the First Tee golf complex nearby adds some green space.

Carytown and Museum District

This hopping retail district shooting straight down a one-way section of West Cary Street just west of the Boulevard is Richmond's reply to every mall out there. This is the way we like to shop; we love a place of our own. One mile of retail and restaurants keeps chugging along, even as some old friends move on. There's always someone else wanting to add to the hip factor of Carytown. Jewelers, women's fashions and accessories, home furnishings, antiques, artsy gifts, a hip knitting store, running store, toy store, and

the historic (and cheap) Byrd Theatre attract the young and old to Carytown. It's the site of several festivals, including the most fun you can have in August, the Carytown Watermelon Festival, which gets noticed in the "Annual Events" chapter.

The Museum District borders Carytown and is home to lovely old townhomes, B&Bs, and the biggest and best museum in town (and Virginia and lots of other places, too), the Virginia Museum of Fine Arts. It and the neighboring Virginia Historical Society make this area a major tourist destination. Some handy retail and very good restaurants are sprinkled throughout the neighborhood.

West End

This very Richmond section west of Carytown between the river and Broad Street is residential, with some classy neighbors such as several house museums (covered in the "Attractions" chapter) and the University of Richmond, one of the leading private liberal arts schools in the country. The university just straddles the Henrico County line. With the addition of the Modlin Center for the Arts and a new football stadium, UR gives the community many and varied reasons to visit the campus. Windsor Farms and nearby neighborhoods that back up to the river are classic old Richmond. They are stately and sedate, and affluent like much, but not all, of the area. Apartments not far from Carytown are handy places to live since you're able to walk to restaurants and shops. Going west on Grove brings you to the fashionable Libbie/Grove retail and restaurant district. There's a movie theater that shows artsy films, or you can head down Cary Street to the River Road Shopping Center. The well-manicured and rolling University of Richmond campus sports a classic, liberal arts

school look—Gothic and brick and beautifully designed. It's nestled among lovely
neighborhoods, and its small lake attracts
fowl and families in equal measure.

South of the James

Manchester/South Side

Manchester used to be its own town and
is getting back on the map now because
of a vibrant mix of arts and culture with
the Plant Zero Art Center, Dogtown Dance
Theatre, and more residential development.
Rambling along the flood wall, this area is
welcoming back the Old Dominion Railway Museum and is gaining restaurants and
residents because of the cool renovations
of old warehouses and factories. Further to
the east along the south side of the James
is the currently underused Port of Richmond
in an industrial area. Heading down a gritty
section of US 1/US 301 you'll see Philip
Morris USA's manufacturing center, where
it has consolidated all of its cigarette manufacturing facilities in the U.S., and the ever-
expanding McGuire Veterans Affairs Medical
Center. Other manufacturing, including the
DuPont Spruance Plant, is down US 1 in
South Richmond.

Woodland Heights/Forest Hill/ Westover Hills

We are still in the city here, but it's harder to
tell as you turn off the Lee Bridge onto Riverside Drive in Woodland Heights. Never far
from the river or the James River Park System,
this area rolls along banks of the river and
surrounds newly renovated Forest Hill Park,
which hosts the popular South of the James
Farmers' Market on Saturday mornings. Early-
to mid-20th-century homes on small lots are
the norm here, with a charming mix of architectural styles. Neighborhood restaurants

and coffee shops on Forest Hill Avenue are
beloved, as is the ease of access into other
parts of the city via the Boulevard, Lee, and
Manchester bridges.

Stratford Hills/Stony Point

Just off Forest Hill Avenue to the west of the
Powhite Parkway, Stratford Hills is home to
the almost too popular Pony Pasture Rapids
section of the James River Park System and
has homes on tree-covered and in many
cases hilly one-acre lots. Retail along Forest Hill Avenue continues to grow, and off
Chippenham Parkway sits the high-end yet
pet-friendly Stony Point Fashion Park mall
with the area's only Saks and CineBistro.
Other stores and restaurants inhabit the Bon
Air/Stony Point section near the intersection
of Forest Hill Avenue and Huguenot Road.
Condos and apartments are available in
all three areas, though single-family homes
predominate.

SUBURBS NORTH OF THE JAMES

Henrico County

Henrico sprawls on top of Richmond, along
I-64 from the westernmost portion of I-295,
to the east all the way over past Richmond
International Airport, and beyond I-295
there. No wonder it has to be spoken of in
either West End or East End terms, with I-95
being the dividing line. The county added
34,190 new residents between 2000 and
2009. Henrico County is home to more
Fortune 500 headquarters in the area than
any other locality, all of them in the West
End, which is likely why it's home to some
very nice hotels, including a Westin and a
new Hilton, the shopping mecca of Short
Pump, and many affluent and middle-class

neighborhoods. The East End has Richmond International Airport and a much more rural feel, though development has come and the pressure for more will increase.

Near West End

The section of the county that borders the University of Richmond and heads out River and Three Chopt Roads until Parham Road is dotted with lovely older homes on rolling hills. Patterson Avenue is one retail corridor for this section, Gayton and Gaskins Roads another, and the Regency Square shopping mall anchors still another. These are quite desirable neighborhoods, and many are architecturally interesting.

Glen Allen

This is an amorphous area, and it's hard to know where it begins and ends, as it straddles the Hanover County line. Parts of Glen Allen are along US 1 north of Richmond, with a mix of older and newer neighborhoods. No matter where you are, though, you're still in one of the "Best 100 Places to Live," according to *Money Magazine* in 2009. The closer you get to Virginia Center Commons, a large mall just off I-95, newer residential areas predominate in the I-295 corridor. Staples Mill Road is a booming retail and residential area out beyond the almost hidden Amtrak station there. J. Sargeant Reynolds Community College's Parham Road campus is not far from I-95. On West Broad Street near the I-64 interchange is the corporate headquarters of Altria. Innsbrook, just off I-295 and I-64 in the Far West End, is the county's premier business park, with more than one hundred buildings on 850 acres. Many corporate headquarters, including Markel's, are here, along with hotels and medical offices, and there's a popular concert series, Innsbrook

After Hours, in the warm weather. This is one business park that actually has some park-like features, such as trees, three lakes, and 3 miles of jogging trails, plus lots of community events.

Short Pump

You're in the Far West End now, no doubt about it—out near where I-295, I-64 and VA 288 converge. Marketers have dubbed it Downtown Short Pump, but they're not fooling anybody. It's a bunch of shopping malls and centers with planned communities off on side streets. It looks like so many other parts of the U.S., which might explain why many newcomers feel at home here right away. The traffic is a bit of a bear (for the Richmond area anyway) along West Broad Street, a combination of drivers going to the mall and heading home, I suppose, but some people love living here in the middle of the highest concentration of stores in the area, including the high-end mall, Short Pump Town Center, home to Nordstrom, Macy's, Dillard's, Crate & Barrel, Pottery Barn, and more of the usual suspects. New hotels, including a Hilton, a Hotel Sierra, and the youthful Aloft have gotten in on the action here recently. Planned communities such as the mixed-use West Broad Village, which seems to have recovered from a bit of a standstill, offer an array of options for living.

East End

The East End of Henrico has a more rural feel than Henrico's West End, more disconnected from downtown even though it's not far at all. Because it hosts **Richmond International Airport,** the immediate area of Sandston has some light industrial and manufacturing. The area right around the airport has several hotels, as is to be expected, but there isn't as much in the way of restaurants and shopping in this end of the county, with the exception of the Laburnum Avenue corridor and its addition of The Shoppes of White Oak Village, which has a Target, Lowe's, and J.C. Penney, among others. Nearby Varina has gone from almost entirely rural to more suburban in a short time, and that doesn't sit well with many residents. Rockett's Landing, an in-progress riverside mixed-use development, is partly in Henrico County and partly in Richmond. North of the airport takes you into Highland Springs, an older community with modest homes. Going north on Laburnum Avenue leads you to a faster-paced place, Richmond International Raceway, a huge economic engine for the area, hosting two NASCAR weekends a year and several home, camping, and boat expos. Civil War sites, including the Dabbs House Museum, which doubles as a regional visitor center, are found throughout the East End.

Hanover County

Spreading above I-64, and bisected by both I-95 and I-295, Hanover County is the largest geographic locality in the Richmond Metropolitan Statistical Area at 470 square miles, and it's a popular place to settle if you want the feel of the country but like easy riding to the city. Eighty percent of Hanover is planned for rural conservation, rural residential, and agricultural use. How else do you expect them to keep cranking out those luscious and famous Hanover tomatoes? The rest of the county, generally those sections closer to Richmond, has a more suburban feel. Some parts of Hanover are as close as 5 miles to the city, but more often than not it's more like 12 to 15 miles away. Across the county there are 34 nationally registered historic sites, including Scotchtown to the west of Ashland, Patrick Henry's home for a time. Though there is more to Hanover County than just Mechanicsville, Hanover Courthouse, and Ashland—including, of course, Kings Dominion, the mega-fun amusement park in Doswell that adds excitement, two million visitors, and jobs to the northern end of the county—most county businesses, stores, and residences are concentrated around those three areas.

Mechanicsville/Cold Harbor

The area of Mechanicsville, with convenient access to I-95 and I-295, has a great quality of life that made it an easy pick in *Money Magazine*'s 2009 list of *"100 Best Places to Live."* The smaller Hanover County Airport sits just off I-95 in an industrial park. Owens & Minor, a Fortune 500 company, has its headquarters and distribution facilities in Mechanicsville. Another Fortune 500 company, SuperValu, has its eastern distributing facilities in the area, and Media General, parent company of the *Richmond Times-Dispatch*, operates its newspaper printing plant near I-295. Bon Secours Memorial Regional Medical Center is the county's No. 1 employer and ranks high in patient care. Neighborhoods of single-family homes, some in wooded developments with rolling hills, others with more modest ranch houses and some apartments and condos, fill in the area between I-95, US 301, and US 360 (Mechanicsville Turnpike). US 301 and US 360 are the main retail corridors, with strip malls providing groceries and other basics. The area is home to several Civil War battlefields, most notably Cold Harbor, where the National Park Service has a staffed visitor center open every day. For those interested in this century, I-295 gives the county easy access to Richmond

International Airport and the beach via I-64. Pole Green Park adds plenty of green space in the eastern section of the county.

Hanover Courthouse

This area is loaded with nationally registered historic sites, including the actual courthouse where Patrick Henry once practiced law. Across the street from the courthouse is Hanover Tavern, which now houses restaurants and a branch of the Barksdale Theatre. This area has Hanover's newest high school, and the nearby parks, along with access from US 301 for boaters on the South Anna and Pamunkey Rivers, make it easy to get out and enjoy nature here. For those who like to wander inside, there are many antiques shops along the US 301 corridor, which you can read about in the "Antiques" chapter, so you can take some history home with you.

Ashland

The "center of the universe" to its 6,000 residents at least, Ashland is an incorporated town right smack in the middle of Hanover County, loaded with great restaurants and quaint shops. Randolph-Macon College brings energy to the charming town, and Amtrak rolls right through and makes several stops a day here. The Ashland Strawberry Faire every May and a Fourth of July celebration that merits coverage in the "Annual Events" chapter are the sort of events that bring in visitors who wish they lived here. Dominion Resources' GreenTech Business Technology Incubator opened in Ashland in early 2010 with the mission of helping start-up companies specializing in energy efficiency and green technology grow and produce jobs. It's a partnership with Hanover County and Virginia Biosciences Development Center of Richmond, as well. Visible

from I-95, Bass Pro Shops with its Richmond region visitor center has made the Winding Brook development a destination within the Ashland zip code.

SUBURBS SOUTH OF THE JAMES

Chesterfield County

Chesterfield is the state's fourth most populous entity and the most populous in the Richmond region. From 2000 to June 2009, the county's population grew 18.3 percent to 307,594. I suppose being between the James River to the north and the Appomattox River to the south, with Lake Chesdin adjacent, doesn't exactly hurt recruiting. The county is a mix of affluent neighborhoods, a few places with a village feel, and rural areas. You can pick strawberries, blueberries, and pumpkins in Chesterfield still. You can also go to the Metro Richmond Zoo, which started small but continues to grow. Chesterfield is also home to two campuses of John Tyler Community College, and Virginia State University is in southern Chesterfield. Of all the big four localities, Chesterfield, because of its proximity to Fort Lee in neighboring Prince George County, will see the greatest population gains with the base realignment that is adding 30,000 new people to the U.S. Army base over the next few years. Associated with that or not, growth continues to surge along several county intersections with VA 288, with more retail development and planned communities on the way.

Bon Air

This is a quaint neighborhood that straddles the city line. Once a summer retreat for Richmond's wealthy residents because of that good air, Bon Air's Victorian homes along Buford Road's tree-lined hills create an

Visitor Information

Richmond Region Visitor Info
www.visitrichmondva.com

Main Visitor Center and Gift Shop
Greater Richmond Convention Center
405 N. 3rd St.
(804) 783-7450

Airport Visitor Center
Richmond International Airport
Lower Level—Baggage Claim Area
(804) 236-3260

Bass Pro Shops Visitor Center
11550 Lakeridge Parkway
Ashland
(804) 615-5412

Dabbs House Visitor Center
3812 Nine Mile Rd.
(804) 652-3406

Ashland/Hanover Visitors Center
112 N. Railroad Ave.
(804) 752-6766

Virginia Travel Information Centers
At Virginia visitor centers, the staff can help you with suggestions, regional maps, and hotel reservations. Gift shops have merchandise with the famous "Virginia is for Lovers" slogan, as well as other souvenirs. If you are the last-minute type and need same-day reservations, they'll help you find a room in a pinch.

Bell Tower Visitor Center on Capitol Square
101 N. 9th St.
(804) 545-5586

Bracey Welcome Center
I-85 North, mile marker 1
(434) 689-2295

Fredericksburg Virginia Welcome Center
I-95 South, mile marker 132
(540) 786-8344

Virginia Welcome Center at Skippers
I-95 North, mile marker 0
(434) 634-4113

---

old-time feel. Bon Air does share some stores and restaurants with city residents, such as those at Stony Point Shopping Center and Buford Road Shopping Center.

Midlothian

This is one of Richmond's most popular and largest suburbs because of its easy access to the city along the Powhite Parkway, US 60, and US 360 all the way from VA 288. Retail development continues to spread throughout the suburb to the west. There are many different sides to Midlothian, from the park-like established neighborhoods closer to

the city to the first planned communities in the region, now old-timers, Brandermill and Woodlake around Swift Creek Reservoir, and the newer ones such as Roseland, all in the Hull Street (US 360) area, a major retail corridor. Midlothian Turnpike (US 60) is another major retail artery, and it includes Chesterfield Towne Center on its way out to the village of Midlothian. Neighborhoods out here are often filled with single family homes on wooded lots, but several developments feature townhomes and condos. A campus of John Tyler Community College, Bon Secours St. Francis Hospital, and of course VA 288 have all been integral in bringing a boom to this neck of the woods.

VA 288 continues to spur development farther out, including the mixed-use Westchester Commons. The $100 million Sports-Quest complex has broken ground on a 250-acre multisport training site near VA 288 and the Powhite Parkway, the first phase of which is scheduled to open late 2010. SportsQuest hopes to lure Olympic athletes to train here in speed skating, cycling, swimming, and other sports, and it will offer memberships and programs to the general public.

Chesterfield Courthouse/Southern Chesterfield

Ukrop Park, a 34-acre soccer facility used by the Richmond Kickers youth teams, is near the intersection of Chippenham Parkway and VA 10, just a few miles from Chesterfield Courthouse. Just a bit further down Chippenham Parkway is the Defense Supply Center Richmond, a government complex that sprawls along the seen-better-days section of US 1. Back on VA 10, a historic part of the county mixes with progress at Chesterfield Courthouse, where county workers ply their trades near a restored mansion and jail. The nearby county airport near VA 288 and VA 10 provides convenient access to the center of the county for charters and corporate jets. Wooded neighborhoods are just off VA 10. Still on VA 10, Chester, though unincorporated, has the feel of an older village, and new development is trying to mimic that—for example, at Chester Village Green, a mix of apartments, stores, restaurants, businesses, and single family homes. John Tyler Community College's main campus is in Chester, just off I-95, and Sabra Dipping Co. just opened a $60 million plant nearby.

Parks in the area are a big draw, especially the enormous Pocahontas State Park near the courthouse and Henricus Historical Park and Dutch Gap Conservation Area on the eastern side of I-95. It's possible to live on or near a lake or a river here. Affluent riverfront and lakefront neighborhoods, as well as more modest neighborhoods close to the Appomattox River, the southern border of the county, offer fishing and boating opportunities. Virginia State University in Ettrick is just across the Appomattox River from Petersburg.

Moseley

This area offers country living in the far reaches of Chesterfield County, and it uses some of its land for family-friendly activities. The Richmond Metro Zoo is here, and farther out is the very popular Chesterfield Berry Farm, which packs in the crowds to pick fruits and vegetables from spring to fall. Residential living here means large lots and much privacy. Recently, a few residential developments have been added to the rural nature of the area.

OUT IN THE COUNTRY

North of the River

Goochland County

To the west of Henrico County, this mostly rural county of 295 square miles spreads out from below I-64 to the James River. I-295 is just 3 miles east of the county line with Henrico. VA 288, leading north to I-64 and south into Powhatan County, bisects the West Creek Business Park, where Fortune 500 member CarMax has its headquarters and Capital One has consolidated its area offices. Most of the 21,000 residents live in quiet, older neighborhoods or on farms, though some large homes have been built recently. It's an area known for its rolling horse farms, its 700-acre Orapax Hunting Preserve, and its popular farmers' market, which is open much of the year. Forestry, agriculture, and mining still account for many area jobs. J. Sargeant Reynolds Community College has its western campus in the Goochland Courthouse Village. Tuckahoe Plantation, Thomas Jefferson's boyhood home, is in the eastern part of the county. See more on that in the "Attractions" chapter. Finally, the county's Field Day of the Past, a county fair–type affair with an old-time farm and industrial equipment, gets attention in the "Kidstuff" chapter.

New Kent County

New Kent County is bounded by the Pamunkey and York Rivers to the north and east and the winding Chickahominy River along its southern and western sections. The county is located 30 miles east of Richmond, just off I-64 on the way to Williamsburg. Though one of the oldest localities in Virginia, New Kent is growing at a faster rate than anywhere else in the region—32.6 percent over the last nine years, to 17,857 residents in 2009. Much of that growth is centered around planned communities. A major one is New Kent Vineyards, a billion-dollar project that includes New Kent Winery, a Rees Jones golf course, and plans for 2,500 homes. With mixed-use residential, office, and retail space, Maidstone and Preservation Park opened not far from the vineyard near the county courthouse. South of I-64 is Colonial Downs, Virginia's only pari-mutuel horse-racing track, which offers thoroughbred and harness racing from April through the fall. A 150-acre industrial park, Weir Creek Commerce Park, has recently opened off VA 33.

South of the River

Powhatan County

Powhatan packs 262 square miles of rural living between its northern and southern boundaries, the James and Appomattox Rivers. Its population has grown more than 25 percent in the past decade to 28,106, with many new residents looking for more land. They'll find it, and more people will find Powhatan with VA 288 zipping through it. While the area has 195 farms, new home developments are sprouting up, and Powhatan will have a job maintaining its rural character; the citizens' group Powhatan Tomorrow hopes to work through the issues sensibly. Though some retailers in the high-end Winterfield Place, on the edge of Chesterfield County off Robious Road, use a Midlothian address, the fully leased, 60,000-square-foot development is in Powhatan. An additional 90,000 square feet of office and retail space is due to be built soon.

The Powhatan Wildlife Management Area off US 60 offers ample land for hiking, horseback riding, or hunting—just not at the same time. The Powhatan Festival of the Grape brings wineries from throughout Virginia to the county each October. Powhatan is the pleasant kind of community that lists the winners of the snowman contest on the home page of the county Web site.

GETTING HERE, GETTING AROUND

Richmond sits at the intersection of I-95 and I-64, which makes it convenient to drive here from much of the East Coast. With a newly expanded airport, averaging 180 flights in and out per day, just 7 miles from downtown and two Amtrak stations, it's easy to get here.

Once here, you'll most likely want a car to get around unless your visit is limited to downtown. Though Richmond installed the first large-scale, successful system of electric streetcars in 1888, public transportation today consists of the award-winning yet under-utilized GRTC bus system. It works great if it goes where you want to go, but it doesn't serve many parts of the region. Using cabs to get around is possible, but you'll have to call in advance for pickup. The city is walkable and bikeable, but the counties less so. Henrico (pronounced Hen-RYE-co) County, with only two pedestrian walk buttons at crosswalks in the entire county, isn't exactly made for walking.

Luckily, the highways and roads in and around Richmond are usually free of major tie-ups. With the average commute for Richmonders under 24 minutes and the pace of traffic moving at a good clip, it's remarkably easy to get from one side of town to the other. Perhaps that's why in 2008 Richmond ranked 10th out of the 75 largest metro areas in the U.S., according to Forbes.com in "10 Best Cities for Commuters."

I-95, which travels from Maine to Florida, connects us southward to Petersburg, then North Carolina and beyond. I-95 north connects Richmond to northern Virginia and Washington, D.C. That's a trip that could take two hours or seemingly forever, depending on congestion up north. We're content to let our northern neighbors wrestle with road rage; we don't have it here. Those who move here from larger metropolitan areas are pleasantly surprised at how painless driving in and around Richmond can be—unless it snows!

BY CAR

The city of Richmond has a grid street system, where North, South, East, and West matter, as do one-way signs. Richmond is not encircled by one continuous beltway, but rather by a network of highways that zig and zag rather than loop, so there are plenty of options to choose from when deciding how to get from point A to point B. No matter which route you choose, driving from the eastern side of the region, say the airport, to the Far West End takes about 30 to 40 minutes at most. The most frequent sources of backups or delays are the tollbooths on some of the highways, or at some James

River bridge crossings, but these are usually mild.

If you rely on the toll roads here, it's easy to get an E-ZPass and attach it to your windshield so that tolls will be deducted from your account automatically. You'll never hunt for coins again. E-ZPass works on other toll roads in Virginia, as well as up the East Coast and elsewhere. For fees and information go to www.ezpassva.com, call (877) 762-7824, or stop by one of Virginia's E-ZPass service centers.

i Richmond's E-ZPass Service Center is open Monday through Friday from 8 a.m. to 6 p.m., but don't be fooled by the mailing address—175 Wadsworth Dr., Richmond, VA 23236—it's really in Chesterfield County.

Now you're ready to hit the road, so here's a cheat sheet for the major highways. The infamous **I-95** cuts through downtown with multiple Richmond exits on its way north and south. Its intersection with the east-west–running **I-64** sometimes creates traffic snarls. From downtown, I-64 heads east to Richmond International Airport and continues towards Williamsburg, one hour away, Hampton Roads, and Virginia Beach, two hours away. I-64 heads west through Henrico County hot spots such as Innsbrook and Short Pump, and on out to Charlottesville, the mountains, and beyond. Commuters driving west to east in the morning and back in the evening must contend with the glare of the sun and related slowdowns on I-64 on both ends of their commutes.

I-295 wraps itself two-thirds of the way around the region, acting as a bypass for downtown for those traveling through on I-95 (though there's usually little reason to add the extra miles). I-295 intersects with I-95 28 miles south of downtown and again 12 miles north of the city. For those heading west, I-295 continues out to Short Pump above I-64. It's useful for connecting Henrico's western and eastern sections with parts of Hanover County, Chesterfield County, and Fort Lee.

VA 288 begins at I-64 in Goochland County, west of where I-295 ends, and heads south into Powhatan County and southeast through Chesterfield County to I-95 south of the city, where it provides the missing link in the loop that isn't quite a loop.

The **Downtown Expressway (I-195),** despite its tollbooth, moves drivers quickly between I-95 in the center of downtown and the **Powhite Parkway (VA 76)** (pronounced POW-hite), which whisks people to South Richmond and Chesterfield County. The **Powhite Parkway Extension** takes drivers to VA 288. (No one but the people who maintain them and collect the tolls considers the Powhites separate highways.)

VA 895, Pocahontas Parkway, is a toll road that provides a route from the airport southward to I-95, bypassing the city. Construction on a new, time-saving airport connector road is underway, scheduled to be completed in 2011, but watch out for shoulder closures and work in the medians. VA 895 connects south of the city to **Chippenham Parkway (VA 150),** not a toll road, which heads northwest in a smaller loop than VA 288, connecting eventually with Parham Road in Henrico County.

Bridge Bits

The **Mayo Bridge** is the oldest highway bridge across the river in Richmond. It's also known as the 14th Street Bridge since US 360 runs along 14th Street in Shockoe Bottom. The **Manchester Bridge** is a favorite of commuters who don't want to pay tolls. The

Toll Roads in Richmond

(Fees for two-axle vehicles)
Boulevard Bridge (VA 161): 35 cents
Downtown Expressway (I-195): 70 cents
Downtown Expressway entrances and exits: 20 to 35 cents
Pocahontas Parkway (VA 895): $1 to $2.75 (due to go up Jan 2011 to $1.25 to $3)
Powhite Parkway (VA 76): 70 cents
Powhite Parkway Extension (VA 76): 25 to 75 cents

Robert E. Lee Memorial Bridge, or the Lee Bridge, is the official carrier of Bicycle Route 1, the main north/south bicycle route along the East Coast. Underneath hangs a popular pedestrian bridge for people, bikes, and dogs on leashes that links the north shore of the James River to Belle Isle, a beautiful, historic spot along the rapids. Don't be surprised to hear locals call the **Boulevard Bridge** the "Nickel Bridge." It costs 35 cents now, but saying "Seven Nickel Bridge" hasn't caught on. Pedestrians and cyclists must use a protected walkway on the west side of the bridge. The **Huguenot Memorial Bridge,** aka Huguenot Bridge, is due for a change. At press time, construction of a new Huguenot Bridge next to the current bridge was scheduled to commence in fall of 2010, with completion in 2013. We'll see.

Major Roads in the Area

East/West

Not all roads lead to bridges in Richmond. Often referred to merely as **Broad Street**

(VA 250), it has an East or West in front of it for a reason. It is a major east-west route from the original section of the city, Church Hill, through downtown and into Henrico County, where it's a retail destination, all the way out to Short Pump.

i For local traffic updates that just might help you decide which bridge or road to avoid, listen to WCVE, 88.9 FM, Monday through Friday at 7:06, 7:39, and 8:06 a.m. and every ten to twenty minutes on the nines from 4:19 to 5:49 p.m. during peak traffic time.

Main Street is actually either East Main or West Main, with Foushee Street downtown being the dividing line. It runs from Church Hill west through downtown and the Fan until it changes names to Ellwood at Boulevard.

Cary Street links the city's tony Near West End, where it is a two-way street to the funky shopping and dining destination Carytown. There it becomes a one-way street heading eastward. It continues through the Fan and VCU's Monroe Park campus downtown to Shockoe Slip and Shockoe Bottom hangouts. Again, Foushee Street is the dividing line for west to east.

Parham Road loops from Chamberlayne Road in Henrico County by J. Sargeant Reynolds Community College to the west end, where it connects with Chippenham Parkway (VA 150).

Laburnum Avenue has the distinction of being West Laburnum, East Laburnum, North Laburnum or South Laburnum as it winds from I-195 through North Side, past Richmond International Raceway, and through eastern Henrico County.

Richmond Area Bridges Across the James River

From east to west:

Bridge Route No.	Northern End	Southern End
Varina/Enon Bridge (I-295)	Henrico County	Chesterfield County
Vietnam Veterans Memorial Bridge (toll) (VA 895/Pocahontas Parkway)	Henrico County	Chesterfield County
I-95 James River Bridge	Richmond	Richmond
Mayo Bridge/14th Street Bridge (US 360)	Richmond	Richmond
Manchester Bridge (US 60)	Richmond	Richmond
Robert E. Lee Memorial Bridge (US 1/US 301)	Richmond	Richmond
Boulevard Bridge (toll) (VA 161)	Richmond	Richmond
Powhite Parkway Bridge (toll) (VA 76/Powhite Parkway)	Richmond	Richmond
Huguenot Memorial Bridge (VA 147)	Henrico County	Richmond
Edward E. Willey Bridge (VA 150/Chippenham Parkway)	Henrico County	Richmond
World War II Veterans Memorial Bridge (VA 288)	Goochland County	Powhatan County
Maidens Bridge (US 522)	Goochland County	Powhatan County

Midlothian Turnpike (US 60) is another major east-west artery that rivals Broad Street for retail usefulness, especially after it heads west from Richmond to Chesterfield County. It crosses into Powhatan County, after it intersects VA 288.

Hull Street (US 360) also begins in the city and heads west to become another east-west shopping artery in Chesterfield County.

North/South

US 1 and US 301 are linked through the city, loosely paralleling I-95 if that's geometrically possible. **Huguenot Road** (VA 147) connects Chesterfield County to the Huguenot Bridge in South Richmond and the city's West End.

i Prefer a carpool for commuting? RideFinders, had 102 vanpools and 1,285 carpools registered as of late 2009. An Emergency Ride Home program guarantees three free rides home or to your car if you have an emergency. Call (804) 643-7433 or go to www.ridefinders.com for more information.

Pay Attention to Direction!

Whether you're in Church Hill, Shockoe Bottom or Slip, downtown, the Fan or Museum District, or south of the river in Manchester or Woodland Heights, pay attention to cardinal directions in street addresses. 100 W. Broad St. is not the same block as 100 E. Broad St. Downtown, the streets change from west to east at Foushee Street south of Broad Street or at St. James Street north of Broad Street. The divider for north-south streets is East or West Main Street until Main Street turns into Ellwood at North Boulevard. Numbered streets add another wrinkle. North and south numbered streets are on Church Hill and its environs, whereas all east and west numbered streets— West 4th Street, for instance—are in the South Side, in neighborhoods such as Manchester, Woodland Heights, and Westover Hills. The east-west dividing road is Hull Street (US 360). In other words, get a good map, and use it!

Staples Mill Road (VA 33) runs primarily north of West Broad Street out to the Henrico section of Glen Allen before becoming Mountain Road and winding up in Hanover County.

Mechanicsville Turnpike (US 360) jogs through parts of Richmond and Henrico County before eventually becoming a retail and business artery in Hanover County.

Parking

On-street parking downtown is usually free after 6 p.m. and on weekends. One- to two-hour metered parking is allowed on weekdays, but from 7 a.m. to 9 a.m. and 4 p.m. to 6 p.m., finding a space at a meter can be a challenge because parking is prohibited on many streets. In some areas of the Fan and Carver neighborhoods, free on-street parking for more than an hour or two is reserved for permit holders, so pay attention to signs. Note as well signs detailing street-cleaning on certain days—your car could be towed if you park where it is prohibited. The good news is that parking at a meter costs only 25 cents per half hour. There are also plenty of parking lots and garages downtown available for a fee.

BY PLANE

RICHMOND INTERNATIONAL AIRPORT
1 Richard E. Byrd Terminal Dr.
Richmond, VA 23250
(804) 226-3000
www.flyrichmond.com

The ease of flying in and out of Richmond International Airport (RIC) cannot be overstated. It's a 10-minute drive to downtown, and though it served 3.35 million passengers in Fiscal Year 2009, you'll rarely hit traffic, have trouble parking, or wait in long lines at ticketing or security. The airport is served by eight commercial carriers. Recently renovated and expanded, with lots of natural light and brick accents, the airport is perhaps the best example of regionalism run right. There's just one terminal, and it's bright, airy, and compact, making navigating it a breeze, with ticketing on the upper level and baggage claim on the lower. Arriving 1½ hours before your flight is usually sufficient.

Enough to Drive You Crazy

Another fun feature of our region is how frequently street names change, sometimes from county to city but also within the boundaries of a city or county. For instance, Jeff Davis Highway becomes Cowardin Avenue, crosses the river via the Lee Bridge, becomes South Belvidere Street, then North Belvidere Street, until becoming Chamberlayne Avenue and eventually, Chamberlayne Road. Sigh. Huguenot Road turns into Courthouse Road at Midlothian Turnpike. Monument Avenue turns into West Franklin Street at North Lombardy Street. I could go on.

The airlines serving RIC combine to provide direct service to Atlanta, Boston, Charlotte, Chicago, Dallas, Detroit, Houston, Miami, New York, Orlando, Philadelphia, St. Louis, Toronto, and Washington, D.C., among other cities, and connecting flights to many more destinations.

Free Wi-Fi is available throughout the terminal, and RIC also has a business center on the lower level of the terminal, open from 5 a.m. to 11 p.m. Next door, a new USO center opened in 2010 to smooth the travels of thousands of Armed Services members who fly in and out every year. A full-service bank is on the second floor, and a small Richmond Visitors Center, moved to more visible digs in 2010, is now between baggage claim areas on the lower level.

If you have time and the inclination, an interfaith chapel is on the lower level as well.

The options for a bite to eat or shopping are more limited than in larger airports, but it's easy enough to grab a burger or vegetarian meal, coffee, beer, or sweet treat at the carts and restaurants. Hudson News has multiple outlets stocking books, periodicals, toys, and Virginia souvenirs.

i Stuck at the baggage carousels waiting for your bags? Take a look at the art exhibits hanging nearby provided by the renowned (and recently renovated and expanded) Virginia Museum of Fine Arts. These changing exhibits always highlight Virginia artists.

Airlines Serving RIC

Air Canada: (888) 247-2262, www.aircanada.com

Air Tran: (800) 247-8726, www.airtran.com

American Airlines: (800) 433-7300, www.aa.com

Continental: (800) 525-0280, www.continental.com

Delta: (800) 221-1212, www.delta.com

JetBlue Airways: (800) 538-2583, www.jetblue.com

United: (800) 241-6522, www.united.com

US Airways: (800) 428-4322, www.usairways.com

i Rather than endlessly circling the airport while waiting to pick up a guest, pull into the 40-space Cell Phone Lot, located near the Arrivals area. Once your visitor calls to let you know he or she has landed, you can be curbside in a minute.

Parking

Is it a tip of the hat to the region's Civil War history or just the luck of the compass that the parking garages that handle daily and hourly parking are named North and South? Whatever the case, it's convenient to park undercover at RIC with just a short walk to the terminal. If you'd rather, valet parking is available at the terminal departure curb for $20 for the first day and $2 an hour for every hour after the first 24. Prearrange it by calling (804) 226-3089. To park your own car, the rate in the daily garages is $12 a day. The hourly lot is cheaper by the hour but more expensive by the day ($24 daily). For less expensive long-term parking options, three economy lots with 24-hour free shuttle service to the terminal are also available for $7 per day. Just follow the signs on the airport entrance road. No need to bother with the AutoExpress kiosks throughout the airport to pay for your parking; it's easy to pay by cash or credit card 24 hours a day at the exits.

> **i** If you prefer your airport reunions inside the terminal, pull into the hourly lot and park. You won't pay a dime (or anything else) if you are in and out of the garage in 59 minutes or less. It's free. Just don't overstay your welcome, or you will be charged for the first hour and any time thereafter.

From the Airport to the City

All ground transportation is available on the lower level of the terminal, near baggage claim, or in the case of taxis, curbside.

Car Rental

Eight national chains provide car rentals at RIC. The airport is so well designed, there are no rental-car shuttles. All vehicles are in a nearby garage, reached by a covered walkway near the No. 1 baggage claim area, once you've made your arrangements at the counter. Several companies have other drop-off and pickup locations in the region, but their hours and offerings are limited.

Rental Car Agencies Serving RIC

Alamo: (888) 826-6893, www.alamo.com
Avis: (800) 331-1212, www.avis.com
Budget: (800) 527-0700, www.budget.com
Dollar: (800) 800-3665, www.dollar.com
Enterprise: (800) 261-7331, www.enterprise .com
Hertz: (800) 654-3001, www.hertz.com
National: (888) 826-6890, www.national .com
Thrifty: (877) 283-0898, www.thrifty.com

Airport Shuttle

Groome Transportation offers 24-hour shuttle service from home, hotel, or airport. They use a zoned system to operate door-to-door, shared ride, and charter services. Their rates vary according to how many people are on board and how far away your destination is, but figure in the $20 to $40 range. Their Web site, www.groometransportation .com, provides the zone map and rates. To schedule a pickup, call (800) 552-7911.

Taxis and Limousines

Taxis

Taxis are available all hours curbside at the lower level of the terminal. According to the Capital Region Taxicab Advisory Board, taxis licensed in the city of Richmond and the counties of Chesterfield, Hanover, and Henrico are required to charge identical rates. All trips that begin at Richmond International Airport cost $10 or the amount registered on the meter, whichever is more. All tolls are the responsibility of the passenger.

The first 0.20 mile costs $2.50 and another 50 cents for each additional 0.20 mile, so that's $4.50 for the first mile and $2.50 a mile after that. Additional charges apply for each 80 seconds of waiting time, for each additional passenger over the age of six and for trips that originate between 9 p.m. and 6 a.m.

Though you will find cabs available at RIC, train and bus stations, and many hotels, cabs are not cruising the streets of the Richmond region looking for fares as they do in New York. In most cases you'll need to call for a pickup.

Allied Central Cab: (804) 266-4008

Deb's Taxi Service: (804) 439–2232, www
.debstaxiservice.com

Gentleman Taxi: (804) 839-8400, www
.gentlemantaxi.com

Innsbrook Cab Company: (804) 909-1990

Manhattan Taxi: (804) 643-6791, www
.manhattantaxicab.com

Napoleon Taxi: (804) 354-TAXI (8294), www
.napoleontaxi.com

Rainbow Taxi: (804) 762-9200

Richmond Taxi: (804) 439-0009, www
.richmondvataxi.com

Veterans Cab: (804) 275-5542, www
.veteranscabrichmond.com

i Airport Taxi operates two ADA-approved wheelchair-accessible taxis in its fleet at Richmond International Airport. The taxis can accommodate people in manual and motorized wheelchairs. If an ADA-equipped vehicle isn't at the taxi stand, call (804) 233-4444 and within 20 minutes Airport Taxi will provide ADA wheelchair-accessible transportation to airport passengers.

Limousines

CMC Limousine is the only limousine company licensed to operate both walk-up sedan service and prearranged limousine service at RIC. To arrange travel with them, call (804) 222-7790. Many other companies can pick you or your group up at the airport or other location if you call ahead.

Classic Limousine Service: (804) 301-5690,
www.vaclassiclimo.com

CMC Limousine: (804) 360-2122, www
.cmclimo.com

Down Under Limousine: (804) 784-4024,
www.downunderlimousine.com

James Limousine: (804) 273-1540, www
.jameslimousine.com

James River Bus Co.: (804) 342-7300, www
.onetransportationsolution.com

TNT Limousine and Executive Sedan:
(804) 965-0990, www.tntlimousine
.com

Tripp's Travel: (804) 347-9318, www.tripps
travellimo.com

Winn Transportation: (804) 358-9466,
www.winnbus.com

BY TRAIN AND BUS

Amtrak

Unlike those in most major cities, Richmond's main train station is not downtown. The beautiful and historic **Richmond-Main Street Station (RVM)** is downtown, but it has only limited passenger service and no checked-baggage service, and just four passenger trains stop there each day. This could change with high-speed rail between Richmond and Washington, D.C., now the region's No. 1 priority, but for the meantime most Amtrak passengers arrive at **Richmond-Staples Mill Road Station (RVR),** which is actually in Henrico County, 1 mile west of I-64, exit 185.

Amtrak runs three routes that serve Richmond, the Carolinian/Piedmont route with service between North Carolina and New York, the Silver Service/Palmetto line with service from New York to Florida, and Northeast Regional route with service from Boston to Lynchburg or Newport News. Currently, only Northeast Regional trains stop at Main Street Station, but not all of them coming through Richmond do. A few trains stop at both Richmond stations, but not all do. Plan your trip carefully so you're not stranded.

The Staples Mill Station (RVR) is unimpressive, small, and not the best gateway to Richmond. It does, however, have what you need to purchase tickets and check baggage. It's open 24 hours a day and has limited food service available from approximately 6:30 a.m. to 6 p.m. seven days a week. Parking is free for the first three hours and $5 a day.

i There are no lockers available in the Staples Mills station to store baggage, so if you have time before your train and want to walk to a nearby store or restaurant without lugging your luggage with you, ask to store your bags in the ticket office.

Though the two Richmond stations are only 8 miles apart, trains take an average of 28 minutes to travel between them, as the trains have to squeeze through the worst railroad bottleneck on the East Coast. So if the train you're taking stops at both stations, avoid the slowdown by leaving from Richmond-Staples Mill (RVR) if you're heading north, and leaving from Richmond-Main Street Station (RVM), if you're heading east to Williamsburg or Newport News.

As convenient as Main Street Station (RVM) is to downtown, there's no ticketing office or checked-baggage availability here. The station is open Mon through Thurs from 9:30 a.m. to 6 p.m., Fri from 9:30 a.m. to 9 p.m., and Sat and Sun from 9 a.m. to 8:30 p.m.

Check schedules and service for both stations by calling (800) 872-7245 (USA-RAIL) or by going online at www.amtrak.com.

Greyhound

The **Greyhound Bus Station** is 3 miles west of downtown, at 2910 N. Blvd. The terminal is somewhat bleak on the outside, but surprisingly bright and spacious inside, with plenty of seating and a fast-food restaurant with booths. The station and ticketing counter are open 24 hours a day every day. Fancy new buses with Wi-Fi and outlets for cell phones and laptops are available from Washington, D.C., and north. For service all over the country and to or from Canada and Mexico, call Greyhound Bus Line at (800) 231-2222 or (804) 254-5910 or visit www.greyhound.com.

Chinatown Buses

An inexpensive way to get to Richmond from Washington, Philadelphia, or New York, or to travel to those cities, is to take one of the Chinatown buses that have set up shop here and run several trips per day. A ticket to D.C. is as little as $15 one way, and a round-trip fare to New York is $60. The online site **www.gotobus.com** serves as a clearinghouse for the different companies, such as Todays Bus and Eastern, which have small stations at three locations in Richmond. Yes, the bus might leave at 1 a.m., but it's an adventure.

BY PUBLIC TRANSPORTATION

The **Greater Richmond Transit Company,** better known as **GRTC,** is a nonprofit transit system owned by the city of Richmond and county of Chesterfield and operated primarily in Richmond and Henrico County. GRTC provides limited service to Chesterfield County and express service Monday through Friday to Mechanicsville, Fredericksburg, and Petersburg. One of the region's flaws is that Chesterfield County offers only limited bus service within its borders. Nevertheless, in 2008 GRTC was voted "Best Transportation in North America" for a midsize city by the American Public Transportation Association, and had more than 10 million passenger trips in 2009.

It's likely that people who discourage you from taking the bus haven't ridden GRTC lately, if ever. With one of the newest fleets in the country, including 170 buses and eight minibuses on 40 routes, GRTC offers convenience and a great deal. At press time, a 25 cents fare increase to $1.50 for local routes (just 75 cents for those 65 and older with proper ID) and $2 for express routes seemed inevitable. Still, riding the bus saves money that would otherwise be spent on parking, gas, and tolls. It's no wonder that when gas prices rise, people flock to the buses. With the advent of Park-N-Ride lots throughout the suburbs, more people than ever can take advantage of this green transportation trend.

i Finish your coffee before the bus comes; no food or drink is allowed on GRTC buses.

Unfortunately, route maps are not available at most bus stops, but in a change that could transform the way Richmonders think of public transportation, new, computerized kiosks are popping up at busy bus stops, providing maps and real-time information about which buses are coming and when. Otherwise, route schedules are available at the front of GRTC buses and at select retail locations, such as supermarkets. But the easiest way to find a route is to surf GRTC's informative Web site, **www.ridegrtc.com.** It's loaded with useful information for the novice bus rider, including videos on how to use both the time-saving Go Cards and the handy bike racks on the front of all fixed-route buses for those who want to do the popular bike-bus combo.

Though exact change is accepted on GRTC buses, the most convenient way to pay bus fare is by using the Go Card, a swipe card available in $5, $10, and $25 increments. Go Cards are available at many CVS pharmacies, Kroger and Martin's supermarkets, and convenience stores and other pharmacies. Fares are deducted from the card each time it is swiped in the fare box upon boarding the bus. Call the Customer Service Center at (804) 358-GRTC (4782) or go to www.ridegrtc.com for more information.

i GRTC Express routes do not operate on Saturday and Sunday, so you will have to rely on local routes to get around via bus on weekends.

CYCLING

Richmond isn't exactly a bike commuter's dream, but progress is being made. One reason Richmond attracts cyclists is because of its unique location at the intersection of Bike Route 1, the north-south on-road route, the East Coast Greenway, and the TransAmerica Trail (also known as U.S. Bicycle Route 76). With ongoing construction of new paved

Virginia Commonwealth University Bus Service

Some GRTC routes are VCU specific—anyone may ride, but VCU students and employees ride these routes around and between the Monroe Park and MCV campuses free by showing their VCU ID. In addition, all VCU full-time students are eligible for free bus passes for use throughout much of the GRTC system. VCU employees can get $150 worth of GRTC bus passes each quarter for just $25 through the VCU Employee Transit Program. That's a deal! Just go to a campus Parking and Transportation customer service office with a valid VCU ID for both programs.

trails leading downtown (the Capital to Capital Trail and Cannon Creek Greenway), Richmond commuters and recreational cyclists will have more options soon. (See more on cycling and trails in the "Recreation" and "Day Trips" chapters.) Most bike commuting takes place around VCU, VUU, and downtown. Sharing the road is the key to everyone's safety and sanity. The bike racks on all GRTC fixed-route buses are well used and help make combo commutes possible.

HISTORY

Richmond's geographic location placed it at a central place in American history—before it was technically America or Richmond—that encompasses exploration and extinction, liberty and enslavement, war and remembrance. So many themes of American history are evident here—the contradictions and the curses, the grievous errors and great achievements, that it's preposterous to think a few pages can do justice to Richmond history. Here goes.

A ROCKY START

Richmond is here because of river, rocks, and—all claims to southern hospitality aside—rudeness. About those rocks and river first. Where the bedrock of the piedmont meets the coastal plain, the river drops 105 feet in 7 miles of rocky roar. For thousands of years before the English settled Jamestown, Indians congregated along rivers for fresh water, food, fertile soil, trade, and travel. Just below the fall line of the James River, at the head of navigable water, was a particularly attractive spot for fishing and finding stones for toolmaking, so the village there was a central part of the chiefdom of Algonquian-speaking tribes. By 1607 the paramount chief, Powhatan, oversaw numerous tribes with upwards of 13,000 Indians from present-day Richmond to the Chesapeake Bay. His son Parahunt was the *werowance,* or local chief, of the settlement at the falls, and it was he whom Captain Christopher Newport, John Smith, and their band of 20 men met on their journey up the James in May 1607, just days after landing at Jamestown.

Newport, Smith, and the rest of the Virginia Company were hoping to find a passage to China, and gold and riches along the way. The rocks had other ideas. Instead, near what is now Fulton Hill, the visitors were welcomed at the Algonquian settlement called Powhatan, where they noted the thatched-roof homes, tended fields, and paths that headed west towards the territory of the Algonquian's enemy, the Monacans, and east to other villages. The Indians offered food. The English offered alcohol. Parahunt agreed to show them the impressive rapids that would impede their further sailing the next day. All seemed friendly enough. The next day the rush and roar of the falls, along with Parahunt's disapproval, dissuaded Newport and company from going further west into Monacan territory.

Now for the rudeness. Smith later recollected his first visit to the falls of the James: "…we were intercepted with great craggy stones in the midst of the river, where the water falleth so rudely, and with such a violence, as not any boat can possibly pass…." Disappointed but wanting to mark his furthest passage westward, Newport planted a wooden cross with "Jacobus Rex 1607" and his name written underneath. When a shout in honor of King James I arose from the English, the Indians became suspicious. Newport craftily lied that the two arms of the cross symbolized friendship and union between Powhatan and himself. In fact, Newport had just claimed everything in sight for King James, and his men had already noted how felicitous the falls would be for mills of every kind.

DON'T BELIEVE DISNEY MOVIES

John Smith returned to the falls in 1609 and bought Parahunt's village, hoping to establish a secure settlement, naming it Nonsuch. Notwithstanding the buying out and bullying of the Powhatans, English settlements near the falls were abandoned by 1610. In 1611, when Sir Thomas Dale looked about for a new spot to settle, he tried his hand 10 miles below the falls, at the more placid (so he hoped) spot of Henricus, now in Chesterfield County. But the area was in the midst of the First Anglo-Powhatan War (1609–14). In 1613, Powhatan's daughter, Pocahontas, was kidnapped by the English and eventually held hostage at Henricus. It sure sounds like a melodrama, but during her captivity Pocahontas converted to Christianity and became not only Rebecca, but also John Rolfe's wife, which brought the First Anglo-Powhatan War to a close.

Poor John Rolfe doesn't get the credit (or the blame) for first successfully cultivating tobacco near Henricus. In 1614 his experimental tobacco plants passed muster in England, and within four years, the colony exported 46,000 pounds of tobacco. As tobacco production expanded and more colonists arrived, the Indians fought to save their land and livelihood. It took three Anglo-Powhatan wars, from 1609–14, 1622–32, and 1644–46, for the English to gain control of

much of eastern Virginia, and still decades of battles lay ahead, with tribes to fight, dispossess, and in some cases, enslave.

SLAVERY BEGINS

The first reference to people of African descent in Virginia (it's unknown whether they were slaves or indentured servants) was made by Rolfe in a 1620 letter, noting that more than 20 had come ashore at Point Comfort in 1619. No doubt Africans had another name for it. Through much of the 17th century, small numbers of slaves worked alongside indentured servants near the falls, but as the plantation system of tobacco growing spread in the late 1600s, the slave trade increased, the laws governing slaves tightened, and the dock at Bermuda Hundred, on the south side of the James River, became a busy slave port. In 1670 perhaps 5 percent of the colony was African. By 1700 more than 25 percent of Virginians were.

Tobacco, trade, and transportation were the keys to Richmond's growth as a commercial center—even before it was Richmond. Tobacco production meant large plantations along the James River, many workers, and many warehouses. The river provided the means to transport tobacco and other goods, especially deerskins, across the ocean.

William Byrd I was at the center of commerce along the falls into the 18th century, with tobacco warehouses, Indian and African slaves, and extensive land holdings on both sides of the James River. When French Huguenots, Protestant refugees who had settled above the falls at Manakin Town, near where the Monacans had once lived, discovered coal deposits in 1701, Byrd got involved in its mining, too. Educated in

London, William Byrd II returned to Virginia to take over his father's vast holdings after William Byrd I's death in 1704. The man who became known as the father of Richmond didn't want a town at the falls. He liked his monopoly on trade there just fine.

Eventually, though, the General Assembly instructed him to set aside land for a town at the falls, at Shacco's (*Shockoe*, the Indian word for flat rock), so in 1737 he had William Mayo survey the town, providing 32 squares of four lots each and streets up to 65 feet wide in a grid pattern. Byrd named the town Richmond, because the view of the river downstream reminded him of Richmond on Thames. When the General Assembly passed the act establishing Richmond in 1742, all of 250 people lived there. William Byrd II died in 1744 at Westover, the mansion he had built east of the settlement, along the north bank of the James River.

FIRST VIRGINIA LOTTERY?

The first coal mine in North America was in Chesterfield County, on the south bank of the James, and by 1763, the Midlothian mines produced 14,000 tons of coal yearly. It was transported to Rocky Ridge, a port on the south side of the river that was incorporated as Manchester in 1769, and shipped as far as Europe. William Byrd III owned the area around Manchester, too, but he wasn't the businessman his father or grandfather had been and instead incurred gambling losses that forced him to offer much of his holdings in a lottery in 1768. The prizes included 10,000 acres split in 100-acre lots, improved lots in town, islands, and leases on warehouses and mills. The lottery contributed to Richmond's growth (574 inhabitants by 1769), but it didn't change Byrd's fortunes. With losses accumulating

and unwilling to support revolution, he shot himself at Westover in 1777. How the mighty had fallen.

REVOLUTION

By 1775 the colonists were uneasy about relations with Britain, and against the Royal Governor's wishes, they called for a Virginia Convention to be held in Richmond, at the only suitable building in town, St. John's Church on Church Hill. There, in the presence of George Washington, Thomas Jefferson, George Mason, Richard Henry Lee, and practically every other distinguished Virginian of the day, Hanover County lawyer Patrick Henry rose to argue that the colony must be prepared to defend itself against the British with a militia of its own, a treasonous proposition to many. Three weeks before shots rang out at Lexington and Concord, Henry thundered, "I know not what course others may take; but as for me, give me liberty or give me death!"

The American Revolution turned Richmond around. It went from merely a trading town to industrial as coal and iron mining and arms manufacturing became more important to the military needs of the new nation, and then it became a political center as Virginia's capital. Westham, just above the falls on the north side of the river, became a foundry, turning out cannons for the war. Richmond's central location helped it become the capital in 1780, leaving Williamsburg to history. Thomas Jefferson, the governor then, was often in Richmond. Indeed, he was just outside Richmond when word came in early 1781 that Benedict Arnold was leading a British force towards Richmond. The militia guarding the town crumbled, and Arnold's force entered the town unopposed. Jefferson had fled west and ordered munitions and records to be taken to Westham for safety. That didn't work. Arnold sent a group to Westham to take out the foundry. After a night of celebrating in Richmond, the Brits set fire to many buildings in town and withdrew the next day.

CAPITAL CITY

With the Revolutionary War over in October 1781, Richmond could focus on being the capital of Virginia. In 1786 it expanded up Shockoe Hill, the site of the new Capitol building under construction, and Church Hill, so that the city held 280 houses and about 1,800 people, half of them slaves. Thomas Jefferson loved classical architecture, and as minister to France, he worked closely with Charles-Louis Clérisseau to design a new state Capitol based on the Maison Carrée, a Roman temple in Nîmes that he had not yet seen in person.

While the building was rising, the General Assembly met in temporary quarters to attend to matters both material and spiritual. It was there that they approved, with George Washington's encouragement, a bill that authorized the James River Company to improve navigation along the James by means of a canal to better transport goods. In 1786 the assembly passed "An Act for Establishing Religious Freedom," or the Virginia Statute for Religious Freedom that Thomas Jefferson had first drafted in 1777, guaranteeing citizens the freedom to practice, or not practice, religion of their choosing, predating the U.S. Constitution and the Bill of Rights.

FREEDOM HAS A PRICE

All the talk of liberty and throwing off the bonds of tyranny had its effect. Some Baptists, Methodists, and Quakers thought it preferable to convert black brothers and sisters rather than enslave them. The Manumission Act of 1782 allowed slave owners to emancipate slaves for the first time in 70 years. Some slaves were rewarded for their military service during the Revolution, others because of the religious leanings of their owners. A Quaker in Henrico not only freed 78 slaves, but also deeded them land in the eastern part of the county.

But slavery was still the lot of most blacks in Virginia. In August 1800, Gabriel, a slave in Henrico County, planned an insurrection to free blacks from bondage. Only a flash flood and a warning to the governor kept Gabriel and his coconspirators from enacting their wide-ranging plan. After gaining access to the armory stores at the Capitol, they had hoped to raise a flag on which they would write, "death or liberty," echoing Patrick Henry's words 25 years before. Liberty would have to wait, however; Gabriel and dozens of his allies were executed. The aborted rebellion led to further restrictions on slaves and free blacks, including revoking the emancipation law and requiring that recently freed slaves leave Virginia within a year of emancipation or be enslaved once more.

COMMERCIAL BOOM

Despite these forebodings of violence, white Richmond felt confident. By 1800 the city had grown to 5,700 residents. Richmond was the capital of the state, where the new nation had begun and where the war to free itself had ended. Its former governor was about to be elected the third president of the United States. It was a leading marketplace, manufacturer, and transportation hub, with the opening of the James River

Canal speeding transportation of goods and people around the falls. The canal that had begun to take shape in 1785 unleashed Richmond's economic potential, and the area near the Great Shiplock and Turning Basin filled with mills and warehouses. Ships often left Richmond's ports loaded with flour destined for Europe, South America, or even Australia, as the James's rushing waters made it a leading flour producer. Ships returned laden with coffee, making Richmond a major coffee market on the East Coast.

Richmond sported the impressive State Capitol, with Houdon's famous statue of George Washington on display within. One of its favorite residents, John Marshall, was about to become chief justice of the Supreme Court. And in 1807 Richmond was at the center of the trial of the century, the treason trial of Aaron Burr, the former vice president, with John Marshall presiding and eminent Richmond lawyers arguing for both the defense and prosecution.

i The Poe Museum at 1914 E. Main St., lauding Edgar Allan Poe, who lived and worked in Richmond as an editor, writer, and master of the macabre, is housed in the Samuel Ege House, the oldest surviving building in Richmond, dating from perhaps 1754.

WORKING ON THE RAILROAD

Commercial progress continued. In 1831 Chesterfield Rail Road began hauling coal from the fields to Falling Creek, using mules and gravity for locomotion. The James River and Kanawha Canal construction continued in fits and starts, using Irish immigrants and slaves to do the dirty work of digging, eventually forging 197 miles into the Virginia mountains, only to be eclipsed by the railroads.

Cotton mills, quarries, iron foundries, arms manufacturers, and tobacco processing plants joined the flour mills at the falls. To further stimulate transport of goods, in 1836 Richmond, Fredericksburg, and Potomac Railroad opened 20 miles of track north from Richmond. With iron foundries along the river producing parts, Richmond soon became a hub of rail transportation with five railroads out into the countryside; foreshadowing the difficulties of regional cooperation, though, none of them were the same gauge, so goods had to be off-loaded before transferring between lines.

AT THE CENTER OF SLAVERY

After the U.S. banned the transatlantic slave trade in 1808, Richmond became the second largest domestic slave market behind New Orleans, and Shockoe Bottom was its center. From 1800 to 1865, 300,000 slaves were sent from Shockoe to work in the Deep South. Thousands more were buried unceremoniously in the Negro Burial Grounds. Most slaves in town worked as domestics, and many were hired out, working in the tobacco, building, and iron industries, for instance, as well as on nearby farms. Various methods were tried to escape the heavy burden of slavery, from contemplating colonizing Liberia with former slaves, to calls for abolition, to the Underground Railroad.

Sometimes the railroad wasn't exactly underground. In 1848, after his wife and children were sold south, Henry "Box" Brown paid a white shoemaker in Richmond, Samuel Smith, to ship him in a wooden crate by RF&P Railroad, boat, and then rail again to Philadelphia. Brown made it to freedom and his story was much publicized, which perhaps explains why two other slaves Smith tried to ship later were caught, and Smith was imprisoned for seven years for his part in the Underground Railroad. By 1860 there were almost 500,000 slaves in Virginia.

WAR

As Gregg Kimball noted in *American City, Southern Place*, antebellum Richmond was "the preeminent industrial city in the Upper South. Richmond solidified its intra-urban connections with the North. Richmond and its sister cities in the South stood largely unconnected with each other and became increasingly dependent on Northern factors and trade." That likely explains why most Richmonders—that is, the white men who could vote—voted to preserve the Union in the 1860 election, knowing how devastating a break with the North would be economically. A peace conference failed, and once Lincoln called for troops to keep the Union together after Fort Sumter was fired upon by Confederate forces, Virginia voted 85–55 to secede from the Union. Robert E. Lee, a U.S. Army officer, turned down a promotion to command U.S. troops and resigned his commission after Virginia seceded. He also turned down command of Confederate forces and instead became commander of Virginia's military in April 1861.

CAPITAL AGAIN

In a show of just how important Richmond knew it was, Virginia refused to join the Confederacy unless Richmond became the capital, so in May 1861, that era began. Since Richmond was the capital of the Confederacy and the supplier of half of the munitions for the South, the Union's rallying cry "On to Richmond" made sense, and much blood and treasure was spent keeping the Yankees out of Richmond. The first threat to

the city came in May 1862 when Union ships came up the James River. The Confederates and their cannons at Drewry's Bluff, 7 miles south of the city, held them off, but the wounded streamed into the city. With battles throughout Virginia, casualties flowed into Richmond. Chimborazo Hospital treated 75,000 wounded over the course of the war.

Over the bloody years of the Civil War, many battles were fought just outside the city, including Cold Harbor, Malvern Hill, and Seven Pines, but the Confederate lines, often dug by slaves and free blacks who were forced into the labor, held. Still, eight Confederate generals died from wounds received in battles to defend Richmond. Only one Union general was lost in these battles.

The city was full of spies and saboteurs, Unionists and POWs; everyone suffered as the war dragged on, and privation was the norm. The stories told by Richmond's Civil War museums are much more complicated and compelling than simply North vs. South. Richmond was a miserable place to be during the war, no matter whose side you were on. As 1865 dawned, the war in Richmond was less about battles and glory and more about surviving. And then, on April 3, Richmond fell.

i Elizabeth Van Lew, a prominent Richmonder who provided valuable service to the Union as a spy during the Civil War, was named postmaster by President Ulysses S. Grant in 1869. She refused the title postmistress. Many Richmonders held a grudge and were in no mood to save the Van Lew Mansion, her grand Church Hill home, from the wrecking ball after her death.

Once Petersburg fell to the South, Richmond could not defend itself, so

Confederate troops evacuated, setting fire to the stores of munitions and goods to keep them out of Yankee hands. It bears emphasizing that the Union Army did not burn Richmond. The blaze burned out of control, burning 20 blocks from the river up to Capitol Square, sparing the Capitol itself. With a raging fire and mobs on the loose, Mayor Joseph Mayo surrendered the city to entering Union troops, who began to bring the fire and the city under control. President Lincoln arrived at Rocketts Landing on April 4 to see the ruins of Richmond and the jubilation of the black population. One young African-American man had taken a Union flag he had kept hidden under his bed and raised it over the Capitol April 3.

i Podcasts are available online to help make Civil War sites come alive. It's like having a park ranger in your ear. Take advantage of a seven-stop tour of Lincoln's visit to Richmond in April 1865, or the Cold Harbor, Gaines Mill, and Petersburg site tours. Go to www.civilwartraveler.com for more information.

RECONSTRUCTION

Richmond rebuilt fairly quickly after the war, and Virginia was welcomed back into the Union. With economic and population growth and continued annexations, the city was the second largest city in the South in 1870. The city's inhabitants were of two minds: those who thought society should return to antebellum ways and those who believed an entirely new sort of social and political order was at hand. Somehow, in the schizophrenic reconstructed South, both sides got their way, for a time. In an astonishing reuse of a building, the Richmond

Theological School for Freedmen, the precursor to Virginia Union University, was founded in Lumpkin's jail in Shockoe Bottom, a former slave jail that the jail owner's widow donated for the education of former slaves. Blacks formed militias, as had their white counterparts in years past, and paraded at the Capitol during celebrations—unthinkable just a year before. Black men could vote for the first time in 1867, yet whites still controlled political and economic power, and segregation still held sway on streetcars and in public education, which the city began funding in 1870.

Richmond never recovered its industrial might after the war. The iron industry and flour milling petered out. Luckily, new enterprises, including the manufacture of wood products and chemicals, started up, with the occasional oddity thrown in—for example, a popular cure-all in the 1870s made from beef marrow was invented and manufactured here: Valentine's Meat Juice (yum).

TOBACCO TOWN

Tobacco once again provided the boost that Richmond needed to rebound, this time with cigarette production beginning here in 1873. Mass production of cigarettes took off in the 1880s, and by the 1900s the tobacco industry employed 10,000 people, though it wasn't until 1919 that the tobacco company most associated with Richmond, Philip Morris, established itself here. Soon packaging and advertising both became integral parts of Richmond's business landscape.

Richmond showed it still was at the forefront of transportation when in 1888 it became the first U.S. city to have a complete electrically powered streetcar system. Designed by Frank Sprague, it took to the streets with 12 miles of track and led to the development of streetcar suburbs and parks throughout Richmond and the surrounding area, eventually encompassing 82 miles.

STRUGGLE AND STRIVING

The struggle for black equality continued amid governmental interference and Confederate commemorations. In 1884 John Mitchell became editor of the *Richmond Planet*, arguing for the rights of black citizens. Some strides were made, and many blacks focused on black enterprise and creating strong black communities, such as in Jackson Ward near downtown. In 1893 the Southern Aid and Insurance Company, the country's first insurance company owned and run by blacks, began operating, headquartered in Richmond. After directing several enterprises dedicated to improving black citizens' prospects, in 1903 Maggie Lena Walker, daughter of a former slave, opened the Saint Luke Penny Savings Bank, becoming the first woman to charter a bank and the first president of the oldest-surviving black-owned bank in the U.S.

The city moved west with the development of the Fan between 1880 and 1920. Monument Avenue had became a stage for Confederate reunions and memorializing, beginning with the placement in 1890 of a statue of Robert E. Lee as the focal point for a new development. It continued with the Lost Cause contingent holding a massive Confederate reunion in 1907, when J. E. B. Stuart's and Jefferson Davis's statues were added to Monument Avenue. The city expanded south of the river as well, annexing Manchester in 1910.

FORWARD AND BACKWARD

With every passing decade there were signs of progress and signs of backwardness.

Richmonders Mary-Cooke Branch Munford and Lila Meade Valentine, founders of the Richmond Education Association, made it their mission to improve schooling for blacks and whites, but it was an uphill battle. In 1902 a new Virginia constitution imposed a poll tax, disenfranchising most blacks and many whites, and mandated only four months of school for black children. In 1906 the General Assembly voted to require segregated streetcars.

Richmond's designation in 1914 as the fifth Federal Reserve Bank district led to its rise as a financial center. Both black and white troops headed off to World War I, and returned to the still-segregated city. The wealthy moved further west, with the development of exclusive Windsor Farms, and both the Country Club of Virginia and the University of Richmond moved to Westhampton, a white enclave then in Henrico County.

In 1924 the governor signed the Act to Preserve Racial Integrity, which subjected all people of mixed-race ancestry to racial segregation laws and didn't allow marriage between the races. Walter Plecker, head of the state's vital records, used the law to officially, at least, wipe out remaining Indians, classifying them as "colored." To further constrain the rights of its citizens, Virginia in 1926 mandated the separation of the races in all places of public assembly.

Culturally, Richmond was mixing things up more. WRVA radio started broadcasting in 1925—showcasing music of Virginia, black and white. In 1935 Leslie Garland Bolling's wood sculptures were exhibited at the Richmond Academy, marking the first time in Virginia that an African-American artist had an exhibit of his own. Five black artists were included in a juried art exhibition at the

James Branch Cabell

Of Richmond's many illustrious writers, James Branch Cabell is easiest to get a sense of by visiting the Cabell rooms in VCU's James Branch Cabell Library Special Collections and Archives, where several pieces of his furniture outfit a beautiful room. There's the bookcase he purchased with the proceeds of his first book, intending to fill it with his future output. He managed to do it, publishing 52 books in his lifetime, including his best known, *Jurgen,* for which he endured an obscenity trial in the 1920s. The first editions are here, along with letters between him and H. L. Mencken, Ellen Glasgow, Sinclair Lewis, and others. Located on the fourth floor of the Cabell Library, the Special Collections and Archives are open Monday through Friday.

Valentine Museum. The Virginia Museum of Fine Arts, the first publicly supported statewide art institution in the country, opened in Richmond in 1936, in the midst of the Great Depression. Douglas Southall Freeman won his first Pulitzer in 1935 for his four-volume work on Robert E. Lee. His literary cohort, Ellen Glasgow, won hers in 1942 for *In This Our Life,* a novel set in Richmond and later made into a movie.

Richmond's diversifying economy helped stave off the effects of the Depression at first, with a big DuPont plant newly opened in Chesterfield County and a Reynolds Metals plant in Richmond. City fathers were resistant to New Deal programs initially but eventually used the funds to create a modern Deepwater Port on the James River, expand the Medical College of Virginia, and build Maggie L. Walker High School and the Library of Virginia, among other projects.

WORLD WAR II

Tobacco production rose during the war, and Richmond profited and worked hard to keep up. The DuPont and Reynolds plants ran three shifts around the clock to keep up with wartime needs. With so many men off to war and much work to be done at home, women took on jobs that were once the province of men, becoming taxi drivers, trolley operators, and mechanics.

Annexation, long the preferred way of growing the city and in turn, diluting black voting power, added 17 square miles and 20,000 mostly white residents to Richmond in 1942. Black Richmond declined to just over 25 percent of the city's population. During World War II, on weekends, more than 30,000 servicemen, black and white, came to Richmond from nearby installations. Black servicemen headed to 2nd Street in Jackson Ward, the entertainment center, where Duke Ellington and Cab Calloway would play.

AT THE CENTER OF THE STRUGGLE

With the war over, black veterans, having fought the same battles overseas as white vets, weren't inclined to go along with the status quo of Jim Crow back home. A group of NAACP lawyers, including Oliver Hill, who in 1948 was the first black member of the Richmond City Council since 1896, had been working for years to address the inequalities of the insidious "separate but equal" charade.

In 1951, when 16-year-old Barbara Johns led a student walkout in Prince Edward County outside of Richmond to protest unequal facilities there, Hill and his law partners had the case they had been looking for. Once again, eminent Richmond lawyers argued on both sides of a case that transfixed the nation. Eventually, her lawsuit against Prince Edward County became one of the five cases incorporated into the transformative *Brown v. Board of Education*.

Sadly, the 1954 ruling did not change policies overnight in Richmond or much of the South. In fact, the *Richmond News Leader* championed the idea of massive resistance for years, advocating closing schools rather than integrating them. In Richmond, heels dragged and integration was slow to nonexistent, but the schools stayed open. As part of the larger civil rights struggle throughout the country, college students from Virginia Union University led sit-ins to protest unequal treatment at venerable Richmond shopping destinations Miller & Rhoads and Thalhimers in early 1960. Though a tense time, Richmond did not see the violence and police brutality that other cities did, and integration came relatively peacefully, if haphazardly and slowly.

As was typical of the times, highway construction and urban-renewal projects in the '50s and '60s plowed through black and working-class white neighborhoods, letting them take the hit for progress and convenience. Jackson Ward and other neighborhoods were torn in two, and in the guise of progress, more than 1,500 antebellum homes were torn down and thousands of people were displaced. Such destruction galvanized preservationists, and people such as Mary Wingfield Scott fought to preserve the rich store of architecture and the fabric of neighborhoods.

Unlike almost every other part of the U.S., cities in Virginia are independent entities, not part of the counties that surround them, so annexation of surrounding county land was for centuries the only way for Richmond to grow. That came to a halt in the 1970s during a contentious seven-year legal battle over the annexation of Chesterfield County. The case was mired in volatile issues of voting rights, segregated schools, and court-ordered busing, which had come into play in 1970 and caused more dissension and white flight from city schools. As a calming measure, a moratorium on annexations was enacted. Over time, the city and counties have worked together to create a regional airport commission and other entities, but still the scars of annexation and Virginia's peculiarities have made regionalization slow going.

COLLEGE TOWN

A $50 million gift to the University of Richmond in 1969 from E. Claiborne Robins, the pharmaceutical manufacturer (of more than $200 million eventually donated by his family), was predicated on UR's becoming independent of the Baptist General Association of Virginia. The university was well on its way to becoming a leading liberal arts university in the South and a more engaged participant in Richmond cultural and intellectual life.

In 1968 Richmond Professional Institute and the Medical College of Virginia merged to form Virginia Commonwealth University. At first, the commuter school in the Fan was uneasily aligned with the venerable Medical College of Virginia downtown, but as you'll see, that has changed dramatically.

Recommended Richmond Reading

American City, Southern Place, by Gregg D. Kimball

At the Falls: Richmond, Virginia and Its People, by Marie Tyler McGraw

Built by Blacks, by Selden Richardson

The Capitol of Virginia, by Fiske Kimball

Nonesuch Place: A History of the Richmond Landscape, by T. Tyler Potterfield

Pennies to Dollars: The Story of Maggie Lena Walker, by Muriel Miller Branch and Dorothy Marie Rice

Richmond: A Historic Walking Tour, by Keisha A. Case

Richmond after the War, 1865–1890, by Michael Chesson

Richmond Burning, by Nelson D. Lankford

Southern Lady, Yankee Spy: The True Story of Elizabeth Van Lew, a Union Agent in the Heart of the Confederacy, by Elizabeth R. Varon

Southern Strategies: Southern Women and the Woman Suffrage Question, by Elna Green

This Business of Relief: Confronting Poverty in a Southern City, 1740–1940, by Elna Greene

True Richmond Stories, by Harry Kollatz Jr.

RIVER RICHES

Richmond has had a rocky relationship with its river, either using and abusing it or ignoring it until a flood swept through town. Late in the 20th century, Richmond realized what a jewel it had and began addressing decades of neglect by cleaning up pollution, transforming the river into a gathering place for people and wildlife, including bald eagles. In 1972 the James River Park System was created, and over the years it has grown to more than 500 acres of urban wilderness in the middle of the city. Learn more about it in both the "Parks" and "A River Runs Through It" chapters.

Henry Marsh became Richmond's first black mayor in 1977, in a time of uncertainty for the city. Richmond Renaissance was created to speak with one voice, black and white, business and government, to build a stronger, more vibrant city. After the damage done to Richmond by three major storms, Camille in 1969, Agnes in 1972, and Juan in 1985, and the inability to foster growth and development in the flood zone, the city finally persuaded the Army Corps of Engineers to build flood walls on both the north and south banks of the river. Even at $135 million, it was a good use of funds; the cleanup from Agnes alone cost $112 million, and the 750 acres now protected are booming entertainment, residential, and light industrial areas.

PROGRESS ON ALL FRONTS

Virginia and Richmond have come a long way in coming to terms with their history of denying opportunity to many citizens. In 1983 Virginia granted official recognition to the Chickahominy, Eastern Chickahominy, Pamunkey, Mattaponi, Upper Mattaponi, and Rappahannock Indian tribes, and to the Nansemond, Monacan, Patawomeck, Nottoway, and Cheroenhaka tribes more recently.

In an especially proud moment for Richmond, in 1989 L. Douglas Wilder, a grandson of ex-slaves and a Richmond lawyer, became the first African American in the nation to be elected governor of a state. So much more was possible than just 20 years before. It was an exciting time for the city. The completion of the flood wall in 1995 spurred development downtown, including the creation of the 1¼-mile Canal Walk, which takes one back through Richmond's past.

In the 1990s and into the 21st century, under the nearly 20-year tenure of former president Eugene Trani, Virginia Commonwealth University transformed itself from a commuter school attached to a nationally respected medical center into a complete public university, 30,000 students strong, expanding out from Monroe Park, adding an engineering school, advertising graduate programs, and building state-of-the-art spaces for its renowned art and sculpture programs. The university sparked a renaissance along Broad Street. MCV, now known as VCU Health Systems, has continued to grow and be a leader in health care, employing thousands downtown in its medical, nursing, dental, pharmacy, and allied health professions schools and its high-tech

hospitals, and at various satellite locations around the city.

High-end shopping, at Stony Point Fashion Park, anchored by Saks and Dillard's, and Short Pump Town Center, anchored by Nordstrom and Macy's, arrived in Richmond in 2003, just as Hurricane Isabel blew through, knocking out power for weeks for some residents. The completion of I-295 two-thirds of the way around Richmond, closing the loop with VA 288 and VA 895 has spread development around the region and made it more convenient to get from one side to the other.

Richmond's political landscape underwent changes in 2004, when the city charter was revised to allow for the direct election of the mayor after years of the city council electing the mayor from among its members. In 2010, with Mayor Dwight Jones in office, the city and counties were working together on occasion to assess how best the region could shake off the effects of the downturn in the economy. The region's politicians and business leaders were making it the region's No. 1 priority to get high-speed rail service between Richmond and Washington, D.C. It all comes back to location, after 400 years.

A FRESH START

The city's reliance on tobacco has diminished considerably, to the point that in late 2009 a smoking ban went into effect in restaurants in Virginia and few people blinked or coughed. Former tobacco warehouses have been converted to hip downtown lofts, offices, and stores. Even with the national economic downturn taking its toll, and the loss of two Fortune 500 companies, Circuit City and LandAmerica, to bankruptcy, Richmond's economic diversity is helping it weather the storm better than most.

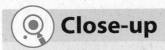

Close-up

Statue Status

In a city so given to using statues as pieces in a game of chess, it was perhaps not surprising that in 1995 controversy erupted over placing a statue of native son, tennis champion, writer, and activist **Arthur Ashe,** on Monument Avenue. After his death in 1993, he was buried in Richmond, the city that denied him the use of the Byrd Park tennis courts when he was growing up, because he was black. When the statue was proposed, some objected to putting anyone other than a Confederate hero on the avenue. Others thought Ashe deserved a place untainted by a racist past. Still others wanted a statue of Ashe—just not the one that was proposed. But in 1996 the statue was erected on Monument Avenue, facing west. He fits in just fine now.

When a statue of President Lincoln and his son Tad was placed on the Tredegar Civil War site in 2003, in the spirit of "binding up the nation's wounds" and commemorating their visit to Richmond in April 1865, some malcontents summoned a different spirit. They chartered a plane that flew overhead with a banner reading SIC SEMPER TYRANNIS, the motto of Virginia that John Wilkes Booth famously shouted in Ford's Theatre after assassinating Lincoln.

More recently, the placement of new statues hasn't stirred controversy, perhaps because they were so long overdue. The *Richmond Slavery Reconciliation Statue,* installed downtown in 2007, not far from the site of a former slave market, acknowledges Richmond's past while proposing healing. Matching bronze sculptures by Stephen Broadbent stand in Liverpool, England, and in Benin, West Africa, to mark the triangle of the slave trade. In 2008 the **Virginia Civil Rights Memorial** in Capitol Square was unveiled, celebrating the courage of those who fought segregation by sitting in, standing up, walking out, or arguing before the courts. And in 2010 the statue of **Connecticut,** a Native American sculpted by Paul DiPasquale, which had been a part of the Diamond for years during the Richmond Braves' tenure there, was due to be moved to the top of the Lucky Strike building in Shockoe Bottom, overlooking the James River. Interestingly enough, *Connecticut* means "beside the tidal river." Another long overdue monument is planned for Capitol Square to commemorate Virginia Indians.

Another Fortune 500 company, MeadWestvaco, just opened its riverfront headquarters in late 2009. Perhaps because the economy is a mix of health care and biotechnology, utilities, packaging, government, financial companies, law, and advertising, in the summer of 2009 *BusinessWeek* said Richmond was the sixth best city in the country to start fresh. A vibrant creative class, anchored by the Martin Agency, which was named the No. 1 advertising agency in the country for 2009 by *Adweek,* is stirring up excitement and jobs. And the city is becoming known as a great outdoors destination, with boosts from signature sporting and artistic events such as the SunTrust Richmond Marathon and the Richmond Folk Festival. A more ethnically diverse population in the city and suburbs only adds to the excitement and possibilities.

PUTTING HISTORY IN ITS PLACE

Before the Jamestown 2007 commemoration, the General Assembly voted unanimously to express profound regret for its part in perpetuating the institution of slavery, establishing the Jim Crow era, and exploiting Native Americans. In 1998 the Richmond mayor at the time, Tim Kaine, apologized for slavery on behalf of the city, which was once a major exporter of slaves. Richmond played its part in the 400th anniversary of the English settlement of Virginia, when Queen Elizabeth II addressed the General Assembly in Richmond before touring Jamestown. Reproductions of the original ships that sailed to Jamestown sailed up the James River, and fireworks over the river marked the occasion. With the backing of the commonwealth, Virginia's tribes are now seeking federal recognition, which 562 other tribes have received. As the tribes aptly note, they were the first to welcome the settlers yet are the last to be recognized.

As the sesquicentennial of both the Civil War and the end of slavery approaches, Richmond is still learning to give history its due. A group of influential Richmonders has sponsored a series of community conversations, as part of The Future of Richmond's Past program to engage people all over the region in discussions of our common and divergent experiences of the past and how our past should be incorporated into our future. Our history has been rocky—not unlike the river that flows through here—but the river renews, and so do the people of the Richmond region.

A RIVER RUNS THROUGH IT

Richmond is the only major city in the U.S. with Class IV white-water rapids shooting right through the middle of downtown. The James River is so beloved now for its beauty and recreational opportunities that it's hard to realize that for so long it was a dirty, industrial waterway that the area used and abused, and otherwise turned its back on. The Clean Water Act of 1972 changed that, thank goodness, and for years now the James has been a great source of pride and a drawing card for the region, a beautiful asset that people want to play in and protect.

From muscle-powered sculls to powerboats, with tubes, rafts, canoes, and kayaks in between, people like to get out on the water. This chapter will give you the 411 on how to stay safe, so no one will have to call 911. The James River is not a water park. There are no lifeguards, and people have drowned in it, so pay attention to water levels and rules of the river, some of which are mentioned in this chapter.

In one day along the James here, you can see herons trying to get lucky, bufflehead ducks cavorting on winter days, and bald eagles within the city limits. In warmer weather you'll see painters painting plein air, white-water rafters rolling through rapids, expert kayakers surfing, mountain bikers carving riverside trails, fly fisherfolk casting off, volunteers spreading mulch on trails and picking up trash, and families frolicking.

Some folks are lucky enough to work with a river view. Don't assume that you can't afford to live near the river; there are so many neighborhoods that offer river views from condos, apartments, townhomes, and single-family homes or feature easy access to the river. With fishing, paddling, tubing, hiking and biking trails, and rocks to climb and scramble over, living near the river is as close as most of us will ever get to living in a full-service resort. Too many outsiders think of Richmond as a city of statues, but we're not about standing still; we're romping along the river.

MUST SEE RIVER VIEWS

No matter where you live or stay, make sure to cross the James—it's the quickest and easiest way to get a sense of the river you've heard about. The Lee and Manchester Bridges downtown offer impressive views. Farther west, the Boulevard, Powhite, Huguenot, and Willey Bridges give you a show, as well. Obviously, it's better to do most of your river-gazing while you're in the passenger seat. Of course, I recommend getting out of the car to really see what the river is all about. The spots listed below are only the top four spots out of numerous ones I could mention. The "Parks" chapter has many more, but these offer different perspectives on the mighty James.

BELLE ISLE PEDESTRIAN BRIDGE

Park at the end of Tredegar Street, under the railroad tracks, and walk or ride onto this fabulous bit of suspended concrete. It's wheelchair accessible and exhilarating. Marvel at the rafters and kayakers zipping through Hollywood Rapids upriver and take in the view of downtown, the history and the high rises, downriver. Crossing over to Belle Isle, a popular part of the James River Park System, a great place to go mountain biking, you can walk alongside the infamous and treacherous Hollywood Rapids as well as see evidence that it was once a notorious Civil War POW camp.

BROWN'S ISLAND

490 Tredegar St.

www.venturerichmond.com

Owned by the city and managed by Venture Richmond, it's not a part of the city parks department, yet Brown's Island functions as a park downtown between the canal and the James River. No need to get wet to access this island. One bridge is near the American Civil War Center, and the other is at 7th and Tredegar Streets. Be sure to walk out onto the April 1865 overlook that walks visitors through the last days of the Civil War, using the words of those who lived it to make the events come alive as the river whooshes by. Brown's Island is the site of numerous festivals, concerts, and races, including Dominion RiverRock, Friday Cheers, and the Richmond Folk Festival. Besides forming the western entry point to the Canal Walk, the island has a more rugged path that connects to the Trestle Trail section of the James River Park, also known as the Pipeline Trail. Parking is available along 5th Street and in nearby lots.

ℹ When Richmonders say they're going to "the rivah" for the weekend, they mean the Northern Neck rivers, the Rappahannock or the York or their many tributaries, well east of Richmond, not the river in the city's backyard.

RICHMOND FLOOD WALL

To get a sense of industry, history, and nature in one walk, you've come to the right place. Though there are flood walls on both the north and south banks of the James in Richmond, the southern portion is built so that walking on top of it is allowed and encouraged. Park at the flood wall lot at the end of Semmes Avenue near the SunTrust buildings and follow the path over the railroad tracks to the overlook atop an old railroad bridge abutment for a cool view of the river and downtown. If you're daring, you could take the trip down the "Mayan Ruins," as runners jokingly refer to them (especially when they are chugging up them), or you could wind back and go down the hill and alongside the railroad tracks to head toward the actual flood wall. Once up there, you can walk for a mile and see herons, cormorants, and other fish-eating birds, as well as plenty of evidence of how the railroads and industry shaped Richmond, and still do.

Floods are spectator sports here in Richmond now that the flood wall protects the city from the river's most damaging effects. When the river hits flood stage at 12 feet, parts of some streets will close, but people will be drawn to the overlooks to see the water raging.

Wheelchair users who want to go on the flood wall should park in the rock climbers' parking lot under the Manchester Bridge, accessible from 7th Street, and with assistance they can navigate the packed gravel until reaching the paved top of the wall. A set of stairs ¾ of a mile in ends the wheelchair-accessible portion.

RIVERSIDE DRIVE

With a name like that, this road really is calling your name, whereas River Road in Henrico County is just teasing because there are no river views to be found there. Riverside Drive is a scenic road, narrow and windy in some sections, that starts just west of the Lee Bridge and meanders from Woodland Heights through Westover Hills, a beautiful stretch of road with some lovely river views, more in the winter than in the summer. This is leisurely driving with many sharp turns, and since walkers, runners, and cyclists like it, too, you might decide to park your car as well. The road ends on Forest Hill Avenue in Westover Hills, only to be picked up again west of the Powhite Parkway in Stratford Hills near Pony Pasture Rapids Park, part of the James River Park System. This last stretch of Riverside Drive going towards and a little past the Huguenot Bridge is full of beautiful views, which are best appreciated by walking or biking on the paths that can often get you much closer to the river than a car can. Running and cycling groups use this scenic section for their training days, and it's easy to see why, but too many people drive too fast here, especially coming home from work, and the summer weekend cruising can be nerve-racking, so pick your forays here wisely.

i Walk across the Boulevard Bridge for some charming river and wildlife views, using the pedestrian walkway. It's narrow, so bikers are supposed to walk their bikes, but don't expect to see that too often. You could connect to the Buttermilk or North Bank Trails from the bridge if you want a longer hike.

BOAT RAMPS ALONG THE RIVER

Whether you need a place to launch your powerboat or a spot to plop in a more

---

James River Etiquette and Safety

When the river is 5 feet or higher, life jackets must be worn on the river, and when it gets to 9 feet, only paddlers with high-water permits are allowed on the water. Even at lower levels, since the river's bottom is uneven, it's possible to wind up over one's head. Use caution and common sense; if you can't swim, stay out of the river. If you do get swept in a rapid, float feet first to keep from bashing your head on a rock. Standing in fast water can get your foot jammed in a rock and can be deadly. Call (804) 646-8228, ext. 4, for water-level information.

Whenever you wander into the river, wear closed-toe shoes such as old running shoes, not flip-flops. Stones, branches, glass, and other sharp debris lurk underwater, and you don't want to make a detour to the emergency room. Along the same lines, glass bottles are prohibited in the James River Park. And whatever you bring out onto the river, please bring it back and put it in a trash or recycling container.

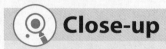 **Close-up**

Nature in and around the James

The variety of wildlife along and in the James is a testament to the river's improved health since the enactment of the Clean Water Act in 1972. It's a wondrous thing to be within the city limits of the capital of Virginia and see bald eagles soaring overhead, and osprey and peregrine falcons, too. Bald eagle sightings are becoming routine along some stretches of the river in the city, though they are never really routine. If you fish or snorkel, you might see gar, shad, perch, striped bass, huge catfish, and even the almost prehistoric sturgeon, because they're all in there. If you walk along the flood wall during the spring fish migration, the birds of prey wheeling about and diving for dinner will attest to that.

Several parks along the river, including Dutch Gap in Chesterfield County and the Wetlands section in the James River Park System, have wonderful birding opportunities beyond the birds of prey. Get your life lists out and get to work. It's common to see cormorants, hawks, owls, and kingfishers, and the list surely goes on. Great blue herons, always a treat to spot flying along the river, have recently shacked up on an island downtown, building more than 40 nests of sticks high up in the trees at their rookery. It's viewable from the Trestle Trail, aka Pipeline Trail, near 12th Street, and in mid-February through March you can see these gawky-on-land, graceful-in-flight, 4-foot-tall birds involved in the particulars of heron courtship. Later in the spring the show changes as the babies hatch and learn to fly. If the river level is low enough, there's a sandy beach where families can play and watch the river rookery.

If you canoe or kayak, you might glide near a beaver, otter, or muskrat, and it's fun to see the large turtles sunning themselves on logs and rocks in the river. Deer are plentiful and are often seen near the river at night. Foxes are sighted occasionally, raccoons more often, and even once a year or so, a small, confused bear.

Every season brings something new to the river. It's most crowded with people in the summer, but most beautiful in the fall and winter when the colors change, the crowds recede, and the sun's angle lights the treetops that tower above the river on fire. In my neighborhood, spotted salamanders come out of hibernation exactly when we don't want to, on rainy late-February nights. Parking at Pony Pasture is allowed then, and Riverside Drive is closed off so that the poor little guys don't get squished as they make their way to little ponds and marshes to mate and lay eggs. Bring a flashlight and walk west along the road, and watch where you step. In February and March, when you need to be reminded that spring is coming, head to the Wetlands section of JRPS to hear the spring peepers and chorus frogs sing their songs of spring.

humble tube, here are the main put-ins along the James in this region. Please know what you're doing and where you're going before you get on the water, as currents can be strong and dams and dangerous rapids are plentiful in some areas. Wear life jackets. Boaters must have a Coast Guard–approved life jacket for each passenger according to regulations. Get more information at www .dgif.virginia.gov/boating.

North Bank of the River

Richmond
14TH STREET TAKEOUT

Hidden away just north of the 14th Street Bridge, this small section of the James River Park System is the takeout used by expert white-water paddlers who have shot the big Class III and IV rapids through downtown. Because it is beneath the rapids at the tidal James River, one could put in here for a float, but the proximity to the sewage treatment plant, however good a job they do over there, usually dissuades people. Because parking is so limited here, you must have either a boat rack or a James River Outdoor Coalition (JROC) or Friends of James River Park (FOJRP) sticker to park here.

Henrico County
DEEP BOTTOM PARK
9525 Deep Bottom Rd.

The farthest east of the area's James River boat launches, this park has two boat ramps that get you onto the James River and a canoe launch for Four Mile Creek. You can launch and bring in boats 24 hours a day, but the park grounds are open from dawn to dusk only.

OSBORNE BOAT LANDING
9680 Osborne Turnpike

This spot features three double boat slips and a canoe launch, and they are available from dawn to dusk. An accessible fishing pier reaches out into the James, and there are trails, a playground, and picnic shelters here as well. Osborne has hosted Bassmasters events in the past, so you know the fishing is good around here.

River Reading Material

To make your walks more enjoyable, purchase interpretive guides published by the **James River Park System.** They are packed with historical and geological information and explain the natural world before you. The $2 pamphlets, written by legendary James River park manager Ralph White, are on such subjects as the Richmond Slave Trail, the flood wall, Pony Pasture, Belle Isle, and fishing along the river. They are available at Blue Ridge Mt. Sports, REI, Riverside Outfitters, Reedy Creek Park Headquarters, City Hall, some museum gift shops, and various river-related events.

Pick up a James River Days brochure at outdoorsy places or access it online at www.james riveradvisorycouncil.com to see hundreds of river-related good times, such as concerts, canoe trips, treasure hunts, snorkeling, and more, planned by Richmond, surrounding counties, and non-profit groups. James River Days run from April through November, so there's no excuse not to get out there at least once.

South Bank of the River

Richmond
ANCARROW'S LANDING/MANCHESTER DOCKS
Maury Street to Brander Street

A busy place because its concrete ramp situates boaters just beneath the fall line, exactly where the fish are, this section of the city's James River Park System is perhaps the most culturally diverse spot in Richmond, especially in the spring when the shad are running. It's a fishermen's paradise (most of them are men, but of course some are women), and on any given afternoon you'll see people lining the bank with their fishing rods, and in boats, angling from that angle. Wheelchair users can use the concrete path next to the boat ramp. It's also the beginning of the Richmond Slave Trail. Find more about that in the "Parks" and "Commemorating the Civil War and Emancipation" chapters. To get here, follow Maury Street past huge oil tanks towards the Manchester Docks signs, going past the city's sewage treatment plant. This area would make a cool movie set.

HUGUENOT FLATWATER
8600 Riverside Dr.
This small parking lot fills up on summer weekends, so get there early to put your canoe or kayak in the water, here in the westernmost section of the James River Park System. There's one boat slide here, and you can paddle up river as far as Bosher's Dam or go beneath the Huguenot Bridge and wander around the islands with no motorboats to contend with. Just pay attention as there are well-marked and dangerous dams downstream and you must portage to the north to avoid the Z Dam. Don't be fooled by the notch; it's for fish coming upriver to spawn, and it's very dangerous for boaters or tubers. Several people have died here because of the dangerous hydraulics. Stay away! Back near the parking lot on Southampton Road there is a small parking area that has a semi-paved path suitable for wheelchair access to a river overlook.

PONY PASTURE RAPIDS PARK
7200 Riverside Dr.
Pony Pasture, one of the most popular sections of Richmond's James River Park System, is a zoo on summer weekends, and people are the animals. Parking can be very difficult on warm weekend days, and parking on nearby streets is illegal. It's usually possible to pull in to drop off or pick up your boat at the boat ramp. It's a wooden boat slide just beneath the biggest rapids at Pony Pasture, and many people head downstream to the Reedy Creek takeout from here. That is one takeout you don't want to miss. The treacherous Hollywood Rapids loom afterwards and should be attempted only by experienced white-water paddlers.

REEDY CREEK
4001 Riverside Dr.
Only expert paddlers should put in here in the main area of the James River Park System. Though it looks calm enough near Park Headquarters, heading downriver takes you to First Break and Hollywood Rapids, neither one to be attempted by anyone other than advanced paddlers. Reedy Creek is a popular takeout for those tubing or kayaking from the west, who know enough to get out while the getting's good.

Chesterfield County
DUTCH GAP BOAT LANDING
441 Coxendale Rd.
The river is tidal here, wide and best suited to powerboats. The concrete ramp will make life easy for you, and it's likely that the fish will, too. The fishing for blue catfish and largemouth bass is outstanding in the area.

ROBIOUS LANDING PARK
3800 James River Rd.
www.chesterfield.gov
This park, just behind James River High School and above Bosher's Dam, has a boat slide suitable for small cartop-size craft such as canoes and Jon boats. It's a popular spot for rowing since the Virginia Boat Club has a boathouse here and the Rapids of James River High School field a crew team.

HISTORY ALONG THE RIVER

The city owes its very existence to the river, though it hasn't always shown it proper gratitude.

Flour and cotton mills and ironworks were powered by the water, canals moved people and goods back and forth, and tragically, ships sailed up and downriver carrying slaves to and from what became the second largest slave market in the South. The Canal Walk tells some of the tales associated with Richmond's river history. See more on that in the "Attractions" chapter. The Richmond Slave Trail, which gets attention in the "Commemorating the Civil War and Emancipation" chapter, tells more.

Just about everywhere you turn along the river, there's some feature of history, whether geological or man-made. Think of this as the Reduced Richmond History, one site for each century since the English made contact with the Native Americans here. Remember the fast-talking guy who could tell the story of *Moby Dick* in a minute? This is the same idea, consolidating an entire century into one river-related site.

1600s

HENRICUS HISTORICAL PARK
251 Henricus Park Rd.
www.henricus.org

Along the river here at this walk back through time, you can get a sense of the Native American society that was here first and see how Sir Thomas Dale's attempt at improving upon the miserable conditions at Jamestown worked out. Tour buildings and interact with costumed interpreters living the 17th-century life.

1700s

WESTOVER
7000 Westover Rd.
Charles City
(804) 829-2882
William Byrd II had Westover built for himself and his family circa 1730. Of course, this impressive spread is in no way representative of how most people at any time in history lived, but Richmond traces its establishment as a town to Byrd, so a pilgrimage here seems only fair. But you don't have to go that far to feel connected to Byrd. Just head up Church Hill to Libby Hill Park at 28th and East Franklin Streets and look to the east to see the view that named Richmond. It is said that Byrd, who spent many years being educated in England, thought the view similar to the view from Richmond on Thames, and that is why we're in Richmond today.

1800s

TREDEGAR SITE (INCLUDING BELLE ISLE)
490 Tredegar St.
The Tredegar site is more than a fabulous place to learn about the causes and effects of the Civil War at both the American Civil War Center and Richmond National Battlefield Park Visitor Center. It also has remnants of Richmond's industrial past— a foundry building, millraces, waterwheels,

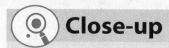

Close-up

River Festivals and Races

Sometimes it's easier to get a sense of the river and its trails by following the crowd. Here are some of the most popular river-related events, but by no means all of them.

DOMINION RIVERROCK

Brown's Island
www.sportsbackers.org

A Filthy 5K one day and the James River Scramble 10K the next offer runners the chance to race riverside paths they might not know exist. Music, food, frivolity, biking and kayaking competitions, and white-water rafting opportunities make this mid-May celebration of the river in Richmond an event you won't want to miss. Find out more in the "Annual Events" chapter.

FRIDAY CHEERS

Nationally known musical acts have been taking over the stage on Brown's Island for more than 25 years during Friday Cheers. Friday night concerts in May and June start the summer right, especially since admission to the concerts is just $2. Food, beer, and wine are available for purchase. Please don't bring your pets, bikes, coolers, alcohol, or skateboards. Get details in the "Performing Arts" chapter.

JAMES RIVER BATTEAU FESTIVAL

http://batteau.org

This event doesn't make its way into the Richmond area until it's almost over on the eighth day, but it celebrates the unusual, almost forgotten shallow boats that plied the James with passengers and cargo from 1775 to 1840. For 25 years enough brave souls have wanted to float and push their way on the James from Lynchburg to Maidens Landing in Powhatan, a distance of 120 river miles, in homemade wooden reproductions of the batteau, dressing the part and camping along the way as part of the festival. Every day's landing is a special event in the river town. Check their Web site for their scheduled landings and departures.

canal infrastructure, and other vestiges of Richmond's reliance on the river for water-power. Across the river on Belle Isle, Union POWs suffered and died. Across the canal on Brown's Island, Confederate munitions were made, and later, former slave and renowned orator John Jasper started Sixth Mount Zion Baptist Church in an abandoned Confederate building there.

1900s

RICHMOND FLOOD WALL

For that last century some of us still remember, the flood wall is our symbol, for without it, much of the downtown economic development of the last 20 years would not have happened, and we wouldn't have had nearly as much fun in Shockoe Bottom and Manchester. After the devastating and expensive

RICHMOND EARTH DAY AND FISH FESTIVAL

320 Hull Street Rd.

www.earthdayrichmond.org

Art and nature combine for a whimsical, fun-filled, and free celebration of the river and the fish that spawn in it. Take a shuttle ride to tour Bosher's Dam's fish ladder, plant a tree, make some art, zip on a zip line for kids, release some tiny shad into the river, or just watch a city troupe do the interpretive dance of the James River Shad while music plays. Food is available for purchase.

RICHMOND FOLK FESTIVAL

Tredegar Street and Brown's Island

www.richmondfolkfestival.com

The river is the backdrop for this free three-day music festival every Fri, Sat, and Sun of Columbus Day weekend. Performers from all over the world let loose on several stages spread out among Brown's Island, the Tredegar site, and up the hill to 2nd Street. This one event brings more people to the river than any other. Don't miss it. Parking is available in nearby surface lots and on the street. Free shuttles run from out of town. Check www.richmondfolkfestival.com for details and see more about the festival in the "Annual Events" chapter.

XTERRA GAMES

www.xterraplanet.com

In June this nationally known touring extravaganza of extreme sports lands in Richmond on Brown's Island for the Xterra East Championship. Richmond's unusual natural and man-made features along the river make it one of the most popular courses in the country and explain why Xterra has been coming to Richmond since 1999. Pro triathletes compete for a large purse and a spot in the World Championship, while lesser mortals strut their stuff in a 10K race, a half marathon, or a sport triathlon. Find more on this in the "Spectator Sports" chapter.

floods in 1969, 1972, and 1985, the city finally won approval for a flood wall. Finished in 1995 by the Army Corps of Engineers, the flood wall protects more than 750 acres of the city on both sides of the river, and the southern section provides great city, wildlife, and river views.

2000s

JAMES RIVER PARK SYSTEM

www.jamesriverpark.org

Richmond's historic 2009 Conservation Easement on approximately 280 acres of the city's 550-acre James River Park System, restricting all future development in eight parcels of the park, means that not only you can walk, run, or bike beautiful river trails or rock-hop or fish, or jump in the river and get wet, but your grandchildren and their grandchildren will be able to, too. That there was a park worth conserving owes much to Joe Schaefer and Jack Keith Jr., locals who accumulated the first parcels of land that would become the park in the 1960s and donated them to the city, and to park manager Ralph White, who has worked miracles over the ensuing decades, improving and caring for this now beloved and protected park. Bringing people back to the river after decades (OK, centuries) of neglect is due in large part to the Clean Water Act in the 20th century and the city's commitment to cleaning up the river with a combined sewer overflow system. The abundance of fish and wildlife, including bald eagles nesting here, a heron rookery, and excellent catfish and bass fisheries attests to improved water quality.

PLAYING ON THE RIVER

Listed below are businesses and organizations that will help get you out on the river in a variety of ways, and get you back safely.

ADVENTURE CHALLENGE
(804) 276-7600
www.adventurechallenge.com
This longtime Richmond company offers white-water instruction and guided kayak or tubing trips.

APPOMATTOX RIVER COMPANY
14213 Midlothian Turnpike, Midlothian
(804) 897-1556
www.paddleva.com
Don't let the name fool you; their equipment will work just fine on the James River, too. With over 200 new canoes and kayaks in stock and many used ones to choose from as well, this place will outfit you for a lifetime of paddling.

BLUE RIDGE MOUNTAIN SPORTS
11500 Midlothian Turnpike
(804) 794-2004
www.brmsstore.com
A great community partner, BRMS offers "Hit the H2O" free kayak demo days several times a year at area parks and occasional day-trip paddles for a fee. Besides kayak and canoes and the associated gear, they also carry rock-climbing equipment for those so inclined. A second location is at 10164 W. Broad St. (804-965-0494).

i For the ultimate river experience, sign up your 8- to 17-year-old children for Passages Adventure Camp this summer. With expert guidance, campers learn to kayak, rock climb, and rappel, all in the James River Park System. Many campers go on to become river guides themselves. Call (804) 897-8283, ext. 310, or visit www.peak experiences.com.

GREEN TOP
10193 Washington Hwy.
(804) 550-2188
www.greentophuntfish.com
For more than 60 years it's been *the* place in central Virginia to go for fishing and hunting gear and expert advice. The staff knows the outdoors and is dedicated to getting you out there. The store, not far from Virginia Center Commons, is open seven days a week.

i The large, national outdoorsy chains REI, Bass Pro Shops, Dick's Sporting Goods, and Gander Mountain have locations in and around Richmond. See the yellow pages for locations.

CHESTERFIELD COUNTY PARKS
(804) 748-1124
www.chesterfield.gov
Paddling instruction in white-water and flat-water canoeing and kayaking for beginners and intermediate folks is available through the county outdoor adventure and nature programs at both Dutch Gap and Pony Pasture in the city. Equipment is provided. Once you have completed certain classes, the county offers play days with supervised kayaking around town.

DISCOVER THE JAMES
(804) 938-2350
www.discoverthejames.com
The best opportunity you'll ever have to see bald eagles in the wild up close and personal is on U.S. Coast Guard–certified captain Mike Ostrander's covered, wheelchair-accessible, 24-foot pontoon boat, complete with space heater and comfortable seating. Choose from among year-round, two-hour Eagle Tours, three-hour photography tours, or two-hour John Smith history tours. You'll come aboard at Deep Bottom Boat Landing in Henrico County on the north side of the river and get close to the water and the birds that are both the symbol of our nation and a symbol of a cleaner environment. Be sure to bring a camera and binoculars, though the eagles will get so close you won't always need the latter. It's $30 per person for a two-hour tour. A minimum of four people is necessary and the maximum is six people.

JAMES RIVER FISHING SCHOOL
(804) 938-2350
www.jamesriverfishing.com
Any time of the year, hit the river for half- or full-day (or even night fishing sometimes) guided catch-and-release fishing trips, guaranteed to make sure the big one gets away only after there's a photo of you holding it. With 25 years of fishing experience, Mike Ostrander finds the hot spots in the James aboard either a 24-foot pontoon boat or a 16-foot runabout in the lower James, or in a raft or Jon boat in the upper section. You'll be amazed at the size of the fish that live in this river, and whether it's blue catfish, flathead catfish, striped bass, or hickory shad that you hook, photos proving your prowess are all part of the deal, as are all fishing gear, tackle, and a light meal. For the novice, fishing instruction is available at various waterways around town.

i Eagle Cruises offers private charters aboard *Eagle I*, their 102-foot vessel that takes groups on lunch and dinner cruises and even moonlight cruises. Passengers embark from 3101 Wharf St. above Rockett's Landing just below downtown, and the boat heads 8 miles down the tidal James River. Call (804) 222-0223 to talk with Captain Bert Lewis or check www.eaglecruises.net for pricing and information.

RIVER CITY RAFTING
100 Stockton St.
(804) 232-RAFT
www.rivercityraft.com
This rafting company offers raft trips to appeal to the thrill seeker or the more tame among us. One trip floats along Class I and II rapids that are barely bump-worthy, and the other trips take you all the way through Hollywood Rapids and the Class IIIs and IVs for the real deal. You'll hear about the well-named Mitchell's Gut rapids and other tidbits of Richmond history while you're along for the ride. Rafting trips must be reserved in advance. Tube rentals

and guided tube trips for groups are also available. See more in the "Kidstuff" chapter.

RIVERSIDE OUTFITTERS
6836 Old Westham Parkway
(804) 560-0068
www.riversideoutfitters.net

This adventure outfit near Pony Pasture is full service, offering canoes, kayaks, tubes, and river boards for rent with a handy and free equipment shuttle thrown in, as well as guided white-water rafting, canoeing, and kayaking trips down the James. The white-water rafting trips are your chance to tackle the Class II, III, and IV rapids that flow through downtown in an exhilarating and adrenaline-producing rollicking ride. The upper raft trip and all of the canoeing and kayaking trips are more serene, offering flat water and in some cases Class I and II riffles. There are even sunset trips to catch the river at its most beautiful. Reservations are required for the guided trips. See more in the "Kidstuff" chapter.

VIRGINIA BOAT CLUB
P.O. Box 8468
Richmond, VA 23226-8468
www.virginiaboatclub.org

This boat club is for those who want to be the motor of the boat, either sweeping (pulling one oar) or sculling (pulling two). Once you join the Virginia Boat Club, you have access to both of the group's convenient boathouses and boats set near miles of rowable water above and below the falls. The downtown boathouse occupies the bottom two levels of the building that houses the Boathouse Restaurant at Rockett's Landing, so that's easy to remember. The Robious Landing boathouse is in Robious Landing Park in Chesterfield County. The club offers recreational and

competitive rowing and welcomes novice and veteran rowers alike. They host the Rockett's Landing Sprints downtown in June. See more in the "Spectator Sports" chapter.

TAKING CARE OF THE JAMES

There's an alphabet soup of organizations devoted to taking care of the James and surrounding lands, because taking care of the river, and in turn the Chesapeake Bay, means careful stewardship of all the land and waterways that are in the river basin. When a drought hits the region, as one did several years ago, we become frighteningly aware of how reliant we are on the James for our health and well-being as it is the region's main source of drinking water. Everything we do, from over-fertilizing lawns, choosing landscaping materials, using rain barrels, using pesticides, composting, keeping the lid on invasive plants, using native plants, watering lawns—heck, having lawns in the first place—and participating in cleanups of streams and rivers either helps or hurts the river that runs through the region—and us.

CHESAPEAKE BAY FOUNDATION
(804) 780-1392
www.cbf.org

Richmond is smack in the middle of the Chesapeake Bay watershed. Because everything connects, and two-thirds of Virginia is drained by rivers and streams that wind up in the bay, the Chesapeake Bay Foundation works to educate those living in the watershed that what we do affects the health of the bay. Restoring oysters and native grasses to area waterways is just part of their work. Encouraging land conservation and working to improve water quality is another. Volunteer projects are ongoing, so call to become a member and/or get involved.

FRIENDS OF JAMES RIVER PARK (FOJRP)

P.O. Box 4453

Richmond, VA 23220

www.jamesriverpark.org

The Friends' mission is to provide ongoing support to the James River Park System, financially and otherwise, so that the park is preserved and maintained and so park users' visits are enhanced and enjoyable. This group is all over the map, literally, conducting an annual survey of the parcels held in the Conservation Easement, holding cleanups in the park, and volunteering at park events like the Parade of Lights event at Libby Hill Park, to spread the good news about what the park has to offer. FOJRP also raises funds to ensure important park educational and outreach programs can continue. For as little as $15 you can be a friend, too.

JAMES RIVER ADVISORY COUNCIL (JRAC)

P.O. Box 40

Chesterfield, VA 23832

(804) 748-1567

www.jamesriveradvisorycouncil.com

A regional body composed of representatives from local counties and cities, business interests, and advocacy groups to coordinate and publicize river-friendly activities, this group promotes and preserves the vitality of the James. It sponsors the James River Parade of Lights in December, James River Days during the summer, and the James River Regional Clean Up in June.

JAMES RIVER ASSOCIATION (JRA)

9 S. 12th St.

(804) 788-8811

www.jamesriverassociation.org

James River Cleanup

The **James River Advisory Council** coordinates a massive annual river and riverbank cleanup the second Saturday in June that covers 70 miles of river and streams at several sites in the region. In the city of Richmond, volunteers meet at Pony Pasture or Reedy Creek Park Headquarters, and wielding trash bags, gloves, and good spirits, spread out from there. Chesterfield sites include Dutch Gap Boat Landing, Falling Creek Ironworks, and Robious Landing Park. Henrico sites are Osborne Park and Boat Landing and the Horsepen Branch. In Powhatan, Maidens Landing is the place, and in Goochland Westview Landing is the spot, though sites could change from year to year. JRAC gets hundreds of volunteers every year and needs them because the trash keeps coming. Some volunteers work on the water in their canoes and boats, but most scour the shoreline for trash and recyclable materials. Wear closed-toe shoes, but be willing to get your feet wet. You won't believe some of the stuff people pull out of the river—baby swings, beach chairs, coolers, tires—much of it dumped elsewhere and washed into the river during floods. Because lunch is provided for volunteers and some sites have a maximum number of volunteers, preregistration on the Web site, www.jamesriveradvisorycouncil.com, is highly encouraged.

This statewide advocacy group works to preserve and protect all 340 miles of the James from its headwaters in Iron Gate to its mouth at the Chesapeake Bay. When you realize that more than one-third of Virginians are connected to the James and its tributaries either by drinking water, recreation, or industry, it's a good thing JRA is here to take care of the river. Two paid river keepers monitor the James's health year-round, and JRA gets the community involved with habitat restoration, land conservation, and extreme stream makeovers. Recently they collaborated with Virginia Commonwealth University to increase sturgeon spawning grounds. You can join JRA for as little as $35 a year.

JAMES RIVER OUTDOOR COALITION (JROC)

P.O. Box 297
Richmond, VA 23219
www.jroc.net

This group is serious about improving the James River Park System and its many amenities, so serious that they often build the improvements themselves. Take the 14th Street boat takeout, for instance, or the changing rooms at several park sites. Where a need is identified, this group isn't afraid to get its hands dirty making the park and river a better place to be. They also hold an annual boat and gear swap and sale during the city's Earth Day celebration in Manchester. Membership costs as little as $20 a year.

RICHMOND AUDUBON SOCIETY

P.O. Box 26648
Richmond, VA 23261
(804) 257-0813
www.richmondaudubon.org/

It's impossible to be down at the river and not see some of our feathered friends, and the RAS does its best to make sure that is always the case. The group's activities include conservation, habitat restoration, planting with birds and butterflies in mind, and working with local schools so kids get the connection between how we treat our world and what lives in it. Members flit around all over town, leading bird walks and watches regularly. Membership is between $15 and $20.

RICHMOND AREA MID-ATLANTIC OFF-ROAD ENTHUSIASTS (RA MORE)

www.richmond-more.org

You might think that mountain biking has nothing to do with the river, but this group has built some of the best trails in town, many with views of the river, including the North Bank Trail, using environmentally friendly methods. RA MORE volunteers have put in hard labor to construct trails, bridges, and alternate routes that keep hikers safe from riders. The stone stairway they built in the main area of the James River Park System is beautiful and fits into the landscape so well you'd swear it was built years ago by the Civilian Conservation Corps. Their work has been instrumental in city trails winning so many awards. Membership gets you hooked in to MORE activities and rides, discounts at several area bike-related businesses, and the satisfaction of supporting a great organization. It's $25 for an individual yearly membership and $40 for a family.

SIERRA CLUB—FALLS OF THE JAMES GROUP

P.O. Box 25201
Richmond, VA 23260
(804) 721-5958
www.virginia.sierraclub.org/foj

The local chapter of the famed Sierra Club is involved in every aspect of environmental advocacy. In town, they lead volksmarches along the trails, hold day and overnight outings for members, have membership socials and meetings monthly at the Science Museum of Virginia, and work to improve recycling, promote urban sustainability, and establish greenways that promote outdoor experiences. Instrumental in getting the JRPS conservation easement in place, this group will keep working to preserve other parts of the park and other land so that view sheds are not lost and Richmond's environment stays healthy.

ACCOMMODATIONS

There are more than 16,000 hotel rooms in the Richmond area, so you shouldn't have too much trouble finding a place to lay down your head. Having said that, if you're visiting the same weekend as NASCAR race weekends in May and September, or the Colonial Athletic Association (CAA) basketball tournament in March, or Columbus Day weekend when the Richmond Folk Festival takes over the town, conveniently located hotel rooms go fast. And downtown hotels tighten up considerably when the General Assembly is in session from January to March. Another thing to keep in mind is that Richmond is a college town, so for big events like parents' weekend or graduations, certain hotels near UR, VCU, or VUU can fill up.

Now that I've scared you into booking early, let me give you the lay of the land as far as hotels in the region go. The hotels that are listed below are just a sample of what is available in the area. If you're here to see the sites of Richmond, I highly recommend staying downtown near the vast majority of the attractions. Many hotels offer shuttle service around downtown, so once you park your car (if you came with one), you can walk or take a hotel shuttle to many attractions and restaurants. Most hotels downtown do charge for parking, but if their rates are too steep, you can usually find nearby lots and garages in the $10- to $12-a-day range.

If you want to be in the suburbs, feel free to stay outside the city, but don't think you've *really* visited Richmond if you don't venture from there. The airport hotels in the East End make useful bases before early flights, but you won't see the best of what the area has to offer out there. Of course, there are dozens more hotels available than could be included here. This is just a cheat sheet.

OVERVIEW

Searching for hotels online is problematic with the Richmond region because the word *Richmond* doesn't always mean the city of Richmond. Many hotels have postal addresses that say Richmond, but they are actually located outside the city in either Chesterfield or Henrico County. Some hotels fudge things by including Mechanicsville-Richmond in their names. It's perfectly fine to stay in one of the county's hotels if that's where you want to be, but many travelers unfamiliar with Richmond's quirky relationship with the U.S. Postal Service book a hotel online that says it's in Richmond, only to find out when they arrive that they are several miles outside of town, not where they meant to be. Another quirk is that a hotel that both hotel marketers and Richmonders believe is in Short Pump might officially be listed as in Glen Allen. It's confusing. This chapter is divided by locality, starting with city hotels and expanding to the surrounding counties.

All of the hotels listed are wheelchair accessible and many have roll-in showers. Lovely as they are, none of the bed-and-breakfasts listed here are wheelchair accessible for overnight guests. For a town where tobacco was top dog until recently, a surprising number of hotels have gone nonsmoking. If smoking is allowed in a hotel, the listing says so. All of the B&Bs are nonsmoking, and they don't accept pets. Hotels that accept pets get a mention in the write-up.

Price Code

Prices are based on a one-night stay in a standard room. Please note that occasionally a range is given to better reflect the pricing. The pricing code is based on March 2010 rates that do not include the 13 percent hotel tax. Some hotels include breakfast in their basic rate. Of course, deals are available online or by checking directly with the hotel. Weekend rates can be substantially less expensive than weekday rates, and special packages are often available.

$..................... under $100
$$ .... $100 to $199
$$$ .... over $199

HOTELS

Downtown

THE BERKELEY HOTEL $$–$$$
1200 E. Cary St.
(804) 780-1300
www.berkeleyhotel.com
The 55-room Berkeley Hotel in Shockoe Slip is Richmond's only true boutique hotel, and though it opened in 1988, its warm and wood-paneled interior with old Virginia touches can fool visitors into thinking they are in a historic building. It was remodeled in 2008 with new mattresses, high-end cherry furnishings, and flat-screen TVs. Garnering AAA's four-diamond award for 21 years in a row, the Berkeley prides itself on giving guests a warm welcome and stellar service.

Seventeen rooms have balconies that overlook old and new Richmond. Wireless Internet is free throughout the hotel, and guest rooms are outfitted with luxury linens, coffeemakers, and terry bathrobes, and receive morning newspaper delivery. Room service is available from 6:30 a.m. to 10 p.m., and nightly turndown service with a homemade chocolate is complemented by complimentary health club privileges at the James Center YMCA, across the street. Smoking is allowed in rooms on the sixth floor by reservation, and valet parking is $17 per day. The Berkeley's cozy lounge is a great place for meetings, though there are also three larger meeting rooms and a ballroom available for events. Shockoe Slip and Bottom have varied dining options just out the door, but the understated yet elegant dining room at the Berkeley shines on its own, receiving AAA's four-diamond accolade as well. You'll find out why in the "Restaurants" chapter.

CROWNE PLAZA
RICHMOND DOWNTOWN $$
555 E. Canal St.
(804) 788-0900
www.crowneplaza.com/ric-downtown
This is one hotel in Richmond where it pays to ask for a room with a view; you could wind up seeing the river or Thomas Jefferson's Capitol. Guests can choose from 299 nonsmoking rooms with either one king or queen or two doubles. Self-parking in the adjacent garage or valet parking are both easy to use. If you're without wheels, the

hotel shuttle will gladly take you where you need to go within 2 miles. Guests have use of complimentary high-speed Internet, a pool, and fitness center. Room service is available from 6 a.m. to 11 p.m., and 13,000 square feet of meeting and banquet space is ready and waiting.

DOUBLETREE HOTEL DOWNTOWN
RICHMOND $$
301 W. Franklin St.
(804) 644-9871
http://doubletree1.hilton.com
Convenient to VCU's Monroe Park campus, this 230-room hotel is certified Virginia Green and offers a seasonally available rooftop pool. Choose either one king bed or two doubles, and enjoy room service from 6:30 a.m. until 11 p.m., or dine downstairs in either the Lobby Lounge or 301 Franklin, a full service restaurant. Check out Richmond's many fine restaurants while using the complimentary shuttle to get around town within 3 miles. This hotel does make one floor of rooms available to smokers and allows pets weighing up to 50 pounds, with a $50 nonrefundable deposit.

HILTON GARDEN INN RICHMOND
DOWNTOWN $$
501 East Broad St.
(804) 344-4300
www.hiltongardeninn/hilton.com
As a completely nonsmoking hotel that reclaimed the long-closed Miller & Rhoads, a beloved Richmond department store, it carries the mantle of old Richmond into the new with an inviting lobby lounge, 250 well-appointed rooms with higher ceilings than typical hotels, and thoughtful tips of the hat to its predecessor with displays of memorabilia throughout the first floor.

This hotel's location couldn't be better for theatergoing at Richmond CenterStage, concertgoing at the National, courthouse-going at the Federal Courthouse, or convention-going at the Greater Richmond Convention Center. The rooms feature either one king or two queen beds and are outfitted with coffeemakers, minifridges, microwaves, and high-end touches like Herman Miller desk chairs. Wireless is complimentary all over the hotel, as is transportation within 3 miles of the hotel. The lobby lounge is a comfortable place for grabbing a drink and a bite, serving a bar menu and full dinner menu from the afternoon until late at night. With its many cozy seating areas, it's a great place for relaxing or watching a fire or TV if you don't want to hide in your room. A 24-hour business center, evening room service, a fitness center, and an indoor pool add to the options. Breakfast at the lobby restaurant is an all-you-can-eat affair with eggs and omelets cooked to your liking.

THE JEFFERSON HOTEL $$$
101 W. Franklin St.
(800) 424-8014
(804) 788-8000
www.jeffersonhotel.com
This really is *The* Jefferson, built in 1895 in the Beaux Arts tradition and one of only a small number of hotels in North America that have received both the Forbes (formerly Mobil) five-star and AAA five-diamond awards. Known as the premier hotel in Richmond for years, it is now one of the finest hotels on the continent. The public rooms are unlike anything else in Richmond, soaring and sumptuous with a life-size TJ himself to greet you, sculpted in Carrara marble by Richmonder Edward Valentine, using some of Jefferson's own clothes to guide him.

Jefferson looks very happy to be here, and you will be, too. He can't gaze upward, but you should be sure to and be wowed at the stained-glass windows and domed ceiling. It's a lobby worth lounging in. Try not to trip down the grand staircase that sweeps you into the Rotunda while you take in the enormous marble columns and another gorgeous ceiling. No matter where you wander, there are cozy and comfortable hideaways to sit in and wait for your fellow travelers. Relax—this is a beautiful hotel, not a stuffy one, and the exemplary service will put you at ease. It's a Richmond tradition for many to come by the Jefferson to view its always-stunning Christmas decorations.

Lemaire and TJ's, the hotel's signature restaurants, continue to dazzle as they aim to be more inclusive and updated. There will be more on both of them in the "Restaurants" chapter, but have no doubt that anything you order from the 24/7 room-service menu will more than satisfy. Guests have a choice of 262 rooms, with either one king, one queen, or two double beds, each room with marble bath, minibar, Egyptian cotton robes and linens, Molton Brown toiletries, flat-screen TVs, and complimentary Wi-Fi. Thirty-seven suites offer the expected roominess, and the unexpected 1,400-square-foot Presidential Suite (truly worthy of the name, since 12 U.S. presidents have stayed at the hotel), includes a baby grand piano and access to the marble balcony overlooking Franklin Street, among other amenities. Smoking is allowed in a few of the guest rooms, and dogs are allowed for $50 per day.

The hotel has built numerous additions over the centuries, including a beautiful indoor pool with skylights, surrounded by cushioned chaise lounges and an outdoor sundeck. There's a good-size fitness center with men's and women's lockers and showers and massage rooms. If you want more, the Jefferson continues to offer guests passes to the Downtown YMCA across the street.

i At The Jefferson, superior rooms are standard, but for only $20 more you can have a deluxe room with a sitting area. Be sure to check out The Jefferson's packages online; great deals are there to be had—don't assume a room here always costs more than rooms around town in less-grand hotels.

A concierge is on duty 24 hours, and a full-service business center is available during the week, with computer workstations available to overnight guests 24 hours a day. Just off the Rotunda is a full-service salon, gift shop, and a florist. The meeting and banquet facilities are, not surprisingly, grand, and there is both valet and self-parking available on site.

OMNI RICHMOND $$$
100 S. 12th St.
(804) 344-7000
www.omnirichmond.com
Connected to the James Center in Shockoe Slip by a light-filled atrium, this hotel is popular with business folk for its convenience and amenities, including microfiber robes, minibars, and the heated indoor pool and outdoor sundeck. Its 361 guest rooms and suites have either two double beds or one king, though a few wraparound rooms have one queen bed. Smoking is allowed in third-floor rooms only, and pets under 25 pounds are allowed with a pet deposit. Call ahead to discuss the fee. Guests may take advantage of the 30,000-square-foot James Center YMCA for free. In-room Wi-Fi

is $9.95 a day, but if visitors enroll in Omni's free Select Guest program, Internet access, a daily newspaper, and two items pressed per day are all complimentary. A Starbucks just off the lobby offers sandwiches and salads in addition to the caffeine, and the Omni's restaurant, Trevi, serves breakfast, lunch, and dinner, with next door's Trevi's Market supplying fast bites for takeout. With recycling and other programs in place, the Omni is a Virginia State Certified Green Hotel.

RICHMOND MARRIOTT $$$
500 E. Broad St.
(804) 643-3400
(800) 228-9290
www.marriott.com

New local owners recently poured $14 million into renovating this nonsmoking hotel, the largest in the region, taking every one of the 410 rooms down to the sheetrock. Now that it's complete, the results are impressive, from the waterfall fountain in the lobby, to the fitness center, to the well-appointed rooms. Located across the street from and connected by skyway to the Greater Richmond Convention Center, this Marriott thinks of itself as Richmond's headquarters hotel. It's so close also to the Federal Courthouse and CenterStage, they may have a point. It has the largest ballroom outside of the Convention Center, at 15,000 square feet, and its lobby is hopping at check-in time. As far as the rooms themselves, they offer plush and comfy bedding on either one king or two doubles, and suites are available. The lobby Starbucks is convenient for a quick jolt, and the large, well-outfitted fitness center is open 24 hours. Their downtown area shuttle is complimentary, and the hotel's public areas offer free Wi-Fi, but it will set you back $12.95 a day for Internet in your room.

T. Miller's, the full-service restaurant and popular sports bar, is unique to Richmond and sports a name that pays homage to the old Richmond department stores that once ruled Broad Street, Thalhimers and Miller & Rhoads. Gather 'round the outdoor fire pit while enjoying outdoor dining some evening if you'd rather not watch the game. The Liberty Bar lounge is limited to evening service for a quieter spot.

West End

EMBASSY SUITES $$
2925 Emerywood Parkway
(804) 672-8585
www.embassysuitesrichmond.com

Renovated in 2008, this all-suite hotel just off West Broad Street, not far from the University of Richmond and other West-End attractions, has 224 suites that offer either one king bed and a sleeper sofa or two double beds and a sleeper sofa. Wireless and wired Internet is available to guests for free. A small percentage of rooms are available for smokers. This property features a full-service restaurant, lounge with a bar, and a complimentary made-to-order breakfast every morning. Its indoor, plant-filled atrium brightens this suburban location, and the indoor pool, hot tub, sauna, and fitness center with Precor equipment make it easier to stay in shape. A nightly manager's reception is also offered.

WESTIN RICHMOND $$
6631 W. Broad St.
(804) 282-8444
www.westin.com

Located in the Near West End near Altria's headquarters, this seven-story, 100 percent nonsmoking property received the highest ranking in guest services of all Westin hotels in North America, in just the first year of operation. In addition, AAA awarded it four diamonds in 2010. The sleek yet soothing guest rooms offer either one king, two queens, or two double beds, and all come equipped with a 37-inch flat-screen TV, ergonomic desk chair, luxury bed linens and robes, and a spacious bathroom. Free wireless Internet is available in the lobby and in the 24-hour business center, but guests will be charged $9.95 per day for in-room Wi-Fi. Crossings, its restaurant, serves breakfast, lunch, and dinner in stylish surroundings, or take advantage of 24-hour room service if you prefer. An indoor pool and fitness center offer easy-access workouts, and the front desk has maps detailing local runs from the hotel. Ten high-tech meeting rooms await your event. A complimentary shuttle will take guests within 5 miles of the hotel during limited hours. Pets under 40 pounds are welcom,e and there is no additional charge.

Far West End/Short Pump

ALOFT RICHMOND WEST $-$$
3939 Duckling Dr.
(804) 433-1888
www.starwoodhotels.com/alofthotels
A hipster hotel just off West Broad Street in Short Pump's West Broad Village (behind Whole Foods) sounds like a bit of a stretch, and people either love it or not. The vibe and decor of this 135-room nonsmoking hotel are nothing like what you'll find at the typical hotel chains in the suburbs. Proximity to Short Pump Town Center for shopping and Innsbrook for business makes it practical, and the trendy names it has for its public areas—re:mix lounge, re:fuel market, and the wxyz lobby bar—make it clear that it craves a happening, relaxed crowd. The rooms have either one king or two queen beds, flat-screen TVs with audio/video hookups for

game players, and a sleek and minimalist style. The lounge has pool tables, complimentary wireless Internet (as does the entire hotel), and a four-panel LCD TV screening wall. Even the indoor pool area has Wi-Fi. This hotel is pet-friendly, but please call if your pet is something other than a dog or your dog weighs over 50 pounds.

ℹ️ Please note, GPS users should use 11173 W. Broad St., Glen Allen, as the address for Aloft Richmond West, or you will be confused.

HILTON RICHMOND HOTEL AND SPA
SHORT PUMP $$
12042 W. Broad St.
(804) 364-3600
www.hilton.com
This new upscale hotel and spa, near Short Pump Town Center, has 254 rooms, all equipped with 42-inch flat-screen televisions, refrigerators, and coffeemakers. Ergonomic desk seating and luxury bed linens provide comfort, while the free wireless Internet access provides convenience. The inclusion of Aura Spa and Salon within the hotel is a pampering plus that no other Richmond hotel can claim. Once you walk into the bright, sleek lobby, you might not even realize you're in the suburbs anymore. The indoor pool area is bright and cheery, and the fitness room is well outfitted. The public rooms set this hotel apart from its West-End counterparts. Its ballroom, with a dramatic 21-foot ceiling and state-of-the-art lighting, is designed to seat up to 850 people. The high-end Shula's 2 restaurant offers diners a classic steak house experience. Some rooms are available for smokers. Pets weighing up to 50 pounds are welcome with a $75 deposit.

HOTEL SIERRA WEST $$
11800 W. Broad St.
(804) 360-7021
www.hotel-sierra.com

This small chain is making a splash in Short Pump, with its year-old, 134-room, non-smoking hotel, and not just because its outdoor infinity pool and hot tub are located near a beautiful fire pit with comfy, cushioned seating. The hotel is adjacent to Short Pump Town Center, right by Dick's Sporting Goods, so the mall's restaurants and stores are an easy walk. Children under 18 stay free in their parents' room, and a made-to-order breakfast is included in your rate. Most rooms have full kitchens, and those that don't have microwaves and refrigerators; plus all rooms feature flat-panel TVs, free Wi-Fi, and bathrobes. A convenience market is open 24 hours, and a bistro serves food Mon through Sat from 5 to 10 p.m., including beer and wine.

RESIDENCE INN BY MARRIOTT RICHMOND NORTHWEST $$
3940 Westerre Parkway
(804) 762-9852
www.residenceinnrichmond.com

Convenient to Innsbrook and other parts of the Far West End, this 104-suite, nonsmoking hotel offers three styles of rooms—studios, one-bedroom suites, or two bedroom suites—that can easily accommodate a family. Every room has a complete kitchen with the works—microwave, stove top, full-size refrigerator, dishwasher, toaster, dishes, and pots and pans—and outdoor grills are available for guest use. Every living room has a pullout sofa bed. An outdoor pool makes it even more family-friendly. This hotel is pet-friendly as well, with pets allowed for a $75 fee per visit. There's complimentary wireless Internet throughout the hotel, and guests can enjoy evening receptions Mon through Thurs from 6 to 7:30 p.m., where hors d'oeuvres and drinks are served. As if that's not enough, a free hot and cold breakfast is served daily. Service above and beyond is this hotel's hallmark.

WINGATE BY WYNDHAM RICHMOND SHORT PUMP $$
13991 N. Gayton Rd.
(804) 421-1600
www.wingatehotels.com

If the Far West End is your destination, this hotel offers many conveniences for a great price, which includes a full, hot breakfast. There is no restaurant on-site but the complimentary shuttle could get you to eateries on nearby West Broad Street. Back at the nonsmoking hotel, there are 102 rooms with one king or two queen beds. Suites are available as well. Wi-Fi is complimentary in the hotel and the business center is open 24/7. The heated indoor pool, Jacuzzi, and small fitness center are open from 6 a.m. to 11 p.m. An unusual feature for the suburbs of Richmond is underground parking, so rain or snow won't be a problem.

East End/Airport

CANDLEWOOD SUITES $
5400 Audubon Dr.
(804) 652-1888
(877) 226 3539
www.candlewoodsuites.com

This all-suite hotel 1 mile from the airport offers the convenience of a long-term property with full kitchens in every room. Guests have a choice of a king bed with a sleeper sofa, two queens, or two doubles. The hotel's 24-hour shuttle takes guests to the airport and to the grocery store if need be.

Complimentary laundry facilities are on the premises, open 24 hours, as are the fitness and business centers. Wireless Internet is free throughout the hotel to guests. A few rooms are available for smokers. Pets weighing under 80 pounds are allowed for $75 for up to six nights. A gazebo has outdoor seating and gas grills for guests' use.

COURTYARD BY MARRIOTT
RICHMOND AIRPORT $$
5400 Williamsburg Rd.
(800) 321-2211
(804) 652-0500
www.marriott.com/courtyard
Recently renovated, this nonsmoking hotel has rooms with either one king or two double beds, and several suites, some with Jacuzzis, are available. Every room has a microwave, fridge, and coffeemaker, and guests can access free wireless Internet throughout the hotel. A fitness room, indoor pool, and a free washer/dryer are additional features. In a new approach for Courtyards, a bistro serves breakfast and dinner, with a full bar open in the evening. The hotel offers a free 24-hour shuttle within 3 miles, so that will get you to the airport and several restaurants.

HAMPTON INN RICHMOND
AIRPORT $$
421 International Center Dr.
(804) 226-1888
www.hamptoninn.com
This 104-room hotel offers proximity to the airport, a 24-hour business center with fax and copier, and a local area shuttle. There is no restaurant on-site, but a complimentary hot breakfast is offered every morning. The public areas have recently been refurbished and are comfortable. You have a choice of either one king or two queen beds, and

there's complimentary wireless Internet as well as a microwave, coffeemaker, and mini-fridge. Rooms for both smokers and non-smokers are available.

HILTON GARDEN INN
RICHMOND AIRPORT $$
441 International Center Dr.
(804) 222-3338
www.hiltongardeninn.com
Take your pick between two queen beds or one king bed in this 130-room hotel a mile from the airport. To satisfy your hunger, take advantage of the many dining choices within the hotel, including evening room service from 5 to 10 p.m. and the full-service Great American Grill. Or take your ease in the Pavilion Lounge. Every room has a microwave and fridge, so you could pick up food in the 24/7 Pavilion Pantry to take back to your room and not worry about leftovers. A 24-hour shuttle will get you to and from the airport and anywhere within 5 miles, and the free wireless Internet will let you catch up on your work in the Mirra desk chair in your room. An indoor pool and fitness center will help you relax. This hotel features a few rooms for smokers.

HYATT PLACE RICHMOND
AIRPORT $$
4401 S. Laburnum Ave.
(804) 549-4865
www.hyatt.com/hyattplace
Located near Richmond International Airport and within the White Oak shopping area to give you walk-to options for shopping and dining, Hyatt Place provides an innovative hotel experience, with a contemporary design and attitude. In the lobby area a light menu, including beer and wine, is available 24 hours a day at the swipe of

your room key. Guest rooms are all semi-suites, since a divider separates a comfortable sitting area with a sleeper sofa and the bedroom that has either a king or two queen beds. The 42-inch flat-screen TV, visible from either section, has a media plug-in panel easily accessible for every hi-tech option, and wireless Internet is free throughout the hotel. A refrigerator and coffeemaker add to the convenience. A 24-hour complimentary shuttle will take you within 5 miles of the hotel, including to the airport.

North

Glen Allen

**COMFORT SUITES AT
  VIRGINIA CENTER COMMONS $**
10601 Telegraph Rd.
(804) 262-2000
www.comfortsuites.com
This all-suite, 100 percent nonsmoking hotel just off I-95 near Virginia Center Commons offers easy access and affordability. Most suites are one bedroom, but two-bedroom suites are available. Some rooms have just a king-size bed, but most king or queen beds are paired with a full-size sleeper sofa. Each suite has a microwave and refrigerator as well. Breakfast is included in the nightly rate, as is free wireless Internet.

**WYNDHAM VIRGINIA CROSSINGS
  HOTEL & CONFERENCE CENTER $$**
1000 Virginia Center Parkway
(804) 727-1400
www.wyndhamvirginiacrossings.com
This AAA four-diamond property includes three colonial-style buildings linked by covered walkways. Don't let the traditional-style buildings fool you—there's plenty of hi-tech here: 23 meeting rooms with state-of-the-art technology and free wireless Internet

throughout for guests, which makes it a good choice for corporate events.

Though it's just off I-95 and I-295, the hotel sits on 20 rolling acres, and there's a championship golf course adjacent to the property that guests may play on for a fee.

The guest rooms are clustered in one building, while the two restaurants, The Glen, known for its lavish seafood buffet every weekend, and Yellow Tavern Pub, with TVs, billiard tables, and a Wii station, are across the way in the Madison building. This place has all the in-room amenities you'd expect in a four-diamond hotel, plus an iPod-docking alarm clock and in-room Nintendo. Outside there's an outdoor pool in season and a squash court and sand volleyball court. The adjacent golf course property is located on the site of the Battle of the Yellow Tavern, where General J. E. B. Stuart was mortally wounded, so it's appropriate that the hotel offers special Civil War packages. The hotel was about to become a nonsmoking hotel at press time.

Mechanicsville

**HOLIDAY INN EXPRESS
  RICHMOND-MECHANICSVILLE $–$$**
7441 Bell Creek Rd.
(804) 559-0022
(888) HOLIDAY
www.hiexpress.com
Just to be clear, you can't be in both Mechanicsville and Richmond at the same time. But if you have business or pleasure in Mechanicsville, or at close-by Richmond International Raceway or Cold Harbor Battlefield, this 105-room hotel could fill the bill. A free breakfast is offered, and Wi-Fi is complimentary as well. If the fitness center doesn't fit your style, a nearby American Family Fitness offers a $5 deal for guests to use their indoor track, pool, and the rest of the equipment. After your

workout, head back to your room with either one king or two double beds. All rooms have microwaves and fridges. Some rooms allow smoking.

Ashland

**HAMPTON INN RICHMOND-
NORTH ASHLAND**   **$$**
705 England St.
(804) 752-8444
www.hamptoninnhilton.com

With 74 rooms and convenient access to I-95, this hotel works for visiting Kings Dominion or nearby Randolph-Macon College. Though it has no on-site restaurant, a continental breakfast is included in your rate. Chain restaurants are close by, and more interesting offerings abound in the center of Ashland. Free wireless Internet is available to guests, and you have a choice of either one king bed, two queens, or one queen. A few rooms have been set aside for smokers. An outdoor pool provides some fun in season.

HENRY CLAY INN   **$–$$**
114 N. Railroad Ave.
(804) 798-3100
www.henryclayinn.com

A small hotel with porches, balconies, and character, this caters to those who want something other than the chain hotel experience. Built in 1992 to match the historic inn that had stood nearby, along quaint Ashland's well-used railroad track, this property has 14 rooms and suites that are furnished with antique reproduction canopy, sleigh, cannonball, or pencil-post beds for a country inn feel. Wireless Internet is available throughout the hotel. The trains do roll through town all night, so ask for a room in the back if you're not staying here for the romance (and rumble) of the railroad. Sit or smoke on the porches if you like, but smoking is not allowed

inside the Inn. Pets are allowed in a couple of first-floor rooms that open to the outside. Rooms on the first floor are wheelchair accessible, though only one has ADA-approved bathroom fixtures. Breakfast is included, but note that if you've stayed here before, the restaurant has closed. Handily, Ashland has numerous restaurants worth frequenting, some within walking distance.

South Side

Chester

FAIRFIELD INN   **$$**
12400 Redwater Creek Rd.
(804) 778-7500
www.marriott.com

Just off I-95 south of Richmond at VA 10 in Chester, this hotel is a good choice for those visiting Virginia State University or seeing Petersburg Civil War sites or Henricus Historical Park. Its 115 rooms have Serta pillow-top mattresses on either one king or two queen beds. Executive-level rooms offer a sleeper sofa as well. A deluxe, free continental breakfast is waiting for you every morning just off the lobby, and wireless Internet is complimentary throughout the hotel. There is an indoor pool and a small fitness center. Per an agreement with the nearby Chester YMCA, guests may be able to use that facility for free with identification and proof of stay. See the front desk for details. Some rooms are available for pets with a $25 deposit. Like all Marriott properties, this hotel is nonsmoking.

Midlothian

**HOLIDAY INN SELECT KOGER CENTER
SOUTH**   **$$**
1021 Koger Center Blvd.
(804) 379-3800
(800) HOLIDAY
www.holidayinnkoger.com

Close to Chesterfield Town Center and Stony Point Fashion Park, this 237-room hotel just off Midlothian Turnpike near Huguenot Road sets you up for a South Side stay. Restaurants and movie theaters are nearby. Whether you stay in a king-bed room or one with two double beds, the plush beds, pillow menus, and bathrobes will help you rest easy. Every room has a microwave and fridge, there is a full service restaurant on-site, and room service is available. Free wired and wireless Internet access is handy, and the indoor pool and fitness room, open from 6 a.m. to 11 p.m., give you a chance to get away from technology. If dancing is your preferred workout, then Visions Dance Club will get your heart pumping—more on that in the "Nightlife" chapter. Some smoking rooms are available.

**HYATT PLACE RICHMOND
ARBORETUM** **$$**
201 Arboretum Place
(804) 560-1566
**www.richmondarboretum.place.hyatt
.com**
Don't let the name fool you—there is no garden here, just an office park off Midlothian Turnpike, a typical suburban shopping strip. Still, if a suburban location suits you, this contemporary-styled nonsmoking hotel offers sleek and satisfying accommodations with a choice of either one king or two double beds, and a sleeper sofa in every room. Those who like playing video games will appreciate the easy-access plug-in panel on the 42-inch flat-screen television. Wireless Internet is free throughout the hotel, and there's an e-room with a couple of computers and a printer for guests' use. A complimentary continental breakfast is offered every morning, and guests can purchase additional items from the Bakery Cafe or the 24/7 Guest Kitchen. The outdoor pool is open Apr through Sept.

BED & BREAKFASTS

Now it's obvious but worth a reminder that with these B&Bs, breakfast for two is included in the prices, as are other amenities and room to spread out. In many cases, a breakfast at one of these inns will likely deter you from eating much if any lunch, and often other snacks are available. As a reminder, these B&Bs are not wheelchair accessible, nor do they allow pets, and they are all non-smoking. Again, this is a sampling of some of the loveliest B&Bs in the area.

The Fan

GRACE MANOR INN **$$–$$$**
1853 W. Grace St.
(804) 353-4334
www.thegracemanorinn.com
One block off Monument Avenue in the Fan, this grand B&B gets a lot of repeat business. Visitors can't get enough of the gorgeous, original woodwork, the rosy chandelier in the dining room, and the baby grand piano in the front room. Dawn's the chef and Albert's in charge of hospitality, as are their three friendly Yorkies who live here, too. Though Yorkies are adorable and considered an allergy-free breed, if you're not a dog lover, you might prefer staying somewhere else. The heated saltwater pool, with loads of comfortable seating, is spectacular. The three suites upstairs all offer work or relaxing space off the bedroom, and everyone can access the back porch for a swing and other seating overlooking the pool. The more contemporary carriage house offers another overnight option. Breakfast is

a three-course affair, starting off with fresh fruit, and then perhaps eggs marinara on fresh bread with pancetta ham hash. Since Dawn owns Carytown Cupcakes, you might be lucky enough to finish off breakfast with one of those treats. Really, what's the difference between a muffin and a cupcake anyway? Off-street parking is available just in back of the Inn.

THE WILLIAM MILLER HOUSE B&B $$–$$$
1129 Floyd Ave.
(804) 254-2928
www.williammillerhouse.com

The William Miller House feels like home as soon as you walk up onto its charming front porch. Sitting on an unusually large yard for the Fan, the beautiful home, built in 1869 and renovated by owners Pat Daniels and Mike Rohde in 1999, is the perfect getaway right in the middle of the city. Once inside, the exquisite marble fireplaces, woodwork, and accessories let you know this is better than home. Its two bedrooms, with either one king or one queen bed, keep the guest number to a maximum of four, so you'll get individualized attention if you need help planning your day.

Both bathrooms have walk-in showers, and the guest rooms have individual climate controls. There's free wireless Internet throughout the house and outside. Sit in the garden room or look over the fishpond in the lovely private side yard while you partake of your complimentary evening wine and cheese. Once back home, you can access several of their recipes online; the crepe with ham and fontina cheese sounds good to me. Please note that Pat and Mike do have a docile dog.

Museum District

THE KENSINGTON BED & BREAKFAST $$
2926 Kensington Ave
(804) 358-9901
www.thekensingtonbedandbreakfast
  .com

Bertie and Bill Selvey have been welcoming guests to their home and inn, previously known as Be Our Guest, for years, but now make plain their in-town location across the street from the Virginia Historical Society and just 1 block from the Virginia Museum of Fine Arts. A comfortable porch overlooking the corner lot gives guests a chance to relax outside. Inside, the public rooms feature beautiful grasscloth wallpaper and striking color combinations. Upstairs, the options include the Italian suite, whose en-suite bathroom has a hydra of a showerhead (seven jets!) and a sweet sitting room off the bedroom, and the French suite overlooks the front of the house and has a nicely renovated bathroom just down the hall. Its bedroom features an amazing three-mirrored armoire that Bertie found in a shop in Carytown. It might inspire you to find something for yourself. Next door is the comfortable sitting room, a good place to access the free wireless Internet. Another option out the back door is the more contemporary-styled Carriage House. Bill handles breakfast duty in their lovely kitchen and serves guests eggs, stuffed French toast, and all sorts of goodies, always with fresh fruit, sometimes with grits. You'll get true southern hospitality here.

MAURY PLACE AT MONUMENT $$–$$$
3101 West Franklin St.
(804) 353-2717
www.mauryplace.com

Maury Place, opened by Jeff Wells and Mac Pence in 2008, is luxury living, if only for a day or two. Overlooking the Maury statue on Monument Avenue, the house, built in 1916, has two porches that dress up the sandy brick exterior. Once inside, it's clear that the owners have spared no expense, as the interior is over-the-top gorgeous, with high, ornately plastered ceilings, intricate woodwork, and lavishly appointed rooms. And then out back there's the 15-by-30-foot heated pool surrounded by plenty of comfortable seating. The suites upstairs range from the fabulous to the divine, including two with private balconies. The Pathfinder Suite, the largest, takes up the front of the house and has a sumptuous king bed, luxe seating and a table area, an elegant and refined bathroom, and the pièce de résistance—access to the balcony overlooking Monument Avenue. Wave regally to the commoners below; they don't know you don't own the place. Three of the four suites have working fireplaces, and all have flat-screen HD TVs and complimentary wireless Internet access. In the bathrooms, you'll appreciate the heated tile floors, the plush robes, and the Gilchrist & Soames toiletries. In the morning, feel at home in the gorgeous dining room while you partake of the lavish gourmet breakfast prepared using local ingredients, including fresh herbs from Mac and Jeff's garden. You will be spoiled here, make no mistake about it, and home might not look so homey once you've stayed here.

MUSEUM DISTRICT B&B $$

2811 Grove Ave.
(804) 359-2332
www.museumdistrictbb.com

Ideally located for a visit to the Virginia Museum of Fine Arts (VMFA), just across the street, and jaunts into nearby Carytown, this B&B has wowed enough guests since opening in 2007 that owner Anna Currence has a stack of thank-you notes from guests, handwritten and effusive, with good reason. Throughout the inn, the wall and fabric colors are soft, warm, and soothing, and her comfortable public rooms have a piano and bookcases full of a wide range of reading material, including several books written by art experts who've stayed here while consulting at VMFA.

Upstairs, the Judge Rhea Suite is a true home away from home, with a sitting area with a working gas fireplace, fridge, TV, separate office space, a queen-size bed, and a luxurious bathroom with walk-in steam shower. The John Lane Suite has two bedrooms and 1½ baths that would be perfect for friends traveling together. Its singular feature is an enormous balcony off the front bedroom that would be the perfect place to enjoy Anna's complimentary wine and cheese in the evening. Out back, the Carriage House offers its own little porch and a more private setting. Anna uses her neighborhood to everyone's advantage, serving bacon from Belmont Butchery and croissants from Can Can as part of her filling breakfasts. Free wireless Internet works everywhere on the property. One last clue about the level of service here: She irons the sheets.

East End

HISTORIC MANKIN MANSION $$–$$$

4300 Oakleys Lane
(804) 737-7773
www.historicmankinmansion.com

To get to the charmingly landscaped five acres of Historic Mankin Mansion, you'll drive through residential and light industrial areas that don't hint at the unexpected oasis of a country estate. Completed in 1924 by Edward Mankin, a well-to-do brick maker who wanted to showcase his brick (and who provided the brick for the rebuilding of Colonial Williamsburg), the mansion offers four different areas for guest accommodations. In the mansion itself are two suites, and there are three more options in various outbuildings. Since 2004 Martin and Paula Ramirez have been restoring the entire estate to its former glory.

The brick is everywhere here, on pathways, four outbuildings, a pergola, and outside and inside the lovely mansion. Entering the Rockefeller Room with its intricate original woodwork and brickwork, you could tinkle the ivories on the baby grand piano or relax on comfortable period furnishings. The dining room offers a sumptuous breakfast every morning. Downstairs, a clue that the hosts are open to younger guests, is an entertainment destination with one room devoted to a poker table, another to watching satellite TV, another to pool playing, plus arcade-style basketball and foosball. The entertainment area is open from 3 to 10 p.m., and snacks and drinks are plentiful. Accommodations are spread around the grounds, reached by beautiful brick pathways. The Gardener's Cottage, Farmer's Cottage, and Carriage House offer space for two to six people. The Gardener's Cottage is a 2½-story cottage with kitchen, living room, a bunk-bed room for children, and another bedroom.

RESTAURANTS

Richmond is too polite to boast about its culinary scene, but word is getting out. The *Washington Post* and *New York Times* have made note recently of several Richmond restaurants, so expect company when you go out to dine. At the more upscale establishments, four trends are notable: Farm-to-table and locally sourced are the catchphrases, everything-but-the-kitchen-sink fusion is popular, ethnic cuisine has expanded well beyond mom-and-pop and sushi places, and even the finest restaurants are being extra hospitable with Sunday suppers, daily specials, and prix fixe menus that encourage diners to get in the door.

The big news in Virginia is that as of December 2009, restaurants and bars are now smoke-free unless they have a designated smoking room—structurally separate and ventilated. Most establishments simply went smoke-free, and most customers have breathed a sigh of relief.

Whether you're looking for family-friendly or foodie central, Richmond cuisine covers all the bases. And there's always something new coming down the pike. Richmond has far too many wonderful restaurants to include in one chapter. This isn't an exhaustive list of the best of Richmond restaurants, though many highlighted here have made that list. Restaurants at all price points are included, from all parts of the area. The city has the highest concentration of worthy destinations, and Shockoe Slip, Shockoe Bottom, the Fan, Carytown, the Near West End, and North Side have restaurant rows, if you will. So if the places listed here are full, you'll likely find several others a few doors down.

OVERVIEW

Restaurants in older buildings in some sections of the city are not always wheelchair accessible. I've noted those that are not in the write-ups, but call ahead elsewhere to be sure you won't have a problem.

In addition to 5 percent state tax, some localities levy a meals tax as well. In our region, Richmond's meals tax is 6 percent, Ashland's is 5 percent, and New Kent County's meals tax is 4 percent. *Mangia.*

Price Code

The price code is based on the average cost of two dinner entrees.

$.....................under $16
$$ .... $16 to $30
$$$ .... $31 to $50
$$$$ .... over $50

AFRICAN

Downtown

**AFRICANNE ON MAIN BY
CHEF MA MUSA** $
200 E. Main St.
(804) 343-1233
www.chefmamusuafricanne.com

Known for its filling, healthy lunch buffet that you pay for by the pound, this cheery restaurant with Afro-centric decor is open Mon through Fri for lunch and serves dinner only on Fri. Everything here is made by chef Ma Musa, who came to Richmond from Liberia in 1980. Customers choose from ginger barbecued chicken, collard greens, and more than 14 other dishes. Chef Ma Musa ships greens as far as Florida and Hawaii. Her restaurant is pork-free, and the offerings are 60 percent vegetarian. Try the homemade ginger tea and spiced lemonade.

The Fan

THE NILE $$
309 N. Laurel St.
(804) 225-5544
www.nilerichmond.com

This family-owned and -operated traditional Ethiopian restaurant (that's unexpectedly also the headquarters of the Ethiopian ski team) has introduced legions of people to finger food, Ethiopian-style. The Nile's injera is made from teff flour, which is loaded with protein, so don't be surprised at how satisfied your stomach is after just a few appetizers. The staff is more than happy to explain ingredients and preparation and help you find something you'll like. FYI, one Buticha Roll won't do. All the vegetarian dishes here are vegan.

AMERICAN AND ECLECTIC

Downtown

LEMAIRE $$$–$$$$
The Jefferson Hotel
101 W. Franklin St.
(804) 649-4644
www.lemairerestaurant.com

Esquire Magazine recently named Lemaire one of the 20 best new restaurants in America, so everything old is new again. Lemaire has been the Jefferson's signature restaurant since 1986, but was redesigned and reborn in 2009 under the steady hand of chef Walter Bundy, who turned the mighty ship around deftly and transformed it from a staid special-occasion establishment to a distinguished yet down-to-earth destination (even dropping the entree prices an average of $10). Speaking of earth, 80 to 90 percent of the outstanding menu is locally sourced, including three varieties of Virginia oysters, and the meat is organic and grass-fed. A decidedly southern attitude makes sense given the farm-to-table ethos here, so fried green tomatoes topped with lump crabmeat, sherry vinegar, and verbena make everyone appreciate the bounty of the South.

It's still the Jefferson, so the Ladies Parlor, the Library, and the bar are all sumptuous, the staff is exemplary, and the details are just so, but there's humor here—in the alligator touches on the barstools, in the menu, and even in the ads that tell Richmond to "leave the pearls at home." This isn't the most expensive restaurant in Richmond—just one of the best. Lemaire is not above offering specials and bottles of wine under $30, so don't miss out. Free valet parking is available at the Franklin Street entrance.

TARRANT'S CAFÉ $$-$$$
1 W. Broad St.
(804) 225-0035
www.tarrantscafe.org

Tarrant's is loaded with proof that drugstores haven't always looked like CVS. Its handsome, well-stocked bar was the pharmacy counter, and Tarrant's still fills prescriptions of a liquid sort. The past here is interesting, but the repasts are even more so. Lunch, dinner, pizza, or brunch—there are lots of ways to go here and they're all sublime. Lunch offers a Tilapia Reuben, dinner can be pan-fried sea bass or filet mignon. Even people who think they don't like bread pudding love Tarrant's whiskey-drenched one.

Shockoe Slip, Shockoe Bottom, and Tobacco Row

THE DINING ROOM AT THE
BERKELEY HOTEL $$$-$$$$
1200 E. Cary St.
(804) 225-5105
www.berkeleyhotel.com

Assured and award-winning, this AAA four-diamond winner makes any occasion special with its mahogany paneling, intimate feel, and fine, locally sourced cuisine. The seasonally changing menu might include butter-basted rockfish or shrimp and grits with a touch of Smithfield ham if you're lucky. Shockoe Slip is just out the window, but this is a place to savor a meal in warm, rich environs. Valet parking is available.

LULU'S $$$
21 N. 17th St.
(804) 343-9771
www.lu-lusrichmond.com

Think of LuLu's as Millie's younger sister, who scored a cool industrial place to hang out in the Bottom. She's got room to spread out and still packs the visitors in for lunch, dinner, and brunch. LuLu's is owned by Millie's veterans, and it produces similarly assured gourmet-flaired comfort food from around the world with an urban vibe, smart service, and happy customers. The bar is open to the kitchen whizzes whirring away, so it's a lively place. Lean toward meat loaf or the osso bucco. What's not to love about LuLu's? Being too full for the homemade chocolate peanut butter pie. There are always five to ten homemade desserts, so plan accordingly.

MILLIE'S $$$$
2603 E. Main St.
(804) 643-5512
www.milliesdiner.com

Known far and wide beyond Tobacco Row for its hustle and bustle, inventive gourmet fare and lines out the door, Millie's quiets down when the food is served, because the fabulous flavors must be admired. It's a great place to bring a bad conversationalist because jukeboxes provide conversation starters and cool tunes and the food will do the talking. Watching the cooks ply their trade is impressive and humbling once you taste their work. Millie's is closed on Mon, perhaps to recover from the brunches they throw down on Sat and Sun.

Church Hill

HILL CAFÉ $$$
2800 E. Broad St.
(804) 348-0360
www.thehillcafe.com

This Church Hill standby, known for its neighborly charm and comfort food, deserves more attention from folks all around town. Sitting in the brick-walled casual spot, perhaps along the bar, you might relish the ginger-scallion crab cakes with mango relish, or maybe you're in a meat-loaf mood. At brunch on Sunthe crab and shrimp omelet gets raves, and so do the grilled fillet medallions served over cheese grits with Creole red gravy. Reservations are a good idea on weekends. Parking is available on-street. It serves lunch and dinner Mon through Sat, and that most worthwhile Sun brunch.

The Fan

ACACIA MID-TOWN $$$–$$$$
2601 W. Cary St.
(804) 562-0138
www.acaciarestaurant.com

Acacia's not in Carytown anymore. Able to stretch out in this 100-seat haven of fine dining, Dale and Aline Reitzer have done it up right. Subtle and savvy, this upscale foodie heaven is unadorned because the food is the thing. Muted colors and minimalism lead the eye to the wide kitchen window so diners can see Reitzer, who was nominated for a James Beard regional award, work his magic. Spoiler alert—he's better behaved than those chefs on TV. The menu changes daily, but be assured you will eat something palate pleasing. He's a master of sauces and seafood, as in sautéed redfish with a pineapple-nutmeg sauce. The beat of the music and the buzz of the diners add to the hotspot vibe. The $23 prix fixe menu makes some of the finest food in town available daily. Valet parking is available. Stop making excuses—it's time to go. Reservations are recommended. Acacia is closed on Sun.

BALLICEAUX $$$
203 N. Lombardy St.
(804) 355-3008
www.balliceauxrva.com

Everyone's in love with Balliceaux—for the food, the decor, the music, the atmosphere,

the drinks, the French-pressed coffee after dinner. There are so many ways to eat happy here, it's like they make you come back again and again to try the spectacular-sounding dozen other dishes on the menu that you didn't order. The menu is divided into Field and Forest, Farm and Pasture, and Waters, with every course offering at least one choice per category. With must-have soups, intriguing salads, creative small-plate options, spot-on sides, and killer entrees like Cremini Mushroom Carbonara and Sausage Duet, I don't know who has the stamina to appreciate the many sublime flavors, not to mention have room for dessert. The back room has great music many nights, and the two bars have a hip vibe.

STRAWBERRY STREET CAFÉ $$
421 N. Strawberry St.
(804) 353-6860
www.strawberrystreetcafe.com

This classic Fan eatery with a cozy atmosphere is famous for its many-splendored salad bar in a bathtub—which looks more appetizing than it sounds. The soup and salad combos are perfect for feeling healthy even if the pile on your plate adds up. There's beautiful fruit in season as well as curry chicken salad, and that's just a taste. Burgers, quesadillas, and classics like chicken potpie give you more options. What many chain restaurants pretend to offer—neighborhood comfort, yummy food, and conversation—this place delivers.

Carytown and Museum District

MEZZANINE $$$–$$$$
3433 W. Cary St.
(804) 353-2186
www.mezzanine3433.com

It's amazing how much good can come out of a 5-by-16-foot kitchen. Elegant yet casual, the setting alone is subtle perfection. And then there's the constantly changing menu that uses fresh-from-the-field ingredients. Mezzanine's handsome good looks—with its painted-brick, two-level interior, and covered patio—and emphasis on local foods took the city by storm. It's hard to keep up with the enthusiastic crowds, drawn here by dishes such as rib eye accompanied by lobster-crushed potatoes and grilled broccolini and finished with a four-day demi-glace. Unless you like the attention, don't sit under the chalkboard menu—the whole restaurant will be eyeing you. The bar stays open till 2 a.m. It would be hard to do better late at night. It's closed on Mon.

WEEZIE'S KITCHEN $$–$$$
3123 W. Cary St.
(804) 726-1270
www.weezieskitchen.com
This understated place is an easy sell for breakfast, lunch, or dinner—even late at night for post-movie snacks or live music on Fri. It's an all-purpose hangout, pulling out the HD projector for football Sun and Mon. The portions are huge, including the biggest child-size dinner I've ever seen, for only $5. The bruschetta starter with blackened chicken on top would fill anyone up before the entrees arrive.

ZEUS GALLERY CAFE $$$$
201 N. Belmont Ave.
(804) 359-3219
Zeus Gallery doubled in size a few years back, so waiting for a table by the bar is more pleasant now. It will be worth the wait. The city's finest B&Bs send their clientele here, knowing Zeus will deliver innovative meals in classy yet comfortable surroundings. It's fittingly not far from the Virginia Museum of Fine Arts—the dishes here are works of art whether you choose the foie gras, duck breast, or beef carpaccio. The desserts are beautiful to behold and even better to eat.

North Side

KITCHEN 64 $$–$$$
3336 N. Blvd.
(804) 358-0064
www.kitchen64.com
A happy place with a bustling covered patio and a cool bar, this restaurant is casual enough to bring the kids along, and serves such a variety that the parents won't deprive themselves of good food just because the little rascals are along. The atmosphere isn't so precious that an occasional kid-shriek will freak anyone out. Diners will be too busy noshing on the Greek nachos, the great burgers, and the black-bean hummus. The portions are huge. The revolving dessert case will distract more than the toddlers, believe me. Entrees like prime rib for under $20 draw crowds.

TASTEBUDS AMERICAN BISTRO $$
4019 MacArthur Ave.
(804) 261-6544
www.tastebudsamericanbistro.com
This unassuming bistro fills up fast on weekends, but the wait doesn't dissuade the people standing in the middle of the dining room. Take your time sampling several savory courses on the constantly changing menu. It's inventive and flavorful—Spring Salad with duck confit, pan-fried rainbow trout, pork tacos with mole sauce—the menu deserves some pondering. A $16 three-course prix-fixe option is available midweek—quite a deal for fantastic food. Tastebuds is closed on Sun and Mon.

Far West End/Innsbrook/Short Pump

PATINA GRILL $$$–$$$$
3416 Lauderdale Dr.
(804) 360-8217
www.patinagrill.com

This popular fusion front-runner keeps the inventiveness coming Tues through Sat. Its classy, neutral interior, jazzed up by walnut and mirrors and copper accents, is the most restrained aspect of this destination that wows with unexpected pairings. Beef tenderloin here soaks up a blackberry-port reduction. Chimichangas pair wild mushrooms and roasted tomatoes. If some of the priciest entrees in the area scare you away, consider the small plates, such as cornmeal-dusted oysters with an apple-mint rémoulade. There are enough flavors in the small plates to make your tongue think it's eaten several courses. Of course, once you start paging through the extravagant martini list, requiring a master's in mixology, showing restraint becomes that much tougher.

Ashland

THE IRON HORSE $$$
100 S. Railroad Ave.
(804) 752-6410
www.ironhorserestaurant.com

Offering modern and southern-tinged versions of fine American cooking overlooking the train tracks, this Ashland favorite serves lunch and dinner in charming surroundings. The cider-braised pork belly shows basic barbecue a thing or two, and the asparagus and chèvre tart begs to be paired with just the right wine from the extensive list. Outdoor seating and live music on weekends jazz up the joint.

ASIAN

Downtown

BEAUREGARD'S THAI ROOM $$–$$$
103 E. Cary St.
(804) 644-2328
www.thairoom.com

OK, so Beauregard's is not your typical Thai restaurant name, but it makes sense because this is not your typical Thai restaurant. Dining here feels like you've entered another world. Perhaps it's the circa-1870 building with the courtyard in the back, possibly the most beautiful outdoor dining spot in Richmond—large and bricked, with gas lamps, lush landscaping, and a fountain. The inside dining rooms are just as refined, as is the food. The Squid in Love or the other traditional Thai dishes are so beautifully presented, it's almost a shame to eat them. Leave room for the famous homemade desserts, including black-walnut and coconut ice cream and mango sorbet. The Thai Room is open for lunch and dinner Mon through Fri, and dinner only on Sat. The restaurant is not wheelchair accessible.

The Fan

STICKY RICE $$
2232 W. Main St.
(804) 358-7870
www.stickyricefan.com

Fun fusion at its best, Sticky Rice serves sushi up fresh every day, along with salads, sandwiches, tons of vegetarian options, and a secret sauce for the Tater Tots. The atmosphere is laced with humor and good times. The staff will happily roll vegan and wheat-free selections. Tofu Max or Hot Hippy hit the spot for vegetarians. The bar's the place to sit for extra attention to detail. At night it becomes a hot spot with karaoke, blingo, and other shenanigans.

Carytown

MOM'S SIAM $$
2811 W. Cary St.
(804) 359-7606
With two levels on the inside, this relaxed Carytown mainstay produces consistently happy customers, whether you're the Siam Jai Curry or ginger-chicken type. The pad thai gets good marks, as do the friendly service and the patio dining when the weather is balmy.

Near West End

OSAKA SUSHI & STEAK $$$
5023 Huguenot Rd.
(804) 288-8801
www.osakasushiva.com
Osaka's sleek and artful interior decor is what happens when sushi chefs get involved in restaurant design. They understand artistry. Since 2006 Osaka has been wowing patrons with its sleek and stunning contemporary design—the stone waterfall and the pearlescent granite sushi bar—as well as with the distinctive and delicious sushi. The possibilities here are endless, but the Hamachi Tataki Salad, the Godzilla with its flaming cucumber centerpiece, Love Boat—a sushi ship for two—and the Godiva Tempura Ice Cream are quite memorable. A second location at 11674 W. Broad St. in the Far West End (804-364-8800) includes some hibachi tables.

West End

FULL KEE $$
6400 Horsepen Rd.
(804) 673-2233
The most authentic Chinese restaurant in Richmond is along the international stew of Horsepen Road. This is where hungry people gather on Sun for the heavy yet heavenly dim sum. Rumor has it that it's even possible to go off-menu at Full Kee and request specialties that take the cuisine farther from American tastes than you thought possible in Richmond.

MEKONG $$
6004 W. Broad St.
(804) 288-8929
www.mekongva.com
Besides being popular for its Vietnamese specialties, this expansive restaurant is known, surprisingly perhaps, for its Belgian and American craft beer selection. Its voluminous menu has the usual suspects, done well, but the chef adds worthy specials often. Mekong is open for lunch and dinner every day.

PHO SO 1 $
6403 Rigsby Rd.
(804) 673-9940
Hidden off Horsepen Road in a mini–United Nations neighborhood, there's no faux *pho* at this Vietnamese noodle house; the lines of people will tell you that. The basic ambience of the place is warmed up by the amazing flavors here. The fragrant *pho ga*, a chicken and noodle soup, is a full meal, and it's fun to concoct your own version with masses of thai basil, fresh lime, and other ingredients that you add to taste. It's the perfect meal for a rainy night.

Far West End/Innsbrook/Short Pump

ANOKHA $$–$$$
4015 Lauderdale Dr.
(804) 360-8686
www.anokha.us
Anokha gives traditional Indian dishes a twist, such as the shrimp that's toasted with

coconut and swimming in pink peppercorn-mint *raita*. Lunch and dinner are served, but you won't find a buffet here. Everything is chic and upscale, including the food. The deep paint colors and comfortable seating make this a place to relax in, and the strong wine list and lounge with full bar encourage that. Besides an exceptional *kheer*, there's a chocolate molten cake on the dessert menu, too. Now that's fusion-friendly.

Mechanicsville

PAD THAI $$
8460 Meadowbridge Rd.
(804) 559-0062
Family-owned and –operated, way off the beaten path, this place is easily missed, but shouldn't be. Looks aren't everything, so walk on in. You might notice the herbs growing around the building—a subtle hint of the freshness to come. Inside, it's no-frills, but that's OK, because the pad thai and duck curry, and desserts like coconut mango rice will knock your socks off with the depth of flavors.

Midlothian

SUSHI O $$$
1228 Alverser Plaza
(804) 897-9878
www.sushiova.com
This chic yet southern member of the Osaka/Wild Ginger family might need a new name after its recent transformation, which adds more than a hint of southernness to this version of farm-to-table food. "Braised short ribs O" just isn't a good name, though. The interior is still spare and a bit severe with the in-your-face signature artwork on the walls, so chef Kevin Lacivita, formerly of Pomegranate, adds warmth with the top-notch sushi.

The curried she-crab soup and short ribs are getting praise, as are the smoked duck tacos with Gorgonzola sour cream. The wine list matches the menu in range, and you can still try a flight of sake. Reservations are a good idea. Sushi O is open Mon through Fri for lunch and dinner, and for dinner only on Sat and Sun.

Midlothian/Powhatan Border

WILD GINGER $$$
3734 Winterfield Rd.
(804) 378-4988
www.wildgingerva.com
As soon as you walk in the door and see that the wine is center stage in a glass-enclosed room, you've been notified this is not your typical Asian restaurant. Opened in 2009, this restaurant isn't content just rolling out rolls. Chef Ken Leiw, Malaysian by way of Singapore, likes to mix it up. Try the seafood curry pot or try not to order the curry-dusted soft-shell crabs. Wild Ginger boasts 2,500 bottles of wine. The porch-like patio is a great place to have some while the fans whir above. Lunch and dinner are available Mon through Fri, but just dinner on Sat and Sun. Reservations are recommended.

BARBECUE
Church Hill

ALAMO BBQ $
2202 Jefferson Ave.
(804) 592-3138
www.alamobbqva.com
This place made an immediate impression upon opening in 2009, and not just because the building looks like the Alamo on Church Hill. Get award-winning, south Texas–style barbecue and beef brisket here. It's takeout with patio seating, and a tent is coming,

but many chowhounds use Jefferson Park as their public dining room. The food will leave you jumping for joy, except you'll be too full. Besides the 'cue, folks go nuts for the grilled portobello sandwich, and the mahimahi tacos. If ribs are your thing, taste the hickory-smoked dry-rub spareribs.

North Side

BUZ AND NED'S REAL BARBECUE $$
1119 N. Blvd.
(804) 355-6055
www.buzandneds.com
Buz was the Flay-slayer on Food Network's *Throwdown with Bobby Flay* in 2007, so this place is worth your time. Ned's not with us anymore, but if you believe the story, he bequeathed Buz old family secrets about barbecue. Buz can keep the secrets as long as he keeps sharing the food. The barbecue is sweet, spicy, and sumptuous. The restaurant looks about like a barbecue joint should, with additional seating outdoors, and wine and a full bar, too. Planning to open a second location on West Broad Street in the West End in the summer of 2010, Buz says he'll try some new offerings with the extra room, so check that out, too.

Stratford Hills

BENNY'S BARBECUE $$
2919 Hathaway Rd.
(804) 320-PIGS
www.bennysbbqonline.com
That easily remembered phone number comes in handy when you're on the way home and have a hankering for Smithfield pork barbecue minced to perfection. It's just plain fun to ask for a pork party pack. If you eat at this neighborhood restaurant, expect a comfortable, easy vibe, good hush puppies, and a bar you can mosey up to if you'd like to watch TV while you munch. Benny's will likely move to a new location in 2011, so make sure to check their Web site for details.

Henrico/East End

HILLBILLY RED'S BBQ $$
353 E. Williamsburg Rd.
(804) 737-2007
www.hillbillyredsbbq.com
One mile from the airport, Red's makes an excellent introduction to barbecue. The sweet potato sticks are the perfect accompaniment to tender and juicy pit-cooked barbecue. The family special, available only for take-out, makes the perfect hostess gift: one quart barbecue, two large sides, a half-pint coleslaw, and 12 buns. Eating here, you can try other vittles, including smoked chickens, beef brisket, catfish platters, and homemade desserts.

Far West End/Short Pump

GRANDPA EDDIE'S ALABAMA RIBS & BBQ $$
11129 Three Chopt Rd.
(804) 270-RIBS
www.grandpaeddiesbbq.com
The smoked, saucy ribs are done up the Alabama way, but there's Texas-style brisket and western North Carolina pulled pork, which is vinegary, so it's a trip around the savory South in this 300-seat popular spot. Try the chicken that won the state barbecue championship, or have a few Pig Sliders for a taste of the barbecue. Homemade sauces, rubs, salad dressing, and desserts only add to the tasty options here, and perfectly attuned live music on weekend nights keeps the place lively and packed until midnight.

Hanover/Ashland

PHAT BOYZ BBQ $$
10185 Washington Hwy.
(804) 550-5707

This family-run joint near GreenTop Sporting Goods features homemade everything. OK, so they don't make the beer, but they keep the barbecue, mac and cheese, hush puppies, and potato salad coming. If you can bear not to eat the pork, try daily specials like chicken and dumplings. They might kill you with kindness, and that's before the bread pudding, coconut pie, and apple dumplings for dessert. Indoor and outdoor seating are available, but parking can be pretty tough.

Mechanicsville

CARTER'S PIGPEN BAR-B-QUE $$
8011 Cold Harbor Rd.
(804) 730-3616

If you're in the area checking out Civil War sites, stop by this homey place in a small house that's been serving Virginia and North Carolina styles of tasty barbecue since 2008. If you're bringing a crowd, call ahead to hold one of the two dining rooms that seat 12 to 14. If you can't decide between barbecue styles, try the ribs instead. Be sure to sample the red-skin potato salad. It gets raves, for good, homemade reasons.

Midlothian

PQ'S BBQ $$
13579 Midlothian Turnpike
(804) 379-5267
www.pqsbbq.com

Open since 1989, PQ's is family-owned and -operated and serves finger-licking barbecue for lunch and dinner. The pork-platter luncheon special is a must-have, with the barbecue and two home-cooked veggies on the side. Save room for dessert because they're all homemade—apple, pumpkin, and coconut pies, cobblers in season. PQ's BBQ is open Tues through Sat.

Q BARBEQUE $$
2077 Wal-Mart Way
(804) 897-9007
www.qbarbeque.com

Perhaps you've seen Tuffy Stone on TV in the TLC show *BBQ Pitmasters,* as the head honcho of his team, Cool Smoke. Here's your chance to taste his award-winning concoctions in his cheerful barbecue hot spot. The guy is saucy, and so is his barbecue. Brisket and ribs—tender, falling off the bone—are a specialty. Eat inside or out and take home all three of his famous sauces: Sa-Weet, Original, and HotZing.

BURGERS AND DOGS

Shockoe Slip

CITY DOGS $
1316 E. Cary St.
(804) 343-3647

Bringing top-notch hot dogs to the center of the city, City Dogs jazzes 'em up with toppings reminiscent of Philly, Santa Fe, Manhattan, Boston, or elsewhere. Or get the hot dog platter with two Richmond Originals, laden with mustard, onions, and chili. Sandwiches and burgers are available, and be sure to try the corn-dog nuggets. There's a full bar, and even with the tight space, there's live music on weekends. It's the rare place where you can get a hot dog until 3 a.m. A second location is at 1309 W. Main St., the Fan (804-359-DOGS).

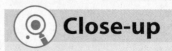 **Close-up**

Bakeries and Pastry Shops

I've spent my life researching this section. Let's do a quick tour.

Start with a cupcake or two or three from **Sally Bell's Kitchen** (www.sallybells kitchen.com) in the Fan. Sure, their boxed lunches are a steal at $8, and I love them, but it's just an excuse to get a cupcake. Go ahead and buy a dozen of the upside-down iced cupcakes so you can mix and match the mocha-iced devil's food ones with the crushed almond or the strawberry, etc.

Farmers' markets are a great source of delicious baked goods. I don't know how they grow chocolate chip cookies, but that's some good fertilizer. See more about farmers' markets in the "Shopping" chapter.

Carytown Cupcakes (www.carytown-cupcakes.com) bakes and frosts inspired cupcakes—not just beautiful, though they are that. Taste matters, and the choices match every taste, from five classics a day and three specials—Mostess, a mint-chocolaty heaven, and raspberry lemon are two.

When you absolutely must have a bouche de Noel, when calories are no object, go to **Jean-Jacques Bakery** (www.carytownbakery.com) in Carytown, because when cream, sugar, and chocolate hang out together, they come to this classic spot. French bread lives here, too. Another Carytown stalwart is **Montana Gold Bakery** (www.montanagoldbread.com). The cherry-apple challah is a revelation, as is the Blue Ridge Mountain herb bread. Hidden away on West Broad Street, **The Mixing Bowl** has been whipping up Richmond's cakes, cupcakes, sweet potato biscuits, and more since 1926. Its second location is in Short Pump.

When I'm in the mood for almond-meringue cookies, **Westhampton Pastry Shop** (5728 Patterson Ave.) is my destination. It's an old-school bakery, with chocolate-covered donuts that will take you back to your childhood (or at least to mine), Boston cream pies, and every retro delicious dessert you never eat now that you're health conscious and no fun. **Pearl's Cupcakes** (www.pearlscupcakeshoppe.com) in the Libbie and Grove area produces exquisitely crafted, tasty cupcakes in a variety of yum flavors like Campfire and banana cream. Vegan and gluten-free options are available as well.

Two Sweet (www.twosweetrichmond.com) bakes popular and delicious high-falutin cupcakes in the Far West End Tues through Sat. Traditional flavors such as German chocolate mix with the intriguing lime coconut.

3 Fellers Bakery (www.3fellersbakery.com) in Goochland is a gluten-free bakery that sells cookie and biscuit dough, corn bread, cake layers, and more. The coconut-cream tart is delicious. Call first for retail hours, and find the gluten-free goodies in Whole Foods, Martin's, and elsewhere around town.

In the South Side, **La Sabrosita Bakery** (www.lasabrositabakery.com) churns out a fine *tres leches* cake, fruit-layered sheet cakes to order, and a changing variety of cheese breads and other Latin American baked treats—not all of them sweet.

Prairie Grain Bakery (www.prairiegrain.com) in the Village Marketplace in Midlothian specializes in whole-wheat breads and rolls. I'm a fan of the herb whole wheat. If you'd rather be more decadent, head to **The Desserterie** (www.thedessert erie.com) off Hull Street for the spectacular pastries made by the European-trained pastry chef. The tiramisu is a star, but the options go way beyond what you've tried elsewhere. Almond pound cake with amaretto cream and dark cherries, topped with almond buttercream icing, sounds stunning.

Carytown

CARYTOWN BURGERS AND FRIES $
3500½ W. Cary St.
(804) 358-5225
www.carytownburgersandfries.com/
Come hungry and leave full. Wait a week; repeat. Order at the counter at this casual eatery. Wait for your grub outside under the tent or upstairs if the weather doesn't suit. The fries are phenomenal, and the burgers— even if you don't order the biggest size—are huge. I have a stomachache just thinking about how full I get here. I'm not sure it's possible to go here and not order fries or a chocolate milk shake.

CAFES, DELIS & SANDWICHES

The Fan

GARNETT'S CAFÉ $
2001 Park Ave.
(804) 367-7909
www.garnettscafe.com
It's a tight squeeze in this old-school–style luncheonette on Meadow Street and Park Avenue, but the Counter Culture coffee, the homemade soups, and the endless menu of delectable sandwiches make this a new Fan fave seven days a week. Garnett's is a coffee shop until 11 a.m., and then the soups and sandwiches take center stage. Cheese plates and beer and wine add to the mix through the night.

North Side

THE DAIRY BAR $
1602 Roseneath Rd.
(804) 355-1937
www.dairybarrestaurant.com
Southern Living says this is one of the five best restaurants in the South for breakfast, so I won't argue, but I'm much more interested in the milk shakes myself. For 64 years this unassuming spot in Scott's Addition off North Boulevard has been offering diner-like food and ambience to generations of Richmonders. The crowd here is a mix of old-timers, business folk, worker guys, and families. Wear the kids out at one of the nearby museums and bring them here. They can add to the bovine-themed art gallery on the wall while you chow down on the popular chicken salad, the subs, or the classic open-faced turkey and roast beef sandwiches, now available seven days a week. The bad news is the DB closes at 3 p.m. Mon through Sat and at 2 on Sun, so time your ice-cream cravings accordingly.

Carytown & Museum District

COPPOLA'S DELI $
2900 W. Cary St.
(804) 359-6969
www.coppolasdeli.com
You are free to order whatever fabulous concoction you'd like, but I am honor bound to order the Mediterranean Magic every time I go here. I've tried to change it up, but the focaccia, the feta, the pesto, the turkey—well, I won't have it any other way. Also offering classic Italian cheeses and delicacies, Coppola's is the kind of tight-packed place people fall in love with. The downtown location is at 1116 E. Main St. (804-225-0454).

Manchester

SAVOR $
201 W. 7th St.
(804) 527-2867
www.savorcompany.com
A worthy detour off the beaten path, Savor serves Rostov's coffee, Counter Culture

Coffee Shops

When you need caffeine in a hurry:

Downtown

Lift Coffee Shop & Café $
218 W. Broad St.
(804) 344-5438
www.liftcoffeeshop.com
Perky and panini.

Church Hill/Tobacco Row

Captain Buzzies Beanery $
2623 E. Broad St.
(804) 377-6655
Pet-friendly and Wi-Fi on Church Hill.

**Globehopper Coffeehouse
   and Lounge** $
2100 E. Main St.
(804) 523-8083
www.globehoppercoffee.com
Espresso and French press and jazz,
oh my.

The Fan

**Crossroads Coffee and
   Ice Cream** $
26 N. Morris St.
(804) 355-3559
www.crossroadsrva.com
Wraps, smoothies, coffee, and sweet
treats near VCU.

**Lamplighter Roasting
   Company and Café** $
116 S. Addison St.
(804) 728-2292
www.richmondcoffee.net
A true hot spot, warming up Richmond and roasting its own coffee.

Carytown

Ellwood's Coffee $
10 S. Thompson St.
(804) 612-1827
www.ellwoodscoffee.com

Making Richmond a cooler place, one
groovy day at a time.

West End

Caffèspresso $
1127 Gaskins Rd.
804-350-4504
www.caffespressocart.com
Northern Italian charm, espresso,
latte, and language classes pair well
with paninis.

South Side/Woodland Heights

**Crossroads Coffee and
   Ice Cream** $
3600 Forest Hill Ave.
(804) 231-2030
www.crossroadsrva.com
Nooks and crannies, couches and
cushioned spots, coffee and Bev's
homemade ice cream, too—plus outdoor seating.

Midlothian

Café Caturra $
13830 Village Place Dr.
(804) 378-4955
www.cafecaturra.com
Only this location of the local chain
that roasts its own beans opens at 8
a.m. for the coffee crowd.

Ashland

Ashland Coffee & Tea $
100 N. Railroad Ave.
(804) 798-1702
www.ashlandcoffeeandtea.com
Cozy up with your coffee in the center of the universe.

espresso, and some of the best sandwiches, soups, and paninis you could hope for. Cranberry-almond chicken salad on focaccia is a very good idea. Several excellent choices are available, ready to go for a picnic or back to work. The Olivado Citrus Salad is so yum, it's won awards.

Near West End

BARREL THIEF $$–$$$
5805 Patterson Ave.
(804) 612-9232
www.barrelthiefwine.com

This is a hybrid between a fine-wine shop and a cool place to have a relaxed bite while sipping your wine. Its Patterson Avenue location has one seating area near the front window and several tables up a couple steps. The menu changes seasonally, but you could keep this a budget night with the appealing selections of starters, sandwiches, and salads (turkey and Brie with apple compote on rosemary focaccia, for instance), or you could up the ante and try entrees like grilled ahi tuna over white-bean cassoulet. With a dozen wines available by the glass, it's easy to try new directions here and sip a little, snack a little. The staff is happy to help you find the directions you want to go. Special wine-tasting nights often sell out. The cafe is closed on Mon, though the retail operation continues. A second location is at 11747 W. Broad St. in the Far West End (804-364-0144).

i What started as a coffee shop—Café Caturra—still roasts and blends all its own coffee at all locations and sells it to the caffeine lover. You can buy it by the pound, whole or ground. At least four or five varieties are available for purchase any given day at the three area locations.

CAFÉ CATURRA $$
5811 Grove Ave.
(804) 285-0690
www.cafecaturra.com

Is it a coffee shop, cafe, or a wine bar? It depends when you come and what you indulge in. The good news is that you'll have plenty of choices for indulging. Open seven days, Café Caturra roasts its own coffee and makes its own soups, rotating through several blends of the former and a dozen of the latter. At lunchtime, the Cuban Panini and the raspberry walnut salad are popular with the business folk and ladies who lunch. Every day once the clock strikes three, Your Hour begins, lasting until six and featuring $3 beers, $4 small plates, and $5 wines. Pouring 24 wines by the glass and offering "try it before you buy it" on all wines, Café Caturra is hoping you can't resist the allure of vino.

A second and third location are at 3332 Pump Rd. in the Far West End (804-360-3377) and 13830 Village Place Dr. in Midlothian (804-378-4955). At least one night a week, each of the three locations presents live music and complimentary wine tastings. The indoor wood-burning fireplaces at all locations only help the cause.

Far West End/Innsbrook/Short Pump

BOYCHIK'S DELI $
4024B Cox Rd.
(804) 747-1030

In Innsbrook, this is the place to go for classic deli breakfasts and lunches. The Boar's Head meats and swift service will hit the spot when you want a serious sandwich on good bread. Don't be surprised if you have to wait, but the turnover is pretty steady.

i When in Ashland, stop in at Homemades by Suzanne, 102 N. Railroad Ave., for the famous boxed lunches, ham biscuits, and other items. Bring something home from this noted caterer's retail spot—the almond chicken salad with apricots would make anyone's day. Call (804) 798-8331 or check out www.homemadesbysuzanne .com.

EUROPEAN ECLECTIC

Downtown

BISTRO 27 $$$
27 W. Broad St.
(804) 780-0086
www.bistrotwentyseven.com
A classy and glassy place with all the windows overlooking Broad Street, 27 ups the ante downtown. The bar is long and luscious, and the tables are spaced well so you're not on top of your fellow diners. From paella to chicken cordon bleu to quail, this bistro covers a lot of culinary ground. Pairing their signature salad with the chocolate mousse is the best way to eat light. There's free parking behind the Renaissance.

CAFE RUSTICA $$–$$$
414 E. Main St.
(804) 225-8811
Cafe Rustica features a cozy atmosphere where the comfort food might take you to Germany, Portugal, or Scotland, depending on the day. The place is small, and the service can be on the slow side, but if you aren't in a rush, the seafood stew and the Mediterranean short stack come highly recommended. There is no wheelchair-accessible bathroom here. Cafe Rustica doesn't serve dinner on Mon and doesn't serve lunch on Sat. The Sun suppers are quite popular.

The Fan

ROWLAND FINE DINING $$$$
2132 W. Main St.
(804) 257-9885
www.rowlandfinedining.com
The husband-and-wife culinary dynamic duo have created something special here: a fusion of southern, Asian, Mediterranean, and Provençal. It might sound messy, but what comes out of the kitchen is superb. Don't wait for a special occasion to go here; the innovative, beautifully presented, and mouthwatering tastes will make any meal here special and spectacular. Get the butterbean cake; it's brilliant. The wine list stands up to the menu very nicely. The desserts, in particular the Bananas Foster, are noteworthy and made on-site, as are the breads and salad dressings. The restaurant is open for dinner every night and offers brunch on Sun.

i If you're hungry and don't know where to eat, heading to West Main Street just west of the Monroe Park Campus of VCU is always a good idea. It's a diner's delight all the way to the Boulevard. Limited space wouldn't permit full write-ups, but Avalon, Bacchus, Davis & Main, deLux, Helen's, Sidewalk Cafe, and Six Burner are all longstanding Fan all-stars, offering great Fan atmosphere and even better food.

FRENCH

Shockoe Slip

BOUCHON $$$$
1209 E. Cary St.
(804) 225-9116
www.bistrobouchon.com
Getting plaudits from the foodies and wine-centric folks who flocked to this bistro the

moment it opened in 2009, Bouchon is the dream come true of a husband and wife team. Wendy Kalif runs the front of the understated and clean-lined house, and Francis Devilliers, the chef, whips up cassoulet of duck confit, stewed lamb and Toulouse sausage and white beans, calves' liver, charcuterie, sweetbreads, fish, and the best chicken ever, using locally sourced food whenever possible. Don't assume this is out of your price range. With specials most nights and a prix fixe menu daily from 5 to 6 p.m. that's $20 for three courses, treat yourself early and often. Go, *vite! Bien sur*, the desserts are homemade. Parking is free at the S. 12th Street deck. Bouchon is closed on Sun.

Carytown

CAN CAN BRASSERIE $$$
3120 W. Cary St.
(804) 358-PARIS
www.cancanbrasserie.com

At the eastern corner of Cary Court Shopping Center, Can Can is the center of the Carytown universe. Its beautiful bar, vibrant energy, and all the festive French touches add up to exactly the right place to stop for breakfast, lunch, or dinner. The breads are delicious, as they should be. Coq au vin, mussels, and the usual French suspects are here, but feel free to be more daring. Open seven days, you'll have plenty of people-watching possibilities here. Reservations are recommended.

Far West End

CHEZ MAX $$$$
10622 Patterson Ave.
(804) 754-3464
www.chezmaxva.com

Freestanding in the Canterbury Shopping Center, not exactly where you'd expect to find classical French cuisine, Chez Max brings fine dining to the Far West End. With the Master Chef of France–trained team working their magic in the kitchen, diners soak in the divine aromas as they sit by the stone fireplace and the dark wooden walls. It's too bad dipping one's finger in other diners' sauces is frowned upon. There are too many to choose from: a Merlot sauce that graces grilled lamb chops, calvados sauce, cognac cream sauce, a lime tartar sauce, caper cream sauce, crawfish butter sauce—you get the idea. And how often do you have to choose between chocolate and Grand Marnier soufflés? It's almost cruel. Chez Max serves dinner only, Tues through Sat.

ICE CREAM & GELATO

Carytown

BEV'S HOMEMADE ICE CREAM $
2911 W. Cary St.
(804) 204-2387

Bev's brings out the poet in me: Um—yum. The um refers to the pregnant pause when one tries to decide between too many fabulous flavors. The yum is self-explanatory. Bev's fills up fast, and the wait can be excruciating after a show at the Byrd lets out. The rich and flavorful ice cream can be found at other spots around town, including Crossroads on the South Side. Bev's has run Ben & Jerry's out of Carytown not once, but twice! Bev's is not wheelchair accessible.

Near West End

BOYER'S ICE CREAM AND COFFEE $
5720 Patterson Ave.
(804) 288-4088

An idea whose time had come, Boyer's brought 16 flavors of Gelati Celesti goodness closer to the city. We appreciate that.

Boyer's is a homey place with some comfortable seating inside and a little bit outside. It also offers Palazzolo's Italian Gelato. Boyer's is closed on Sun.

West End

DELUCA GELATO $
1362 Gaskins Rd.
(804) 741-3202
www.delucagelato.com

This family-owned and -operated *gelateria* makes all the gelato right here—65 amazing flavors, with 36 offered daily, including several dairy-free sorbets and two sugar-free options. Most days you can see the process through the production window. My favorite part of the process is tasting the results. Balliceaux serves the finished product, so you know it's good. I'm especially fond of the Frutti di Bosco—mixed berries. For the truly enamored, sign up for a flavor alert: Send them an e-mail with the flavor you can't wait to see return in the subject line, and they'll reply when it's available. Other specialty Italian desserts are also homemade.

GELATI CELESTI ICE
  CREAM MAKERS $
8906 W. Broad St.
(804) 346-0038

You always remember your first gelato. And this classic spot was Richmond's first. A West End institution, it's often packed, but worth the wait. You'll need the time to decide which of the distinctive and delicious flavors you're going to choose. For a special occasion, be a hero and order one of their gelato cakes or pies with your choice of flavors.

ITALIAN
Shockoe Slip

LA GROTTA RISTORANTE $$$
1218 E. Cary St.
(804) 644-2466

Since 1994, this charming family-run restaurant has been welcoming diners into the warm, woody, and rustic downstairs dining room for true Italian feasts. Chef Antonio Capece cuts all his own meat and prides himself on his use of wild meats such as wild boar, buffalo, and even kangaroo. All pasta, bread, and desserts are made on the premises. For a special event you can dine in the wine cellar, which holds close to 200 varieties of Italian and American vino. La Grotta serves lunch and dinner Mon through Fri, with dinner only on Sat. Complimentary parking is available at night in Central Parking, 100 Virginia St. The only downside is that La Grotta isn't wheelchair accessible, as stairs are involved from the entrance.

i Bottom's Up Pizza (www.bottomsuppizza.com), an institution in Shockoe Bottom at 1700 Dock St., is a place to go when you're really ravenous. Any other time would be a waste of the deep-dish pies that are weighted down with barbecued chicken, caramelized onions, and cheddar cheese, or crabmeat and artichoke hearts. More standard fare and thin-crust pizza are available, too, in this fun, lively spot with an outdoor patio and deck.

The Fan & Oregon Hill

EDO'S SQUID $$$
411 N. Harrison St.
(804) 864-5488

Up a narrow flight of stairs, Edo's charms not with charm, but with delicious garlicky food at a reasonable price. The tables are tightly packed, the service is notoriously disinterested, and the brick adds ambience and bounces noise around, so if it's crowded, and it usually is, it's hard to carry on a conversation without raising your voice. Still it's likely your mouth will be stuffed with some of the best pasta carbonara, squid, rockfish, and broccoli rabe you've ever tasted, so who cares? Parties of four or more must order family-style, but that just makes tasting everyone's food that much easier. Edo's is not wheelchair accessible.

MAMMA 'ZU $$$
501 S. Pine St.
(804) 788-4205
Some people are too fastidious for this dive, with its cash- or Amex-only policy, tight squeeze, and brusque and busy service, but clearly the line out the door indicates Richmond has a wild side—or we're addicted to garlic. *Style Weekly's* "Restaurant of the Decade," Mamma 'Zu's packs the people who love what garlic, olive oil, and wine can do to fish, flesh, or pasta. The chalkboard menu makes no mistakes—simplicity done spectacularly. It's closed on Sun. Lunch is an easier sell if you don't like the waiting outside.

Carytown

MARY ANGELA'S $-$$
3345 W. Cary St.
(804) 353-2333
www.maryangelaspizzeria.com
A Carytown staple for more than 20 years, Mary Angela's features New York– and Sicilian-style pizza, and pasta specialties in a family-friendly, bustling place. The subs and calzones are worth the calories. Parking is available on the street. Expect the pre- and post-movie crowd to be here.

Near West End

AZZURRO $$$
6221 River Rd.
(804) 282-1509
www.azzurros.com
Giving the River Road Shopping Center a touch of Italia, Azzurro has it all—fireplace inside and patio in the back and a warm, refined atmosphere that makes it easy to enjoy lunch or dinner. One ever-so-slightly bossy friend of mine loves the sage-butter ravioli so much here that she orders it even when it's not on the menu. Besides pastas, lamb chops, and other fine choices, brick-oven pizza is always an option—as simple and satisfying as the Margherita or as sumptuous as shrimp and roasted peppers.

West End

CAPRICCIOS PIZZERIA & RISTORANTE $$
9127-A W. Broad St.
(804) 346-0184
www.capricciorestaurantva.com
Many of my northern brethren smile more now that this New York–style pizzeria, run by a native of Sicily who lived in New York and New Jersey, has come to town. Simple ingredients, a little sauce, thin crust—done. Gravy, hoagies, and homemade cannoli let you know this guy knows the ways of the North.

Far West End/Innsbrook/Short Pump

MAMA CUCINA $$-$$$
4028-O Cox Rd.
(804) 346-3350
You won't be wowed by the latest trendy decor here, but the fine southern Italian

cuisine will do that trick once you open your mouth. The veal dishes are especially impressive. No need for the chains out here when Mama Cucina is on the job.

Midlothian/Powhatan Border

MEDITERRANEO $$$
3730 Winterfield Plaza
(804) 794-5350
www.mediterraneocuisine.com
The Mary Angela's family gussied itself up for the suburban folks here on the border of Midlothian and Powhatan. This is a comfortable, busy spot where you can focus on pizza—and this family knows pizza. Or you can kick the cuisine up a few notches and have entrees of rockfish or robust pasta—the shrimp and garlic pasta with fish-stock base is quite nice. The pesto and Gorgonzola pizza with a thin crust is just gooey enough. The covered patio with ceiling fans is a nice touch in good weather.

LATIN AMERICAN

Shockoe Bottom

HAVANA 59 $$$
16 N. 17th St.
(804) 780-CUBA
www.havana59.net
The decor alone makes this place worth a visit just across from the 17th Street Farmers' Market, and the hopping atmosphere and tantalizing food—perhaps the '59 Paella—will keep you coming back. The rooftop patio with palms now works all year round, but that's where the cigar bar is, so be warned. The bartenders work magic with mojitos and margaritas. It's closed on Sun and Mon.

The Fan

EMILIO'S RESTAURANTE
ESPANOL $$–$$$
1847 W. Broad St.
(804) 359-1224
www.emiliosrichmond.com
Whether you are in the mood for tapas or a big plate of paella, Emilio's has the authentic Spanish cuisine your heart and taste buds desire. Emilio, from Sueca in the Valencia region of Spain, where paella originated, fires up his traditional dishes, including dozens of delicious tapas choices. Second and third locations are at 200 Towne Center West Blvd. in Short Pump (804-360-8080) and 7016 Woodlake Commons Loop in Midlothian (804-639-8099). Check out the Web site to see which location has the salsa dancing, Flamenco performers, open mics, and live music.

KUBA KUBA $$
1601 Park Ave.
(804) 355-8817
www.kubakuba.info
Known beyond Richmond for good reason, Kuba Kuba has the perfect hole-in-the-wall bodega feel, and I mean that as a real compliment. No pretension here, just great food, a lively scene, and a friendly waitstaff. For an hour or two, you won't believe you're in Richmond, yet the fact that you're noshing on a mouth-watering Cuban sandwich, slurping the rich black-bean soup, inhaling the vegetable paella, or devouring the mind-blowing tres leches cake is one of the reasons you're so happy you are in Richmond. Kuba Kuba is open for breakfast, lunch, and dinner, with brunch on Sat and Sun.

THE JERK PIT $
2713 W. Broad St.
(804) 353-7755
www.jerkpit.net

Remember, size doesn't matter. This place is small, near the Science Museum of Virginia, but it's known for spicy chicken, shrimp, and veggie jerk kabobs. It's primarily for take-out, and the food, especially the beef patties and the goat curry, fly out the door.

i If you forgot to pick up a rotisserie chicken at the grocery store, Chicken Fiesta (www.chicken fiesta.com) could change your dinner plans single-grilledly. At either the West Broad Street or Midlothian Turnpike location, the rotisserie chickens are always cranking, and the garlic and other spices transform humble chickens into stars. Other goodies are available for eat-in or take-out. Dipping the cassava into the yummy garlicky mayo and mustard sauce seems healthier than downing french fries.

Carytown

NACHO MAMA'S $$
3449 W. Cary St.
(804) 358-6262
www.nachomamasva.com

Fun and funky with the bright yellow umbrellas out front, two levels inside, and Latin music pumping throughout, this is a go-to spot for a good mix of Mexican, Caribbean, southwestern, and Cuban-inspired dishes. The 20 varieties of margaritas add to the festive feeling in the air. A second location is at 7610 Left Flank Rd. in Mechanicsville (804-730-7311).

Stratford Hills

MEXICO $$
7001 Forest Hill Ave.
(804) 320-1069
www.mexico-restaurant.com

Go to this local chain when you're really hungry and can't wait more than a couple of minutes for your food, because you will be served immediately. Typical Mexican food and pleasant margaritas come faster than perhaps is strictly a good idea, but children are welcome here, the fajitas sizzling on the griddle at your table are enormous, and the staff will let you or your kids practice your Spanish. The chicken soup flavored with cilantro is a tasty way to get out of here without consuming tons of cheese and refried beans. Second, third, and fourth locations are at 11621 W. Broad St. in the Far West End (804-360-9446), 5213 Williamsburg Rd. in the East End (804-226-2388), and 7162 Mechanicsville Turnpike in Mechanicsville (804-559-8126). Space doesn't allow listing the rest of the area locations, but the Web site tells all.

i A lot of triathletes frequent Palani Drive (www.palanidrive .com) in the Near West End for the healthy and tasty protein-packed quesadillas, breakfast burritos available all day, and smoothies and cappuccino. At night, the black-bean quesadilla and pasta with Gorgonzola are sure-fire hits. Perhaps eating the food at this low key, inexpensive, and sharp-looking place is the key to unleashing the athlete within.

MEDITERRANEAN

The Fan

COUS COUS $$
900 W. Franklin St.
(804) 358-0868
www.couscous900.com

For great meals in a funky Mediterranean setting, with dark wood and luscious fabrics, you've found the place. The extensive menu begs to be shared, though it might be hard to part with the gnocchi in Gorgonzola cream sauce or the Chicken B'stilla, a Moroccan pot-pie. The cocktail list is exotic and expansive. Pear-pomegranate sangria and hot summer days in Richmond are a perfect match.

West End

**2-M MEDITERRANEAN MARKET
AND DELI** $
7103 Staples Mill Rd.
(804) 262-9950

In the Dumbarton Square shopping center, two brothers from Bosnia own this combo market and small restaurant, cranking out fresh specials every day. It's a charmer, with halal meats and gyros, and the perfect spot to grab some baba ghanoush, fresh pita, and of course, the hummus. Pick up top-shelf ingredients for your next feast here.

Bon Air

JOE'S INN AND JOE'S OUT $$
2616 Buford Rd.
(804) 320-9700
www.joesinn.com

The Greek salad, the souvlaki, and white pizza here are what lands this friendly, neighborhood gathering place in this section and not the Italian section, where it also could go. If there's feta on it, get it. Spaghetti a la

Greek is a winner. A second location is at 205 N. Shields St., the Fan (804-355-2282). The Buford Rd. location has a bustling take-out business adjacent. Both locations serve breakfast, lunch, and dinner.

MIDDLE EASTERN

Shockoe Bottom/Tobacco Row

AZIZA'S $$–$$$
2110 E. Main St.
(804) 344-1523
www.azizasonmain.com

In Tobacco Row you'll find this appealing though noisy spot with its brick-walled interior and tin ceiling. One room is the restaurant, the other a deli with out-of-the-ordinary chicken salads, hummus, and other great picnic fare. The cream puffs are killer good. At present, dinner is only Thurs through Sat, and it gets high marks for serious fare such as rack of lamb. I recommend the brunch—the pancetta and fontina, or olive, feta, and spinach frittatas, are delectable, and they are accompanied by the best seasoned potatoes I've ever had.

PUBS

Downtown

PENNY LANE PUB $$
421 E. Franklin St.
(804) 780-1682
www.pennylanepub.com

Have your fish-and-chips or bangers and mash and a pint in a place that's loaded with reminders of life across the pond. Football is likely on the telly, but not the wimpy American kind where the boys wear helmets and pads. Just try to find a seat during the World Cup here. It's open for lunch and dinner Mon through Fri, for dinner only on Sat, and occasionally for Sun brunch when big football matches are on. Smoking is allowed on the patio and in the upper room, which leaves the downstairs bar and dining room smoke-free.

Shockoe Slip

SINE IRISH PUB AND RESTAURANT $$
1327 E. Cary St.
(804) 649-7767
www.sineirishpub.com

Lots of wood inside warms up this spot, which doesn't confine its menu to dishes from the Old Sod. Two words: Irish nachos. Snacks and salads go well with a pint, and with several levels of seating and a popular deck out the back, there can be a different atmosphere in different sections.

Westover Hills

O'TOOLE'S $$–$$$
4800 Forest Hill Ave.
(804) 233-1781
www.otoolesrestaurant.com

This family-owned place was recently expanded, but it still has the cozy, friendly atmosphere that brings the regulars back for dependable appetizers, including the reliably filling Guinness. There's more here than just Irish pub food. Soups are homemade, and there's an appealing variety of salads and reasonably priced entrees. Some of the bartenders and waitstaff have worked here for more than a decade and treat everyone like regulars. O'Toole's is open every day for lunch and dinner and offers Sun brunch.

West End

RARE OLDE TIMES $$
10602 Patterson Ave.
(804) 750-1346
www.rareoldetimespub.com

This warm and inviting pub has the requisite Irishman at the helm, so some good *craic* is on tap here, as well as the Guinness. Andy and Cindy, the owners who perform as Andy and Cindy and Thensome, have opened with the best of them—Paddy Riley, Tommy Makem, and the Clancy Brothers—so you just might be wanting to go over and hear them some Fri or Sat night. If Andy isn't on stage, he's back in the kitchen cooking bangers and mash or fish-and-chips and other pub fare. There's music Thurs through Sat, and Uisce Beatha plays most Thurs.

REGIONAL & SOUTHERN

Downtown

COMFORT $$$
200 W. Broad St.
(804) 780-0004
www.comfortrestaurant.com

Oh my, just thinking about the chocolate mousse and the Surry sausage here, not necessarily eaten in that order, makes me hungry. This hip, narrow downtown place has been doing the comfort-food thing to perfection since 2002. They don't take reservations, so on weekends especially, you'll be crowding around the full bar with the other foodies, trying your best to stay out of everyone's way, hoping a booth or table opens up. Entrees, such as the mouthwatering pork tenderloin, the popular shrimp and grits, and the classic roasted chicken are priced according to whether you want two or three sides. You'll want three. Choose from mac and cheese, braised greens, roasted beets, and on and on. You can even go with an all-vegetable plate if three aren't enough. Meat loaf must pair well with whiskey because Comfort has an extensive whiskey list. It can be loud here, though not so much at lunch.

Comfort serves a killer brunch on Sun. My friends think people should share dessert. No, that mousse is mine. Parking is on-street.

LOUISIANA FLAIR $-$$
322 E. Grace St.
(804) 612-9066
www.louisianaflair.com

Chef Nate cranks out the real Cajun deal just across from the Media General building. Breakfast, lunch, and early dinner or take-out will have to suffice because Louisiana Flair closes at 6 p.m. on weekdays and 4 p.m. on Sat. The fresh beignets on Wed with the blueberry syrup are legendary. The out-of-this-world gumbo recipe is 85 years old, from the chef's grandmother, and the oyster po'boys are to die for. Jambalaya, fried trout, and catfish—it's all cooked fresh by Nate, and the service will have you thinking you're a member of the family. Grown men weep when there's no more bread pudding with whiskey sauce.

TJ'S $$$
The Jefferson Hotel
101 W. Franklin St.
(804) 649-4672
www.jeffersonhotel.com

Watching my Virginia peanut soup being poured onto the peanuts and poached bing cherries, I had my doubts, but I forgot where I was. TJ's is a southern bistro that knows how to take the homely peanut and make it shine. What might have been a liquid peanut butter and jelly turned into a mature taste once the chives got involved. Imagine what TJ's does with Shrimp-n-Grits or Apple Cider Brined Pork Rib Eye. Local ingredients, savory flavors, and helpful, knowledgeable servers ensure a memorable meal. Before or after dinner, lounging at the long, dark,

and handsome bar with its fine selection of microbrewed beers extends the evening most pleasantly.

ℹ️ For lunch during the week, here are two sure things: Perly's (111 E. Grace St., 804-649-2729), a solid citizen of downtown, is a reliable purveyor of biscuits and southern breakfast and lunch specialties that locals love. Chez Foushee (203 N. Foushee St., 804-648-3225, www.chezfoushee.com), also downtown, is a dreamy spot open for dinner only on Friday and Saturday nights, so lunch will have to do the rest of the week, and it's done up right. The food is divine. Bring home dessert if you can't eat it there.

Shockoe Bottom

JULEP'S NEW
SOUTHERN CUISINE $$$$
1719-21 E. Franklin St.
(804) 377-3968
www.juleps.net

Julep's has been earning rave reviews for its southern charm and cuisine ever since opening in 2003 in an elegantly renovated 1817 building. The restaurant reminds diners that Richmond deserves a place at the table among southern-food capitals like Charleston and New Orleans. Julep's intuitively prepared southern delicacies consistently win over restaurant reviewers. Pair that with nabbing *Wine Spectator's* "Award of Excellence" in 2008 and 2009, and Julep's is a can't-miss. Mon is wine night, with half off all bottles of wine for groups of six or less. Chef Branden Levine's reinvented fried green tomatoes are divine, as is the Creole mustard-and-herb-crusted rack of lamb with sour cherry *gastrique*. Julep's is closed on Sun.

Jackson Ward

MAMA J'S $-$$
415 N. 1st St.
(804) 225-7449
www.mamajskitchen.com
Serving up lunch and dinner standbys in a comfortable red-walled and dark-wood setting, Mama J's caters to the crowds that want good, honest, home-cooked food but want to have the fun of being here instead. Fried catfish, ribs, burgers, and sides like candied yams and seafood salad keep the regulars coming back. That homemade pineapple coconut cake sounds deadly but is divine.

Carver

THE BLACK SHEEP $$
901 W. Marshall St.
(804) 648-1300
www.theblacksheeprva.com
In what used to be known as Sheep Hill, The Black Sheep is a restaurant you can count on seven days a week for all three meals. New Orleans–inspired, it serves Community Coffee, and breakfast is served until 2 p.m. After a Bayou Breakfast, you won't need dinner. Famous for naming their intriguing subs for battleships, the good-humored, brick-walled spot often overflows with customers willing to do battle with the massive portions.

East End

LUCILLE'S SOUTHERN CUISINE $$
1203 N. Laburnum Ave.
(804) 644-1646
Lucille's offers home cooking for you and your friends without the hassle of cleaning up after yourselves. The crab cakes and collard greens are local favorites, and the smothered pork chops, barbecue, short ribs, and fried catfish do the trick, too. Live bands

play at this location every Fri and Sat night. A second location is at 7515 Brook Rd. on the North Side (804-515-8740).

Hanover

**HANOVER TAVERN RESTAURANT
AND PUB** $$$
13181 Hanover Courthouse Rd.
(804) 537-5250
www.hanovertavern.org
For those antiquing along US 301, this 1791 building (with 19th- and 20th-century additions) is the biggest antique you'll find. The she-crab soup is stellar, and the variety of wraps, salads, and sandwiches, especially the fried green tomato BLT, should fortify you for additional treasure hunting. If you have tickets to a Barksdale at Hanover show, the theater menu offers a three-course special that includes entrees such as pink peppercorn–crusted salmon or potato gnocchi. Reservations are recommended for dinner. The restaurant is closed on Mon.

Powhatan

THE COUNTY SEAT $$
3883 Old Buckingham Rd.
(804) 598-5000
www.thecountyseat.com
This family-friendly gathering place across from the county courthouse is run by four generations of the same family, so it's no surprise that it offers classic southern breakfasts, with breakfast buffets on Sat and Sun. Watching the video on the Web site of 90-year-old Mattie Clayton talking about her holiday tradition might not turn you on to fruitcake, but it certainly will convince you that the County Seat is a wonderfully authentic southern, home-style, not-to-be-missed spot. And keep in mind that it covers

all the bases, serving lunch and dinner, too, with live music till 10 p.m. on Sat. The dinner menu has several seafood offerings—like Rappahannock fried oysters or crab and tilapia—mixed in with the home-style meat loaf or smothered chicken.

SEAFOOD

Shockoe Slip/Tobacco Row

THE BOATHOUSE AT ROCKETT'S LANDING $$$
4708 E. Old Main St.
(804) 622-BOAT
www.boathouserichmond.com

It took this remarkable restoration of an old power plant into a stunning riverside destination to give a spark to the Rockett's Landing development just east of downtown. The Boathouse is Richmond's only riverfront restaurant, and its setting along the tidal James, with dramatic views of downtown, makes for an electric atmosphere—and a crowded one, especially on weekends. Patrons waiting for tables will be draped all over the multilevel stairways and railings, having a drink and watching the water. Dinner—seafood specialties, steaks, and brick-oven pizza—is served nightly and Sun brunch is every bit as popular.

i The popular Boathouse at Rockett's Landing is packed most nights, but remember its sister spot is the Boathouse at Sunday Park on Swift Creek Reservoir in Midlothian. The views aren't of the James River, but the sunset still works its charms.

THE HARD SHELL $$$–$$$$
1411 E. Cary St.
(804) 643-2333
www.thehardshell.com

The Raw Bar here alone is enough to turn a landlubber into a seafood connoisseur, and I don't know who can resist the Hard Shell's stellar she-crab soup. There's almost always an energetic buzz in the air here, with people who know they've made the right choice for the evening enjoying some of the best seafood in town. The restaurant serves lunch and dinner every day, and with the raw bar, soups, salads, and appetizers filling in the gaps, the Hard Shell doesn't have to do the hard sell to keep customers coming back. It's a sure seafood thing, as simple or as sophisticated as you'd like.

i Europa (www.europarichmond .com), sister restaurant to The Hard Shell and right next door on East Cary Street in Shockoe Slip, is widely praised for its flavorful tapas. It's a destination of choice for groups looking for a friendly atmosphere, inventive food, and great wine pairings.

Near West End

COAST $$$–$$$$
5806 Grove Ave.
(804) 288-8466
www.coastrva.com

Ensconced in the Libbie and Grove area of town, Coast's decor is subtle and sublime, light and fresh, just like the expertly prepared seafood it features. Whether you choose mussels *marinière* or bouillabaisse, or even the steak, note that sides are ordered separately here. No one said anything about dessert having to be light, so caramelized pear *croustillant* will do quite nicely. Expect a knowing wine list since Coast's beloved sister restaurant, Enoteca Sogno, is an Italian wine bar. The latter is due to reopen on the North Side in 2010. Coast is closed on Sun and Mon.

Manchester

CROAKER'S SPOT $$
1020 Hull St.
(804) 269-0464
www.croakersspot.com
Its Jackson Ward location closed in 2010, but thank goodness this South Side spot, full of nostalgic touches and character, is still bringing on the "soulful seafood" that includes everybody's favorite fish boat. Pick how many pieces of fried lake trout you can handle, and the secret-sauced, sautéed peppers and Vidalia onions, corn bread, and house potatoes will surround them. Try the seafood chili—scallops, shrimp, and fish swimming with beans, veggies, and spices— po'boy sandwiches, and vegetarian choices.

Midlothian

CRAB LOUIE'S SEAFOOD TAVERN $$$
1352 Sycamore Sq.
(804) 275-2722
A classic seafood restaurant in a warm and woody, historic tavern, Crab Louie's has been filling the South Side's hankering for shrimp and grits and crab cakes since 1981. Its varied selections of fresh fish at lunch and dinner can be prepared in a multitude of ways—with cilantro lime butter, hazelnut crusted, blackened with southwestern rémoulade—or you can dive into the signature dishes such as the seafood latkes and lump-meat crab cakes, of course. Perhaps the most decadent dish is the Seafood Au Gratin, which combines fresh Virginia crabmeat, scallops, and shrimp in a sherry cream sauce covered in Havarti cheese. Loaves of homemade breads such as apple cheddar and zucchini pineapple are available for purchase. The main entrance has a wheelchair ramp and there is a wheelchair-accessible bathroom. Some areas within the tavern do have stairs, though.

PESCADOS $$$
13126 Midlothian Turnpike
(804) 379-7121
www.pescadosseafood.com
Delivering fresh, savory seafood south of the river with a south-of-the-border twist, Pescados has been changing the tastes of Midlothian diners and forcing the city dwellers to come hither to sample the innovative flavors, whether it's the tilapia tacos or the Haitian-inspired voodoo shrimp. Quirky mojito selections fit right in with the lighthearted, casual atmosphere.

> **i** A second location of Pescados opened summer 2010 in Oregon Hill at 626 China St., where the crowd allows chef Louise Lane to up the ante from the Midlothian version. An outdoor patio will no doubt become a hot spot, the perfect place for cool ceviche.

STEAK HOUSES

West End

BUCKHEAD'S RESTAURANT AND CHOP HOUSE $$$$
8510 Patterson Ave.
(804) 750-2000
www.buckheads.com
The dark and elegant atmosphere pairs well with the mouthwatering aged and hand-cut beef. Sure, there are fancy chain steak houses all over town now, but Buckhead's has them matched at every turn. You'll hope you need to wait at the bar, it's so handsome. And the dining rooms make you forget you're in a West End shopping center. Seafood, such as pan-seared scallops or Atlantic salmon

with beurre blanc, might tempt you away from the beef, and won't disappoint, but you came here for the perfectly seasoned steaks. The wine list is extensive—more than 700 bottles—so *Wine Spectator* bestowed the 2009 Best of Award of Excellence on Buckhead's.

Goochland

THE NORTH POLE   **$$$–$$$$**
1558 River Rd. West
(804) 784-4222
www.thenorthpolerestaurant.com
Kitschy and colorful, without the typical steak-house decor, the North Pole hand cuts the filet mignons and rib eyes when you order them. It's a drive out VA 6, past VA 288, to the Crozier section of Goochland County, but the fireplace and the portions of heart-warming food make the drive worthwhile. The North Pole is open for dinner Thurs through Sat.

VEGETARIAN

The Fan

IPANEMA CAFE   **$$**
917 W. Grace St.
(804) 213-0190
www.ipanemaveg.com
Don't let the vegetarians have all the fun here at this VCU-area cozy nook that serves some of the most delicious food around. Yes, the *udon* noodles swimming in a coconut and peanut sauce with sautéed vegetables and tofu are bound to make vegetarians and vegans happy, but honestly I can't see how anyone would miss the meat here. The rich menu of salads, sandwiches, classy apps like pistachio-crusted risotto cakes, and entrees like grilled Indian pizza, along with the laid-back atmosphere, makes every bite enjoy-able. Put the brunch on your bucket list. A DJ is in the house on weekends. Sadly, it's not wheelchair accessible.

NIGHTLIFE

Don't tell me the spot that produced GWAR, Lamb of God, Carbon Leaf, Jason Mraz, and Elliott Yamin has no nightlife. Richmond's music scene has been strong for decades, helping Pat Benatar hone her skills in clubs in the '70s and giving Bruce Springsteen's early band, Steel Mill, a lot of love and places to crash in the old days.

The nightlife scene changes so rapidly that I've kept it simple in this chapter with some sure things geared to a wide range of ages and styles. I've stayed away from highlighting the chains, such as Buffalo Wild Wings, BlackFinn, or Stool Pigeons. No offense, chains, but we know the score there already.

College and young singles hit up the VCU area for the Grace Street nightlife, with clubs and bars that cater to that crowd. Shockoe Slip and Bottom draw crowds—high school kids going to a show at Alley Katz, college kids or serious clubbers at the Canal Club, and the older crowd hitting the bars, music venues, and dance clubs. Comedy is growing—with more open mics around town all the time—and special events at some unexpected spots.

As with so many Richmond venues, you'll notice lots of renovation and reuse of cool old buildings, from seeing a movie in an old locomotive factory to dancing in old warehouses. For outdoor concerts and the big-time acts that hit the Coliseum or Landmark Theater, see the "Performing Arts" chapter.

It seems as if almost anywhere you can buy food and drink in Richmond, from City Dogs to Balliceaux, has live music some nights, so you'll want to pick up the latest *Style Weekly* (www.styleweekly.com) or *Brick* (www.brickweekly.com) for up-to-the-minute goings-on. There's live music several places in town every night; I haven't come close to listing all the good options.

The "Restaurants" chapter includes many more spots that are worthwhile for their food, ambience, beverages, and music, including wine cafes.

BARS, PUBS, BREWERIES, AND LOUNGES

Downtown

CAPITAL ALE HOUSE
623 E. Main St.
(804) 780-ALES
www.capitalalehouse.com
With prints of old Richmond on the walls, dark wood, and a bar that's cooler than most with its famous ice strip down the middle, this place has all the right touches. It might take you a while to slog through the 30-page beer menu, with 300 beer possibilities. Dozens are on tap, and the servers will be happy to narrow the choices down for you. The 80-seat beer garden outside is popular and

shaded, and the fountain and the beer might keep you cool when the temperature rises. Grab dinner here before slipping into the adjacent Music Hall for a show.

LEMAIRE
101 W. Franklin St.
(804) 649-4644
www.lemairerestaurant.com
When you want a cosmopolitan spot either early or till last call, the bar at the Jefferson Hotel's signature restaurant is the swanky, sophisticated place to be a grown-up. If you're game, grab one of the burnt-tangerine banquettes near the granite-and-mahogany bar, and you and your friends can sample wondrous bites from the abbreviated bar menu from 4 to 5 p.m. and from 10 p.m. to midnight. In between, the sky is the limit. Try specialty cocktails that mimic the farm-to-table ethos here or choose from more than 150 bottles of wine or 20 available by the glass, half bottle, or *quartino*. Small plates start at just $5.

Shockoe Bottom

ROSIE CONNOLLY'S PUB AND RESTAURANT
1548A E. Main St.
(804) 343-1063
www.rosieconnollys.com
This pub looks the part on this stretch of road where you can be in Havana one minute and Eire the next. Sit outside and watch the clash of cultures. Named after the owner's grandmother, Rosie's offers basic pub fare along with a dose of Guinness, Harp, Smithwick's, and more on tap. Owner Tommy Goulding will be happy to mix you a Poor Man's Black Velvet—Guinness and cider—or any number of concoctions. The entrance is on N. 17th Street across from the farmers' market.

The Fan

COMMERCIAL TAPHOUSE AND GRILL
111 N. Robinson St.
(804) 359-6544
Serving lunch and dinner while bringing the best microbrewed beers of the world to Richmond, the Taphouse features 15 beers on draft seven days a week, 'til midnight most nights. This is a low-key, cozy haunt for the beer connoisseur looking for Blue Mountain Evil 8, Left Hand 400 Pound Monkey, Hofbrau Maibock, Nugget Nectar, Stoudt's Karnival Kolsch, Terrapin Rye Pale Ale, or Jefferson Reserve Bourbon Barrel Stout—an astounding number of ever-changing offerings. Find this place on Facebook to see what's on tap.

MARTINI KITCHEN AND BUBBLE BAR
1911 W. Main St.
(804) 254-4904
www.martinikitchenrichmondva.com
Aiming for sophistication, this larger-than-typical Fan spot has live music several nights a week, more than 80 martini concoctions, leather sofas, and a beautiful bar. The music here can range from R & B to funk to go-go to hip-hop, and the room can handle a big band and a big crowd. On-site parking is available.

THE REPUBLIC
2053 W. Broad St.
(804) 592-4444
www.therepublicrva.com
Here's a hip place where smokers and non-smokers unite, and perhaps delight if they sample some of the internationally inspired small plates while they're at the bar. Having two bars in separate rooms, one where the smokers ignite and the other for the free-breathers, works because once diners have finished up, the place is popular with the 25 to 55 crowd late into the night. Hear bands

playing the blues, country, or other types of music here two to three times a week, in the room with the smoke. To be a true citizen of the Republic, try VIP packages that are available to move you up in the inevitable lines and offer discounts on meals.

i A reliable source of late-night revelry are the Fan joints that line West Main Street west of VCU. Your choices include City Dogs, 3 Monkeys, Star-Lite, and many more. Decide which spot's patio looks like your kind of crowd, and have a good time.

Manchester

LEGEND BREWERY
321 W. 7th St.
(804) 232-3446
www.legendbrewing.com
Legend, Richmond's largest and oldest microbrewery, pours legendary microbrews in a comfortable, roomy, 150-seat pub. It's often more crowded on the 200-seat outdoor deck because of the views of downtown near the flood wall. Legend brews five kinds of beer year-round—Porter, Pilsner, Golden India Pale Ale, Lager, and Brown Ale—and specialty brews when the brew muse strikes. The brewery features live music Fri through Sun and lots of seafood specials throughout the week that make the food a couple of cuts above pub food. The portions are huge. You can take a tour of the brewery on Sat at 1 p.m.

Far West End/Innsbrook

BIG AL'S SPORTS BAR AND GRILL
3641-F Cox Rd.
(804) 270-4454
www.bigalsrichmond.com

Big Al has quite a following around town, with his morning sports-talk radio show, *SportsPhone,* and he's become a brand now with his popular sports bar in the West End. With 15 high-definition TVs here, including the 133-inch screen, you won't miss a play here unless it's because you're in the middle of talking about sports. Wii sports are on the big screen on Tues, and Fiesta Friday offers free food on the patio.

CAPITAL ALE HOUSE
4024-A Cox Rd., Glen Allen
13831 Village Place Dr., Midlothian
(804) 780-ALES
www.capitalalehouse.com
With five taps and over 200 bottled beers, I'm guessing you can find something you'd like to drink here in these 10,000-square-foot versions of the downtown original. In the Glen Allen location, a pool table and dart boards allow friendly competition, and the 150-seat patio overlooks a small pond. The Midlothian one features two patios, one nonsmoking and the other smoking.

Mechanicsville

SPORTSPAGE BAR & GRILLE
8319 Bell Creek Rd.
(804) 559-4700
www.sportspagebarandgrille.com
With 55 HDTVs here, a 15-inch flat screen in every booth, you won't miss a play of the game while you're chowing down on wings and treats from the raw bar. Pool tables, darts, and video games keep everyone occupied. A second location is at 14245 Midlothian Turnpike in Midlothian (804-379-1844).

i Bowling is better at Plaza Bowl (521 E. Belt Blvd., 804-233-8799) in Southside Plaza because the music is live and loud and the bowling is secondary. Almost as quirky as the bowling alley in the old NBC show *Ed*, but with smaller balls (duckpins), it's a fun spot to move beyond your spare, strike, and gutter-ball dances. Check www.myspace.com/plazabowlrva for updates.

COMEDY CLUBS

West End

MYSTERY DINNER PLAYHOUSE
Crowne Plaza Hotel-Richmond West
6531 W. Broad St.
(888) 471-4802
www.mysterydinner.com/richmond
Mystery Dinner Playhouse has been feeding clues and dinners to customers for 17 years, playing any topic, including the Civil War, for laughs, as in *Frankly Scarlett, You're Dead!* If you like dinner-theater shows with a little intrigue and a lot of laughs, perhaps *And the Killer Is…*, a takeoff on awards-show shenanigans, will fill the bill. Shows run every Fri and Sat night from Labor Day to May 1 and every Sat in the summer. Dinner and the show costs $42 plus tax for adults, with discounts for groups, seniors, and children. Reservations are required and must be secured with a credit card.

Far West End

FUNNY BONE COMEDY CLUB AND RESTAURANT
Short Pump Town Center
11800 W. Broad St.
(804) 521-8900
www.richmondfunnybone.com

Bringing stand-up comedy to Richmond since 2003, the Funny Bone is part of the national chain that showcases internationally and nationally touring comics such as Aisha Tyler and Pablo Francisco for shows Wed through Sun. Apollo Night is often featured on Thurs, with comics from Comedy Central, HBO's *Def Comedy Jam*, or BET's *Comic View*. Tickets for shows are between $12 and $20. Dinner, mainly burgers and pub food, is available for purchase. Seating is on a first-come, first-served basis, and tables seat four. If your party is not a multiple of four, other people may be seated with you. This is a 21-and-over club.

i On the last Saturday of the month, the 9:55 Club (www.955comedy.com) commandeers the second floor of Bottom's Up Pizza, at 1700 Dock St. in Shockoe Bottom, for a monthly no-cover show that features local comedians, many of whom have performed on college campuses and clubs. One former local, Lee Camp, is living the dream, appearing occasionally on *The Daily Show*. The Richmond Comedy Coalition stages improv and sketch comedy once a month at Gallery 5. See www.rvacomedy.com for the latest.

HATTHEATRE
1124 Westbriar Dr.
(804) 343-6364
www.randomactsimprovcomedy.com
On the last Fri and Sat of every month, this improv group steals the show at this 70-seat, Far West End black-box theater. The two shows a night depend on audience participation. The 7:30 p.m. show is for all ages, but the 9 p.m. is for more mature audiences. Tickets are $7 a show or $10 for both.

DANCE CLUBS

Shockoe Slip/Shockoe Bottom

MARS BAR
115 N. 18th St.
(804) 644-MARS
www.marsbarrestaurant.com
This is the place for all-'80s-all-the-time music, and I mean all the time, since it's open seven days a week till 2 a.m. It draws a diverse, young crowd of people age 18 and up, though some folks into their 30s have been spotted gyrating to Milli Vanilli in the usually packed club. Karaoke rules on Mon and Tues, and you'll get plenty of '80s pop and new wave during the dance party Fri and Sat nights. There's never a cover, and it's a restaurant, too, with a full menu.

i To the Bottom and Back (www .2bnb.org) is a free bus service that runs from Carytown to Shockoe Bottom Thurs through Sat from 6 p.m. to 3 a.m. The aim here is to provide a fun and safe way to get from bar to home or hotel and keep drunk drivers off the roads. The buses run continuous loops from Ellwood Thompson's in Carytown to The Market at Tobacco Row on E. Main Street and will drop off and pick up people anywhere along the route. Look for the black and green buses with "2BNB" across them, and thank the driver and sponsors that keep this service rolling.

THE TOBACCO COMPANY CLUB
1201 E. Cary St.
(804) 782-9555
Part of, yet separate from, the touristy Tobacco Company Restaurant, this 21-and-over dance club attracts a dressy crowd.

Starting at 8 p.m., the house DJ will mix it up depending on what the crowd is in the mood for, so you could hear top 40 to house music to R & B—whatever it takes to get people moving. Open Thurs through Sat, the club has a $3 cover, and its entrance is on 12th Street. Be warned, this club has a strict dress code that does not allow, among other sins, tennis shoes, work boots, hats, or "an overall unkempt appearance."

Downtown

VAULT
1005 E. Main St.
(804) 648-3070
www.bankandvault.com
This industrial-chic, two-floor dance club is connected to the sophisticated and refined Bank, which is a restaurant and club. Vault's recycled metal bar winds its way through the cavernous, warehouse-like space. Bank has a martini lounge upstairs if you'd rather not be a dancing fool. Complimentary parking at 8th and Cary Streets after 6 p.m. helps the cause. Valet parking is available on Fri and Sat nights.

West End

DANCE SPACE
6004 W. Broad St.
(804) 673-3326
www.thedancespace.com
If you don't need alcohol to loosen up your dancing feet, you might like this alcohol-free venue. There's ballroom dancing every Fri night, with the first 30 minutes set aside for a group class and the rest for general dancing from foxtrot and tango to the hustle and salsa. Saturday Swing Dance takes over the first, second, and third Sat nights. The bamboo floors feel great underfoot, and

the soft lighting and great sound system set the mood. Light refreshments are served, and the cost ranges from $5 to $8 a person; students get in for $5.

Chesterfield County

VISIONS DANCE CLUB
Holiday Inn Select Koger Conference
  Center
1021 Koger Center Blvd.
(804) 379-3800
www.holidayinnkoger.com/attractions_
  visions.aspx
Just about every Sat night, a rotating roster of popular bands such as the Janitors and Flashback takes the stage to play rock, top 40, R & B, and beach music. One band has a four-piece horn section. It's an $8 cover and the bands start at 9 p.m. There's dancing every night—from new-style line dancing to shag to country line dancing to tango lessons. Complimentary appetizers are offered Mon through Fri until 7 p.m.

GAY AND LESBIAN BARS & CLUBS

Downtown

BARCODEVA
6 E. Grace St.
(804) 648-2040
This classy mainstay serves lunch to the business crowd, but by night it morphs into a favorite watering hole courtesy of its big bar and fabulous outdoor patio. No-cover karaoke on Sun nights is popular and goes until 2 a.m.

GODFREY'S
308 E. Grace St.
(804) 648-3957
www.godreysva.com

Drag's the thing here, with a drag dinner the first and third Sat hosted by Tiffany Devereaux and Alvion Davenport. Every Sat it's Saturday Sirens dance party and show. The college crowd loves it here, and the music is pumped up for dancing on Thurs and Fri. Godfrey's is famous, or infamous, for its Sunday Drag Brunch, which draws plenty o' straights, who go more for the spectacle than for the food.

i For the latest hot spots and special events, check out www.gayrva .com/nightlife or find out what social and cultural events the Gay Community Center of Richmond has going on at (804) 622-4646 or www.gayrichmond .com.

Carytown and Museum District

BABES OF CARYTOWN
3166 W. Cary St.
(804) 355-9330
www.myspace.com/babesofcarytown
The only bar in Richmond geared towards lesbians, Babes has something going on every night it's open, from drag shows and bingo on occasion to country line dancing every Tues night and Wii bowling after that. There's karaoke on Wed, and Sat night the DJ gets the club music going. The patio is open year-round, and volleyball is popular there. Babe's is closed on Mon.

NATIONS
2729 W. Broad St.
(804) 257-9891
www.myspace.com/nationsofrichmond
Fairly new to the scene, this upscale nightclub and restaurant is worth a visit for the food alone, but the large dance floor, big TVs,

pool table, and Thurs night karaoke make it more exciting than just dinner and drinks. Fri and Sat nights, the DJ gets the men moving. Other evenings, nationally known entertainers strut their stuff, and perhaps most fun of all is that other kind of drag race, the Ms. Nations Pageant.

LIVE MUSIC
Downtown

CAPITAL ALE HOUSE DOWNTOWN MUSIC HALL
623 E. Main St.
(804) 780-ALES
Next door to the original Capital Ale House, this brick-and-beamed, wood-floored venue brings in a mix of touring and local musicians Thurs through Sat, with the music starting at 5 p.m. on Fri for the first of two shows. Occasionally, the Richmond Jazz Society brings in some heavy hitters for concerts here. Some shows are seated, cabaret style, but many are standing room only. Wed nights the mood changes to accommodate showings of classic comedies like *Caddyshack*. There's free parking at the Lanier deck at 6th and Cary Streets.

THE NATIONAL
708 E. Broad St.
(804) 612-1900
www.thenationalva.com
The National is a beautifully renovated, crowd-pleasing place with big-name acts—Ben Folds, Wilco, Snoop Dogg, George Thorogood—and local groups of consistent quality. The acoustics are great, and the venue is perfect for mingling and moving to the beat. Some shows have reserved seating, while others are general admission. To get close to the stage, consider having dinner

at Gibson's Grill before the show. With your ticket and a receipt from Gibson's for $10 or more, you get escorted into the National 15 minutes before those who didn't plan so well. Call (804) 644-2637 for reservations. Ticket prices range from $10 to $45. Get tickets at the box office or from www.ticket master.com.

Shockoe Slip/Shockoe Bottom

HAT FACTORY
140 Virginia St.
(804) 788-4281
www.hatfactoryva.com
The latest reincarnation of the former Lady Byrd Hat Factory by the canal has live music several nights a week, snagging musicians as diverse as Dweezil Zappa, Sister Hazel, the Wailers, and Leon Russell. On Fri nights, the 22,000-square-foot club is the site of the Richmond RoundUp—country and western shenanigans including bikini bull-riding, country music videos, and live bands.

The Fan

BALLICEAUX
203 N. Lombardy St.
(804) 355-3008
www.balliceauxrva.com
See more on this hip spot in the "Restaurant" chapter, but the back room here is a great place to catch music several nights a week, and there's never a charge.

BOGART'S IN THE FAN
1903 W. Cary St.
(804) 353-9280
www.bogartsinthefan.com
Back with jazz at its new, larger location, Bogart's (not to be confused with the West End Bogart's) is the place to hear the Oregon Hill

Funk All-Stars one night and a nationally touring jazz artist another. Karaoke and open-mic nights fill out the week. Bogart's has been perfecting the speakeasy feel for 40 years, so have dinner and enjoy the music. There's free parking behind the Cary Street Lofts.

THE CAMEL
1621 W. Broad St.
(804) 353-4901
www.thecamel.org

The Camel is a two-room spot that offers live music in a wide array of musical styles just about every night in one room and pizza, salads, and paninis along with a full bar in the other. Depending on the night, you could hear folkies, a hip-hop show, the funky No BS Brass Band, local rock, or VCU jazz. It's a comfortable, casual place that attracts a diverse crowd, from young to old, who appreciate the music and the food and drinks. There is usually a cover.

North Side

SHENANIGANS
4017 MacArthur Ave.
(804) 264-5010
www.greenpub.com

Nothing fancy here, just good music, dependable food and drinks, and a relaxed and happy older crowd that can't help but get up and dance when certain bands are playing. The spot is open every day, and live music lives here Tues through Sat, when quality bands take the stage for honky-tonk, Cajun dance-hall music, or the blues.

Ashland

ASHLAND COFFEE & TEA
100 N. Railroad Ave.
(804) 798-1702
www.ashlandcoffeeandtea.com

Arguably central Virginia's premier listening room, cozy Ashland Coffee & Tea packs 'em in Wed through Sat nights for performances by homegrown artists like Susan Greenbaum and the Taters, and touring, Grammy-winning performers like Dave Alvin. You might think you are in Nashville for a minute if you wind up here on a Tues night for the Songwriters' Showdown. It's a contest that gets underway at 7 p.m. and has a guest judge. It's $5 at the door for the audience, $3 for a performer.

Other nights you'll be treated to Celtic rock, bluegrass, alt rock, or nationally acclaimed artists such as Ellis Paul and Patty Larkin. Save by buying tickets in advance. There's often a $5 cover or $12 charge for a concert. It's open daily, but never stays open real late, so there's no good reason to miss the music.

ℹ️ Lucille's is known for southern specialties for lunch and dinner, but her 1203 N. Laburnum Ave. location in the East End becomes a nighttime hotspot with live bands most Friday and Saturday nights. Other nights, folks let loose with karaoke and amateur nights. Lucille's 7515 Brook Rd. location offers comedy on occasion, in addition to karaoke. Check www.lucillesoutherncuisine .com for updates.

MOVIES IN STYLE

Most movie theaters in the area are the typical multiplexes run by Regal or UA; some are fancier than others, with stadium seating and cup holders and all the rest. They are easy enough to locate on Fandango. The city has just recently scored a beautiful movie theater for first-run films to add to the two old-school movie houses it already had. These more unusual spots are the ones that

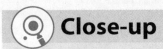

Close-up

First Fridays Art Walk

Thousands of people flock downtown for the **First Fridays Art Walk,** the popular event managed by **Curated Culture.** The walk strings together art galleries, restaurants, and other cultural venues along Broad Street, east and west, and includes partners in art on nearby streets as well. The often-crowded event recently expanded to include special happenings a few blocks east. The University of Richmond has been sponsoring the Art Walk for years, but now it's taking its involvement to the streets by being a part of First Fridays East. From 5 to 8 p.m., UR's Downtown Center at 7th and Broad Streets, the Library of Virginia, Richmond CenterStage, and other facilities are all hoping to encourage folks to check out their artistic offerings. Lasting past 8 p.m., the party continues on down the road as art galleries and cultural centers like the Black History Museum and Cultural Center host openings of new work. Some venues offer drinks and eats and live music, while others let the art do the enticing. Gallery 5 often puts on quite a show for First Fridays, including fire twirlers or burlesque, so that's an especially popular spot. Find updates about Richmond's moving medley of arts and culture at www.firstfridaysrichmond.com.

get the nod here. A first-run movie in Richmond will usually set you back $8 a person.

North Side

MOVIELAND AT BOULEVARD SQUARE
1301 N. Blvd. at West Leigh Street
(804) 354-6008
www.bowtiecinemas.com
Bringing first-run movies back to the center city in much-appreciated comfort, this complex houses 17 screens in a 53,000-square-foot former locomotive assembly plant. The theaters here are large and boast stadium seating with plenty of legroom. The food offerings are more substantial than popcorn, with pizza available, for instance, and a bar. And they do *Rocky Horror* showings every weekend, but you might as well wait for the every-other-weekend version, which features a live cast. OK, so it's not nightlife, but every Sat and Sun morning, Movies &

Mimosas lets you watch a classic film such as *North by Northwest* or *The Princess Bride* on the big screen and enjoy a mimosa before the show.

i Before or after a flick at Movieland, pop in to Stronghill Dining Company, just around the corner from the theater at 1200 N Blvd. (804-359-0202, www.stronghillrestaurant.com) for a bite at the bar with inspired small plates. Or time it right for a complete dinner from the cutting-edge, "creative southern" menu. And the desserts here beat Milk Duds any day.

Carytown

THE BYRD THEATRE
2908 W. Cary St.
(804) 353-9911
www.byrdtheatre.com

This historic, 1,300-seat Carytown theater, built in 1928, is a National Historic Landmark and a true movie palace, but you don't need to dress like royalty to go here. Make sure you show up before the house lights get dimmed because seeing the gorgeous interior is well worth the price of admission. The 18-foot, two-and-a-half-ton, Czechoslovakian crystal chandelier, the sumptuous curtains, the gold leaf, and—OK, now I'll admit it—the uncomfortable seats with not quite enough legroom all add up to a trip back in time. The Byrd runs two shows a night, and several film festivals, including the popular French Film Festival, take over the Byrd throughout the year. Hear the mighty Wurlitzer organ played before Sat evening shows, and on holidays like the Fourth of July and St. Patrick's Day, you'll get the chance to sing along. The Byrd is open 365 days a year, and there are no previews here. Tickets are just $1.99 for the second-run movies. The Byrd's lobby is so small that you aren't allowed to wait there until the previous show has let out. So buy your ticket and wait in the line for entry. Once the theatergoers from the previous viewing have exited, it's your turn to go in (and wait in line for popcorn).

Near West End

REGAL WESTHAMPTON CINEMA 1 & 2
5706 Grove Ave.
(804) 288-9007
www.regmovies.com
This theater in the Libbie and Grove shopping area is a walk back in time to a more civilized era. It's a 1950s-style theater with a great neighborhood feel, and though it's part of a chain, it's actually the only theater

in Richmond that regularly shows independent and art-house-style films, including foreign-language films. You'll find two first-run movies playing at a time in two large, comfortable theaters. It's such a stress-free way to see a movie. Parking in the back or on the streets is easy, and there are restaurants within walking distance.

i CineBistro, an upscale movie theater that serves much better food than popcorn, beer, wine, and cocktails, opens in the fall of 2010 next to Dillard's at Stony Point Fashion Park. Moviegoers age 21 and over can sink into leather chairs with built-in tables in six intimate theaters to watch the latest blockbusters and art-house movies, while enjoying dinner with the films. A lobby lounge serving cocktails, snacks, and desserts makes pre- and post-movie socializing convenient. See www.cobb cinebistro.com for details.

Ashland

ASHLAND FIREHOUSE THEATER
201 Duncan St.
(804) 798-9721
www.ashlandfirehousetheater.org
There's room for 125 movie lovers inside the old firehouse, which the Ashland Community Theater Foundation has refurbished for community fun. Classic movies from Hitchcock thrillers to *Raiders of the Lost Ark* are shown most Sat nights, and matinees geared towards children and families are held some Sat afternoons. Tickets are $6, and subscriptions are available to make it even more of a bargain for a night out. Concessions are available.

Goochland County

GOOCHLAND COUNTY DRIVE-IN
4344 Old Fredericksburg Rd.
The only movie theater in the county, out in the western reaches of the area, near exit 152 off I-64 in Hadensville, is the recently opened and popular Goochland Drive-in, which shows first-run movies under the stars. Outdoor movie season begins at the end of March. Of course, you'll need an FM radio for the sound to work. Some of their many rules include no alcohol, no smoking, no admittance 30 minutes after the first movie begins, and no outside food or drink. Admission for a double feature is $7 for adults and $3 for children age 12 and younger. Everything at the snack bar—barbecue, Gooch dogs, and popcorn—is $3.50 or less.

ARCHITECTURE

Despite sustaining devastating floods in 1771 and every century since, and suffering war-related fires in 1781 and 1865, more damage was done to Richmond's architectural fabric during peacetime by men than nature and war combined. Between the end of World War II and 1968, flawed attempts at urban renewal accounted for the loss of more than 1,500 of the city's pre-1850 buildings. Sumptuous Old City Hall was threatened with demolition twice, in 1915 and the late 1970s. We're slow learners. Luckily, committed citizens have stepped up when needed. Mary Wingfield Scott became alarmed in 1935 about plans to demolish the 18th-century Adam Craig House, so she formed a group that purchased and saved it. So began the William Byrd Branch of what is now Preservation Virginia.

After World War II, the decline of the neighborhood around St. John's Church led citizens to form the Historic Richmond Foundation, which encouraged the city council to create the St. John's Church Old and Historic District in 1957, the first of its kind in Richmond, establishing architectural controls on exteriors within the district. Fourteen additional local historic districts have followed, preserving the character of neighborhoods while encouraging investment and adaptive reuse.

The Historic Richmond Foundation, Preservation Virginia, the Alliance to Conserve Old Richmond Neighborhoods (ACORN), and hundreds of dedicated private citizens and businesses have committed to the renovation and reuse of historic structures and saved hundreds of buildings, protecting much of what is unique to Richmond, safekeeping the stories that buildings tell about a city and its people, and advocating a responsible, green approach before it was trendy. ACORN recently became involved in saving Emily Winfree's cottage in Manchester, a rare urban example of a former slave's house. Saved from destruction, the house was moved in hopes that it will become a part of the Richmond Slave Trail.

OVERVIEW

This chapter focuses on the rich store of architecture that's still here, pointing out some of the many architecturally significant buildings in Richmond's center, emphasizing ones that are open to the public. Special opportunities to tour private homes on seasonal house tours are noted, and you can find out about Historic Garden Week in April in the "Annual Events" chapter. For some of the earliest architecture in the region, you'll have to hit the road to the James River Plantations in Charles City County. See all about them in the "Day Trips" chapter.

Several sites receive additional notice in the "Attractions" or "Museums" chapters. Richmond is an architecture classroom, filled

Architectural Preservation Groups

ACORN (Alliance to Conserve Old Richmond Neighborhoods)
104 Shockoe Slip, (lower level), Suite C
(804) 644-5040
www.richmondneighborhoods.org
By championing the use of tax credits and educating homeowners and renovators about historic renovation, ACORN, a nonprofit group dedicated to saving buildings and history while improving neighborhoods, preaches and practices "prosperity through preservation."

Historic Richmond Foundation
4 E. Main St.
(804) 643-7407
www.historicrichmond.com
Now a branch of Preservation Virginia, 2010 marked the 75th anniversary of preservation in the city, which HRF proudly continues by purchasing and restoring endangered buildings, finding conservation-minded buyers for others, and educating the region's citizens and politicians about the unique architectural resources Richmond possesses and must preserve for the good of the entire region.

Preservation Virginia
204 W. Franklin St.
(804) 648-1889
www.preservationvirginia.org
A statewide nonprofit group, formerly known as APVA, Preservation Virginia began its work preserving the state's irreplaceable architectural and landscape treasures in 1889. It preserves and manages 23 properties around the state, including Historic Jamestowne and several in Richmond. Its state headquarters is housed in one of its historic properties, the circa-1800 Cole Diggs House.

with more architectural styles than most are aware of—International, Art Deco, Mediterranean, Tudor, Greek Revival, and more. You just have to know where to look and what you're seeing. In this chapter we start at Church Hill, one of the best preserved and earliest sections of the city, and move west.

CHURCH HILL

When you walk or drive around **Church Hill,** it's easy to feel you're in an earlier century,

since it's the oldest intact neighborhood in the city and home to the most antebellum structures in Richmond. You'll see a variety of styles—Greek Revival, Neoclassical, Federal, Queen Anne, Italianate, Gothic Revival, Romanesque Revival, Art Deco, and more. Walk around to see the ornamentation and detailed ironwork of the mostly private homes. Begin your tour at **St. John's Church,** at 2401 E. Broad St., built in 1742 as a rectangular building. In 1772 the church built a large addition, so in 1775 when Virginia's second convention met here, it was in a T-shaped St. John's that Patrick Henry gave his most famous speech. Surely you know it by heart. No matter the changes and additions made over the years, the church is the only surviving colonial building on Church Hill.

It's a surprise to many that Richmond has a **Philip Johnson**–designed International-style building, and even more surprising that the concrete and steel 1968 building is on top of Church Hill at East Grace Street between 21st and 22nd Streets amid old-school architecture. What used to be the **WRVA** radio studio and tower and is now a nonprofit group's office affords a classic view of downtown and Shockoe Valley. To appreciate the connections between the low-slung office and the tower, stand across 22nd Street. Walking down Grace Street towards Libby Hill Park will take you by dozens of 19th-century homes that are more typical of Church Hill architecture.

i An amazing resource for understanding the intertwining of architecture and history in and around Richmond is the National Park Service's Web site devoted to Richmond travel itineraries. Check out www.nps .gov/nr/travel/richmond/index.html to get pointed in more directions than you could possibly go in one trip.

TOBACCO ROW

Down the hill from Church Hill are numerous tobacco warehouses and cigarette factories built in the late 19th and early 20th century, now renovated into apartments, restaurants, and offices.

Across from Tobacco Row is the circa-1754 **Old Stone House,** at 1916 E. Main St. Considered the oldest house in Richmond,

built out of stones dredged from the James River, it houses the **Edgar Allan Poe Museum.**

SHOCKOE BOTTOM

At 1807 E. Franklin St. is the 1787 **Masons Hall,** with its notable cupola. It's the oldest Masonic Hall in continuous use in the U.S., and George Washington and John Marshall were members. The **Beaux Arts Main Street Station,** at 1520 E. Main St., was built in 1900 and has withstood fires and the constant rumbling of traffic, as I-95 comes precariously close to its beautiful clock tower. Though its steep terra-cotta roof gives it the air of a chateau, it's still a working Amtrak train station, and worth a visit whether or not you're hopping aboard a train.

CANAL WALK

At 14th and Canal Streets, we're at one of many entry points to the Canal Walk, so head down the stairs to take a look at the reconstructed **Kanawha Canal,** one of two along the river that powered mills, transported goods and people, and were originally dug by slaves and immigrants—the original dirty work. Though most of what you walk along is the prettified 20th-century version, there is an original section, complete with a lock, near 12th Street. If you continue west and walk along the **Haxall Canal,** through the old hydroelectric plant that once powered Richmond's streetcars, you'll be on **Brown's Island** and eventually have a great view of both the James River and the 1973 **Federal Reserve Bank of Richmond,** designed by Minoru Yamasaki and built the same year his World Trade Center Towers rose much higher in New York City. You might think you know where the money is here, but 50 percent of the building is underground.

Match Game

I've done the matching for you, so you've already won the prize.

Notable Architects	built this in Richmond	and that somewhere else
Carrère and Hastings	Jefferson Hotel	New York Public Library, New York City
Thomas Jefferson	State Capitol of Virginia	Monticello, Charlottesville
Philip Johnson	WRVA Building	Glass House, New Canaan, Conn.
John A. Lankford	W. L. Taylor House	True Reformers Building, Washington, D.C.
Elijah E. Meyers	Old City Hall	State Capitols of Texas, Michigan, Colorado
Robert Mills	Monumental Church	Washington Monument, Washington, D.C.
Richard Neutra	Rice House	Lovell House, Los Angeles
Alexander Parris	Wickham House	Faneuil Hall Market, Boston
John Russell Pope	Broad Street Station (Science Museum)	Jefferson Memorial, Washington, D.C.
Robert A. M. Stern	Federal Courthouse	Museum for African Art, New York City
Thomas S. Stewart	Egyptian Building	Church of St. Luke and the Epiphany, Philadelphia
Minoru Yamasaki	Federal Reserve Bank	World Trade Center Towers, New York City

CAPITOL SQUARE

Entrusted with the design of the **State Capitol** while in France, Thomas Jefferson based the building on the Maison Carrée, a Roman temple in Nîmes, France. Jean-Pierre Fouquet's plaster model based on Charles-Louis Clérisseau's plans sits in the Capitol today. Built of brick, when it was "finished" in 1788, the Capitol had not yet been stuccoed

Architecture Tours

Segway of Richmond Tours
1301 E. Cary St.
(804) 343-1850
www.segwayofrichmond.biz

If you're Segway-inclined, zoom along (at 12½ mph top speed) on a variety of guided tours that usually start with a short training session near the Shockoe Slip shop. I've seen 70-year-olds Segwaying, so there's nothing to lose but your pride—everyone looks goofy on a Segway. Tours cover many parts of Richmond, including Church Hill, Hollywood Cemetery, and the wide-ranging Landmark tour. It costs $65 for a two-hour romp that includes the Canal Walk, Tredegar, Court End, Capitol Square, and more. You don't go inside any of the attractions—it's a lay of the land sort of tour. Several tours are offered in conjunction with Historic Richmond Tours at the Valentine History Center.

Historic Richmond Foundation
4 E. Main St.
(804) 643-7407
www.historicrichmond.com

HRF is always a part of Virginia Garden Week in April and offers tours by appointment of Monumental Church. In addition, HRF hosts special events for the young at heart as part of its Quoit Club. Party like it's 1899 by joining this group that socializes at historic sites while supporting the foundation's work preserving the city's heritage. Seasonal events feature guided tours of Richmond's Pumphouse, Hollywood Cemetery, etc., with local experts. It's $80 for an eight-event season or $15 for a single event.

Historic Richmond Tours through Valentine Richmond History Center
Various locations
(804) 649-0711, ext. 301
www.richmondhistorycenter.com

In any given year this group offers more than 350 chances to learn the ins and outs of Richmond. Wander all over the city—Canal Walk, Jackson Ward, Hollywood Cemetery, Forest Hill, Highland Park, The Fan, Ginter Park—to learn the backstory of Richmond's architectural riches—with knowledgeable tour guides. No matter what your interest—stained glass, social history, architecture—there are tours to match them. Most tours are walking tours, but bus tours and Segway tours are available, as well as some dog-friendly History Hounds walking tours. Hollywood Cemetery tours are offered daily from Apr through Oct, Mon through Sat at 10 a.m., and on weekends into Nov. The cost is $10 for adults and $5 for members and kids under age 12.

Richmond City Van Tours
(804) 744-1718
www.richmondcitytours.com

Private tours for small groups in the company's vans include half-day ($75) and full-day ($150) options. Tours include historic gardens, museums, and history- and architecture-themed trips. Hotel pickup is available.

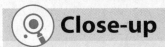

Close-up

Monumental Church

Monumental Church (1224 E. Broad St.) was built as a monument to the 72 victims, including the governor and many prominent Richmonders and their slaves, who died in the Richmond Theatre Fire of 1811. The December 26th calamity, which killed men and women, white and black, galvanized the city and the nation. Chief Justice John Marshall, who became a parishioner, led the fund-raising campaign for a church to be built upon the site of the catastrophe in memory of those who perished. Thomas Jefferson's only architectural pupil and the first American-born architect, Robert Mills, designed an unusual octagonal structure with a dome on top in Greek Revival style. Under the church's portico is a replica of the original monument to the dead, as the original succumbed to environmental hazards of city life. Beneath the monument, the remains of the dead are interred in a bricked-in crypt. Symbols of mourning—urns, upside-down torches, hourglasses, wreaths, and burial shrouds—are evident inside and outside the church. Of particular interest is the invisible skylight that lights the altar area. **Historic Richmond Foundation** owns the building, which was decommissioned as a church in the 1965, and continues to renovate and restore it. Tours of Monumental Church are available by calling (804) 643-7407. It's open for free during Court End Christmas.

white and had no stairs to the grand entrance. Those didn't come until the 1906 expansion that added the wings, which house the Senate and House of Delegates chambers. Its original surroundings—visible from all sides, even from the river below—were more spectacular than they are today, but it's still most impressive. Take either a self-guided tour or a guided one. The building is open seven days a week and tours are free. There's more on the Capitol in the "Attractions" chapter.

If tours are available, pop in to the Alexander Parris–designed **Executive Mansion,** the oldest governor's mansion in continuous use in the country and survivor of two fires and many governors' families. Whether you're a churchgoer or not, if you're in the vicinity of Capitol Square, walk into the church where Robert E. Lee and Jefferson Davis worshipped, **St. Paul's Episcopal Church.** It was designed by Philadelphia

architect Thomas S. Stewart, who also is responsible for the Egyptian Building. If the Corinthian columns and ornate plasterwork inside aren't enough to tempt you to enter, then the prospect of ten Tiffany windows and an altar mosaic ought to.

North of the Capitol stands what is now known as **Old City Hall,** though when it was finished in 1894 it was the new one, replacing the 1816 Robert Mills–designed city hall that was wrongly feared to be structurally unsound. Architect Elijah Meyers designed and delivered this massive and ornate High Victorian Gothic building at 1001 E. Broad St., the largest granite building in Richmond, using stone quarried from the James River, $1 million over budget. Some things never change. An office building now, the spectacular first floor is open to the public Mon through Fri during business hours.

ℹ️ For haunted tours of Richmond's creepy sites, try Haunts of Richmond's Shadows of Shockoe or Haunted Capitol Hill, which run May through early November, Thursday through Saturday, though private tours can be arranged other times. Call (804) 343-3700 or see www.hauntsofrichmond .com. Eerie Nights, www.eerienights.com or (804) 833-1845, also offers Shockoe Bottom tours several nights a week June through October and on Friday only in May.

COURT END

Across Broad Street is **First African Baptist Church,** at 301 College St., built in 1877 to replace an earlier church that had once served whites, slaves, and free blacks in one congregation. When the white members of First Baptist built a new church in 1841, the black members continued to worship at the original church until they replaced it with this Greek Revival building, now owned by VCU. Another of VCU's treasures, on the Medical College of Virginia (MCV) campus at 1223 E. Marshall St., is the **Egyptian Building,** one of the best examples of Egyptian Revival architecture in the country. An exotic temple, the first permanent home of what became the Medical College of Virginia, it has been used for medical education since it was built in 1845. The cast-iron fence with mummies and palm-leaf capitals are only some of the Egyptian motifs visible. The hieroglyphics-filled lobby and the Egyptian-themed first-floor lecture hall were completed in 1939.

Surrounded by MCV, the **John Brockenbrough House,** now known as the White House of the Confederacy, at 1201 E. Clay St., is open for tours in conjunction with the adjacent Museum of the Confederacy. Originally a two-story Federal home as designed by Robert Mills in 1818, the third floor was added in the mid-19th century. The home's interior is interpreted as it would have looked during Jefferson Davis's time living here while he was the president of the Confederacy.

At 1015 E. Clay St. on the most beautiful stretch of Court End, you'll see the **Wickham-Valentine House.** Architect Alexander Parris, who studied with Charles Bulfinch, designed this Federal masterpiece for John Wickham, a prominent lawyer. The elliptical staircase is especially lovely. It pays to look closely here at the woodwork—you'll see magnolia, dogwood, and tobacco in the exquisite carvings, and the decorative paintings on the parlor walls of scenes from *The Illiad* show how important classical references were in this era. You can tour the home with admission to the **Valentine Richmond History Center.** There's more on both in the "Attractions" chapter.

Continuing west in Court End, you'll come to the **John Marshall House** at 818 E. Marshall St., a Georgian treasure where the famous chief justice lived until his death in 1835. Preservation Virginia owns the home and operates it as a historic-house museum with many Marshall family artifacts and furnishings within.

ℹ️ The Court End Passport gains you admittance for one year to the John Marshall House, Valentine Richmond History Center, including the Wickham House, and the Black History Museum and Cultural Center.

JACKSON WARD

Continue westward into **Jackson Ward,** another area of town that is known as an

---

Holiday House Tours

Here's your chance to see some of the great store of architecture all dressed up for the holidays. Many of the events are free and some offer access not usually available the rest of the year.

Church Hill Historic Holiday House Tour ($15 to $20)
www.churchhillrichmond.com

Court End Christmas (free)
Various locations
www.richmondhistorycenter.com

Executive Mansion Holiday Open House (free)
Capitol Square
www.executivemansion.virginia.gov/

Fan District Holiday House Tour ($25 to $30)
www.fandistrict.org

Hanover Tavern Holiday Open House (free)
13181 Hanover Courthouse Rd.
(804) 537-5050
www.hanovertavern.org

Maggie L. Walker National Historic Site Holiday Event (free)
600 N. 2nd St.
(804) 771-2017, ext. 24.

Maymont Mansion Holiday Tours ($5)
1700 Hampton Ave.
(804) 358-7166
www.maymont.org

Mountain Road Corridor Holiday Celebration (free)
2892 Mountain Rd.
(804) 501-5121

Tuckahoe Plantation Weekend Candlelight House Tours ($12)
12601 River Rd.
(804) 971-8329
www.tuckahoeplantation.com

Woodland Heights Holiday House Tour ($10 to $15)
www.hillsandheights.org

---

architecturally and historically rich neighborhood, with a large concentration of antebellum homes. Free blacks settled here before the Civil War, and afterwards it became the center of black culture and commerce as families, businesses, and social and fraternal societies acquired the area's Greek Revival and Queen Anne town houses and Classical and Romanesque Revival structures. Jackson Ward has more ornate ironwork, mainly on cast-iron porches and fences, than anywhere in the county except New Orleans.

2nd Street, where much of the action of Jackson Ward took place, is also where some of its most important architecture remains. The Art Deco **Hippodrome Theater,** undergoing renovation, is next to the 26-room Queen Anne–style **W. L. Taylor House** at 522 N. 2nd St. The house was purported to be the largest African-American residence when it was built in 1907, and it was designed by John Lankford, the first African-American licensed architect in Virginia. Much of Lankford's important work in

Richmond, including his Southern Aid Building, has been demolished. The more recent **Southern Aid Building,** a 1931 Georgian Revival structure at 212 E. Clay St., has been renovated into mixed-use condos. Banker **Maggie L. Walker's House,** at 110½ Leigh St., is an example of Italianate architecture and is open to the public as a National Park Service site. It was built in 1888 by a black builder, George Boyd, who also was responsible in 1884 for **Sixth Mount Zion Church,** the church founded by Rev. John Jasper. It stands at 14 W. Duval St.

DOWNTOWN

The wealthy tobacco industrialist, Lewis Ginter, commissioned the New York firm of Carrère and Hastings to build Richmond the finest hotel in the South, **The Jefferson Hotel** at 101 W. Franklin St. Completed in 1895, it was the grandest place in town. It still is. Its Beaux Arts exterior is a sign to all that you enter another world here. Go inside and see what I mean. Fire destroyed some of the hotel in 1901, and it was altered and rebuilt more grandly, with the addition of the famed staircase.

i The Virginia Museum of Fine Arts' fabulous Tiffany collection isn't the only one in town. Just go to church at St. James, St. Paul's, Grace & Holy Trinity, or All Saints Episcopal Churches. Or visit Beth Ahabah Synagogue to see Mount Sinai in all its glory, or Maymont or Ginter Park Baptist and Second Presbyterian Churches, and even Lewis Ginter's Mausoleum at Hollywood Cemetery. While in Petersburg, visit Old Blandford Church to see 15 Tiffany windows and Washington Street United Methodist to see five more.

THE FAN

Crossing over Belvidere into the Fan, peek in at two massive architectural highlights along Monroe Park. First, the Marcellus Wright Sr.–designed **Landmark Theater,** formerly known as the Mosque, stands at 6 N. Laurel St. With its exterior exotic turrets and exquisite mosaics and gilded detailing inside, it's hard to imagine Richmond's reaction to it in 1927, when it was built for the Shriners. Just to the north is the **Cathedral of the Sacred Heart,** at 18 N. Laurel St., completed in 1906, a soaring example of Renaissance Revival architecture. Hope for a sunny day so the stained glass looks its best.

i Three county historic homes worth a visit are Hanover Tavern (804-537-5050, www.hanovertavern .org), where Patrick Henry didn't exactly live since this version postdates his time there; the Federal plantation home Magnolia Grange in Chesterfield County (804-796-1479, www.chesterfieldhistory .com); and Walkerton Tavern in Henrico County (804-261-6898), a beautifully restored early-19th-century home business that features an unusual swinging wall.

The Fan, the largest intact Victorian community in the country at more than 100 city blocks, is cheek-by-jowl full of beautiful architecture. You almost can't go wrong, so wander freely. Franklin Street through VCU's Monroe Park Campus has many fine examples of restored 19th-century buildings. To really appreciate the details, get out of your car. Keep going west on Monument Avenue to see the varied yet stately collection of architectural styles that makes it a sought-after address.

i 15th Century Agecroft Hall and Virginia House, and 18th century Wilton, all in Richmond's West End, were moved to their present locations to save them from destruction well before the terms historic preservation or adaptive reuse were bandied about. They get their due in the "Attractions" chapter.

There are too many wonderful private homes to note, including seven designed by acclaimed architect W. L. Bottomley—six Georgian Revival and one Mediterranean—but the grandest home, the only one on Monument Avenue individually listed on the National Register of Historic Places, is the 1917 Tudor Revival **Branch House,** at 2501 Monument Ave., designed by John Russell Pope and now the **Virginia Center for Architecture,** and open to the public. Its sheer size, at 27,000 square feet, is impressive, but the amount of detail within

and without is what makes it worth a visit. The wooden screen in the Great Hall is the most intricate piece you're likely to see, carved by Italian craftsmen and beautiful beyond belief. The plasterwork above is mind-boggling, and the details on doorknobs and fireplaces make walking through here a treasure hunt, and that's not including the exhibits.

See another building by Pope by heading to the **Science Museum of Richmond** at 2500 W. Broad St., housed in what used to be **Broad Street Station.** The only train station Pope designed, he employed a Neoclassical theme on a grand scale, adding a colonnade and a Pantheon-like dome to the building. When passenger service moved out to Henrico County, the state bought the building, intending to raze it. The rotunda was measured and marked for demolition. Thankfully, the Science Museum of Virginia needed a home and was allowed to reuse this grand building.

PERFORMING ARTS

Richmond is as much the cultural capital of Virginia as it is the political one. With its own ballet and symphony, a share of Virginia Opera, and numerous professional theaters, dance companies, and musicians, Richmond is a more artsy and creative place than many people realize. The theater scene here is vibrant and innovative. Richmond is the only city in the mid-Atlantic with a full-time professional theater, Richmond Triangle Players, devoted to producing plays relevant to the gay experience. The Firehouse Theatre is the site of the Festival of New American Plays every year, drawing 200 entries. With more than a dozen professional theaters and theater companies staging productions throughout the region, there's no need to wait for the touring Broadway shows to come to town to scratch Richmond's itch for theater. Modern dance and contemporary music here get bursts of energy from the faculty and students at the universities around town—especially the University of Richmond and Virginia Commonwealth University.

One of the charms of our historic region is that you can see ballet and opera in an old movie palace and catch a play in an old firehouse, in the nation's oldest gristmill, in a historic tavern, or in the courtyard of a Tudor mansion. Who needs scenery? Anything goes. I've lost count of how many buildings have been donated to arts groups by generous individuals and corporations. The shows go on, in much swankier facilities than just 10 years ago. Richmond Triangle Players has a new building in Scott's Addition, and Dogtown Dance has just renovated an old school gymnasium in Manchester. CenterStage has brought the Carpenter Theatre back to its former glory and added the Gottwald Playhouse to the mix.

Collaboration is the word on the street these days in the arts. Richmond Shakespeare collaborated with African-American Repertory to produce *Othello* at the Gottwald. The Latin Ballet of Virginia paired with the Barksdale recently as well. Those touring Broadway shows take up residence at either the Landmark or the Carpenter Theatre, and the University of Richmond's excellent Modlin Center for the Arts series stages some performances on campus, some at the Landmark, and others at the Carpenter Theatre. Be sure you know where you're going before you leave your house. All the moving around from venue to venue can be confusing, but it's really an embarrassment of riches.

OVERVIEW

Catch concerts in cool settings such as the Hat Factory or the National. Like your music alfresco? Innsbrook's After Hours Series will set you up all spring and summer long, as will Sunsets at Kanawha, Dogwood Dell Festival of the Arts, and Friday Cheers on Brown's Island. The biggest outdoor concert series in Richmond is the Richmond Folk Festival, with music of all kinds wafting through the air along the river in October. It gets attention in the "Annual Events" chapter. Though the local music scene gets some mention here, music in smaller clubs, bars, and coffeehouses gets a look in the "Nightlife" chapter.

Most of the arts are centered downtown in Richmond, but Chesterfield, Henrico, and Hanover counties all have at least one theater within their borders.

BALLET

RICHMOND BALLET
407 E. Canal St.
(804) 344-0906
www.richmondballet.com
Under the direction of artistic director Stoner Winslett for 30 years, the company is innovative and acclaimed, and it's been invited back to the Joyce Theatre in New York twice now. As one of the resident producing companies at CenterStage downtown, the ballet stages two productions in the grand Carpenter Theatre, a storybook ballet such as *Romeo and Juliet, Cinderella,* or *Sleeping Beauty* in February, and the spectacular, sugarcoated extravaganza otherwise known as *The Nutcracker* for at least a dozen performances leading up to Christmas. In its own studio on Canal Street, the ballet presents the more laid-back Studio Series several

times a year, where patrons can get up close in the intimate performance space and see premieres of original works and previews of the company's touring productions. The Studio Series, with a 6:30 p.m. start, is popular with the after-work crowd because you can grab a drink at the Ballet Barre (get it?) and see two pieces of ballet in a relaxed setting. Tickets for the Studio Series are $30, while performances at the Carpenter Theatre cost from $15 to $125. Call (800) 982-2787 to purchase tickets or buy them at the ballet's box office in the lobby on Canal Street.

i Perfect for dance aficionados, the Choreographer's Club gets you insider access to the Richmond Ballet. You'll be invited to exclusive Tuesday evening previews of the very popular Studio Series productions, and after the show, stay for a Q & A with the company and then enjoy a cocktail reception.

CONTEMPORARY DANCE

DOGTOWN DANCE THEATRE
109 W. 15th St.
www.dogtowndancetheatre.com
Dogtown Dance Theatre in Manchester, way off both Broadway and Broad Street, staged a grand opening in May 2010, celebrating the recycling and renewal of what was a school gymnasium into a practice and performance space designed for small dance companies and independent artists. With a 46-by-31-foot stage and seating for up to 200 patrons, this venue should provide dance enthusiasts with the flexible performance facility that has been missing in Richmond. Ground Zero Dance Company will be involved, so you know the work will be top-notch. Plenty of free parking is available in the adjacent lot and surrounding streets.

Moving Performances

These dance companies move gracefully all over town.

Amaranth Contemporary Dance
809 N. 26th St.
(804) 647-8890
www.amarantharts.com
This 10-dancer company, founded in 2006 by artistic director Scott Putnam, has made a splash in Richmond's contemporary dance scene, creating more than 20 new works. They perform all over town from Godfrey's, to CenterStage, to the Firehouse, to Dogwood Dell, if they're not performing in Colorado or at the Arezzo Festival in Italy.

Elegba Folklore Society
101 E. Broad St.
(804) 644-3900
www.efsinc.org
Performing African and African-American dance at community events around the city, this group's exuberant and heart-pumping work is integral to the Capital City Kwanzaa event and the Juneteenth Celebration at Manchester Docks. See more about both events in the "Annual Events" chapter.

Ground Zero Dance Company
www.groundzerodance.org
Known for producing choreographer and founding member Rob Petres's ground- and gravity-breaking *Moment of Flight*, this company brings modern dance to a wider audience in Richmond, and beyond, participating twice in the Philadelphia Fringe Festival and being an instrumental part of Performatica, a festival of contemporary dance in Mexico. Get rid of your preconceptions of what dance is and isn't: Auditions ask for "modern dancers, martial artists, capoeiristas, runners, soccer players, and extreme sports enthusiasts—anyone with strength, agility."

K Dance
(804) 270-4944
www.kdance.org
One of the top contemporary dance companies in Virginia, K Dance produces *Yes, Virginia—Dance!*, an invitational that brings professional dancers and choreographers together for an explosion of contemporary dance at Grace Street Theatre near VCU. Other performances take place at the Firehouse Theatre.

Latin Ballet of Virginia
Cultural Arts Center of Glen Allen
(804) 379-2555
www.latinballet.com
This company performs approximately six passionate productions a year that bring the traditions of Hispanic culture alive. Past productions have included *El Día de los Muertos, The Little Prince*, and the ever-popular *Legend of the Poinsettia*. Though officially based at the Cultural Arts Center of Glen Allen, the company is branching out and heading all over town. The work is fiery and fresh, and technically strong whether the dances are flamenco, tango, modern dance, or classical ballet.

Starr Foster Dance Project
(804) 343-0250
www.sfdproject.org
This award-winning company produces and performs the annual Richmond Choreographers Showcase, among other way cool events.

MUSIC

CHAMBER MUSIC SOCIETY OF CENTRAL VIRGINIA
(804) 519-2098
www.cmscva.org

This all-volunteer organization is led by artistic director James Wilson, a former member of the illustrious Shanghai Quartet. The society brings in internationally known musicians for the Richmond Festival of Music in the winter and gives several concerts a year, spanning a wide range of performances from electric music to Baroque opera. Many concerts are performed at First Unitarian Universalist Church, though other venues are occasionally used. Ticket prices range from $5 for students to $25 for adults and can be purchased at the Web site.

RICHMOND JAZZ SOCIETY
(804) 643-1972
www.vajazz.org

Awarded the Governor's Award for the Arts in 2008, this 30-year-old organization is devoted to preserving the history of Richmond jazz, presenting performances, and educating people about the joys of jazz. With the talent of the VCU Jazz Masters and jazz faculty right down the street, it's not hard to hear some smoking jazz in Richmond 12 months of the year. Several times a year the society brings in high-powered headliners to the Downtown Music Hall at the Capital Alehouse downtown. Previous performers from the world of jazz include Freddy Cole, the Amina Figarova Sextet, young sax upstart Grace Kelly, and Richmond's beloved Rene Marie. Ticket prices vary.

i Grammy-winning new music sextet eighth blackbird has been the ensemble-in-residence at the University of Richmond since 2004. They regularly perform their innovative and provocative yet accessible repertoire on campus and as part of the Modlin Center for the Arts. Call (804) 289-8980 for updates.

RICHMOND PHILHARMONIC
W. E. Singleton Center for the Performing Arts
922 Park Ave.
www.richmondphilharmonic.org

Home base for this all-volunteer group is VCU's W. E. Singleton Center for the Performing Arts, but don't be surprised to hear them at the James Center, out in Brandermill, and at various other locales around the region during their performing season, from Oct to June, sharing their love of orchestral music. With music director Robert Mirakian at the helm, the orchestra has received two grants from the National Endowment for the Arts. Some concerts are free, while others ask for $10 a family, so it's a painless way to introduce the family to fine music.

RICHMOND SYMPHONY ORCHESTRA
Richmond CenterStage
600 E. Grace St.
(804) 788-1212
www.richmondsymphony.com

In its first year of existence, 1957, the Richmond Symphony performed in concert three times. Times have changed, and now RSO, with 36 full-time and more than 40 part-time musicians, plays more than 200 events each year, reaching 125,000 patrons at concerts and many more music lovers through school programs and weekly radio

Richmond CenterStage

Richmond CenterStage, the downtown arts center that houses two theaters, a music hall, and an education complex, opened in Sept 2009 after a $75 million renovation and expansion of what had been the Carpenter Center. Now inside is the sparkling and historic 1,800-seat Carpenter Theatre, which originally was a Loew's Theater, the 200-seat Gottwald Playhouse, and the multiuse Rhythm Hall. CenterStage has nine resident companies: the African-American Repertory Theatre, Elegba Folklore Society, Richmond Ballet, Richmond Jazz Society, Richmond Shakespeare, Richmond Symphony, School of the Performing Arts in the Richmond Community (SPARC), Theatre IV/ Barksdale, and Virginia Opera. That doesn't mean that these groups perform only at CenterStage. In fact, every one of them performs elsewhere, too, some even in their own facilities. When you buy a ticket to a show, make sure you know where it's playing. It's a fairly new setup, sharing all that downtown space, so here's hoping that everyone plays nicely, makes beautiful music together, bangs the drum slowly, and avoids all other clichés. CenterStage is located at 600 E. Grace St.; (804) 225-9000; www.richmondcenterstage.com.

broadcasts on WCVE. Most of the symphony's performances now take place in the gorgeous and acoustically wonderful Carpenter Theatre in the CenterStage complex. The symphony recently appointed a new music director and conductor, Steven Smith, to lead the orchestra. He had been the director of the Santa Fe Symphony and Chorus. It will be interesting to see and hear where his baton will take the symphony.

The Altria Masterworks program brings the classical music canon, from Beethoven to Prokofiev to Stravinsky, downtown Sat nights and for Sun matinees. On occasion, the symphony is accompanied by the 120-voice Richmond Symphony Chorus, and preconcert talks often take place in the Gottwald Playhouse one hour before curtain time for interested audience members. For those in the mood for a pops series, the Genworth Financial Pops program is a combination of Richmond traditions—for example, *Let it Snow!* and the sort of adventurous programming RSO has been recognized for by the American Society of Composers and Publishers. The program brings in guest artists from the world of jazz, gospel, and popular music, and sometimes just has a good time re-creating classic movie scores while Hitchcock scenes scare the audience out of their seats. Guest artists in the past have included Aretha Franklin, Marvin Hamlisch, Itzhak Perlman, Andre Watts, and most recently, Arturo Sandoval. The Metro Collection brings chamber orchestra concerts to high schools, art centers, college campuses, churches, and parks all over the region. Finally, the Lollipop series is aimed at children, with family-friendly offerings three Sat a year, such as Beethoven Lives Upstairs and a festival-like atmosphere before the performance, including the popular musical-instrument petting zoo. Ticket prices vary depending on the series, but single tickets for children up to age 18 are $12, while adult tickets can range from $17 to $77, though seniors get a discount. The Metro series has a top ticket price of $20. Season subscribers save 20 percent off the price of single tickets. Single tickets are available through Ticketmaster at www.ticketmaster.com or at the CenterStage box office.

i Catch the Richmond Symphony for free at its annual appearance at Dogwood Dell in Byrd Park in Richmond during the Dogwood Dell Festival of the Arts. Music and moonlight—what more could you want?

OPERA

VIRGINIA OPERA
Richmond CenterStage
600 E. Grace St.
(804) 644-8168
www.vaopera.org
For 35 years and counting, Virginia Opera has wowed audiences all over Virginia, performing in northern Virginia, Norfolk, and Richmond, now in the acoustically ideal Carpenter Theatre. Every year the company stages four operas, such as *La Boheme, Porgy and Bess,* and *Don Giovanni* to enthusiastic crowds. For those new to opera, Virginia Opera's Web site overflows with scene-by-scene explications and historical background, so that when you arrive for the show, you might not even need the English supertitles. There's also a section about misconceptions about opera and handy terms to know. Another way to enjoy the show is to hear Dr. Glenn Winters

of Virginia Opera tell all in a pre-opera talk 45 minutes before the curtain rises. He'll have you cheering "Bravi!" (but only at the appropriate time) in no time. Ticket prices range from $29 to $99 and are available at www.ticketmaster.com or by calling (800) 982-2787.

i The lineup for the 2010–11 season of Broadway in Richmond includes *A Chorus Line, The Color Purple,* and *Disney's Beauty and the Beast,* among others, at the Landmark Theater. Subscriptions are available for the five-show season online at www.broadwayinrichmond.com or by calling (804) 592-3401.

PERFORMANCE VENUES

CARPENTER THEATRE
600 E. Grace Street
(804) 225-9000
www.richmondcenterstage.com
Originally a Loew's movie theater built in 1929, this historic and flamboyant building with its atmospheric architecture has been renovated and restored to its original glorious colors. With 1,800 seats and more legroom and lumbar support, it's a pleasure to sit and soak up the beauty of the space even before the curtain goes up. Look up at the acoustical clouds and you'll see LED stars shining through. When the curtain does rise, you might notice that the stage is twice as deep, and larger across as well, the sight lines are fantastic, and the sound is symphonic quality. And it's comforting to know that during the restoration, the builders quadrupled the number of restrooms.

Holiday Happenings

For some families, the following events are annual traditions and rites of passage. Try one to see if it will become a part of your holiday routine.

Richmond Ballet's
The Nutcracker
Richmond CenterStage
(804) 262-8003
www.ticketmaster.com

Concert Ballet of Richmond
The Nutcracker
Various venues
(804) 798-0945

Amahl and the Night Visitors
Landmark Theater
6 N. Laurel St.
(804) 646-4213
A free Sunday performance in Dec.

Legend of the Poinsettia
Latin Ballet of Virginia
Cultural Arts Center of Glen Allen
(804) 379-2555

THE CULTURAL ARTS CENTER OF GLEN ALLEN
2880 Mountain Rd.
(804) 261-2787
www.artsglenallen.com
This is the Henrico County home of the Center Season, which brings internationally known performers to Glen Allen. Talents as diverse as Janis Ian, the Shangri-la Chinese Acrobats, Livingston Taylor, the Harlem Gospel Choir, and Celtic Crossroads have taken the stage here. CAGA also provides a warm welcome to the Latin Ballet of Virginia for several productions a year and other local groups as well. 2nd Stage is a new venue that brings in local and regional musicians and occasionally improvisational comedy through ComedySportz. 2nd Stage tickets are $10 in advance, $12 at the door. Center Season rates vary, but generally are between $12 and $30. Check the Web site for details. Dinner before some shows can be purchased at the door, but reservations beforehand are appreciated.

i The Groovin' in the Garden music series at Lewis Ginter Botanical Garden brings top-notch performers like Old Crow Medicine Show and Sharon Jones and the Dap Kings, and turns one of the loveliest spots in town into one of the liveliest. The series of concerts runs on Thursday evenings in May and June, rain or shine. Ticket prices vary, and food and drink are available for purchase. See www.lewisginter.org for details.

DOGWOOD DELL
Byrd Park
6000 S. Blvd.
(804) 646-DELL
Starting in June, happy crowds fill up the 2,400-seat amphitheater throughout the summer for family-friendly concerts, plays, and performances that run the gamut of styles from dance, drama, comedy, and musical theater to classical music, reggae, pop, swing, rhythm and blues, jazz, and bluegrass. Did I mention that all performances are free? Robin and Linda Williams are regulars, and with a little bug spray handy, it's a great place to visit with friends and catch a concert or a play. Many people bring lawn chairs for a picnic, though a blanket will work, too. Before a show, consider picking up food from Sally Bell's at the Landing near Fountain Lake, open Tues through Sun, 11 a.m.–8 p.m..

EMPIRE THEATRE
114 W. Broad St.
(804) 282-2620

Part of the Barksdale/Theatre IV group of theaters, the Empire is home to Theatre IV's Family Playhouse Season, though the occasional grown-up show shows up here, too. When the child in your life is ready for the excitement of live theater, and a night (or a day) on the town, put on your Sunday clothes and head to this historic theater for a special treat. See more in the "Kidstuff" chapter.

GOTTWALD PLAYHOUSE
Richmond CenterStage
600 E. Grace St.
(804) 225-9000
www.richmondcenterstage.com

Sharing CenterStage with the Carpenter Theatre, this spare and soundproofed smaller theater has 150 to 200 seats, depending on the configuration, providing audiences with a more intimate experience than the Carpenter Theatre. Richmond Shakespeare and African-American Repertory are just two of the companies using the space to the community's advantage.

i Looking for something cultural and free to do? Go to www.modlin.richmond.edu and click on the Free Spot button. Upcoming free concerts, lectures, and dance performances pop up in one place, courtesy of the University of Richmond's Modlin Center for the Arts.

HAT FACTORY
140 Virginia St.
(804) 788-4281
www.hatfactoryva.com

Formerly Toad's Place, this is the place to catch nationally and internationally touring acts such as Leon Russell, The Wailers, and JET and the Crash Kings. Some up-and-coming musicians, known only to your teenager, as well as local talent, get their chances to break out here, too. It's a general admission venue, standing room only, and it rocks along the canal.

i From May through June, people flock to Brown's Island on Friday nights for Friday Cheers, a series of concerts that brings nationally known musical acts to the riverfront stage for three hours of music and revelry for just $2. Food, beer, and wine are available for purchase, but please leave your pets and coolers at home. Call (804) 788-6466 for details or check out www.venturerichmond.com.

THE LANDMARK THEATER
6 N. Laurel St.
(804) 643-4213
www.landmarktheater.net

The largest theater in Richmond, with 3,616 seats and one of the largest proscenium stages on the East Coast, this exotic-looking building across from Monroe Park has hosted a who's who of the entertainment business since its opening in 1927, when it was known as the Mosque. True to its original name, there are minarets outside and lavish decor inside, including imported tile from Spain, Italy, and Tunisia. It now hosts plays, concerts, comedians such as Steve Harvey and Jerry Seinfeld, the Richmond Forum and other lectures, and the Broadway in Richmond series, which in 2010 included the touring production of Stephen Schwartz's *Wicked*. The 2011 series includes *The Wizard of Oz* and *Beauty and the Beast*. Tickets for events at the Landmark Theater are available at area Ticketmaster outlets, which include participating Macy's, Stony Point Fashion Park, and Regency Square Mall. Tickets may be charged by phone at (800) 745-3000 or purchased online at www.ticket master.com. Tickets may also be purchased at the Landmark Theater box office.

THE NATIONAL
708 E. Broad St.
(804) 612-1900
www.thenationalva.com
The mood's a little more casual on this side of Broad Street in the lovingly renovated National. Most shows are general admission, and with video screens and monitors throughout, you'll have a great view no matter where you hang out. Nationally and internationally acclaimed touring acts such as Snoop Dogg, Elvis Costello, and Leo Kottke stop here to put on some of the best shows in town now that Richmond is back on the radar. The National has a club feel with a bar in the back, and there's even a restaurant, Gibson's Grill, adjacent for a full night out. Sadly the 10-person hot tub behind the stage is for performers only. Get tickets at the box office or at www.ticketmaster.com.

RICHMOND COLISEUM
601 E. Leigh St.
(804) 780-4970
www.richmondcoliseum.net
This is where Springsteen rocks when he comes to town, where Carrie Underwood belts it out, and Tyler Perry lets loose. Sure, you can see the circus and monster trucks here, too, in the biggest venue in town. It's a bit outdated and in need of love or replacement, but when the right group is blowing the roof off, the audience doesn't seem to

mind. Parking in any of the numerous nearby lots or garages will set you back $5 to $15. See the Web site for parking specifics.

i Fridays at Sunset, a summer concert series held at Kanawha Plaza, brings artists such as Busta Rhymes, India Arie, Chuck Brown, and David Sanborn to the center of town. Bring a chair or blanket to sit on and bring cash, as no other form of payment is accepted for tickets, food, and drink. Tickets are approximately $20, though that can vary. Children under age 10 are admitted free outdoors, but if weather dictates a move to the inside, everyone needs a ticket. Check out www.friday satsunset.com for more information.

SNAGAJOB.COM PAVILION
4901 Lakebrook Dr., Innsbrook
(804) 423-1775
www.innsbrookafterhours.com
Site of the Innsbrook After Hours concert series in the West End, this outdoor venue presents 15 to 20 shows when the weather warms up. Nationally known touring acts, such as Barenaked Ladies and Earth, Wind, and Fire, perform here in the open air. Single show tickets range from $12.50 in advance to $25 at the gate. Gold Circle tickets ($25 to $45) let you get closer to the stage with first-come, first-serve seating. Otherwise, you sit or stand on the lawn. Concerts go on rain or shine, and children under age 10 are admitted free to most concerts. Parking is free unless you want to pay $3 for premium parking, and food and drinks are available for purchase. No coolers or pets, please.

The Arts Go to College

University of Richmond

Modlin Center for the Arts
Jepson Theatre
28 Westhampton Way
(804) 289-8980
www.modlin.richmond.edu

The University of Richmond is home to the Modlin Center for the Arts, which brings internationally acclaimed artists to Richmond in a series that runs from Sept to May each year. An eclectic mix of the best in music, theater, and dance, the series offers such diverse performers as Cirque Éloize, The Klezmatics, the Reduced Shakespeare Company, Les Ballets Trockadero de Monte Carlo, and Alvin Ailey American Dance Theater. Many events take place in the Alice Jepson Theatre in the Modlin Center on UR's West End campus. Others are presented downtown at the Carpenter Theatre or the Landmark Theater under the Modlin banner. Besides performances of music and dance, the Modlin Center has brought David Sedaris, Garrison Keillor, and Stephen Sondheim to town to the delight of sold-out audiences.

Virginia Commonwealth University

W. E. Singleton Center for the Performing Arts
922 Park Ave.
(804) 828-1514
www.vcu.music.org
(804) 828-6026
www.vcu.edu/arts/theatre/dept

A veritable smorgasbord of performing arts takes place here year-round, from cutting-edge student work, to Richmond Philharmonic concerts, to VCU Music's popular Guitar and Other Strings series (one of the best tickets in town—only $10 a show) in July. The lauded Mary Ann Rennolds Chamber Series is also housed here, and tickets for it range from $10 for children to $32 for adults.

---

i In conjunction with the Mary Anne Rennolds Chamber Series, a couple times a year internationally acclaimed visiting musicians give master classes in the Sonia Vlahcevic Concert Hall in the W. E. Singleton Center. These are free and open to the public. Go to www.vcu.edu/arts/music for details.

THEATRE

AFRICAN AMERICAN REPERTORY THEATRE
Gottwald Playhouse
600 E. Grace St.
(804) 355-2187
www.richmondcenterstage.com

Dedicated to illuminating the African-American experience through theater, this company is one of the resident companies of Richmond CenterStage downtown. Its collaborations have included working with Richmond Shakespeare on a production of *Othello* and with the Barksdale-Willow Lawn for a holiday production of *Black Nativity*.

BARKSDALE THEATRE AT WILLOW LAWN
1601 Willow Lawn Dr.
(804) 282-2620
www.barksdalerichmond.org

It's hard to keep up with the Barksdale anymore, led by Bruce Miller and Phil Whiteway, because it's everywhere in the theater community. The Barksdale's signature season takes the stage at Willow Lawn, and larger musicals take over the Empire Theatre downtown, as does their popular children's theater, Theatre IV. (See more about Theatre IV in "Kidstuff.") The Barksdale operates another theater in Hanover County and collaborates on productions at CenterStage downtown.

The Willow Lawn theater is an in-the-round, or rather square, theater that seats 207, and conjures up magic once the lights dim. Audiences might go *Into the Woods* or *Driving Miss Daisy* or any number of imaginative places. Rush tickets are sometimes available at the box office between 90 minutes and 20 minutes before showtime for only $20. College students may buy tickets for $10 each. Many shows sell out, so plan ahead.

BARKSDALE THEATRE AT HANOVER TAVERN
13181 Hanover Courthouse Rd.
(804) 282-2620
www.barksdalerichmond.org

The Barksdale Theatre's origins go back to this historic building when, in the early 1950s, young actors saved Hanover Tavern from falling down and started what became the country's oldest dinner theater. The tradition continues, but the joint has been spruced up quite a bit over the years. Before catching one of the five Barksdale productions staged here annually in the intimate brick-walled theatre downstairs, patrons now have the option of dining in the full-service restaurants at Hanover Tavern, choosing from a specific theater menu. Supersaver subscriptions can save theatergoers as much as $91 over the course of a five-show season.

CHAMBERLAYNE ACTORS THEATRE
319 N. Wilkinson Rd.
(804) 262-9760
www.cattheatre.com

A fringe theater by virtue of its out-of-the-way location off Chamberlayne Road in Henrico County, this group has put on more than 100 plays over the course of 40 years performing in the North Chamberlayne Civic Association building. In 1999 CAT went from a strictly community theater model to paying stipends to its actors and designers, and its work is getting more notice every year. Recent plays include *I'm Not Rappaport, All My Sons,* and *Crimes of the Heart*. Season subscriptions are available, and opening nights offer buffet dinners for an extra fee. They have embarked on a fund-raising campaign to upgrade the audience experience, i.e., acquire more comfortable chairs!

FIREHOUSE THEATRE PROJECT
1609 W. Broad St.
(804) 355-2001
www.firehousetheatre.org

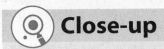

Close-up

Acts of Faith Festival

www.theactsoffaith.org

This homegrown, January-through-March theater festival warms up winter, not with fire and brimstone, but instead building bridges between the theater and faith communities, by offering stimulating theater to audiences who might not normally patronize some of the smaller theaters. I seem to remember a lot of drama in the Old Testament.

With a dozen or more professionally produced plays such as *Altar Boyz*, *The Chosen*, *Buffalo Soldier*, *Grapes of Wrath*, *First Baptist of Ivy Gap*, *Rabbit Hole*, and *Children of a Lesser God*, chosen by the participating companies, not the faith communities, the festival encourages the edgy as well as the expected. Back in 2004 when this idea sprouted at Second Presbyterian Church in Richmond, some faith communities were hesitant about the idea, wondering if their congregations would be offended by some of the themes and language, but the festival has been true to its original idea that it would encourage free artistic expression.

Acts of Faith has become the largest faith-inspired drama festival in the U.S. And faith is far more encompassing than religion, so the vibe of the festival isn't religious or preachy in the least, and nonbelievers are involved as much as anyone. The spirit of the festival is an ecumenical one of exploring and seeking, which is why some performances are followed by talk-back discussions that include the audience, actors, director, and community members who are special guests. It's a two-way street. Theaters get audiences in the seats that they might not otherwise, and the churches and synagogues often use the themes and issues in the plays for workshops and other programs at their own facilities.

Several churches and synagogues cosponsor the festival with monetary donations, and even more act as participating faith communities. Cosponsors in 2010 included the founder, Second Presbyterian Church, along with Lutheran, Baptist, Catholic, Jewish, Episcopal, and other Presbyterian congregations. In addition, participating faith communities encourage their congregations to attend and help spread the word, and again that list includes Christian and Jewish organizations. Of course, the full range of religious experience or lack thereof in Richmond isn't mirrored by this list, but festival organizers would love to see more faiths represented. A free preview of the festival is held in January. It's a combination of performances from some of the upcoming productions and directors giving their take on what their productions are about. It's an easy way to give the Acts of Faith Festival a try.

Known for producing thought-provoking, contemporary American works that are new to Richmond, the Firehouse Theatre, housed in a building that once was a city firehouse, really does have the hottest ticket in town. It's an intimate theatergoing experience, with some seats practically onstage and every seat with good sightlines.

A true community effort that started on a shoestring in the early '90s, the Firehouse has for more than 15 years brought challenging and entertaining plays by David

Mamet, Edward Albee, John Patrick Shanley, Sam Shepard, Sheila Callaghan, and others from off-Broadway to Broad Street. Founder and artistic director Carol Piersol has cultivated close working relationships with several established playwrights, including Israel Horovitz, Bill C. Davis, and Clay McLeod Chapman, hosting world premieres of their works.

The theater also encourages new playwrights with the annual Festival of New American Plays, which routinely receives more than 200 submissions a year. This is also the place for staged readings of new plays, screening of independent films, and other theatrical and literary events. Wine is available for purchase before the show, and opening nights often feature festive pairings with local restaurants. Free parking is available along Broad Street and in the Lowe's parking lot across the street from the theater. If you catch the theater bug while you're here, the Firehouse offers acting classes.

i The Firehouse Theatre has "pay what you will" Sunday matinees, so if you're hesitant to pay full price or can't afford it, this is your chance to see innovative theatre for a song, so to speak.

HATTHEATRE
1124 Westbriar Dr.
(804) 343-6364
www.hattheatre.org
Bringing shows to the area that no one else has, this 70-seat, black-box-style theater in the West End keeps its prices affordable while bringing audiences two quality productions a year, some for families and others not so much. *Why Do Fools Fall in Love?* and *Cheaper by the Dozen,* are just two past

productions, and you can see holiday shows, one-acts, comedy improv, and shows by local playwrights on occasion here. Tickets range from $10 to $15. Call or e-mail info@ hattheatre.org to reserve your seats. Tickets cannot be purchased at the door.

RICHMOND SHAKESPEARE
Gottwald Playhouse
(804) 592-3400
Agecroft Hall
(866) BARD-TIX
www.richmondshakespeare.com
This longstanding Richmond company has taken up residence downtown during the colder months at the Gottwald Playhouse in CenterStage, where a jam-packed schedule of the bard's work fills the winter months, including one production that's a part of the Acts of Faith Festival. Collaboration with the African-American Repertory Theatre produced a compelling *Othello* recently. A re-worked classic, *A Christmas Carol for Two Actors,* does an annual run during the Christmas holidays.

Every summer Shakespeare heads outside to be part of the Richmond Shakespeare Festival in the courtyard at Agecroft Hall. Two Shakespeare-related plays run in June, July, and sometimes into Aug. Recent hits have included *Hamlet* and *Twelfth Night.* Agecroft is a wonderful place to watch a play under the moonlight, soaking in the atmosphere of the 500-year-old building crated over from jolly old England. Ole William was a bawdy bard, and the cast doesn't miss an opportunity to poke fun, so to speak.

RICHMOND TRIANGLE PLAYERS
1300 Altamont Ave.
(804) 346-8113
www.rtriangle.org

How interesting that the only full-time professional theater in the mid-Atlantic devoted to producing plays relevant to the gay, lesbian, bisexual, and transgendered experience is not in D.C., or Raleigh, or Baltimore, or Charlotte, but right here in so-called conservative Richmond, VA. This nonprofit professional company stages eloquent, challenging, entertaining, and critically acclaimed works that speak to a wide audience. A participant in the Acts of Faith Festival, RTP produces five plays a year, including such fare as *Altar Boyz, Facing East,* and *Kiss of the Spider Woman*. Its production of *The Stops* garnered awards at the 2006 Columbus National Gay and Lesbian Theatre Festival. Now in its new Scott's Addition 4,000-square-foot theater that unlike its previous, cramped place is fully ADA compliant, RTP can expand their offerings with touring shows. They are aiming to have something entertaining going on here nearly every weekend. Traditional seating takes up half the audience space, with cabaret tables filling out the other half, the better for patrons to enjoy the offerings of the bar. Reserved tickets are available on the Web site.

SWIFT CREEK MILL THEATRE
17401 Jefferson Davis Hwy.
(804) 748-5203
www.swiftcreekmill.com

This Chesterfield County theater produces six plays a year for general audiences and several more per year with children in mind, in the underbelly of the nation's oldest gristmill. Taking in a show here can be a dinner-theater experience with a buffet before the show, or for $15 less you can just see the show. The fare here is entertaining and approachable, with past productions including *Pete 'n' Keely, A Grand Night for Singing,* and *Animal Farm.*

i If you know children who have the performing bug, consider connecting them with SPARC (School of the Performing Arts in the Richmond Community), a nonprofit organization that offers professional theater-arts education to 5- to 18-year-olds. Voice, dance, and acting classes are available during the school year and in summer camps. Though some SPARC alumni—paging Jason Mraz—have gone on to professional success in the arts, SPARC's mission is to light a spark in young people so they become more confident students, stronger speakers, and better team players.

SPEAKER SERIES

JCC FORUM
Oates Theater
Collegiate School
N. Mooreland Road
(804) 545-8608
www.weinsteinjcc.org

Sponsored by the Weinstein Jewish Community Center, this series of talks, performances, and panel discussions brings fascinating newsmakers, writers, artists, and observers to Richmond not only to comment on the current political and cultural scene but also to add to it. Previous participants have included Elie Wiesel, Cokie Roberts, Tiki Barber, the Capitol Steps, and Richmond's own Elliott Yamin. Multiple events guaranteed to entertain and inform are included each season, and single event tickets are available after Sept for $35 each. Purchasing season subscriptions is recommended to ensure you see what you want to see.

The Literary Lifestyle

Richmond is a writers' town, so you won't be at a loss for words here. Between the **VCU Visiting Writers Series,** the **Poetic Principles** series at the Virginia Museum of Fine Arts, the **Fresh Ink** literary series at the **Visual Arts Center of Richmond,** and special events at the **University of Richmond** and the **Library of Virginia,** top-notch writers give readings and talks frequently. Then there are the speakers and writers that bookstores and the **Richmond Forum** or the **JCC Forum** bring in. **James River Writers**, www.jamesriverwriters.org, puts on monthly meet-and-greet Writers Wednesdays and the entertaining and educational Writing Show at venues around town. If a poetry slam is what you're after, **Slam Richmond** throws words around every Saturday at **Artspace,** 0 E. 4th St. A writing workshop starts at 5 p.m. for those interested in working on their work. Sign up for open mic and the slam starting at 7:30 p.m., and the show starts at 8 p.m. Call (804) 232-6464 for details.

RICHMOND FORUM
Landmark Theater
6 N. Laurel St.
(804) 330-3993
www.richmondforum.org
Bringing movers and shakers to town five times a year to enlighten and occasionally entertain, the Richmond Forum is a subscription series that releases extra single tickets about three weeks before the event. Get on their e-mail list so you can be notified of available tickets. Previous high-profile folks who have taken the Landmark Theater's stage include Tony Blair. Former first lady Laura Bush, magician David Blaine, and news anchor Anderson Cooper are among the speakers scheduled for 2010–11.

MUSEUMS AND
ART GALLERIES

With the reopening of the stellar Virginia Museum of Fine Arts, Richmond will ascend to new heights, going beyond its place as the arts capital of Virginia to become an arts destination. It's a creative cauldron here, fueled by the best public arts graduate school in the country, the renowned VCU School of the Arts with 3,000 students in 16 programs. VCU Arts grads have received three MacArthur Fellow "Genius" Awards in the past five years, three Guggenheim fellowships and numerous other accolades, so it's clear VCU attracts and develops major talent. And then there's the faculty who teach, create, and start galleries. We residents and tourists just get to reap the rewards. People know how to do things with their hands here in Richmond, and not just text and tweet. In addition to art, what they make often includes community-building events such as First Fridays Art Walk and InLight.

Of course museums don't always mean art, and Richmond has been known to make a bit of history as well, and hold onto it in its many museums. Some museums are clustered, like the Virginia Museum of Fine Arts and next-door neighbor the Virginia Historical Society, and just around the bend on Broad Street, the Science Museum of Virginia sits right next to the Children's Museum of Richmond (see "Kidstuff" chapter). Two Civil War museums have banded together downtown at the Tredegar site, and Richmond history and Confederate history intertwine in historic Court End. Art galleries are similarly clustered along Broad Street and W. Main Street, and then there's the whole Manchester art explosion just south of downtown that includes Art Works and Artspace at Plant Zero, art centers with studios for working artists. You could spend days wandering through museums and galleries here and never see it all. Then they go and change the exhibits, so you have to start over. Which reminds me—the expanded Virginia Museum of Fine Arts is scheduled to bring in some blockbuster shows, some of them making their only U.S. stop in Richmond, so check www.vmfa.state.va.us regularly so you don't miss a thing.

Historic house museums, such as Agecroft Hall and the John Marshall House, are listed in the "Attractions" chapter, under "Historic Homes."

MUSEUMS

AMERICAN CIVIL WAR CENTER AT HISTORIC TREDEGAR
500 Tredegar St.
(804) 780-1865
www.tredegar.org

The newest kid on the Civil War block in Richmond, this museum opened in 2006 with the revolutionary and reconciliatory mission of showing the Civil War from the sides of all who endured it, participated in it, and still share its legacies. In considerable depth and comprehensive breadth, it tells the story of the entire country's experience of the war, not just one city's or state's. Its groundbreaking exhibit, In the Cause of Liberty, brings three perspectives—African-American, Confederate, and Union—together in one building, the historic Civil War–era Tredegar Ironworks Foundry, and encourages visitors to see more than they might have been inclined to before coming here. Through four films, interactive displays, hundreds of artifacts, and the illuminating words of those who lived and died in the war, the exhibit traces the causes, follows the course, and examines the effects of the war, intertwining the varied experiences of Southerners, Northerners, slaves, and free blacks. Parking is free with museum admission. The center is open seven days a week. Children under six are admitted free, it's just $2 for children 7 through 12, and adult tickets cost $8.

i When you become a member of the American Civil War Center, you have access to free parking during the center's operating hours. So, for those who frequent the Tredegar exhibits, go to Brown's Island for events, or like to walk across to Belle Isle or sit along the James River, you have a perfect place to park.

BLACK HISTORY MUSEUM AND CULTURAL CENTER OF VIRGINIA
00 Clay St.
(804) 780-9093
www.blackhistorymuseum.org

In a beautiful building that once was the black branch of the Richmond Public Library in the heart of Jackson Ward, the bustling center of black life in Richmond through the mid-20th century, this museum has several exhibits that get at the heart of the pride and pain of the black experience in Richmond. As a repository of important photographs, written records, and artifacts relating to black life in Virginia and a collector of African and African-American art, the museum highlights people and events that we should know more about. Impressive artifacts on display include the Woolworth's lunch counter and stools that once stood at the center of the civil-rights struggle in Richmond. The museum hosts traveling exhibits as well, covering such territory as Negro League baseball and the African-American experience in the military during Jim Crow. The gift shop has a wonderful selection of books and artwork for sale. Admission is $5 for adults, with discounts for seniors, students, and teachers. Admission for children 12 and under is $3.

EDGAR ALLAN POE MUSEUM
1914-16 E. Main St.
(804) 648-5523
www.poemuseum.org

Though master of the macabre Edgar Allan Poe lived in Richmond almost a third of his life, and considered himself from Richmond, he never lived in the Old Stone House, or any of the four buildings that make up this museum. Later, he married in Richmond, and while establishing his literary reputation, worked at the *Southern Literary Messenger,* which was headquartered at 15th and Main Streets. The exhibits here display a world-class collection of Poe's manuscripts, letters, and first editions of his works, as well as personal and family belongings and memorabilia associated with him and his lasting work. His literary output was much more wide-ranging than scary stories and gloomy poems, and you'll get a sense of that here. Be sure to check out the model of Richmond in the time of Poe in the Model Building, and as you move to the building named in honor of Poe's mother, Elizabeth, examine his work and his possessions, including a lock of his hair, his boyhood bed, and his engraved walking stick that he mistakenly left in Richmond just days before his death. The Exhibits Building houses changing displays that explore the effect Poe and his work have had and continue to have on our culture. Save time to soak in the ambience of the recently restored Enchanted Garden, which was designed in 1921 to re-create a garden that Poe described in one of his poems. The museum celebrates Poe's death day, Oct 7, fittingly with a macabre march and candlelight walk. If you have an MP3 player, download the audio tour of the museum from www.poemuseum.org before

i The best way to introduce someone to Poe's work is to attend one of the monthly Unhappy Hours that are held on the fourth Thursday of the month, Apr through Oct. Admission is free to the Poe Museum then, and there are guided tours, refreshments, and a cash bar. Activities could include a telltale heart scavenger hunt or a *CSI*-type gory activity. Best of all, hear Poe's work come alive through performances. All ages are welcome, and yes, they have one near Halloween.

you go to make your visit come alive. Otherwise, there are self-guided tour sheets that you can follow. Admission is $5-$6. Parking is available in the museum lot or on neighboring streets. The museum is closed on Mon.

MUSEUM AND WHITE HOUSE OF THE CONFEDERACY
1201 E. Clay St.
(804) 649-1861
www.moc.org
Almost surrounded by VCU's Medical College of Virginia campus, this museum offers some choices: Tour the museum and tour Jefferson Davis's White House, or just pick one. This three-story museum gathers the most comprehensive collection of artifacts related to the Confederate States of America, including extensive weaponry, uniform pieces, and wartime flags. Exhibits incorporate details and artifacts from soldiers, slaves, and freed blacks, famous generals, and the president of the Confederacy, Jefferson Davis. Imagine the work involved to move a 2,000-pound cannon. Shake your head at the Southerner's boast that "We can lick 'em with cornstalks." There's plenty of colorful history in here. The museum is open seven days a week. Free parking is available in the MCVH Visitor Patient Parking deck on 12th Street. Just bring your ticket to the museum's front desk for validation.

i The Richmond Civil War Pass allows entry to three sites crucial to visitors' understanding of the Civil War. For $15, the pass allows entry to the American Civil War Center at Historic Tredegar, the Museum of the Confederacy, and the National Park Service's Richmond National Battlefield site at Tredegar. That's a $4 savings, and the pass is available at all three sites.

OLD DOMINION RAILWAY MUSEUM
102 Hull St.
www.odcnrhs.org

Just across the Mayo Bridge in Manchester, and on schedule to open in the summer of 2010, this museum renovated the Southern Railway station that served Richmond from 1914 to 1957. Besides being able to tour the station and see how things, including telegraph machines, worked back in the day, visitors will be able to hop aboard several actual railcars. See more on this in the "Kid-stuff" chapter.

RICHMOND NATIONAL BATTLEFIELD
   PARK VISITOR CENTER AT TREDEGAR
470 Tredegar St.
(804) 771-2145
www.nps.gov/rich

The focus here, in the Pattern Building on the 8.3-acre historic Tredegar site, next to the American Civil War Center, is Richmond's role in the Civil War, primarily in relation to the seven engagements that took place on the surrounding battlefields. This three-story center orients visitors to the war in this region and offers much information and advice for those who want to drive around the surrounding Civil War battlefields and sites.

By spring 2011 the visitor experience will change, and the entrance to the building will be on the first floor, where there will be ticketing, orientation, exhibits, and a bookstore all done in concert with the American Civil War Center. The second floor, with its large battlefield and campaign maps, is a must-see for those who want a more in-depth understanding of where the major battles for the prize of Richmond were and how best to visit the sites. Take the opportunity to ask questions of a National Park Service

ranger. These people know their stuff and will vastly improve the quality of your visit. The third floor will house the orientation film that previously was on the first floor and will continue to display the moving multimedia exhibit, Richmond Speaks. Take the time to hear the words of those who lived or passed through Richmond during and after the war. See more on this site in the " Commemorating the Civil War and Emancipation" chapter. The site is open every day except Thanksgiving, Christmas, and New Year's Day. Buy the Civil War pass for free parking at the site and admission to the American Civil War Center and the Museum and White House of the Confederacy. Admission is free.

i The Federal Reserve Bank of Richmond at 701 E. Byrd St. downtown has recently opened the all-new "Fed Experience." Using interactive exhibits and simulations, visitors explore the nuts and bolts of the economy. The museum's goal is to help visitors see connections between what the Federal Reserve Banks do with the big bucks and what consumers do with dollars and cents. Actions have consequences. Open Monday through Friday, the Fed Experience is free, though visitors are encouraged to register in advance. Photo IDs are required for visitors over age 17. Check the Web site at www.thefedexperience.org or call (804) 697-8110.

SCIENCE MUSEUM OF VIRGINIA
2500 W. Broad St.
(804) 864-1400
www.smv.org

This comprehensive museum features exhibits that educate children and adults about the seen and unseen, from the microscopic to the edges of the universe, illuminating scientific concepts in an interactive way. If you have an interest in trains, be sure to peek into the RF&P Railroad Founders Room to see the photographs of the building back when it was Broad Street Station. If you are interested in traveling farther afield, check out the daily (including some in the evening) offerings in the IMAX Dome. Destination: Universe is a 20-minute planetarium show held at 1 p.m. daily that costs just $3 for nonmembers. The IMAX Dome and planetarium shows are a great way to travel to Everest, the Grand Canyon, or into space without leaving the comforts of Richmond. These films change every few months, so check the Web site for updates. There's more on this museum in the "Kidstuff" chapter.

i If a starry night appeals to you, then Sky Watch, held the third Friday of every month, weather permitting, on the Science Museum's front lawn, is for you. It's free, and members from the Richmond Astronomical Society share their powerful telescopes and help the rest of us pick out features of the night sky. Inside, at 6 p.m. the same night for $5 a person, an astronomer guides the planetarium's audience through the night's sky.

VALENTINE RICHMOND HISTORY CENTER
1015 E. Clay St.
(804) 649-0711
www.richmondhistorycenter.com

Preserving Richmond's history since 1894, when the Valentine family began the museum in historic Court End, the center has amassed an enormous collection of Richmond-related artifacts, including 900,000 bits and pieces of Richmond's past, an internationally admired textile collection more than 40,000 pieces strong, and an important African-American history collection, among others. The changing exhibits pull from these collections to bring to light fascinating and forgotten parts of Richmond's history. The permanent exhibits focus on the two families who made this complex what it is today, the Wickhams and the Valentines, both of whom once lived in what is known as the Wickham House, which is adjacent to the history center. As part of your visit, be sure to tour the exquisite house, which gets attention in the "Attractions" chapter. Other permanent exhibits include a walk through Richmond's first 300 years in Settlement to Streetcar Suburbs: Richmond and its People, a replica of Edward V. Valentine's sculpture studio, a look at how the Valentines and others made history and preserved it, and Signs of the Times, vintage neon signs from Richmond's bygone days. Serving salads, sandwiches, and paninis, Café Richmond, located within the history center, offers outdoor dining in the lovely garden or indoor dining year-round. The museum is closed on most Mon, but check the Web site for details. Admission is $8.

i For only $10, a Court End Passport entitles you to admission to the Valentine Richmond History Center, the Wickham House, the John Marshall House, and the Black History Museum and Cultural Center of Virginia for an entire year! That is an amazing deal, and it's available at all of the participating sites.

MUSEUMS AND ART GALLERIES

VIRGINIA AVIATION MUSEUM
5701 Huntsman Rd.
(804) 236-3622
www.vam.smv.org

For flights of fancy, head here to see what the early days of flying were really like—hint: not fancy at all. This museum, with its gliders and military and civilian aircraft, gives a good introduction to the science of flight and illustrates how we got from human-powered flight as a fantasy to reality—however fantastic that is. For the serious aircraft enthusiast, check out the U.S. Air Force SR-71 Blackbird that is the museum's pride and joy and the Grumman F-14D Tomcat, both outside. Inside, the collection has quite an array of barnstormers, Wright brothers' glider replicas, aircraft connected to famous Virginians such as Paul Galanti and explorer Richard Byrd, and other historic artifacts for those who aim high. The museum is open Tues through Sun and some holiday Mon. Admission is $5-$6.

i While at Historic Polegreen Church, use your cell phone to get a self-guided audio tour of the site. Just call (804) 205-9836, and using the guide that's available at the kiosk, select the prompts you'd like to hear. It's narrated by Professor Dan Roberts, of the University of Richmond and WCVE's locally produced *A Moment in Time*.

VIRGINIA CENTER FOR ARCHITECTURE
2501 Monument Ave.
(804) 644-3041
www.virginiaarchitecture.org

Designed by John Russell Pope for the Branch family, this Tudor Revival showplace was a winter retreat—their spring place was in Italy, and their summer home a farm in upstate New York. Something tells me they weren't exactly homeless in the fall. For years the headquarters of an insurance company—hard to believe, but true—the Branch House has been reborn as the Virginia Center for Architecture, one of the few architecture museums in the Southeast. Besides showcasing the amazing bit of architecture sitting right here on Monument Avenue, the idea at the Virginia Center for Architecture is to focus on the importance of the built environment in general.

The Long Gallery is the main exhibition space and is glorious to be in even if it's empty. A typical exhibit is the annual Design Awards display that tips its hat to the year's award winners in the mid-Atlantic region. Children love to build, so it makes sense that there's plenty here to appeal to younger children. Dominating the Chapel Gallery is a Lego model of the Branch House that kids would love the chance to replicate. Occasional family days offer a variety of activities in the education room, which isn't wheelchair accessible. Look closely wherever you go in this building—up is especially important as the ceilings are often plaster masterpieces, but observe door handles, doors, and windowpanes. Every surface tells something about design and form and function. For more, check out the "Architecture" chapter.

VIRGINIA HISTORICAL SOCIETY
428 N. Blvd.
(804) 358-4901
www.vahistorical.org

To do this museum justice, plan on at least two hours to wander about. The Story of Virginia, An American Experience—a multimedia, multi-gallery march through

Religious Museums

As the birthplace of religious freedom, it's fitting that there are so many museums in Richmond commemorating the free exercise of religious expression.

Beth Ahabah Museum and Archives
1109 W. Franklin St.
(804) 353-2668
www.bethahabah.org
Open Sun through Thurs, the three galleries display permanent exhibits that trace the Jewish experience in Virginia, including a copy of a letter from George Washington, and other 18th-, 19th-, and 20th-century documents and objects, both sacred and secular, that bring to life the contributions of Jews in Richmond. A donation is requested.

Virginia Baptist Historical Society
University of Richmond
Westhampton Way
(804) 289-8434
www.baptistheritage.org
Open for tours by appointment, the society's Heritage Gallery houses a 36-panel mural of Virginia Baptist history.

First Freedom Center
1321 E. Main St.
(804) 643-1786
www.firstfreedom.org
Open Mon through Fri, the center holds panel discussions and special events to highlight the importance of freedom of conscience and expression. An online exhibit is available as well as one on-site.

Historic Polegreen Church
6421 Heatherwood Dr., Mechanicsville
(804) 266-6186
www.historicpolegreen.org

Not an actual museum, but a work of airy art itself, seemingly floating in the woods, Polegreen Church commemorates a particular piece of religious history in Hanover County while putting it in context of the thousands-of-years struggle for religious freedom throughout the world.

Museum of Virginia Catholic History
18 N. Laurel St.
(804) 359-5661
www.richmonddiocese.org/archives
Open by appointment only, this museum is tucked by the crypt of the Cathedral of the Sacred Heart near Monroe Park. It traces the history of the diocese, founded in 1820, as well as the history of the cathedral itself.

John Jasper Museum at Sixth Mount Zion Baptist Church
14 W. Duval St.
(804) 648-7511
www.smzbc.org
Founded by former slave Rev. John Jasper in 1867 on Brown's Island, this church has a small museum that dates from 1926. It is devoted to the story of John Jasper and church history, complete with 19th-century artifacts and church archives. They are open every day for free tours of the church, including the museum, but they prefer that you make an appointment.

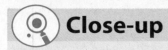

Close-up

Virginia Museum of Fine Arts

The big news here is a $150 million project that includes 165,000 square feet of space, large windows, natural light, a three-level atrium, two restaurants, an outdoor sculpture garden, the largest party deck in Virginia, comfortable sitting areas, free Wi-Fi— hmmm. Has a new resort opened on Boulevard? Not exactly, but a star is born, or born again rather, with the newly renovated, expanded, and reopened **Virginia Museum of Fine Arts** (200 N. Blvd., 804-340-1400, www.vmfa.state.va.us), now a destination unto itself in Richmond. With its extensive and rich permanent collection that spans 5,000 years and its glorious new Rick Mather–designed digs that match the sterling quality of its collection, Richmond is now home to one of the country's great museums. The Virginia Museum of Fine Arts is one of the 10 largest comprehensive art museums in the country and one of the best and most innovative. If VMFA counted the square footage of its parking deck like some museums do, it would be the sixth largest. But let's not quibble about numbers.

The art is the thing, and that's clear from the moment you walk up to the sleek and stunning entrance of the museum, the new James W. and Frances G. McGlothlin Wing off Boulevard. Upon entering you'll see the bold 8-by-32-foot, 16-panel painting, *Art History is Not Linear*, by Ryan McGinness. Art history may not be linear, but it sure is colorful and vibrant. Commissioned specifically for this welcoming space, the piece layers 200 iconographic images of works from the museum's collection. It's the artistic equivalent of a generous host opening the door and exulting, *"Mi casa es su casa."* With free admission every day the museum is open, it is meant to be yours, mine, and ours.

The five-story McGlothlin Wing expands the gallery space of the museum by 50 percent. It has a 150-seat lecture hall and a 12,000-square-foot gallery on the lower level that can be configured to hold multiple exhibits. With 40-foot spans and 15-foot-high ceilings, VMFA won't have to turn down a blockbuster exhibit because it can't fit. It is director Alex Nyerges's plan to "bring the world to Richmond," so recently the museum was the only U.S. museum to host the dazzling exhibit, Tiffany: Color and Light, after it had been at the Musée du Luxembourg in Paris and the Montreal Museum of Fine Arts. In 2011 the VMFA will host Dynasty and Divinity: Ife Art in Ancient Nigeria, 12th- to 15th-century bronze, terra-cotta, stone, and glass sculptures that recently wowed critics and audiences at the British Museum. An exhibit of internationally acclaimed photographer **Sally Mann's** work will arrive here in 2011. This is the company the VMFA keeps and will keep visitors coming back for more.

American and South Asian galleries and a gallery devoted to 21st-century art are also part of the new wing, as well as the casual **Best Café** and coffee bar, a museum

thousands of years of Virginia history, from well before it was Virginia or America to the day before yesterday—could take much longer if you watched every video and read every explanation. If among the hundreds of artifacts in this massive and comprehensive history of Virginia you can't find something to interest you, you aren't trying. Tales of hardship and struggle mix in with those of triumph and creativity.

Sit and watch the 12-minute introductory film to get your bearings. Interactive exhibits

shop, and research library, one of the finest on the East Coast. In a city dependent on bridges over the James Rivers, it makes sense that five bridges cross the three-story Louise B. and J. Harwood Cochrane Atrium to connect the McGlothlin Wing with the existing building. The museum has many reconfigured spaces and galleries and continues to display treasures as important as the museum's world-renowned Fabergé collection, the largest outside of Russia, its stellar Lewis collection of Art Nouveau and Art Deco furniture (rivaled only by the Musée d'Orsay in Paris), including the stunning Tiffany lamps and objects, 42 in all. Then there's the Mellon collection of Impressionist and Post-Impressionist art that includes several original waxes and bronzes by Degas and works by Monet, Cassatt, and more. If you're interested in ancient, classical, and Egyptian art, they've got you covered. And the museum is home to the finest collection of English silver in the country. Now there's room to hang medieval tapestries and display top-notch collections of African, Indian, Nepalese, and Tibetan art, including an elegant, white-marble, 19th-century pavilion from Rajasthan, India. It's too much for one visit, if you didn't know that already. Think of it as a mini-Metropolitan.

It's tempting to hide overnight in here à la the sister and brother in *From the Mixed-Up Files of Mrs. Basil E. Frankweiler,* who slept over in the Met. You would have to live here a while to begin to get a sense of the collection. Interestingly enough, the museum is encouraging guests, if not overnight ones, to drop by for the comfortable lounges with free wireless Internet access, for a quick bite at the Best Café, or to linger at the bar over by Amuse restaurant overlooking the sculpture garden. It's clear that the amount of glass and open space and vistas here encourage looking, seeing, and continuing on to the next intriguing space to see what's there.

All the glass will surely pique the curiosity of those outside the museum and reward those inside with views of city life and of the E. Claiborne and Lora Robins Sculpture Garden out back. It wasn't completed at press time, but it's due to be a 3½-acre outdoor oasis featuring pieces from the museum's permanent collection as well as changing exhibits. Visitors will wander beneath shade trees on the sloping, landscaped grounds. Two reflecting pools, connected by a watery staircase, will add depth and drama, and in an interesting use of space, the sculpture garden partially covers the parking deck.

What about that party deck on top? We'll have to see how that becomes a part of Richmond's cultural landscape, but I'm willing to bet that like everything else about the new VMFA, it will be a showstopper and a city-starter. Admission to VMFA is free, but there are charges for special exhibits and events. The museum is open daily. Parking in the museum's garage is free for members and $3 a day for all others.

help engage children (or adults), including a Powhatan farmhouse, a dollhouse-like replica of Wilton, and a streetcar you can walk into. The vastness of the exhibit and the themes covered in it—prehistoric peoples, Native American life, the age of exploration, contact with the English, westward expansion, slavery, war, segregation, transportation, women's rights—make you almost believe that all of human history happened in Virginia. The Virginia Historical Society is closed on Mon. Free admission.

VIRGINIA HOLOCAUST MUSEUM
2000 E. Cary St.
(804) 257-5400
www.va-holocaust.com

At once personal and universal, painful and profound, this museum engages visitors in a history of the Holocaust so that it can never be forgotten or repeated. Through its many dramatic and moving permanent exhibits, the museum tells the larger story of Nazi barbarity by drawing on the personal stories of many Virginians who were Holocaust survivors, liberators, or witnesses. There are many lives remembered here, but sadly too many did not survive the Nazis. One who did, museum founder and director Jay Ipson, narrates the 70-minute audio guide that takes you through the many exhibits. It's a powerful thing to walk by stark reminders of the dark time with the voice of a victim in your ear, but as you follow his family's story, you are reminded that his is the voice of a survivor.

The museum is an interactive place that encourages visitors to walk in the shoes of those who endured so much. There is a ghetto to walk through, a cattle car to ride in, a hiding place to crawl through, and a reproduction of the Nuremberg courtroom to stand in. If you would prefer a docent-guided tour, please call in advance to arrange it. Because of the serious and graphic nature of the content of the museum, the museum recommends that children be at least 9 years old to visit. Open every day except for Rosh Hashanah, Yom Kippur, Thanksgiving, Christmas, and New Year's, this museum has no admission charge, though donations are accepted.

i One of the most important offerings of the Holocaust Museum is visitors' ability to interact with survivors at lectures and special events or online through its "Ask a Survivor" feature on its Web site. Local survivors of the Holocaust are committed to making sure future generations understand the gravity of what happened and work to bring about a more tolerant world. In that regard, the museum often hosts films, art exhibits, lectures, and other special events that educate the public about genocide ongoing in the world today.

ART GALLERIES

ART6
6 E. Broad St.
(804) 343-1406
www.art6.org

A member-run nonprofit organization devoted to the visual and performing arts, Art6 produces exhibits such as Shoot the James, a photographic look at the area's greatest natural treasure. Its annual Think Small exhibit features small works by local, national, and international artists. Contemporary reactions to the Holocaust, elections, and Juneteenth are all part of Art6's purview.

i First Fridays Art Walk, held downtown the first Friday of every month, is a self-guided gallery stroll that draws big crowds and big fun to the streets of River City. Galleries schedule openings and special events to coincide with First Fridays, and people come from far and wide to check out the art and each other. See www.first fridaysrichmond.com for a full list of participating venues.

University Museums

These museums keep less regular hours and schedules than others, as they are tied to college calendars. All have free admission.

University of Richmond Museums
(804) 289-8276
www.museums.richmond.edu
The Joel and Lila Harnett Museum of Art hosts approximately a dozen exhibitions a year, in its 4,000-square-foot public galleries. **The Joel and Lila Harnett Print Study Center** is the home of the permanent collection of prints, drawings, and photographs of the University of Richmond Museums. Both are located within the **George M. Modlin Center for the Arts.**

The Lora Robins Gallery of Design from Nature has a vast, 100,000-piece collection of natural objects, cultural artifacts, and decorative arts. The range is staggering, from Jurassic dinosaur fossils, to ancient coins, to Dale Chihuly's contemporary glass art.

Anderson Gallery at Virginia Commonwealth University
907½ W. Franklin St.
(804) 828-1522
www.vcu.edu/arts/gallery
Always contemporary, often cutting edge, this gallery is a part of what *U.S. New & World Report* says is the No. 1 public university art and design school in the country. The gallery is closed on Mon.

Museum Galleries at Virginia Union University
1500 N. Lombardy St.
(804) 257-5660
Inside the L. Douglas Wilder Library on campus since 2004, this set of galleries displays mainly African, African-American, and South Pacific art. The museum is free and open to the public Tues and Thurs and by appointment.

ADA GALLERY
228 W. Broad St. (exhibition space)
1829 W. Main St. (mailing address)
(804) 644-0100
www.adagallery.com
ADA has been showing contemporary fine art since 2003 on Broad Street but was considering a move to its other space at 1829 W. Main St. when this went to press, so give the gallery a call before you go. Taking advantage of the plethora of talent from VCU School of the Arts, and with a roster of emerging and nationally known artists, this gallery features mixed media and works on paper. The gallery is open Wed through Sat and by appointment.

ART WORKS
320 Hull St.
(804) 291-1400
www.artworksrichmond.com
Open Tues through Sun, and a major player in Manchester's free monthly Fourth Fridays event among art galleries, running from 7

to 10 p.m., Art Works is home to dozens of artists who have studio space here. Five galleries on two levels host a jam-packed mix of juried local mixed-media shows, traveling international exhibits, and special exhibits designed to bring all kinds of art to all.

i Just across the river from downtown, Manchester offers its own art walk on the fourth Friday of every month except December that runs from 7 to 10 p.m. and includes openings of new work and performance art at Art Works, Artspace at Plant Zero, and other nearby galleries. Neighborhood restaurants get in the act, too.

ASTRA DESIGN
3110 W. Marshall St.
(804) 257-5467
www.astradesign.com

The studio and gallery for sculptor and metalworker Tom Chenoweth and jeweler Louise Ellis showcases their hand-wrought and exciting work that blends old materials with innovative design. Chenoweth's large-scale, fantastical sculptural pieces mix with smaller-scale lighting fixtures and functional furniture for indoors and out, including somehow rugged yet whimsical gates and railings. Ellis incorporates gold, silver, gems, antique buttons, and braided horsehair into bangles, rings, necklaces, and earrings of stunning craftsmanship The gallery is open by appointment only.

ELEGBA FOLKLORE SOCIETY
101 E. Broad St.
(804) 644-3900
www.efsinc.org

Always a part of First Fridays, this cultural center provides African and African-American perspectives with art shows, crafts, wearable art, dance, and drum performances. A truly hands-on place, artists lead art-making workshops on weekends. Gallery tours are available by prearrangement.

i Crossroads Art Center at 2016 Staples Mill Rd. has indoor art walks starting in January, on the third Friday of every other month year-round. Admission is free, and you can sip something from the cash bar and sample food from local restaurants while perusing the work of the featured artists. See www.crossroadsartcenter.org for details.

ERIC SCHINDLER ART GALLERY
2305 E. Broad St.
(804) 644-5005
www.ericschindlergallery.com

Located in historic Church Hill, this gallery is the oldest commercial fine-arts gallery in Richmond, operating continuously since 1960. It currently has more than twenty artists on its roster, with a specialty in regional painters and ceramic artists such as Lisa Taranto. To catch the traffic downtown, the gallery has opened Schindler Satellite at 8 W. Broad St. for First Fridays. The original gallery is open Wed through Sat and by appointment.

43RD STREET GALLERY
1412 W. 43rd St.
(804) 233-1758
www.43rdstgallery.com

Just off Forest Hill Avenue, this is the go-to place for contemporary crafts from over 50 artists and artisans, including pottery by owner Robin Cage, whose studio is on the premises, work by Lee Hazelgrove and

Barbara Dill, and rustic furniture, whimsical accessories, and jewelry by many artists. The gallery is typically closed on Sun and Mon, though holiday hours vary. For almost 20 years, it's sponsored the 43rd Street Festival of the Arts in Sept.

GALLERY5
200 W. Marshall St.
(804) 644-0005
www.gallery5arts.org
A typical Gallery5 opening might have fire twirlers, live nudes with paint covering their bodies, or . . . in other words, there is no typical here. Daring and cutting edge (for Richmond at least), it's the life-of-the party gallery, showcasing art in the oldest firehouse and police station in Virginia. The gallery stages offbeat art, performance, film, and music, engaging the entire community. In 2009 Gallery5 was voted by *Richmond Magazine* readers the "Gallery with the Most Attitude," and in 2008 it was awarded the Theresa Pollak Prize for Excellence in the Arts as an "Arts Innovator."

GHOSTPRINT GALLERY
220 W. Broad St.
(804) 344-1557
www.ghostprintgallery.com
A relative newcomer to the Broad Street scene, this gallery brings to Richmond the work of internationally known artists in all sorts of media, in an attempt to redefine "fine art." Interested as well in discovering the cutting edge in our own backyard, this gallery showcases high design from Italy one month and emerging illustrators from Richmond another. It's open Wed through Sat and by appointment.

GLAVE KOCEN GALLERY
1620 W. Main St.
(804) 358-1990
www.glavekocengallery.com
Open and casual, this gallery represents more than 30 local and regional artists, including Richmond favorites Steve Hedberg and Laura Loe. Exhibits in their 3,200-square-foot space run the gamut from photography to paintings, to clay, to wood, to mixed media by contemporary American artists. An annual small works show in Jan is well-attended, and online exhibits change frequently. The gallery is closed on Sun and Mon.

PAGE BOND GALLERY
1625 W. Main St.
(804) 359-3633
www.pagebondgallery.com
In this renovated garage in the Fan, you'll find contemporary art in a wide variety of media, from local artists with emerging national and international reputations to those whose names the world already knows. A recent print exhibit included works by Helen Frankenthaler, Ellsworth Kelly, Martin Puryear, and Richard Serra, and both Sally Mann's and Cy Twombly's work has been on view here. Supportive of Richmond artists as well, the gallery has mounted shows of acclaimed local artists Andras Bality and Kathleen Markowitz as well. The gallery is open Tues through Sat and by appointment.

QUIRK GALLERY
311 W. Broad St.
(804) 644-5450
www.quirkgallery.com
Open Mon through Sat or by appointment, Quirk features a wide array of art for sale, from wearable art to paintings and

photography, to ceramics and accessories, all offbeat and at a refreshing range of price points. One recent exhibit featured several of Richmonder Noah Scalin's skull creations from his Skull-A-Day project, which won him an international following and a book deal. The gallery brings work from all over the world to Richmond and puts on events and exhibits, including an annual guys' night in Dec, designed to foster the burgeoning Broad Street art scene.

RED DOOR GALLERY
1607 W. Main St.
(804) 358-0211
www.reddoorgalleryrichmond.com
Specializing in established contemporary painters and sculptors with national reputations, this gallery's roster includes local talent Ed Trask and Matt Lively, and from farther afield, Jordan Faye Block, Marshall Burns, and Deborah Colter, among many other artists. The gallery is closed on Sun and Mon.

REYNOLDS GALLERY
1514 W. Main St.
(804) 355-6553
www.reynoldsgallery.com
This is the crème de la crème of galleries in Richmond. Owner Beverly Reynolds has been bringing the work of artists with national and international reputations—Sally Mann and Jasper Johns, to name two—to her two-level gallery for 30 years. With 15 exhibits a year, a 4,000-square-foot exhibit space, and a top-notch roster of 40 artists, the gallery has a history of supporting local artists and getting many of them national attention. A recent exhibition included a wall installation by 1993 VCU sculpture grad and New York sculptor Teresita Fernández, who has received both MacArthur and Guggenheim

Fellowships. The gallery is open Tues through Sat, Sept through May, and Mon through Fri, June through Aug.

i Every year in October, Gallery 44, Richmond's longest-running, juried arts and crafts show, brings more than 170 Virginia artists to First Unitarian Universalist Church of Richmond near the Carillon for a show and sale. You'll find multimedia works, fiber arts, photography, pottery, wood-turned bowls, and so much more during the five-day show at 1000 Blanton Ave., and there is free parking in the lot and along the streets. Call (804) 355-0777 or check out www.richmonduu.org for exact dates and times.

RICHMOND PUBLIC LIBRARY
101 E. Franklin St.
(804) 646-4740
www.richmondpubliclibrary.org
The six exhibit spaces of the grand public library offer impressive permanent collections and frequently changing exhibits of paintings, mixed media, photography, and sculpture. A part of First Fridays, it's an important but sometimes overlooked stop on the evening Art Walk.

SARA D. NOVEMBER GALLERY
Weinstein Jewish Community Center
5403 Monument Ave.
(804) 545-8659
www.weinsteinjcc.org
Open every day but Sat, the gallery is dedicated to preserving and sharing Jewish culture by presenting exhibits that feature the work of Jewish artists and Judaica. Every few months the gallery sponsors juried exhibits for undiscovered artists over the age of 16.

InLight

InLight Richmond, a curated one-night light exhibit downtown, is an annual event, though it bounces around the calendar (and the city) in the fall. The venerable yet funky **1708 Gallery** started the event here to celebrate its 30th anniversary in 2008, hoping to engage the city and transform unnoticed downtown spaces into canvases of light. Calling it a curated light exhibit just doesn't do it justice; it's more of a jazzy lit-up extravaganza. In 2009, 26 light-inspired multimedia installations lit up the streets, the buildings, the sky, and the people who were lucky enough to be in Richmond for it. There were video hands playfully popping in and out of a vacant building's windows, photography, light installations, sculpture, performance art, a lantern parade, and a wearable art fashion show. It's not just about seeing, either. There's music on multiple stages and a beer and wine garden, so you can take a break from all that dancing and staring. Flickering and fleeting, rain or shine, this delightful event lights up the night in Richmond. Check out www.1708gallery.org/inlight to get up-to-date information.

1708 GALLERY
319 W. Broad St.
(804) 643-1708
www.1708gallery.org
One of the oldest artist-run galleries in the U.S., 1708 has been at the forefront of Richmond's vibrant art scene since its founding in 1978 by VCU arts faculty. During First Fridays, it's easy to find the 1708 Gallery—just look for the solar-powered stars shining in the sidewalk installation called InLight Walk, a permanent example of 1708 using art to build community and transform downtown. 1708's annual art auction in May is a big deal and a big draw, since 50 artists donate art to be bid on. And their annual Small Works invitational show in Nov and Dec makes the best of Richmond available to the public in small doses. A new, fast-paced event is *20*, when twice a year eight artists share 20 pieces of work in the allotted 20 seconds per slide. The gallery is closed on Sun and Mon.

i It's never too late to bring your inner artist out to play at the **Visual Arts Center of Richmond. Classes in woodworking, fiber art, metalworking, drawing, clay, painting, cartooning, and many more areas are offered, some in one-day sessions, others on a weekly basis during the day or in the evening. VAC members get discounts. Go to www.visarts.org to see the current schedule.**

VISUAL ARTS CENTER OF RICHMOND
1812 W. Main St.
(804) 353-0094
www.visarts.org
Where adults and children go to take classes in a variety of disciplines, the Visual Arts Center hosts frequent art exhibits by teachers and students and houses the True F. Luck Gallery, which mounts curated exhibitions several times a year. The gallery is open Mon through Sun. In addition, near the lobby is the fun and fabulous Art-o-mat, a

vending machine that in its former life spit out cigarettes. Now, for a mere $5, anyone can own an original piece of artwork dispensed from the machine. Call it inconspicuous consumption.

VISUAL ART STUDIO
208 W. Broad St.
(804) 644-1368
www.visualartstudio.org
This is always a vibrant place to be on First Fridays, with good music, good cheer, and really cool art in a price range that appeals to the gift giver and the more serious art collector. Besides the larger exhibits of local and internationally exhibited artists' work, the studio features local pottery, handmade jewelry, decorative arts, and small paintings for sale, many for under $100. The studio is closed on Sun and Mon.

ATTRACTIONS

The destinations spotlighted in this chapter are a mix of indoor and outdoor attractions, some free and some with admission fees. Within this chapter are the classic stops that visitors (and residents, let's be honest) ought to put on their lists to get a sense of what the city and surrounding areas have to offer. A separate section lists several historic houses that are often destinations unto themselves. It won't surprise you to know that while in the Richmond region you can tour wonderful specimens of homes from the 17th to the 20th century, but it might bewilder you to realize that you can also tour two buildings from the 15th century, right in Richmond's West End. Keep reading to find out how that's possible.

If you are looking for the famous James River plantations, you'll find them mentioned in the "Day Trips" chapter, since they are a bit farther afield in Charles City County. Kings Dominion amusement park gets two write-ups in the "Kidstuff" chapter, for its water park and its drier options, so flip to that if you're interested in thrills and chills.

For the attractions that don't provide visitor parking, don't fret. Parking garages and lots are numerous downtown; hourly rates are in the $3 range, and daily rates run between $10 and $15. In many cases, on-street parking is available, and meters in Richmond do not need to be fed on weekends, except during special events.

Price Code

The price code is based on admission for one adult.

$. . . . . under $6
$$ . . . .$6 to $10
$$$ . . . . over $10

THE CLASSIC AND CLASSICAL

CANAL WALK   **FREE**
Between 5th and 17th Streets,
   near the river
(804) 788-6466
www.venturerichmond.com
With entrances at just about every block between 5th and 17th Streets, there are

any number of ways to wander along Richmond's Canal Walk downtown near the river. The restored canals, both the Haxall and the James River and Kanawha, owe their existence to George Washington, who wanted to connect the Atlantic to the Mississippi to transport goods and people. It didn't get quite that far, but by 1860 more than 240,000 tons of goods were shipped along these canals, and packet boats carried passengers as far as Lynchburg.

Starting at Brown's Island, which itself was created by the canal system, near the American Civil War Center, is the Haxall Canal, the westernmost portion of the restored canals, which have 1¼ miles of pathway for strolling through 400 years of Richmond history. All along the way there are river and city views, historic buildings to see, traces of mills and railroads that used to line the rushing river, statues that celebrate history, and markers that let you learn about it. While on Brown's Island, don't miss the April 1865 exhibit on a bridge that juts out into the river and into Richmond's past. It's a dramatic setting for commemorating Richmond's most dramatic days. Several markers on the island highlight parts of Richmond history that too few people know, including how John Jasper, a former slave who became a renowned preacher, founded Sixth Baptist Church in a former Confederate laboratory right here. Wheelchair-accessible entrances are at 5th, 10th, 12th, 14th, and 16th Streets.

i Runners and walkers can do a fun 3¼-mile loop that incorporates the Canal Walk and trails along the flood wall to give a little ambience to your workout.

Keep walking and you'll eventually see both the end of the Haxall Canal and the Christopher Newport Cross, which commemorates his arrival here in 1607, when he claimed the area for King James. Just around the bend at 12th Street, you'll see one of two remaining locks on the canal, the Tidewater Locks. This is where boats went up and down 69 feet in the space of 3½ blocks, using a series of water stairs. From here to the east is the James River and Kanawha Canal. It continues its journey to a new Turning Basin, where from spring to fall and on the night of Grand Illumination in December, canal boats transport passengers once again, but this time not overnight. In 2009, thousands of people took the 45-minute guided tour. Make sure

you see Box Brown Plaza to read about Henry "Box" Brown's daring escape to freedom up North. The end of the line is at one of Richmond's claims to fame, our own Triple Crossing, something for the railway enthusiasts among us. Sadly, biking is not allowed along the Canal Walk, but you will see Segways. Not sure I understand the logic there.

i For a fun party April through November, charter a canal boat or two and while away the hours floating downtown. Contact Venture Richmond at www.venturerichmond.com/experiences/canalcruises.html for information.

HENRICUS HISTORICAL PARK $-$$
251 Henricus Park Rd.
(804) 748-1613
www.henricus.org
As the second permanent English settlement in Virginia, it doesn't get the press that Jamestown does, but with the 400th anniversary of the founding of Henricus coming up in 2011, big doings are afoot, with special events planned from Sept 2010 through Sept 2011. Sir Thomas Dale brought 300 settlers here in 1611, thinking the high ground above the James River was superior to the miserable and unhealthy Jamestown. Though the Arrohateck Indians, members of the Powhatan confederacy, had been friendly to the group of explorers including John Smith in 1607, they weren't too keen on the larger numbers of intruders, so the settlers built a palisade for protection. Dale was a taskmaster and instituted private land ownership, so many settlers moved out of Henricus to launch their own farms. Tobacco cultivation, successfully started here by John Rolfe, was instrumental in the farms' successes. Just about everyone has heard the

story of Pocahontas, but not so many know that it was at Henricus where she was held captive, converted to Christianity, and then married John Rolfe. Henricus was destroyed during the Indian Wars of 1622, though that certainly didn't change the pattern of English settlement in Virginia.

Every month different activities are held to highlight important aspects of life at the 32-acre Henricus Historical Park, be it Militia Month, Harvest Month, or Native American Month. No matter the month, visitors stroll between and in several reproduction, wattle-and-daub buildings that shine light on 17th-century life. Hint—it was really hard. See Mount Malady, the first and best-named hospital ever, and a soldier's house, blacksmith's forge, a planter's house and tobacco barn, and more. Costumed interpreters engage in the tasks of the 17th century and might ask you to lend a hand. Publick Days in Sept is always a big, free event with extra added activities, including military reenactments, Native American heritage activities, storytelling, and most frightening of all, 17th-century medical demonstrations. There are fees for make-and-take crafts. The park is part of and adjacent to the 842-acre Dutch Gap Conservation Area, which is a great place to take a nature walk and do some birding. Henricus Historical Park is open Tues through Sun from 10 a.m. to 5 p.m. Ticket sales end at 4 p.m. daily to allow visitors time to explore the site before it closes. Admission is $7 for those over 12 and $5 for those 3 through 12. Discounts apply to Chesterfield and Henrico residents, senior citizens, and other groups.

HOLLYWOOD CEMETERY   **FREE**
412 S. Cherry St.
(804) 648-8501
www.hollywoodcemetery.org

Laid out in 1848 in the pastoral style, Hollywood takes its name from the stands of holly trees throughout its 135 acres of rolling, tree-shaded hills and valleys. Its winding paths, elaborate statuary, ornate ironwork, and famous residents, including James Monroe and John Tyler, two of Virginia's many U.S. presidents, make Hollywood a popular tourist destination. Monroe's grave is ensconced in one of the best examples of ornamental cast ironwork in the U.S. Another of the cemetery's most notable monuments is the 90-foot-high stone pyramid made of James River granite that honors the 18,000 Confederate dead buried nearby. Besides the unknown soldiers, more than 20 Confederate generals, including J. E. B. Stuart and George Pickett, are buried here, as well as Jefferson Davis and members of his family.

Pick up a map of the cemetery at the entrance to make sense of the meandering roads. Following the blue line will take you to many of the highlights. It doesn't take much time in Richmond to recognize these names—Lewis Ginter, William Mayo, T. C. Williams, James Branch Cabell, Douglas Southall Freeman, Ellen Glasgow, Mary Munford, Lewis Powell. So much of the history of Richmond, so much of Richmond today connects back to the work and generosity of those buried here in this outdoor museum. But it can be as moving to wind in and around the gravesites to read lesser-known names on the granite markers and see the expressions of both grief and hope in the epitaphs and angels.

The cemetery is open every day from 8 a.m. to 5 p.m., and to 6 p.m. during daylight saving time. From Apr through Oct, daily except on Sun, guided walking tours are offered at 10 a.m. for a fee. Contact the Valentine Richmond History Center at (804) 649-0711, ext. 334, for more information.

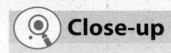

Close-up

Capitol Square

I'm afraid too many people, Richmonders especially, think that **Capitol Square** (1000 Bank St., 804-698-1788, www.virginiacapitol.gov) is a place only for legislators, lobbyists, and the lofty. Yes, Capitol Square is where the **Virginia General Assembly,** the oldest continuous representative government in the New World, meets in the State Capitol, Thomas Jefferson's temple to classicism.. And yes, the square is home to the **Executive Mansion** for the governor. But this 12-acre space is also meant to be used by the people for all sorts of activities. The grounds, older than Central Park, are a place of celebration and protest, of commemoration and recreation. It's a public park. It's the first family of Virginia's front yard. It's where the nation's first elected African-American governor, **L. Douglas Wilder,** was inaugurated. Winston Churchill and Queen Elizabeth II both visited, and you should, too. You won't get to walk in the Capitol building via the front steps as they did, but you can go inside one of the most beautiful buildings in the United States, for free.

Capitol Square is also a classroom for school groups or anyone interested in government and history. Remember, as Thomas Jefferson said, "Whenever the people are well-informed, they can be trusted with their own government." Thousands of people do come down during General Assembly sessions (Jan through Feb or Mar, depending upon the year) to inform and be informed. Listening in on sessions, either in the actual chambers or via a live feed in other rooms, is encouraged and accommodated. Interestingly enough, they don't have valet parking, but they do offer valet protesting. If you file an application for your protest group with the Department of General Services, state workers will set up a podium and amplifier for you—by appointment, of course—often near the historic **Bell Tower** to the southwest of the Capitol, also a Virginia visitor center. The grounds are full of statues commemorating Virginia heroes. There's the famous **statue of George Washington on his horse**, reportedly showing unscrupulous legislators the way to the old State Penitentiary, and there's the moving **Virginia Civil Rights Memorial,** dedicated in 2008, that recognizes the contributions of 16-year-old Barbara Johns, Oliver Hill, Thurgood Marshall, and so many others who fought so long to bring about equality for all Virginians.

To get inside the splendid **State Capitol,** the Thomas Jefferson–designed temple based on the Roman Maison Carrée in Nîmes, France, enter at the main entrance on Bank Street, south of the building. The Capitol extension, completed in 2007, is underground to preserve the view of Thomas Jefferson's masterpiece. You'll have to go

---

i Other cemeteries worth checking out for their history include Oakwood, Shockoe Hill, and the Hebrew Confederate Cemetery on Shockoe Hill, which is the only Jewish military cemetery in the world outside the state of Israel. The cemetery is maintained by Congregation Beth Ahabah.

JAMES RIVER PARK SYSTEM **FREE**
4001 Riverside Dr.
(804) 646-8911
www.jamesriverpark.org

Quite the attractive attraction, it really is one of the biggest draws in Richmond, visited by more than 500,000 people each year, and it stretches for miles from east of downtown to

through airport-like security to enter, and then you can decide if you want a self-guided or guided tour. If time permits, take the guided tour; you'll learn and see so much more. Call ahead to schedule tours for large groups.

Jean-Antoine Houdon's famous statue of George Washington dominates the **Hall of Presidents** in the two-story Rotunda. It's the only statue Washington posed for, and it is considered an exceptional likeness. Carved of Carrara marble, it weighs 18 tons with its base. Houdon's bust of Lafayette is also here, so esteemed that Lafayette is allowed to keep company with Virginians who became president. In all, the Capitol has 26 sculptures and 90 paintings on display, so it's an art museum, too. Look up at the dome, another work of art. First Lady of Virginia Elizabeth Swanson took on the interior design in 1906 and went wild on the dome's decorative painting. She was the type who hand-painted her own china. You might feel as if you are in the wrong building for a minute. There is no dome on the outside of the building, and it wasn't called for in Jefferson's plan. It's unclear who sneaked it into the building, but it seems to suit GW just fine.

One of the many advantages of taking a guided tour is that guides have keys and can let you in the **Senate and Delegate chambers** to see the glorious skylights there. On a self-guided tour, you'll have to be content with looking through a glass door. It's easy to see why the State Capitol has more than once stood in for the U.S. Capitol in movies such as *Dave* and Gore Vidal's *Lincoln*.

Look around for official seals of Virginia, above in the Hall of Presidents, even on the doorknobs. Tyrants should get the message that Virginia won't put up with them. You can also look for fossils in the white-and-black floor of the Hall of Presidents.

Be sure to head upstairs to the governors' gallery, not so much to see the 16 official portraits of the most recent Virginia governors lining the walls, but to get a closer look at the dome above and to look down at the dizzying view of George Washington. That railing that's keeping you from landing in the Hall of Presidents below is some of the oldest woodwork in the building—it's very sturdy, I swear.

Free guided tours of the State Capitol are offered every day except Thanksgiving, Christmas, and New Year's. It behooves every Virginian to get the most out of your tax dollars to take advantage of such a valuable freebie. **Meriwether's Cafe** serves food during the week, and the gift shop is closed on Sun. Parking is available in nearby lots or on the street. Of course it's harder to come by easily during General Assembly sessions. The grounds are open from 7 a.m. to 11 p.m., and the Capitol itself is open from 9 a.m. until 5 p.m.

just west of the Huguenot Bridge. It's where Richmonders and everybody else go to walk, run, mountain bike, paddle, fish, bird-watch, rock-hop, and just watch the river run and the trees change colors. There's much more about this gem of the James in both the "Parks" and "A River Runs Through It" chapters.

LEWIS GINTER BOTANICAL GARDEN $$
1800 Lakeside Ave.
(804) 262-9887
www.lewisginter.org

This 80-acre property has more than 50 acres of gardens arranged in more than 10 garden areas, so you'll need a lot of time to see them all. It has grown tremendously over its 25 years, adding an attractive visitor center, education building, and an 11,000-square-foot conservatory to its already lovely gardens. It is named after Lewis Ginter, the wealthy cigarette manufacturer, developer, and builder of the Jefferson Hotel. Lewis's sister, Grace Arents, lived on the grounds here in Bloemendaal House (which means "valley of the flowers"). A group of botanists, horticulturists, and interested citizens took on the task of turning the property into a botanical garden, as Grace had instructed in her will, and the Lewis Ginter Botanical Garden was planned and planted.

Now maturing nicely, the three-acre Flagler Perennial Garden is one of the best on the East Coast, and you'll wander amid lovely gardens devoted to roses, conifers, healing plants, wetlands, Asian landscape, and more. Winding paths, ponds, bridges, and of course the whimsical children's Tree House make a walk through the gardens not just about what's growing.

But a lot is growing, and going on. "A Million Blooms," from Apr into June, is probably not even an exaggeration. You'll want to see the tulips in Apr, the daylilies throughout the summer, and the exotic plants that you wish you could make work in your garden. There's always a crowd here for the Mother's Day concert and Father's Day fun. Flowers after 5, Fidos after 5, Families after 5, and the popular concert series Groovin' in the Garden all offer the chance to enjoy the garden on beautiful spring and summer evenings. Listen to music, sip wine, stroll the garden paths. When the weather turns cold, the garden warms up the holidays with GardenFest of Lights, a colorful holiday display of 500,000 lights in and around the gardens. If hot chocolate isn't enough, dinner is available at the Robins Tea House,

but reservations are recommended. Lunch is available in the Robins Tea House daily.

Spring and fall plant sales are a wonderful opportunity to expand your gardening repertoire while picking up some deals. There's always a booth of plants donated by Ginter volunteers that is a great place to score some good-quality plants inexpensively. Proceeds go to the garden. The garden's gift shop in the visitor center is worth spending time and money in. There's a great children's section, a wonderful collection of practical and decorative items for the garden, and gorgeous pieces of art that you might not need but will want. Admission is $10 for adults, $9 for seniors, and $6 for children 3 through 12. Those under age 3 and members are free. The garden is open daily from 9 a.m. to 5 p.m.

i Lewis Ginter has reciprocal admission with dozens of gardens around the country and discounts, once you are a member. Plus you'll be more inclined to stop by to see what's blooming if you know admission is free.

LIBRARY OF VIRGINIA FREE
800 E. Broad St.
(804) 692-3500
www.lva.virginia.gov
Founded in 1823 at Thomas Jefferson's request as the repository of the state's books and official records, the library's collection is now both massive—97 million pieces and counting—and priceless. Housed in a beautiful, airy building since 1997, the library is much more than a collection of books. With maps, books, documents, letters, government records, photographs, posters, and family lore from the 1600s to the present housed on 55 miles of shelves,

it is recognized as the most comprehensive resource in the world with regards to Virginia history, culture, and government. Within the collection is a Declaration of Independence written on sheepskin and inscribed to Mr. Thomas Jefferson, a collection of George Washington's letters, one of only 12 manuscript copies of the original Bill of Rights, and the minutes of the last meeting of the House of Burgesses that end with a knowing 4-inch-tall *FINIS* written with a flourish. But you don't have to be connected to the famous to be included in this library's collection. Vast amounts of information about the daily lives of Virginians over the centuries are here, and the library regularly mounts exhibits that highlight Virginia's storied past. The library also collects the works of Virginia writers, including Sherwood Anderson, Edgar Allan Poe, Ellen Glasgow, and William Styron, and helps the literary tradition continue with literary events, lectures, and book signings.

Some visitors use the library for its extensive genealogical resources, including a military records collection that dates from the American Revolution, and the staff here is dedicated to helping you along your search. Most of the collection is in the stacks, and you will need a photo ID to access what you want. Wireless Internet is available on the first two floors of the library. Forty-five minute tours can be arranged in advance by calling the library, which is open from 9 a.m. to 5 p.m., Mon through Sat. Free parking for patrons is available underground during library hours. A gift shop filled with Virginia-related books and merchandise is near the front entrance.

MAYMONT   **FREE–$**
1700 Hampton St.
(804) 358-7166
www.maymont.org

A 100-acre Victorian county estate might sound like a stuffy place, but that's not at all the essence of Maymont, a delightful oasis in the city overlooking the James River. There's something for everyone here—a Children's Farm, wildlife exhibits, exquisite gardens, a 33-room house museum, a carriage collection, nature center, and a collection of exotic trees. Don't think you can do it justice in one day. The animal experiences are detailed in the "Kidstuff" chapter, and the house tour gets attention below in the Historic Houses section. Then there are the gardens and grounds. Every season makes for a worthwhile visit here, but there's something about spring in Maymont that is a must-do.

In 1886 Major and Mrs. James H. Dooley bought a former dairy farm overlooking the James and, with meticulous attention and a lot of money, created magnificent gardens and a stunning arboretum out of fields and pastures. Entering from the Hampton Street entrance makes the most sense. Sallie Dooley liked to get her hands dirty, planting rosebushes herself, but she also had 20 groundskeepers and several landscape designers at her beck and call. It shows. The Italian Garden features a beautiful wisteria-covered pergola, geometrically arranged flower beds, and massive stone stairs with a water feature. Views of gazebos and statues only add to the otherworldly feel here. Going down stairs eventually brings you into another world, just as beautiful, but in a completely different way, in the Japanese Garden. Stepping stones over the fishpond, bridges, pathways, and a grotto all lend a calming air down here, even with the gushing waterfall. You'll want to be here when the azaleas are blooming. Maymont has other, smaller gardens, including a Cactus Garden not far from the Japanese Garden and an herb garden near the Hampton Street entrance. Closer to the Children's Barn is a Daylily and Daffodil Garden with 150 varieties of the former and 55 of the latter, blooming from Apr through Sept, and a Butterfly Garden, so it's likely you'll find something blossoming. And if not, the trees at Maymont are worth a visit themselves in any season, as tree lovers of all ages attest. Besides thousands of trees native to Virginia here, the Dooleys planted more than 200 exotic species of trees; some, such as a blue atlas cedar and Persian ironwood, are exotic champions. Special events—for instance, full-moon hikes and Herbs Galore—are regularly offered at Maymont. See more in the "Annual Events" chapter. There is no admission fee to visit the grounds and garden, which are open 10 a.m. to 5 p.m. daily, though donations are appreciated.

i If you can't get out to Maymont or Hollywood Cemetery at the moment, take a look at Nancy Ross Hugo and Jeff Kirwan's gorgeous book, *Remarkable Trees of Virginia*. An astounding tulip poplar from Maymont gets the cover shot, and a black gum tree in all its autumnal glory spreads over two pages inside. Several magnificent trees throughout the region are given their due, and you'll want to get up close and personal with every one once you get the chance.

METRO RICHMOND ZOO $$$
8300 Beaver Bridge Rd.
(804) 739-5666
www.metrorichmondzoo.com
This is not like other big city zoos. First of all, it's out in the country in Chesterfield County, and it has a bit of a county-fair feel with some kiddie rides. But with 1,500 animals—more than 150 species, including orangutans, Bengal tigers, tapirs, rhinos, and cheetahs—and the unusual opportunity to feed giraffes, you'll be glad it's unique. See the animals from the sky on the Safari Sky Ride, watch the African penguins get fed, and ask the keeper questions afterwards. The budgie aviary gives the adorable birds a chance to check out us, perhaps while they're perching on a shoulder or head. A Safari Train ride into the African savanna gives you a guided tour while giving your legs a rest. The zoo is open Mon through Sat year-round, except on Thanksgiving, Christmas Eve, Christmas, and New Year's Day. Parking is free, but the rides are $2 to $3 extra. Admission is free for those under the age of two.

RICHMOND NATIONAL
BATTLEFIELD PARK FREE
Numerous sites
(804) 771-2145
www.nps.gov/rich
The Civil War battles for Richmond that are the raison d'être of this sprawling battlefield park were fought over the course of three years in two major campaigns, the 1862 Peninsula Campaign led by George McClellan and the 1864 Overland Campaign led by Ulysses S. Grant. The number of historic sites involved is mind-boggling, but here's a clue: Driving to every site within Richmond National Battlefield Park will put 80 miles on your odometer. Because of the time commitment involved, most visitors pick and choose among the park's 12 sites. The best bet is to start your visit at the Battlefield Park's Civil War Visitor Center at 470 Tredegar St. downtown—which is open every day but Thanksgiving, Christmas, and New Year's Day—and

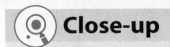

Close-up

Monument Avenue

Nothing more than a tobacco field even after Robert E. Lee's statue was erected in 1890, and now included on the National Register of Historic Places, this stately avenue was designated one of the 10 great streets in America by the American Planning Association in 2007. The street is on a perfect lateral axis with the State Capitol; that was some good planning, though of course its name changes to Franklin after you pass ole J. E. B. Stuart going east.

I think the statues get too much of the credit for the grandeur of the street. The 40-foot-wide, tree-lined median and the 36-foot-wide streets on either side, with 10-foot-wide sidewalks lined by an impressive inventory of late 19th- and early-20th-century architecture entice people to spend time here, returning every year for the famous 10K race or the Easter on Parade event, or coming more often for neighborly jogs and dog-walking. The architecture is an amazing collection of styles, including Colonial Revival, Craftsman, Classical Revival, Mediterranean, Romanesque, and Tudor Revival, so it's impossible to be bored while you're walking along here. It's a good thing it's not against the law to drool while driving, because it's hard not to when you see these gorgeous homes, one after another.

And then there are those six statues, of Robert E. Lee, Stonewall Jackson, J. E. B. Stuart, Jefferson Davis, Matthew Fontaine Maury, and Arthur Ashe. What started as a way to memorialize the Confederate past while jump-starting development to the west of town in the late 19th and early 20th centuries took on a life of its own, mythologizing the Lost Cause. For the record, the vast majority of people in and around Richmond do not venerate those dead Confederate guys. We mostly joke about them or ignore them, along with the NO LEFT TURN signs at some of the street's intersections. It is no joke that they represent a painful past that Richmond and the rest of the country are still coming to grips with. They do add focal points and drama to the avenue, and sometimes even a protest or two.

In 1968 Helen Marie Taylor took a stand against a paving machine that would have covered the original Belgian blocks on the road. She jump-started the movement to preserve and protect the avenue's unique character. In the 1990s a controversy erupted when plans went forth to add to Monument Avenue a statue of Arthur Ashe, a Richmond native, tennis champion, international human rights activist, and writer who died in 1993. Some objected to putting anyone other than a Confederate hero on the avenue. Others thought Ashe deserved a place not tainted by the cult of Confederate past. Still others wanted a statue of Ashe there, just not the statue that was proposed and in 1996 erected on Monument Avenue, facing west. He fits in just fine now, though there is some concern that the statue looks like he is about to whack a child with his tennis racket.

has exhibits, maps, and park rangers who will steer you right. Find more about that site in the "Museums and Art Galleries" chapter.

The second tip is to go to Cold Harbor National Battlefield in Hanover County next.

A park ranger is on duty at the visitor center there every day but those three major holidays, and there's a 1½-mile driving tour and a 1¼-mile walking tour with markers along the way to make the trip more meaningful.

It's also close to the Gaines' Mill site for a two-attractions-for-one-trip deal. Of course, you'll need a map of the campaigns and sites, which is available at any of the park visitor centers.

Once you've decided which sites to drive to, understand that to really see what you want to see, you will need to get out and walk. Some sites do have driving tours, but others, such as Drewry's Bluff, can only be seen and appreciated by walking a ways into the woods on a path that isn't exactly wheelchair friendly. There is no charge at any of the battlefield park sites. More information about local sites will appear in the "Commemorating the Civil War and Emancipation" chapter.

ST. JOHN'S CHURCH   FREE–$$
2401 E. Broad St.
(804) 648-5015
www.historicstjohnschurch.org
Famous not for any sermon preached here but for Patrick Henry's trailblazing oratory during the Second Virginia Convention in March 1775, St. John's role in the American Revolution is remembered every day here atop Church Hill. If you'd like a tour, purchase tickets at the visitor center at the rear of the property. Thirty-minute guided tours, beginning on the hour and half hour, explain the history of the church and put the events that transpired here in the context of our nation's history. There's more history here than that momentous occasion, though, and the graveyard yields hint of that. Remembering is one thing, reenacting quite another. If you can, attend one of the free public reenactments held every Sun afternoon from Memorial Day weekend through Labor Day weekend and on the Sun in March closest

to March 23, the date of the original speech. Tickets are distributed at the front door starting at 1 p.m., an hour before the historical drama begins, and you can take a seat at 1:15 p.m. The church does fill up, so don't dally. Patriotic music played on a rare Adam Stein organ will entertain you while you wait for Patrick Henry and his illustrious contemporaries to arrive and animate American history right before your eyes.

Tours are available Mon through Sun, though not on several holidays. Of course, because the church is an active Episcopal parish, tours might be unavailable because of weddings, funerals, etc.

VIRGINIA WAR MEMORIAL   FREE
621 S. Belvidere St.
(804) 786-2060
www.vawarmemorial.org
Most people in Richmond have driven past this moving memorial to Virginians who have died in battle that commands a hill near the James River. Engraved on walls of stone and glass are the more than 11,000 names of Virginians who made the ultimate sacrifice. It's a solemn and sobering place, with the haunting 23-foot-high statue, Memory, standing by. Inside, touch-screen computers help people access information about thousands of Virginia veterans, and artifacts and exhibits about Virginians' roles in various wars are on display. The Paul and Phyllis Galanti Education Center, opened in mid-2010, is an 18,000-square-foot addition that includes exhibit space, visitor services, and an 850-seat amphitheater. Special programs of remembrance are held on Veterans Day and Memorial Day. The memorial is open every day, and free parking is available.

HISTORIC HOUSES

AGECROFT HALL $$
4305 Sulgrave Rd.
(804) 353-4241
www.agecrofthall.com

Agecroft Hall is a 15th-century Tudor manor house that now sits above the James River here in a posh neighborhood in Richmond's West End. How did that happen? It was dismantled and shipped here from England in 1926 because T. C. Williams wanted it as a centerpiece to his English village neighborhood, Windsor Farms. Rebuilt as a modern home, this house features exquisite wood carvings and gorgeous leaded-glass windows that survived the trip. The period artifacts that adorn the house add to the sense of time travel. Special events include concerts, puppet shows, teas, holiday activities, and the ever-popular Richmond Shakespeare Festival, which performs two plays every summer outside in Agecroft's courtyard. The gardens are always worth wandering about. The Elizabethan Knot is a wonder. It's a magical place for anyone, but children especially love inhabiting another world. See more about Agecroft in the "Kidstuff" chapter. Admission is free for those under age six. Agecroft is closed on Mon and national holidays.

EXECUTIVE MANSION   FREE
Capitol Square
(804) 371-8687
www.executivemansion.virginia.gov

Built during the War of 1812, this classic Federal-style home is the oldest governor's mansion still used as such. As originally designed by Alexander Parris, who also designed Wickham House, the house had only four rooms on the first floor. Extensive additions and renovations have taken place

over the years, of course. As the home, office, and entertaining headquarters for governors, this place has been witness to history. Stonewall Jackson, Arthur Ashe, and Oliver Hill have lain in state in the mansion. Generals Lee and Grant both visited, but under different circumstances and on different days, you can be sure. Winston Churchill slept here, and Queen Elizabeth II visited, too. Free 25-minute tours are available on a first-come, first-served basis a few days a week, but check the Web site to get updated information. Groups of 10 or more may call to schedule tours in advance. Special events, such as an open house the day after gubernatorial inaugurations and the first weekend in Dec are well-attended, since the governor sometimes greets visitors.

JOHN MARSHALL HOUSE
AND GARDEN $$
818 E. Marshall St.
(804) 648-7998
www.preservationvirginia.org/marshall

Built in 1790 by John Marshall, who became the third chief justice of the U.S. Supreme Court and lived here until his death in 1835, this Federal-style house contains many of his family's original possessions, including the gown he wore as chief justice. Besides his remarkable and crucial tenure on the Supreme Court, Marshall fought in the American Revolution, studied law at William & Mary, served on city council and in the legislature in Richmond, was minister to France, congressman, secretary of state, and presided over Aaron Burr's treason trial right here in Richmond. Then he served as chief justice for 34 years. He did it all while having a fulfilling marriage to his dear Polly, who bore 10 children, 6 of whom survived to adulthood.

The house hosts many special events, such as reenactments of inaugurations (because Marshall presided over nine presidential ones) and discussions of his practice and philosophy of jurisprudence. On a lighter note, it has programs on colonial dancing and gardening, and of course is a part of Court End's holiday open house in Dec. The house is open Wed through Sun, Feb through Oct, and by appointment in Dec and Jan. The Court End Passport, at $10 for an adult and $7 for children and seniors, is good for an entire year at four nearby historic sites.

MAGGIE L. WALKER NATIONAL
   HISTORIC SITE   FREE
600 N. 2nd St.
(804) 771-2017
www.nps.gov/mawa

The symbolic centerpiece of this site is the impressive home of the even more impressive woman Maggie L. Walker. She was the grand secretary of the Order of St. Luke, an influential fraternal organization dedicated to helping African Americans improve their economic standing in the age of Jim Crow. She went on to cofound the local chapter of the NAACP and charter a bank. This National Park Service site highlights the work and accomplishments of this Richmond native, the daughter of a slave who never let being a black woman in the segregated South slow her down. Though her 28-room mansion is on Leigh Street, you begin the visit at the park's visitors center on 2nd Street by watching the orientation film that puts her life's work in the context of American history. Then the guided tour walks you through her life story, from poverty to powerful citizen, businesswoman, and banker—the first African-American woman to charter a bank.

Then it's on to her home, which is furnished as it was in 1930. This site is open Mon through Sat.

MAYMONT MANSION $
1700 Hampton St.
(804) 358-7166
www.maymont.org

This 33-room Gilded Age home of Major James and Sallie May Dooley, on the lovely grounds of Maymont, can be toured year-round. The public rooms of the house feature exotic and over-the-top intricate ornamentation and are very much as they were when the Dooleys lived here. The Dooleys were millionaires and noted collectors, so there's something to see everywhere you look. As the tour of the upper two floors is guided, surely the enormous Tiffany window will be pointed out to you, as will the famous swan bedroom-furniture set. Downstairs, in the servants' area, eight rooms with displays interpret the nonstop action of the life of the servants, shedding light on the humanity of those downstairs and how the grand life upstairs was possible. Special teas and tours are offered on occasion. The suggested donation for the basic tour is $5. The mansion is closed on Mon.

SCOTCHTOWN $$
16120 Chiswell Lane, Beaverdam
(804) 227-3500
www.preservationvirginia.org/
   scotchtown

Like the John Marshall House in Richmond, Patrick Henry's home in Hanover County is owned and operated by Preservation Virginia. What stands at Scotchtown now was built by the Chiswell family, who owned the land and erected a house sometime in the mid-18th century. The house changed hands several times before and after Henry's family lived here for about seven years around the time of the Revolutionary War. Patrick Henry's first wife, Sarah, was ill and died here. He rode to St. John's Church for his most famous speech in Richmond from here, but once he was elected governor, he moved his family to Williamsburg and sold the house. Built in the 18th century, the house is interpreted as the Henry home with period furniture and artifacts. Especially interesting is the basement, which housed the dairy, wine cellar, slave quarters, and the bedroom where Sarah was confined and cared for until her death. The house is open Fri through Sun, Mar through Dec.

TUCKAHOE PLANTATION $–$$
12601 River Rd.
(804) 784-5736
www.tuckahoeplantation.com
The grounds of Tuckahoe Plantation, built by the prominent Randolph family between 1733 and 1740, are open daily from 9 a.m. to 5 p.m. for a self-guided tour. Now it could well be that we owe everything Thomas Jefferson ever did to the seven years he lived with his family at Tuckahoe, since his schooling began in the schoolhouse that still stands here. Special events are held throughout the year, including a guided spring garden tour, house and grounds tours during Virginia Garden Week, a peony sale before Mother's Day, and a Christmas candlelight open house. As it is privately owned, the house is open for guided tours by appointment only. A $5 donation is suggested for the self-guided grounds tour. An honor box is near the gate.

VIRGINIA HOUSE $
4301 Sulgrave Rd.
(804) 353-4251
www.vahistorical.org

Alexander Weddell, a U.S. diplomat, and his wife, Virginia, purchased the 15th-century Priory of Warwick at a demolition sale in England in the 1920s and had it dismantled and shipped here. The priory pieces were used to build Virginia House, a modern yet ancient-looking home on rolling land that leads down to the James River. The Weddells' hope was that it would one day be the home of the Virginia Historical Society, so some of the home's rooms, a gallery, and library seem like spaces in a public building. The gardens, designed by Charles Gillette, are spectacular in the spring. The house is open by appointment only.

WHITE HOUSE OF
THE CONFEDERACY $$
1201 E. Clay St.
(804) 649-1861
www.moc.org
A tour of this house, originally called the Brockenbrough house, a Neoclassical standout, can be included with admission to the adjacent Museum of the Confederacy with a combination ticket. Built in 1818 and attributed to Robert Mills, this house became the home of Jefferson Davis's family from August 1861 to March 1865 while he served as president of the Confederate States of America, and it is furnished as it was during that time period. Davis often used it as his headquarters and office, so many meetings and state visits took place here. President Lincoln toured the house after the fall of Richmond. Admission varies depending on whether visitors tour the house and the Museum of the Confederacy. The best deal is to buy the Civil War pass for $15; then you get admission to the house, museum, and the American Civil War Center at Tredegar. The house is closed in Jan.

WICKHAM HOUSE $$
1015 E. Clay St.
(804) 649-0711
www.richmondhistorycenter.com

Part of Valentine Richmond History Center, this neoclassical masterpiece was built in 1812, and a tour of it is included with Valentine admission. Three floors of the palatial place are open to visitors, with a self-guided tour of the basement slaves' quarters. As many as 15 slaves worked for the Wickham family here, but most of them would have lived above the carriage house or other outbuildings on their property. They had plenty to do, as John and Elizabeth Wickham had 19 children between them. Maybe the house wasn't so big after all. This home was for grand entertaining, and no guest would have doubted for a moment that the Wickhams were in the top echelon of society. Find more on this house in the "Architecture" chapter.

WILTON HOUSE $$
215 S. Wilton Rd.
(804) 282-5936
www.wiltonhousemuseum.org

Being at Wilton is a bit like being a time traveler. Visitors travel through time in an 18th-century house that traveled from its original setting east of Richmond to this tranquil setting in a West End Richmond neighborhood in the 20th century. Confused? Then you should visit Wilton to make sense of it all. It is a beautiful example of Georgian architecture, but keep telling yourself that all of the events that transpired within the walls—including George Washington staying here after hearing Patrick Henry's famous "Give me liberty" speech and a visit from Marquis de Lafayette—didn't actually happen *here*. The house was moved to its current site in 1934 by the preservation-minded Colonial Dames to save it from being overrun by industrialization east of town. Now the house is furnished according to an 1815 survey and is stocked with fine silver, ceramic, textiles, and period furniture. The floor-to-ceiling paneling is especially noteworthy. Costumed tour guides bring the past to life, including discussing how the 2,000-acre plantation was worked by 100 slaves.

Special events here include indoor and outdoor concerts, Halloween and Christmas time to-dos, and lectures. Upcoming exhibits will include *Death Comes to Wilton* and the popular dollhouse and miniature decorative arts exhibit. Non-reserved tours are available Tues through Fri in the afternoon, with additional hours on Sat and Sun.

COMMEMORATING THE
CIVIL WAR AND EMANCIPATION

With the 150th anniversary of the Civil War and Emancipation upon us, I fear that many people remember that Richmond was the capital of the Confederacy and think that sums up Richmond—then and now. Well, shoot—pardon the pun—but somewhere between ignorance and mythology lies a mature understanding of what the years and legacies of the Civil War mean to our nation and to our city, one that includes all sides of the complex and continuing story. In the 1860s it wasn't as simple as North and South, black and white, and it still isn't. In April 1861 the Virginia Secession Convention held in Richmond first voted *against* secession, but flip-flopped after Fort Sumter and then voted to secede. After Stonewall Jackson's death, his body lay in state before grieving crowds in the Executive Mansion. The next beloved Virginian to get that treatment was Arthur Ashe Jr. upon his death in 1993. Statues of both men stand on Monument Avenue now.

If Richmond had a middle name, it would be Contradiction. At the top of Church Hill, Patrick Henry gave his famous "Give me liberty or give me death" speech in a city where the slave trade powered the economy down the hill in Shockoe Bottom. Twenty-five years after Henry's rallying cry for freedom, a slave named Gabriel was executed near East Broad Street for daring to fight for his and other slaves' liberty as leader of a foiled slave rebellion.

The sesquicentennial of the Civil War, 2011–15, presents Richmond with an important opportunity. Earlier commemorations idolized Confederate warriors and white survivors of the Confederacy while ignoring every other perspective, especially that of the black citizenry still scarred by slavery and Jim Crow policies. That was then. Now it's Richmond's chance to be an example of how to tell the whole truth, incorporating a sometimes painful past and Richmond's robust African-American history into the story of our city and nation.

Richmond is well suited to the task, finally. As if Richmond's iron-making capacity didn't make Richmond enough of a target, becoming the Confederate capital made the city the object of Union assaults for four years, which explains why one quarter of Civil War battles were fought within a 75-mile radius of the Richmond-Petersburg region and 60 percent of the war's casualties occurred here as well. As an important player in colonial and Revolutionary history, the center of the East Coast slave trade, capital of Virginia and the Confederacy, and much later, the site where the first elected African-American governor in the U.S. was sworn in to office, Richmond should be considered hallowed ground by all Americans, for many, often conflicting, reasons.

OVERVIEW

This time around, Richmond is poised to make the multiyear commemoration of the 150th anniversary of the Civil War transformative by combining it with a commemoration of the end of slavery as well—to tell it whole and tell it true. It's an intuitive yet long-elusive link proposed by University of Richmond president and historian Edward L. Ayers, and it has people talking and engaged, which is exactly the point.

As the years come and go, expect to see special events and tie-ins emphasizing the twin sesquicentennials at numerous sites all over the region. There will be living-history events, lectures, guided tours, musical offerings, archaeology, panel discussions, and art exhibits, all designed to explore Richmond's role in the central and deadliest conflict in American history and its multifaceted reaction to emancipation.

DISPATCHES FROM THE FIELD

ON TO RICHMOND
www.ontorichmond.com

"On to Richmond" was the clarion call of Union newspapers during the Civil War. If Richmond, capital of the Confederacy and manufacturing headquarters for the South, fell, the war would be over. One hundred and fifty years later, this Yankee yell has been appropriated by the Richmond Metropolitan Convention and Visitors Bureau (www.visitrichmondva.com), in collaboration with Petersburg Regional Tourism (www.petersburgarea.org) and the Virginia Sesquicentennial Commission, as they work to bring tourists to the area for the 150th anniversary of the Civil War.

This comprehensive Web site gathers information about the region's vast store of museums, battlefields, trails, cemeteries, and historic sites in one place. Itineraries—focusing on battlefields and commanders, slavery and freedom, evacuation and fire, prisoners and spies—are featured, but feel free to mix and match.

THE FUTURE OF RICHMOND'S PAST
(804) 289-8002
www.futureofrichmondspast.org

This collaboration among Virginia Commonwealth University, Virginia Union University, and the University of Richmond is a local outgrowth of the Virginia Sesquicentennial Commission's first signature conference, held at the University of Richmond in 2009 and chaired by University of Richmond president and Civil War historian Edward L. Ayers. By giving equal billing to the Civil War and the end of slavery in the U.S. in its approach to the anniversary, this group has facilitated community conversations about race, memory, and history in hopes of a richer, brighter future. It's an inspired pairing that ensures this latest commemoration of the Civil War is vastly different from previous ones—including anyone who's interested and perhaps interesting those who thought they weren't. Check the Web site for upcoming events and discussions.

i For the Civil War aficionado, Owens & Ramsey is a hidden gem tucked in the back of a shopping center at 2728 Tinsley Dr. in Bon Air. Stocking 5,000 titles in an old-timey shop and doing a serious mail-order business, these people are experts. They also offer guided tours of Richmond area Civil War history. Call (804) 272-8888 or check www.owensandramsey.com for details.

VIRGINIA CIVIL WAR TRAILS
www.civilwartraveler.com

If you've driven in Virginia or several other states, you've seen the red, white, and blue Civil War Trails signs that point people in the direction of well-known and obscure Civil War sites. Richmond has more than 60 Civil War Trails signs, one-sixth of Virginia's. Maps showing the trails are available at the Richmond National Battlefield Park Civil War Visitor Center. The relevant trails here are the 1862 Peninsula Campaign; Lee vs. Grant: The 1864 Campaign; and Lee's Retreat: The Final Campaigns. The Web site has excellent resources, including maps and walking tour podcasts.

ℹ️ *Rappahannock County,* a multimedia musical based on actual Civil War-era diaries, letters, and accounts, has been commissioned by University of Richmond's Modlin Center, the Virginia Arts Festival, and the Virginia Opera. The Ricky Ian Gordon-composed song cycle, with libretto by Mark Campbell, features five principal singers performing 30 roles—slaves, plantation owners, soldiers, and survivors—as the work explores the war and its impact on one Virginia community. It opens in Norfolk for the Virginia Arts Festival in April 2011 and continues in Richmond in September 2011, before heading to the Texas Performing Arts Center in Austin.

VIRGINIA SESQUICENTENNIAL COMMISSION
www.virginiacivilwar.org

Set up by the General Assembly to coordinate and sponsor events throughout the state and support local commissions, the Virginia Sesquicentennial Commission produces annual conferences—the first, in 2009, was "America on the Eve of the Civil War" at the University of Richmond. The second, "Race, Slavery and the Civil War: The Tough Stuff of American History and Memory," is set for Sept 24, 2010, at Norfolk State University. Unlike previous glorifying remembrances of the war, these conferences are wide-ranging and inclusive and won't shy away from the painful and complicated past. A different Virginia university hosts the yearly academic conference (which is open to the public), streaming it live online and providing the fascinating content on the Web forever. A law school symposium coinciding with the 2013 anniversary of the Emancipation Proclamation will delve into the legacies of the 13th, 14th, and 15th Amendments to the Constitution.

ℹ️ The Richmond Civil War Pass allows entry to three sites crucial to visitors' understanding of the Civil War. For $15, the pass allows entry to the American Civil War Center at Historic Tredegar, the Museum of the Confederacy, and the National Park Service's Richmond National Battlefield Visitor Center at Tredegar. The pass is available at all three sites.

THE BIG GUNS

Any look at the Civil War and its aftermath here begins with these essential Richmond museums and Richmond and Petersburg National Battlefields. See even more about the Richmond entries in the "Museums" and "Attractions" chapters.

AMERICAN CIVIL WAR CENTER AT HISTORIC TREDEGAR
500 Tredegar St.
(804) 780-1865
www.tredegar.org

Chronology of Conflict

Here's an abbreviated list of important Civil War dates in Richmond history:

1861

Apr 4: Virginia Secession Convention votes against secession at the State Capitol.

Apr 12: Shots are fired at Fort Sumter, S.C.; the Civil War begins.

Apr 17: Virginia Secession Convention passes the Ordinance of Secession.

Apr 23: Robert E. Lee accepts command of Virginia military forces in the State Capitol.

May 20: Richmond is made the capital of the Confederacy.

May 29: Jefferson Davis arrives in Richmond and takes up residence in Court End.

Oct 17: Chimborazo Hospital opens on Church Hill.

1862

May 15: The Union's *Monitor* is outgunned by the Confederate sailors at Drewry's Bluff.

June 1: Robert E. Lee takes command of the Army of Northern Virginia.

June 25: Seven Days' Battles begin, involving sites such as Gaines' Mill and Malvern Hill.

1863

Jan 1: Lincoln issues the Emancipation Proclamation.

Apr 1: Women riot downtown for bread, stopping only when Jefferson Davis himself threatens to have soldiers fire on them.

Summer: Slave labor and troops continue work on earthwork defenses around Richmond.

1864

Feb 9: 109 Union prisoners escape rat-infested Libby Prison via a 60-foot-long tunnel they had dug.

May 5: The Overland Campaign begins as Union troops land at Bermuda Hundred.

May 31–June 12: Battle of Cold Harbor finally ends. Grant heads toward Petersburg.

June 18: Siege of Petersburg begins, the longest in American history.

1865

Apr 1: Five Forks Battle is waged southwest of Petersburg.

Apr 2: Lee and his troops withdraw from Petersburg and Richmond.

Apr 2–3: Richmond falls. Departing Confederate troops burn munitions, and the evacuation fire burns out of control.

Apr 3: Union troops enter the city and take control of the fire and mobs.

Apr 4: President Lincoln visits Richmond.

Apr 9: Lee surrenders at Appomattox Courthouse.

Apr 14: Lincoln is assassinated in Ford's Theatre in Washington, D.C., and dies the next day.

Apr 26: The Civil War ends.

Dec 6: 13th Amendment abolishing slavery is ratified.

Housed in the 1861 Tredegar Gun Foundry, this museum is dedicated to the idea that the Civil War must be studied from all sides—Union, Confederate, and African-American. Its main, multifaceted exhibit, In the Cause of Liberty, echoes Pulitzer Prize–winning historian James McPherson's comment at a center-sponsored symposium that "the central tragedy, the great irony of the war, is that all three groups were fighting for the legacy of the American Revolution, but they profoundly disagreed about what that legacy was." Much in this interactive museum will challenge your expectations and enliven your understanding of an era that affects our country still. It wasn't so simplistic as South vs. North. Watch the film *1863: The War Comes Home* about the New York City race riot if you doubt that. If you can't make it to the museum or if you want to learn more, check out the Tredegar Digital Dispatches section of the museum's Web site for access to more than two dozen podcasts about artifacts in the collection and personal recollections of actual events, again from every perspective. Starting in spring 2011, the American Civil War Center will mesh more closely with Richmond National Battlefield Park at Tredegar by combining ticketing, the visitor center, and the gift shop next door in the Pattern Building. Notwithstanding the changes, this will remain a separate museum that charges admission, but a Civil War Pass provides free parking for visitors to both museums as well as entrance to the Museum of the Confederacy.

BLACK HISTORY MUSEUM AND CULTURAL CENTER OF VIRGINIA
00 Clay St.
(804) 780-9093
www.blackhistorymuseum.org

A visit here is essential to begin to understand the obstacles black Richmonders had to overcome after Emancipation and to appreciate their achievements in a world that still didn't offer equality. Permanent exhibits shed light on the post–Civil War black experience in Richmond, including the rich cultural heritage of Jackson Ward, and traveling exhibits explore the rocky road to freedom. Admission is charged, but a Court End Passport can save you money.

MAGGIE L. WALKER NATIONAL HISTORIC SITE
600 N. 2nd St.
(804) 771-2017
www.nps.gov/mawa

Born a slave, Maggie L. Walker overcame poverty and personal tragedy to be one of the most successful businesswomen and community leaders of her time, founding a bank and the local chapter of the NAACP, among other accomplishments. A visit to her 28-room mansion and the park's visitor center will put her startling achievements in the segregated South in perspective. A powerful presence in Richmond, she once loaned the white-run city money so the schools could remain open. Find out more about this remarkable woman here Mon through Sat. Admission is free. See more about this site in the "Attractions" chapter under Historic Houses.

MUSEUM AND WHITE HOUSE OF THE CONFEDERACY
1201 E. Clay St.
(804) 649-1861
www.moc.org

This isn't your grandfather's Museum of the Confederacy. Though certainly a destination for Rebel flag-wavers, as the repository of the most comprehensive collection of artifacts related to the Confederate States, the museum provides crucial pieces of information about what happened all over the U.S. and within Virginia. Three floors of exhibits include The Confederate Years, Between the Battles—a look at camp and home life—and The Confederacy in Virginia, among others. Tours of the adjacent home that served as Jefferson Davis's home and office during the war are also available. The museum's Web site has several educational videos, including subjects as varied as the making of an ironclad, amputations in the war, and servants and slaves in the White House. There's even a recipe for hardtack there. MOC is building a satellite at Appomattox, due to be completed in 2011. Parking is free at the VCU Medical Center Visitor Deck with ticket validation. The museum is open seven days a week, and there is an admission fee, but getting the Civil War Pass saves money.

PETERSBURG NATIONAL BATTLEFIELD
5001 Siege Rd.
(804) 732-3531
www.nps.gov/pete

Grant said, "The key to taking Richmond is Petersburg," which is why a visit here, at the Eastern Front Visitor Center, one of four National Park Service Petersburg Battlefield sites, is a must. Once you get oriented at the visitor center, take the 4-mile driving tour with several stops along the way. This site, which features miles of trails for hiking, biking, and horseback riding, tells the story of the nearby battles, including the famous Battle of the Crater, which occurred right here, and the brutal 9½-month siege of Petersburg that began in June 1864 once Grant's forces were stymied. It's a horrific tale, and I'll let the park do the talking.

Pamplin Historical Park & the National Museum of the Civil War Soldier

If you're willing to go farther afield to Dinwiddie County, visit the 422-acre National Historic Landmark, Pamplin Historical Park & the National Museum of the Civil War Soldier. Its combination of four high-tech museums, four antebellum homes, and living history will keep you busy for hours. Every April, the park holds an annual Breakthrough Tour, a guided walking tour that covers the Union Army's attack route that led to the fall of Petersburg and then Richmond. The tour begins in the predawn hours and is followed by breakfast. Registration is required, and there's a fee. For more information call (804) 861-2408 or visit www.pamplinpark.org.

After you've explored this site, consider a trip to City Point in Hopewell, where the James and Appomattox Rivers meet, and where Grant's headquarters and the Union supply base for troops fighting around Richmond and Petersburg were. City Point has a ranger on duty every day but Thanksgiving, Christmas, and New Year's. Five Forks Battlefield, the Western Front Visitor Contact Station at Poplar Grove Cemetery, and City Point do not charge admission fees. The Eastern Front Visitor Center charges $5 per car or $3 for individuals. The pass is good for one week.

ℹ️ After a visit to the Petersburg National Battlefield Visitor Center, take a trip into downtown Petersburg to see nearby Old Blandford Church at 111 Rochelle Lane. It became a Confederate Memorial Chapel in the early 20th century and features 15 Tiffany windows. Admission is charged. See www.petersburg-va.org/tourism for hours of operation.

RICHMOND NATIONAL BATTLEFIELD PARK VISITOR CENTER AT TREDEGAR
470 Tredegar St.
(804) 771-2145
www.nps.gov/rich

Visiting this site, devoted to Richmond's part in the Civil War saga, provides an excellent introduction to the scope of Richmond's involvement. Rangers can help you plan a tour of the battlefield park that encompasses 12 sites and an 80-mile drive. No matter how much or how little you explore, hardship and heartache is close to the bone here, but an amazing resiliency is evident, too. The moving multimedia exhibit Richmond Speaks, which chronicles life in Richmond during the war, will share the top floor with the orientation film as of spring 2011, while the second floor is devoted to orienting visitors to the numerous battlefield sites and educating them about the Peninsula and Overland Campaigns that had Richmond as their goal.

For a fuller experience, try to venture out to some of the other sites. Cold Harbor Battlefield has a staffed visitor center with an excellent electronic map and trails that lead to interpretive signs in fields and through woods. The first weekend in June Cold Harbor stages a living-history event with artillery fire, reenactors, and a popular candlelight tour.

Chimborazo Medical Museum on Church Hill tells the story of the largest Confederate hospital, which served 76,000 poor souls. South of downtown is Drewry's Bluff, the site of the Confederate Naval Academy and a great battlefield site for children, with wooded paths, earthworks (not to be climbed on, though), a cannon, and an impressive overlook of the James River. Some sites and Civil War Trail stops are so out of the way you'll swear you're lost before you come upon them. Imagine how difficult it would have been to transport men, horses, mules, cannon, etc., through thick woods, swamps, and dirt roads at best.

This visitor center is joining forces with the American Civil War Center to open a joint visitor center and gift shop on the first floor of the Pattern building. There are no entrance fees to Richmond National Battlefield Park sites. However, there is a parking fee for the American Civil War Center at Tredegar Iron Works. Free parking is available nearby. Park battlefields are open sunrise to sunset. The park is closed on Thanksgiving, Chirstmas, and New Year's Day.

ℹ️ Through a collaboration between Richmond and Petersburg National Battlefields and Civil War Traveler, podcasts of battlefield tours are available at the latter's Web site, www.civilwartraveler.com. Download them in advance of your trip and you can wander all over the park with a knowledgeable park ranger in your ear. Topics include a seven-stop tour of Lincoln's Apr 4, 1865, visit to Richmond, the Battle of the Crater, and Cold Harbor.

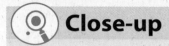 **Close-up**

Richmond Slave Trail

Manchester Docks/Ancarrow's Landing
Maury Street to Brander Street
(804) 646-8911 or (804) 698-1070
www.library.vcu.edu/jbc/speccoll/slavery/

Richmond has been slow to identify, care for, interpret, and publicize elements of its horrific slave-trade past—out of ignorance, shame, and lack of funds and/or interest—but that's changing, due mostly to the work of Richmond's Slave Trail Commission, the Alliance to Conserve Old Neighborhoods, the Elegba Folklore Society, and the James River Park System's care of the **Richmond Slave Trail.** Interpretive signs are being added along the trail, which begins on the south side of the James at **Manchester Docks** near **Ancarrow's Landing,** where slaves once arrived from Africa and later departed for the Deep South. The trail, which takes two to three hours round-trip, retraces the slaves' sad steps as they walked, chained together—under cover of night to spare the white population any discomfort—across the Mayo Bridge. There in Shockoe Bottom they were penned in ghastly slave jails and warehouses, treated worse than animals, and eventually auctioned off. Walking the trail is an educational and emotionally draining way to begin to comprehend how insidiously intertwined the slave trade is in Richmond's history. It's worth pondering that the ominous phrase "sold down the river" refers to the James, because once slaves were auctioned in Richmond, they were bound for the Deep South, farther from family and freedom.

Though Virginia banned the import of slaves from Africa in 1778, slavery continued unabated. Since the heavy work of settling Virginia was done by then, the state had an excess of slaves. The states to the south and west had the demand, so Richmond became the hub of an immoral economic engine and supplied that demand for the

i Hollywood Cemetery has long been a Civil War pilgrimage stop—and justly so with more than 18,000 soldiers buried here—but there are many more historic cemeteries here as well. Among them are Oakwood, Richmond National Battlefield Cemetery, Cold Harbor, City Point, and Poplar Grove, which is near Petersburg, where luminaries are lit in honor of Veterans Day every year.

IMPORTANT ENGAGEMENTS

Here's a sampling of upcoming exhibitions related to the Civil War era. Expect many

museums and sites, including the Black History Museum and Cultural Center of Virginia, Maggie L. Walker National Historic Site, historic churches, and everybody's uncle to mount sesquicentennial events and exhibits as the years go on.

UNIVERSITY OF RICHMOND MUSEUMS
(804) 289-8276
www.museums.richmond.edu
The Joel and Lila Harnett Museum of Art will host multiple sesquicentennial-related exhibits over the next few years. First up is Lincoln 1861-1865: A Print Series by Tomas

interstate slave trade. By 1820 Richmond was the leading exporter of surplus slaves. In the 1850s, as many as 10,000 slaves were sold here monthly.

There were dozens of slave dealers, auction houses, and jails in Shockoe Bottom between 15th and 19th Streets and from the river to Broad Street. Now, the only building in Richmond known to have been a slave auction house is at 15th and East Cary Streets. However, north of **Main Street Station,** under layers of earth and a parking lot, the site of a large slave jail complex has been discovered, **Lumpkin's Jail.** The notorious Devil's Half-Acre, as it was known, warehoused thousands of slaves in misery. Adding another layer of interest to the site is that after the war, Lumpkin's widow, a former slave, turned the site into a school for former slaves. That school was a forerunner of **Virginia Union University,** one of whose African-American graduates later became governor. There's a move afoot to fully excavate the site to preserve and interpret it, and to pay homage to those buried unceremoniously in the nearby **Negro Burial Grounds,** which is also paved over.

It's a moving experience, and when you stand at Main and 15th Streets to view the **Reconciliation Statue**—one of three identical statues placed here and in Benin, West Africa, and Liverpool, England—perhaps it can be a healing one. Just a few blocks up the hill, the first African-American elected governor in U.S. history, **L. Douglas Wilder Jr.,** a grandson of slaves, was sworn in on the steps of the Capitol in 1990. The **Slave Trail Commission** is moving forward with plans for a slavery museum in Shockoe Bottom, ground zero of the slave trade. Interpretive signs and sculptures that illuminate long-shrouded pieces of African-American and Richmond history are also along the **Canal Walk** and the **Virginia Capital Trail.** A slave-trail brochure with a map is available from the Slave Trail Commission and at the Web site above. If your schedule permits, call for a guided tour. They are offered on Sat during Feb, as part of the Juneteenth celebration by torchlight, and occasionally throughout the year by the Elegba Folklore Society *(www.efsinc.org)* and the James River Park System (804-646-8911).

Lasansky, Oct 3, 2010, to June 26, 2011. From Dec 11, 2010, to Mar 28, 2011, UR Museums, in collaboration with the Virginia Museum of Fine Art, will play host to First Hand: Civil War Drawings from the Becker Collection, approximately 60 drawings sketched by war reporters and artists. Avel de Knight's Drawings for Army Life in a Black Regiment, illustrations meant to accompany a book about the Union's first black unit, will appear in the Joel and Lila Harnett Print Study Center, Oct 11, 2011, to Apr 6, 2012.

THE VIRGINIA HISTORICAL SOCIETY
428 N. Blvd.
(804) 358-4901
www.vahistorical.org
Besides being the home of French mural artist Charles Hoffbauer's series Four Seasons of the Confederacy and the exhibit Arming the Confederacy, not to mention the wide-ranging Story of Virginia, the historical society will be the headquarters from Feb 4, 2011, to Dec 30 2011, of the Virginia Civil War Sesquicentennial Commission's huge exhibition An American Turning Point: The Civil

War in Virginia. Spread out over 3,000 square feet, showcasing more than 200 artifacts, and using a multimedia approach, the two-part exhibit will travel around Virginia once its run here is over. Part 1, Surviving War, illuminates the civilian and political sides of the war. In Waging War, soldiers' experiences take center stage. The point here isn't a dry recitation of battles and commanders. Heart-wrenching stories of bravery and bravado, service and sacrifice, bring to light little-known elements of the war, and make it easy for visitors to put themselves in the shoes of those who lived through or died during the four-year conflict.

VIRGINIA MUSEUM OF FINE ARTS
200 N. Blvd.
(804) 340-1400
www.vmfa.state.va.us
Dec 11, 2010, to Mar 28, 2011, the museum joins with the University of Richmond Museums to host First Hand: Civil War Drawings from the Becker Collection. Each site will showcase 60 drawings produced by Joseph Becker and other mid-19th-century artists/reporters who were on assignment, sometimes in Virginia, for Frank Leslie's *Illustrated Weekly*, giving eyewitness accounts of the war bothon the battlefield and in camp.

PARKS

There is no excuse for staying inside and vegetating when hundreds of parks in the Richmond area beckon with infinite possibilities for enjoyment. Recreation gets its due in the next chapter. Of course there will be some overlap, but this chapter provides an introduction to the region's main parks as well as the unique offerings at some lesser-known parks. Keep in mind that battlefield parks get attention in the "Commemorating the Civil War and Emancipation" chapter. Parks that function primarily as boating access to the James River have their day in the sun in the "A River Runs Through It" chapter. Some parks are the sites of major festivals, races, and concert series. Find more on those events in the "Annual Events" chapter.

With the exception of Pocahontas State Park and the National Battlefield Parks, the parks in our area fall under the jurisdiction of the local parks and recreation department. Regionalization hasn't caught on in this neck of the woods, so you'll have to check out each locality's Web site for more park information. This chapter starts at the state park level and works its way through City of Richmond parks, both north and south of the river and then to Henrico, Hanover, and Chesterfield Counties, and finally to the outlying counties of Goochland and Powhatan.

OVERVIEW

Richmond's first three parks were acquired in the 1850s. Since then the list has grown considerably, so that the Richmond Department of Parks, Recreation and Community Facilities oversees 169 parks, tot lots, playgrounds, and open spaces sprinkled throughout the city. With forested trails, ponds, dog parks, river access, and athletic opportunities, we haven't paved paradise in the city. The gem of this impressive collection is the **James River Park System,** a 550-acre oasis that stretches for miles along the banks of the James River in the middle of the city, but don't confine yourself to it. There are adorable urban pocket parks, disc golf courses, fields, basketball and tennis courts, horseshoe pits, playgrounds, community gathering spots and gardens, and trails of all sorts, so get out there and explore. Parks are open dawn to dusk, glass and alcohol are prohibited, dogs must be on leashes except in dog parks, and golf and archery are not allowed. See www.richmond.gov/parks for a complete list of park locations, amenities, and rules.

The "big three" counties, **Chesterfield, Hanover,** and **Henrico,** which encircle Richmond, sport an impressive array of parkland with amenities all over the map, quite literally. There are equestrian facilities, basketball and tennis courts, skate parks, and in an encouraging move, several parks that offer special facilities for special-needs children or those in wheelchairs.

Most of the county parks are open from dawn to dusk. It should go without saying to please pick up after yourself and use the trash receptacles. Dogs should be on leashes, and they need to be picked up after, too. Chesterfield boasts 3,152 park acres, Hanover 1,153, and Henrico comes in at 3,630 acres. I couldn't possibly tell you about every acre in every park, so the ball's in your court, so to speak.

STATE PARKS

POCAHONTAS STATE PARK
10301 State Park Rd.
(804) 796-4255
www.dcr.virginia.gov/state_parks
Richmond's closest state park is the nearly 8,000-acre Pocahontas State Park, about 20 miles from downtown Richmond, in the center of Chesterfield County. It was built as part of the Civilian Conservation Corps (CCC) project during the Great Depression and has a museum devoted to the role the CCC played around the country.

Open year-round from 7 a.m. to sunset, Pocahontas offers the requisite woods, trails, and camping, but with two lakes that offer boating and fishing, bridle trails, an amazing pool and mini–water park, and an outdoor amphitheater, it's no wonder it's one of the state's most popular. Keep in mind that camping isn't available Dec, Jan, and Feb, and swimming and boat rentals are available Memorial Day through Labor Day. There's a $4 entrance fee for each car weekdays—$5 on weekends—plus fees for camping, swimming, and special events in season. If you are a frequent user, Pocahontas offers annual parking passes for $36, good only at Pocahontas. A $61 pass covers your parking in all Virginia state parks for a year.

Pocahontas is prized for its miles of maintained single-track mountain-biking trails, some for beginners and others that will test even advanced riders. Plenty of trails are great for hiking, too. One popular special event here is the annual Muddy Buddy race, a messy mix of mountain biking and trail running in May. If you'd like to ride a horse on the 9 miles of bridle trails and don't have one of your own, nearby Beaver Hollow Farm will set you up with horses and transportation if you call (804) 240-2545 or visit www.beaverhollowfarm.com. Fishing, with a valid Virginia license, is permitted on both the 150-acre Swift Creek and 24-acre Beaver Lakes during daylight hours. Gas-powered boats are not allowed, but private boats with electric motors may put in at Swift Creek Lake.

i If you're planning to camp at Pocahontas for the annual Muddy Buddy or NASCAR races in May, make your reservations early. For the last couple of years, the events have fallen on the same weekend, and both sets of racing enthusiasts know a great camping place when they see it.

CITY PARKS

JOSEPH BRYAN PARK
4300 Hermitage Rd.
(804) 646-5733
Nestled between two interstates, 260-acre Joseph Bryan Park, known as Bryan Park, still manages to be a refuge against the fast-paced 21st century, with forest, open space, gardens, ponds, and wetlands framing athletic fields, tennis courts, an 18-hole disc golf course, and a playground, not to mention some of the best sledding hills in Richmond.

This park was once primarily known for its 17-acre Azalea Garden, started in 1952 by Robert Harvey, a former Richmond parks and recreation supervisor who undertook the monumental task of planting many

Park Contact Info

City of Richmond Department of Parks, Recreation and Community Facilities: www.richmondgov.com/parks, (804) 646-5733

Chesterfield County Parks and Recreation: www.chesterfield.gov, (804) 748-1623

Hanover County Parks and Recreation: www.co.hanover.va.us, (804) 365-4695

Henrico County Recreation and Parks: www.co.henrico.va.us, (804) 501-7275

Virginia Dept. of Conservation and Recreation: www.dcr.virginia.gov/state_parks, (800) 933-PARK

thousands of azaleas in scores of beds around a small pond, eventually making the Azalea Garden a major tourist attraction. Though time and neglect has taken its toll, volunteers and the city are working hard to restore the garden to its earlier glory, and with the recent completion of the gazebo, it's more beautiful every spring.

i The road around the azalea gardens is usually closed to traffic, though bikers, walkers, and runners are free to enter the loop. It opens to vehicular traffic from Apr 1 to May 15 every year. Dogs are not allowed in the azalea gardens, so please keep them leashed and on the road.

In the late 1990s the Central Virginia Soccer Association put in several well-kept soccer fields for use by children and adults. They are heavily used for league play and practice during spring through fall. Permits are needed for use of the fields. The handsome stonework of the bridges, ponds, and roadways, built by the Works Progress Administration (WPA) during the Great Depression along the park's rolling hills, gives the park much more charm than the typical athletic complex. Down near the lower ponds is an 18-hole disc golf course, giving a visitor more than one reason to exclaim, "Duck!"

The Richmond Audubon Society holds bird walks on the first Sun morning of every month, 30 minutes after sunrise. Great horned owls, bluebirds, rose-breasted grosbeaks, and indigo buntings, among many other birds, can be found here. From May through Nov on Tues afternoons, a farmers' market has taken up residence here as well. The Friends of Bryan Park's Web site has more information to help you get the most out of this excellent example of nature and nurture. Find out more at www.friendsofbryanpark.org.

WILLIAM BYRD PARK
0 S. Blvd.
(804) 646-5733
This 287-acre park in Richmond near Carytown and the Fan, almost always shortened to Byrd Park, sprawls along both sides of the Boulevard, starting at the Columbus statue and heading towards the Boulevard Bridge. Named after the founder of Richmond, this park hosts the city's Fourth of July celebration and many other cultural events, and features one of the area's few dog parks, Barker Field. Music lovers, dog lovers, tennis lovers, and more can all find something to love here.

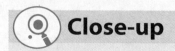

Close-up

James River Park System

Park Headquarters
4001 Riverside Dr.
(804) 646-8911
www.jamesriverpark.org

The James River Park System, part of Richmond's Department of Parks, Recreation and Community Facilities, gets some attention in the "A River Runs Through It" chapter, but there's so much to discover in Richmond's urban wilderness, a detailed write-up here makes sense. Fourteen parcels and growing, the park contains 550 acres of urban wilderness on both sides of the river. The only urban Class IV white water in the country runs through the park and downtown, making it a playground for paddlers and white-water rafters. For those with other interests, the park's beautiful shoreline, meadows, woods, islands, and rocks, so much of which are in or near downtown, give residents and visitors alike myriad opportunities to hike, bike, paddle, tube, rock climb, fish, boat, swim, bird-watch, and just be in a wild and beautiful place..

The park gets more accolades than funding, but under the devoted care of local legend and park manager Ralph White, the little park that couldn't has overcome obstacles to become the big backyard of all Richmond, and a source of pride for its uniqueness, beauty, and adventure-recreation possibilities. Ever since two civic-minded, self-described "river rats," Jack Keith and Joe Schaefer, decided to take possession of islands and shoreline that were in private hands and donate them to the city in the late 1960s, Richmond has had a gem in its midst.

What had been a difficult place to access because of railroad and private land ownership has, since 1972 when the James River Park System was officially created, opened the river up to Richmond and the surrounding communities. With improved sewage treatment and pollution controls, the water quality in the James has improved to the point that several species of fish are on the comeback trail, as evidenced by the many bald eagles and osprey that prowl the river for their next meal.

People are often on the trails here, too, and more multiuse trails are being built all the time with the help of dedicated volunteers. It's possible to hike for miles right here in the city, and to link the park's many sections with the city's flood wall to create lengthy loop trails, utilizing the Mayo, Belle Isle Pedestrian, and/or Boulevard Bridges.

At the eastern edge, **Ancarrow's Landing** offers fishing and is especially popular in the spring when the shad are running. It is also the starting point of the solemn and moving Richmond Slave Trail, highlighted in the "Commemorating the Civil War and Emancipation" chapter.

Within the park west of Ancarrow's, urban outdoor rock climbing is available at the **Manchester Climbing Wall** for those who know what they're doing. Farther west is **Belle Isle,** one of the most popular spots in the park, and accessible from the north shore via the Belle Isle Pedestrian Bridge or from the south shore along the access bridge. This is the spot for up-close views of **Hollywood Rapids** and a trail system that walkers and mountain bikers relish. Stay out of the rapids there, as they are Class III, IV, and even V on occasion. Only expert paddlers should attempt shooting those rapids. If you can't resist getting a piece of that action, call up one of the city's white-water rafting companies, Riverside Outfitters or River City Rafters. Find more information about them in the "A River Runs Through It" and "Kidstuff" chapters.

The Buttermilk Trail, a favorite of mountain bikers, wanders along the main area of the park, which also has massive rocks to clamber on and narrow paths to **Reedy Creek** and the river. The **Park Headquarters** building is at Reedy Creek, too. Impressive geological features dot this section, along with beautiful stonework, wooden bridges, and landscaping, much of it installed by volunteers. One may cross the **Boulevard Bridge** and pick up the North Bank trail just west of the tollbooth and head east back towards downtown. Once you pass Maymont, the trail follows Kansas Street in a neighborhood for a few blocks before picking up the off-road trail at the Texas Beach entrance. Options abound here. Head to Texas Beach over the railroad tracks if you'd like, and head west for a look at remnants of **Foushee's Mill,** or continue east toward downtown. The North Bank trail snakes below three Richmond cemeteries, including the most famous, **Hollywood Cemetery,** and comes out near the pedestrian bridge onto Belle Isle. If you are so inclined and are sure-footed, you could head to Brown's Island and pick up the Trestle Trail, aka Pipeline Trail. It affords a view of the heron rookery in the late winter and early spring. Expert paddlers, shooting through Hollywood and Pipeline Rapids, will be happy to get to the 14th Street takeout, near the Mayo Bridge, the end of the line for the James River Park System at this point. By stringing together these many and varied parts of the park, and using the Boulevard, Belle Isle Pedestrian, and the Mayo Bridges, it is possible to hike for as many as 11 miles through history along the James River in the park system. Shorter routes are easily configured.

I'm tired, and I haven't even mentioned one of the park's great attractions. Back on the south side, from the park's main section, continue west by car or bike, to the **Wetlands** and/or **Pony Pasture** sections, which connect via trails. The Wetlands area is a placid place with trails perfect for biking (bring the kids), slow-moving water for good swimming, and pond-side duck blinds ideal for bird-watching.

Pony Pasture is a happening, youthful place, overcrowded on hot summer weekends. The wait for legal parking can sometimes be a hassle. Come back during the week for a calmer visit. When the water is low enough, people frolic in the rapids there, or sunbathe on large rocks. Take to the paths east to find a less crowded spot or put in a canoe or tube to float out into the riffles. Just make sure you know where you're going. The takeout for everyone but the most experienced paddlers is at Reedy Creek, to the right after passing under the Boulevard Bridge. Try an early-morning visit when you'll likely have the rocks to yourself. The winter months open up vistas unavailable other times of year, so don't forget to come back every season. And please pick up litter on your visits. The Friends of James River Park, a local nonprofit that supports the park, thanks you for that.

For the easiest boating experience, put in at **Huguenot Flatwater,** and as the name suggests, you won't have more than a few riffles to contend with as you paddle up as far as Bosher's Dam or down under the Huguenot Bridge. If you're floating to the Pony Pasture, make sure you get over to the left bank to portage well before William's dam. DO NOT attempt to go over this or any dam. The river is beautiful, and the cascading water alluring, but the hydraulics near a dam are not to be toyed with, and people have died there.

The park is open from sunrise to sunset. No alcoholic beverages, glass containers, or unleashed pets are allowed in city parks. By law, when water levels are at 5 feet and above, everyone on the river must wear a life jacket. When water levels are at 9 feet or above, no one is allowed on the river without a permit. To check the river level, call (804) 646-8228, choose option 4, and listen for the Westham reading.

Special Interest Parks

BMX

Gillies Creek Park
Hobbs Lane and Admiral Gravely Boulevard, Richmond

The city of Richmond sports an impressive BMX course that hosts races almost year-round. Helmets, please! The course has a completely different entrance than the disc golf course; hence the different addresses.

Disc Golf

This game is similar to the golf you see on TV, but players send a "Frisbee-like" disc flying towards (one hopes) the basketlike target.

18-hole disc golf courses
Bryan Park, 4300 block of Hermitage Road, North Side
Gillies Creek Park, Williamsburg Road and Stoney Run Drive, East End
Dorey Park, 2999 Darbytown Rd., Henrico, East End
Fighting Creek Park, 2200 Mann Rd., Powhatan

Nine-hole course
Dunncroft/Castle Point Park, 4901 Francistown Rd., Glen Allen

Dog Parks

Dogs who like to socialize have several options around the area:
Barker Field, in Byrd Park, Richmond
Chimborazo Dog Park, just east and down the hill from the Richmond National Battlefield Park Headquarters Building on Church Hill

Ruff House Dog Park, in Rockwood Park, 3401 Courthouse Rd., Midlothian
Hanover Animal Control Dog Park, in Taylor Park, 13017 Taylor Complex Lane, Ashland, offers a place for exercise and agility training.

Petanque

Chimborazo Playground
29th Street and East Grace Street, Richmond
(804) 649-3939

If you're in the mood for something new, try petanque, (pronounced "pay-tahnk"), a cousin of horseshoes and bocce, where players lob boules at a target. Les Boulefrogs of Church Hill play SaT afternoons and Thurs evenings year-round at Chimborazo Playground. No special skill is required, and the club has extra equipment for new learners and visitors. For more information go online to http://boulefrogs.word press.com/about.

Roller Hockey

Hanover Courthouse Park
7232 Courtland Farm Rd., Hanover
Lace up your in-line skates. For free outdoor roller-skating and roller hockey, head to Hanover Courthouse Park in Hanover County, where the Matthew & Daniel Barton Memorial Roller Hockey Rink is.

Closest to the Columbus statue, Fountain Lake features pedal-boat rides in the summer and sports a new concession building, the Landing, with free Wi-Fi and food from Sally Bell's in the summer. The popular tennis complex features push-button lighting for play anytime, and there are two baseball fields nearby. Two more lakes, Swan and Shields, provide leisurely fishing, with a Virginia fishing license. Nearby grills and shelters make that area a popular place for picnics and gatherings.

i Please don't feed the geese in the park. Overpopulation and its typical messy effects are a problem here, and feeding them is not allowed.

Farther west is the 1-mile Vita Course, a stone dust track that will be shadier each year because of the city's Tree the Track initiative. The Carillon, across the Boulevard, is the most prominent feature of the park. It is a memorial to those who died in World War I and houses a 56-bell clavier that has been played on Veterans Day, the Fourth of July, and other special occasions over the last 50 years by city carillonneur Lawrence Robinson. The sunken grassy area in front of the Carillon was originally designed to be a reflecting pool and perhaps one day will be. For now, Frisbee and football games, sunbathing, and the athletic antics of the SEAL Team (an extremely motivated exercise group that cavorts around several city parks) are likely to be going on there.

FOREST HILL PARK
4100 Forest Hill Ave.
(804) 646-5733
A former quarry, estate, and amusement park, this park is a go-to destination when it snows for some serious sledding fun. More

typically, however, Forest Hill Park is a lovely spot to burn calories walking, running, or mountain biking, as well as a great place to ingest calories sampling the delicious local flavors at the South of the James Market, a farmers' market held on Sat from 8 a.m. to 1 p.m. from May through Nov, possibly even into Dec.

Be sure to walk down the cobbled paths to see for yourself the centerpiece of this charming park, a lake that recently underwent a $1.7 million renovation and now sparkles and brims with turtles and fish. The stonework around the lake and the impressive stone gazebo with fireplaces are especially photogenic. It's hard to believe you are in the city. Walk around the lake and head onto the dirt trails at the southeast section of the park. The huge boulders that tumble down into Reedy Creek, which feeds the lake, will have you thinking you're in the mountains. Paths vary from paved and level to steep, natural, and narrow, and more are coming. Volunteers—mostly from Richmond Area MORE, under the direction of park trails manager Nathan Burrell—are carving more single-track mountain-bike trails up and down the sloping hills. If you're up for a longer hike, it's easy to connect with the James River Park trails at the northern edge of the lake.

If you are otherwise inclined, there are also tennis courts, picnic shelters, and a children's playground. During the summer, free Sun concerts are a pleasant addition to this gathering place in Westover Hills.

COUNTY PARKS
Henrico County

DEEP RUN PARK
9900 Ridgefield Parkway

This Far West End park has tangles of multi-use dirt trails that turn back on themselves, but they currently are not opened to mountain biking. The county is talking with Richmond MORE to try to make the park a mountain-biking destination in the future.

A two-level duck pond that's more likely teeming with Canada geese has a wooden boardwalk across the dam so you can be right in the thick of the wildlife action. The pond is encircled by a paved path with benches, and there's a nature pavilion at one end for leisurely viewing or fishing. An impressive playground, soccer fields, and a fitness trail complete the picture.

DOREY PARK
2999 Darbytown Rd.

I could say this park in eastern Henrico County has a little bit of everything, but honestly it has a lot of everything, from lighted athletic fields and baseball and softball diamonds, to miles of trails, a disc golf course, a stocked fishing pond, and an equestrian ring.

Some of the trails in the woods here are twisty and turny, as if they were meant for mountain biking, but currently mountain biking is not permitted on them, no matter what mountain-biking Web sites say. The county and Richmond MORE are in negotiations to try to get bikers back on track, so to speak. For now, trail runners and walkers use these shaded trails. There is also a fitness trail with pull-up bars and the like and a paved path around the five-acre pond.

The Virginia Department of Game and Inland Fisheries stocks the pond with trout, so those angling to make a catch must have a Virginia trout license between Nov 1 and Apr 30, in addition to a Virginia fishing license. Children under the age of 16 do not need a license. For more information call (540) 899-4169.

The horse ring is used for shows and special events many weekends, and if you have your own horse, there are 5 miles of horse trails to trot through.

LAUREL SKATE PARK
10301 Hungary Spring Rd.
(804) 672-6273

Though this park does have a couple of athletic fields, its raison d'être is that it's the place for both youth and adults to whip out their skateboards, in-line skates and/or BMX bikes. With 6,700 square feet of free skate area loaded with ramps, rails, a half-pipe, and a combination bowl, be prepared to see some action. If you're game and you have the required safety equipment—helmets, elbow and knee pads, and wrist and shin guards for bike riders—this is a great place for you to bust out a new move on your skateboard, in-line skates, or BMX/freestyle bike.

Bikes must have at least one hand brake. Heelys and scooters are not allowed. Laurel Skate Park is staffed during operating hours, Mon through Fri from 3:30 to 9 p.m., Sat from 12:30 to 6 p.m., and Sun from 1 to 6 p.m. Admission is free.

THREE LAKES PARK & NATURE CENTER
400 Sausiluta Dr.
(804) 262-5055

Its name tells you that there are water features to roam around outside here, but it doesn't hint at how much water is *inside*. Don't miss the 50,000-gallon aquarium in the nature center, stocked with critters who live in the neighborhood. Wetlands and woodlands are the featured habitats, and exhibits are designed to foster a hands-on approach to plants and animals. The center offers nature programs for children from preschoolers to age 12.

Outside, there are viewing platforms and connected trails around the three lakes that add up to 1.3 miles. Be on the lookout and you might spot otters, beavers, mink, deer weasels, and turkeys, depending on the time of year. Fishing is permitted in two of the three lakes with a valid Virginia fishing license. Children under 16 don't need a license to fish. Bass, catfish, crappie, and sunfish are waiting to get hooked. The middle lake is closed to fishing as it's used for stocking the aquarium.

From Mar through Nov, the nature center is open Tues through Sun from noon to 4:30 p.m. June through Aug, it opens at 10 a.m., Tues through Fri. It operates on weekends only from Dec through Feb.

Hanover County

POLE GREEN PARK
8996 Pole Green Park Lane

This 217-acre park has an array of amenities that attest to Hanover's rural heritage and its growing suburban status. It has both an equestrian ring and stable area and a skate park, not to mention the ball fields, volleyball courts, horseshoe pits, picnic shelters, and trails typical of a county park. It also boasts an all-inclusive playground designed for wheelchair accessibility so that differently abled children and adults can have fun on a playground together. Special features include a rubberized surface that's easy on the wheelchairs and anyone who takes a tumble, adaptive swings so children can be securely strapped in, ramps to make slides wheelchair accessible, and more.

The famous Hanover Tomato Festival is held here every July (more on that in the "Annual Events" chapter). Many of the region's high school cross-country meets are held here, so the trails are great for running, just not on those Sat in the fall when meets are held. The park is open from dawn to dusk year-round, with extended hours for lighted athletic events.

POOR FARM PARK
3400 Liberty School Rd.

It's much more fun to explore this 254-acre park than it must have been to farm it all those years ago. A few miles west of Ashland center, Poor Farm has hills and forests beyond the large flat areas that are home to lighted soccer, softball, and baseball fields, and a football field. Horseshoe pits, a tot lot, open play areas, picnic shelters, beach volleyball courts, and a seasonal concession stand with restrooms fill out the wide-open section. Hidden a bit by the trees are an amphitheater, archery range, and an extensive network of trails, suitable for nature hikes, trail running, and mountain biking.

The main hiking trail starts near the horseshoe pits and runs in a loop, though it's possible to zigzag inside the maze of trails within the loop, too. The mountain bikers have concocted a tangle of easy-to-moderate single-track that winds through the shady hardwood forest over hill and dale and down towards Stagg Creek. Crossing the creek takes you onto private property, so don't do it even when you see trails sneaking that way.

A very special feature of the park is the Operation Hope Playground that provides a wheelchair-accessible place for special-needs children to enjoy the simple pleasures of swinging and sliding with their friends and families. Annual events at the park include the Patrick Henry Half Marathon, which starts and finishes here on what often seems to be the hottest day in Aug. A community Easter Egg Hunt is fun for the younger set. The park is open from dawn to dusk all year-round.

Chesterfield County

DUTCH GAP CONSERVATION AREA
411 Coxendale Rd.
(804) 748-1623

Dutch Gap, surrounding the Citie of Henricus, is so named for Sir Thomas Dale's use of a moat known as a Dutch Gap to protect the second successful English settlement in the New World. Situated on the south bank of the James River, its 800-plus acres of woodlands and water features are home to a blue heron rookery, beavers, muskrats and other wildlife. This watery spot, with a freshwater tidal lagoon, marsh, and swamp, is a bird-watcher's dream, with eagles, osprey, owls, and rare birds such as yellow-billed cuckoos among the 140 species seen here. Along the 8-mile-long, narrow, out-and-back Dutch Gap trail, there's ornithology information sprinkled along the way to help aspiring bird-watchers. Be sure to apply some bug repellent, as the mosquitoes like the place, too.

i Shelters are available to rent for picnics and large gatherings at eight Chesterfield County parks. They provide several picnic tables and grills. Volleyball courts and horseshoe pits are included with most shelters. Electricity and water availability varies. To schedule your fun time, call (804) 751-4696.

Dutch Gap is open daily during daylight hours and is free. The county offers special programs, which do have fees associated with them, including a wonderfully titled graveyard paddle that explores the remains of a sunken tugboat and moonlight paddles that sound just as spooky. For more information about Chesterfield County Park programs at Dutch Gap, call (804) 318-8735 or go online to www.chesterfield.gov.

HARRY G. DANIEL PARK AT IRON BRIDGE
6600 Whitepine Rd.
(804) 748-1623

Across VA 10 from the Chesterfield County Airport, near VA 288, this is Chesterfield County's largest park at 365 acres. It features the typical baseball, softball, soccer and football fields, basketball and tennis courts, trails, picnic shelters, and a playground, but it offers amenities many parks don't, including handball, racquetball, and volleyball courts, and good wheelchair accessibility at several shelters, as well as a therapeutic fitness trail for those with special needs.

In addition to all this, Iron Bridge has an 18-hole First Tee Golf Course, which aims to develop young golfers, from the age of five on up, with golf and life lessons. The course, driving range, and par 3 holes are open to adults as well as juniors, for a fee, of course. Check out the Web site for details, as there are discounts for county residents, juniors, and seniors. Look for more details in the "Recreation" chapter. Call (804) 275-8050 or check out www.thefirstteerichmondchesterfield.org.

R. GARLAND DODD PARK AT POINT OF ROCKS
201 Enon Church Rd.
(804) 748-1623

This is a 188-acre park with two distinct personalities. As you drive into the park, sports fields, athletic facilities, a playground, and picnic shelters are spread over a wide area. To reach the more scenic, hikeable section, park at Shelter 1 or 2 and take the path down into the woods. The trails are not well marked, but as the Appomattox River winds around the park, it's hard to get too far afield, though you might come across an actual field at one point. Point of Rocks refers to a geographical feature that no longer exists here. Prominent rocky cliffs once were visible from the Appomattox River, but the rock was blasted after the Civil War to use as headstones at City Point National Cemetery. The system of trails, gravel and dirt, makes for a pleasant hour hike, and informational signs at strategic overlooks add to the experience. Make sure to walk out onto the impressive, 0.3-mile, C-shaped metal boardwalk that looks like it vanishes into the freshwater tidal marsh but actually comes back around to land. It's your chance to walk on water and see darters and dragonflies, and perhaps egrets, herons, and kingfishers in their habitat.

ROCKWOOD PARK
3401 Courthouse Rd.
(804) 748-1623
This heavily used, 163-acre suburban park near the corner of Hull Street Road (I know, that's redundant) and Courthouse Road has several wooded trails, mostly paved that are popular with dog walkers. Between paved and dirt paths, you could easily string together a pleasant 4-mile run, chugging by Gregory's Pond, which hugs one side of the park. It is private and no fishing is allowed. If you are looking for a softer running surface, a 1½-mile stone dust trail loops around the park.

Dogs must be on a leash unless you're at the Ruff House Dog Park section of the park, a double-gated, off-leash exercise place for dogs. Owners must stay with the dogs at all times and, of course, clean up after them.

The Nature Center has turtles and snakes and other natural offerings that will delight young visitors, and programs that often give hands-on experience. Ball fields, horseshoe pits, shelters with grills, and volleyball and tennis courts spread out over the rest of the park. An unusual feature is the archery range that is shockingly close to one of the main paths. Signs are posted to alert people to avoid straying into the woods, and they aren't kidding. The 12 targets vary in distance from 12 to 65 yards, and it would be impressive, if a little scary, to see someone take aim. Only qualified archers are allowed, understandably. A community garden sprouts here in the spring.

OUTLYING COUNTY PARKS
Goochland County

522 SKATE PARK AT GOOCHLAND SPORTS COMPLEX
1800 Sandy Hook Rd.
(804) 556-5854
www.co.goochland.va.us
Located in what used to be the tennis courts for the old Goochland High School, this skate park is open every day for users, but you must call or come by the Parks office in the same complex to sign a waiver before you skate. With that taken care of, they will give you a sticker for your helmet. If you don't have a helmet or the sticker, you won't be able to skate. The park area also has baseball and softball fields, a football and soccer field, and a gym where other activities are held. Check out the Program Guide on the Web site for more details.

Powhatan County

FIGHTING CREEK PARK
2200 Mann Rd.
(804) 598-5612
www.powhatanparksand recreation.com
This brand-new facility is near the court-house complex and encompasses 220 acres. Mixed in with the county library, YMCA, and other facilities, it's a great addition to central Powhatan. There's a playground, complete with fun facilities for disabled children, baseball, softball, and soccer fields, and the largest 18-hole disc golf course in Virginia. That's quite a boast. For now, walking trails meander over a picturesque wooden bridge and by sharp-looking wooden picnic shelters. Dogs and horses are not allowed here, and the park closes at sunset.

RECREATION

Both adrenaline junkies and those inclined towards more traditional (and tame) recreational pursuits will find plenty of ways to be active in this part of the world. The weather is such that people might be out on their bikes in January and golfing in February. Besides the usual suspects, Richmond has some unexpected offerings for a metropolitan area, including superior single-track mountain-biking trails in the city along the James River. Richmond is the rare city where you can go white-water rafting, rock climbing, and recreational tree climbing, as long as you're hooked up with the right outfit.

If you don't find your preferred activities in this chapter, remember that many other options are covered in the "A River Runs Through It," "Parks," "Kidstuff," and "Annual Events" chapters. Paddling, rowing, and white-water rafting are covered in the "A River Runs Through It" chapter. Mountain biking gets attention in the "Parks" and "A River Runs Through It" chapters. The cursory attention to camping given here doesn't indicate its popularity among area residents. It's just that most people head to the state parks in the mountains or near the beach to camp. For listings of all the state parks, check out www.dcr.virginia.gov/state_parks.

There are simply too many recreation leagues in too many sports to list them here. Soccer, baseball, softball, and tennis are all popular activities, often available through the various parks and recreation departments in our area. YMCAs and other gyms and recreation centers are everywhere you turn around. You would think no one here ever sits on a couch in front of a television. Besides offering the traditional softball and volleyball leagues, the area also feature groups that participate in wheelchair basketball, kickball, hula hooping, fire twirling, rugby, and on and on. *Discover Richmond,* an annual publication of the *Richmond Times-Dispatch,* has a handy listing of dozens of organizations that offer youth and adult programs in a wide variety of sports.

Besides a few municipal pools in the city of Richmond, public pools are not the way of the world here. Many neighborhoods are home to recreation associations that feature pools and often tennis courts and charge yearly membership dues.

BOATING AND FISHING

Boating and fishing regulations are long and involved. Please familiarize yourself with them before heading onto the water. Approved life vests are required for boating. See www.dgif.virginia.gov/boating or www.huntfishva.com. For more information about boating or fishing on the James River, including boat ramps along the James, see the "River" chapter.

i In 2010 the Virginia Boat Show combined with the Richmond Boat Show for one February event at the Richmond Raceway Complex. Dozens of boat dealers show off ski boats, pontoons, jet boats, bass boats, and more. Scads of other exhibitors offer everything boat-related you can think of—safety equipment, marine electronics, and water-sports loot. It's unclear if in coming years there will be two events or one, so check back early next year. Go to www.agievents.com/shows for updates.

HANOVER COUNTY BOAT RAMPS
US 1/North Anna Ramp
17600 Washington Hwy.
US 33/South Anna Ramp (Ground Squirrel Ramp)
15008 Mountain Rd.
VA 54/South Anna Ramp
13151 W. Patrick Henry Rd.
US 301/Pamunkey Ramp (Littlepage Ramp)
13600 Hanover Courthouse Rd.
The Pamunkey and North and South Anna Rivers are awfully nice places to paddle. These are the places to go to float your boat.

LAKE CHESDIN
This 3,100-acre reservoir attracts plenty of people for its array of water sports and fishing. Largemouth bass, black and white crappie, channel catfish, walleye, and striped bass are potential catches here. A public boat ramp and fishing pier are available at 12900 Lake Chesdin Parkway on the north side of the lake in Lake Chesdin Park, a Chesterfield County park. See www.chesterfield .gov for more information.

Boating and Fishing Organizations

Coastal Canoeists (www.coastals .org) is a group for those who love paddle sports, whether whitewater or flat, ocean, river, or lake. Many local opportunities, including classes and trips, are available around Richmond once you connect with other members. Members receive discounts at boat-related stores around town and can get to know new rivers and people. Yearly dues are $20.

Dedicated to spreading the word about fly fishing, **Fly Fishers of Virginia** (www.flyfishersofvirginia .org) hosts fishing trips all over the state and six dinner meetings a year with an expert speaker at Salisbury Country Club in Midlothian. Their most important work is volunteering with the Healing Waters program, helping members of the armed forces who are in rehab at the McGuire Richmond VA Medical Center learn the ins and outs of fly fishing and fly-tying as part of their healing process.

JAMES RIVER FISHING SCHOOL
(804) 938-2350
www.jamesriverfishing.com
Though his guided fishing trips are on the James River (see more in the "A River Runs Through It" chapter), Captain Mike Ostrander will be happy to provide instruction on other bodies of water for the novice or experienced fishing enthusiasts hoping to improve their freshwater fishing techniques. He'll meet you at streams, ponds, or rivers that are convenient to you.

POWHATAN WILDLIFE MANAGEMENT AREA

www.dgif.virginia.gov/fishing/index.asp

The 66-acre Powhatan Lakes and smaller Powhatan ponds that range from two to nine acres within the Powhatan Wildlife Management Area are quite popular for fishing—for largemouth bass, channel catfish, black crappies, redear sunfish, and more—and launching small boats. Both lakes and two of the ponds have boat-launching facilities, though gas motors are prohibited.

CAMPING

POCAHONTAS STATE PARK
10301 State Park Rd.
(804) 796-4255
www.dcr.virginia.gov/state_parks

Eight thousand acres not far from area residents' doorsteps makes Pocahontas a great place for introducing camping to novices. During Mar through Nov, tent or RV camping is available on 129 campsites with electrical and water hookups for $25 plus tax a night. For those disinclined to sleep on the ground, Pocahontas offers several rustic camping cabins that sleep four in bunk beds. An in-season swimming pool, two lakes for fishing, and trails for hiking, biking, and even horseback riding (using a nearby stable and with advance reservations) are options here. See more about this park in the "Parks" chapter.

CLIMBING

Recreational Tree Climbing

RIVERSIDE OUTFITTERS
6836 Old Westham Parkway
(804) 560-0068
www.riversideoutfitters.net

For a rare chance to climb up a tree like a squirrel, except more slowly, sign up for a half day of recreational tree climbing with Riverside Outfitters. The rigs and ropes are strong enough to hold 8,000 pounds, so you should be fine. If you've wanted to know what a bird's-eye view is, this is your big chance. But since you don't have wings, your quads will get quite a workout as you pull yourself up the trunk. The rappel down is pure pleasure.

Challenge Discovery

When you're ready to climb to new heights, check out Fearless Fridays at Challenge Discovery's Odyssey Course at the University of Richmond. Challenge Discovery is known for its team-building work with groups at its High Ropes courses in Doswell and Richmond. Fearless Fridays offers high-flying adventure to those not part of a corporate or church group. Anyone 12 and older is welcome to partake of the exciting challenges and inspiring teamwork. It's only $15 for three hours of fun that's sure to give your weekend a lift. Go to www.challengediscovery.com for the latest information.

Rock Climbing

PEAK EXPERIENCES
11421 Polo Circle
(804) 897-6800
www.peakexperiences.com

The largest indoor climbing gym on the East Coast is a mecca for climbers and newbies. With bouldering areas, a 50-foot wall, 14,000 square feet of climbing space, and a high ropes course in front of your face, it would take quite a while before you mastered every one of the 135 different climbing routes. It's open seven days a week and offers equipment rental, belaying, and when you're ready, a shop for gear purchases. Day passes or memberships are available. Whether you're starting at the beginning in Climbing 101 or ready for outdoor nuts and bolts, so to speak, instructors will guide you through the process, so you can join the climbers on Belle Isle and the Manchester climbing wall some day. See more in the "Kidstuff" chapter.

CYCLING

ANTHEM MOONLIGHT RIDE
Sports Backers Stadium
100 Avenue of Champions
(804) 285-9495
www.sportsbackers.org
If a nighttime bike ride on a moonlit night along North Side and the Near West End sounds intriguing, then strap on your helmet. This event is held on a Sat in Aug, but has to move around from year to year to keep up with the moon. It isn't a race, but it offers an 8-mile or 17-mile option with a concert and refreshments after the ride. Children may ride, but see the age and bike requirements in the "Kidstuff" chapter. The first year, one family showed up on a bicycle built for five. Costumes are encouraged; bike lights are required.

HEART OF VIRGINIA
Richmond Area Bicycling Association
(804) 358-5801
www.raba.org
The Heart of Virginia, sponsored by the Richmond Area Bicycle Association, is central Virginia's premier road-biking event and is

usually held the middle weekend in Sept. The routes include centuries—English and metric—a 40-miler, and a 30-mile route especially for families. Rest stops and lunch are included. Remember, it's about the journey, which will have some hills, not the destination, which is the same place you start, usually the Patrick Henry YMCA. All routes start near Ashland and spread out over Hanover County's beautiful countryside. Registration fees vary per event.

GOLF COURSES

If you haven't become golfing buddies with members of the many private golf clubs in the region, don't worry. The more than 20 golf courses open to the public here are spread throughout the area and offer a variety of amenities, including river views, short courses, and instruction. What follows is a small sampling. To see all public courses in the area, go to www.virginiagolf.com. Several par 3 courses at family sports centers are mentioned in the "Kidstuff" chapter.

BELMONT GOLF COURSE
1600 Hilliard Rd.
(804) 501-4653
www.belmontgolfcourse.com
Belmont Golf Course, located in and owned by Henrico County, features an 18-hole PGA Championship golf course that's a par 71. Originally built in 1916, after alterations it was the site of the 1949 PGA Championship won by Sam Snead. Further alterations get the thumbs up from *Golf Digest,* which ranks it four stars. The full-service pro shop is open daily, and private golf lessons are available by appointment. Tee times, which can be reserved in person, by phone, or online, are required. The greens fees for adults range from $16 to $27, depending on the time of

year, day of the week, and age of the golfer. It's a steal to play after 2 p.m., Oct through Feb—just $6. A cart costs $14, but walking is allowed. Henrico County residents get a discount on greens fees and can buy passes to save even more.

THE GOLF CLUB AT BRICKSHIRE
5520 Virginia Park Dr.
(804) 966-7888
www.brickshiregolfclub.com
Near Colonial Downs Race Track in New Kent County, this golf club is all about the drive—to exit 214 off I-64— and the drives you'll need to hit to handle the fairways that range in length from 5,151 to 7,291 yards, depending on which of five tees you use. Curtis Strange designed this championship course, which opened in 2002, in collaboration with Tom Clark as a combination of some of his favorite holes in golf. Right from the first hole ,you can pretend you're playing the No. 3 hole at Augusta. Holes from Pinehurst, St. Andrew's, and the Riviera Club mix in with challenging and beautiful holes with wetlands, uneven lies, and a very pretty finishing hole with a great watery view. Not surprisingly, it ranks as one of *Golf Digest's* "Best Places to Play." A cart is mandatory here, and the $65 greens fee includes one.

HUNTING HAWK GOLF CLUB
15201 Ashland Rd.
(804) 749-1900
www.huntinghawkgolf.com
Tucked in a secluded, wooded section of Hanover County along the Chickahominy River, Hunting Hawk is a championship course that makes you feel a million miles away. Actually, this W. R. Love–designed course is close to I-95 and I-64, but because it doesn't have any houses or developments

overlooking the course, it's a bit of a nature walk out here, with wetlands around every bend and mature trees lining the fairways. Soon after the course opened, *Golf Digest* named it No. 3 of best new affordable courses, and *GolfStyles* put Hunting Hawk on its "100 must-play courses of the Middle Atlantic." Greens fee with cart is $67 for

---

First Tee

First Tee Richmond
400 School St.
(804) 646-4074
www.thefirstteerichmondchesterfield
.org

First Tee Chesterfield
Harry G. Daniels Ironbridge Park
6736 Hunting Creek Dr.
(804) 275-8050
www.thefirstteerichmondchesterfield
.org

Both of these facilities were built with the goal of introducing children to golf, using the discipline of the sport to build character and instill confidence. It's possible to play at either short course and get a feel for the game before making the commitment to an 18-hole outing.

First Tee Richmond, on Richmond's North Side just off Chamberlayne Avenue, has a six-hole, par 3 course and a driving range. The Chesterfield facility features three Scottish links–style par 3 holes that range from 70 to 118 yards and a lighted driving range. When you're ready, so is the 18-hole, par 66 championship course dotted with two small lakes. Call the shop to make a reservation up to seven days in advance.

weekend play during peak season. Several less expensive options are available, including playing (and paying for) just nine holes or year-round twilight rates—$10 a round of 18 after 2 p.m. A credit card is required to reserve a tee time.

INDEPENDENCE GOLF CLUB
600 Founders Bridge Blvd.
(804) 594-0261
www.independencegolfclub.com
In the Founders Bridge neighborhood, at the border between Chesterfield County and Powhatan County, is Virginia's only daily-fee championship and short course designed by Tom Fazio. This upscale facility, rated at four-and-a-half stars by *Golf Digest,* is owned and operated by the Virginia State Golf Association Foundation. Independence has picked up many accolades since opening in 2001, including being named the No. 1 public practice facility in the U.S. by *Golf World,* with a double-ended driving range, chipping green, sand bunker, and putting green. Independence is consistently named one of the best places to play golf by *Golf Digest.* Its stylish clubhouse is home of Virginia State Golf Association and the Museum of Virginia Golf History. The greens fee is $65, with various discounts for time of day, walking, etc.

RIVER'S BEND GOLF COURSE
11700 Hogan's Alley
(804) 530-1000
www.riversbendgolfclub.com
This course is well named and well situated in Chesterfield County above the James River, 15 minutes south of downtown. Designed by Steve Smyers, this par 71 championship course ranges from 4,932 to 6,671 yards and has four sets of tees. The first three holes and the last offer beautiful views

of the river, and you'll encounter other water features along the way. You'll also see plenty of houses as you traverse the course, as River's Bend is a golf community with large homes lining parts of the course. The terrain is quite up and down with many bluffs. The expansive river view from the 18th tee is well worth the hike up the 60 steps to the tee box. *Golf Digest* ranks it four stars. The greens fee is $50 in peak season with off-peak discounts available.

HUNTING

VIRGINIA DEPARTMENT OF GAME AND INLAND FISHERIES
(866) 721-6911
www.huntfishva.com
Hunting and trapping license requirements and fees are somewhat involved, with different rules for residents and nonresidents, so to make sure you have the required licenses for the relevant season, get information at www.huntfishva.com. It's the Virginia Department of Game and Inland Fisheries' Web site and has all the information you'll need, including prices, hunting seasons, and helpful links. Licenses may be purchased online, by phone during business hours, or at scads of agents in retail stores. Hunting on public lands is not allowed on Sun in Virginia, and remember the blaze orange clothes. For hunting and fishing gear and apparel, Green Top, Dick's Sporting Goods, Gander Mountain, Bass Pro Shops, and Orvis, all retailers in the region, ought to scratch that itch.

POCAHONTAS STATE PARK
10301 State Park Rd.
(804) 796-4255
www.dcr.virginia.gov/state_parks

 **Close-up**

Horseback Riding

You might not think horseback riding has a place in a city, but this is Virginia, after all. Haven't you noticed how many statues of horses there are around here? The **Friends of Richmond Mounted Squad** (www.frmsva.com) hold the annual **Richmond Ride** the Sunday before Strawberry Hills Races at Colonial Downs in conjunction with the Mounted Police division. The four-hour, 10-mile ride with a break for lunch starts at a different site every year, but previous rides have started at Bryan Park, Byrd Park, and the Federal Reserve Building, and toured parts of Richmond where horses would once have been common sights. It's quite a sight to see. Of course it's bring-your-own-horse, and the $25 entry fee raises money for the Mounted Police squad. Riders must be at least 12 years old, and horses must have a negative Coggins certificate.

Every year in June, the **Richmond Police Department's Horse Barn** at 801 Brook Rd. has an open house so the department's Mounted Police Division can show off the horses they're so proud of. It's a treat for young and old.

The counties are loaded with trails and horse barns. No matter where you live, it's likely you're within 20 minutes of a barn that offers lessons for children and adults and boarding for those who own a horse. If you have a horse, **Dorey Park** in Henrico County, **Pocahontas State Park** in Chesterfield County, and **Powhatan Wildlife Management Area** all offer horse trails.

For the horseless among us, **Beaver Hollow Farm** in Chesterfield County offers guided one- or two-hour trail rides through Pocahontas State Park or Petersburg National Battlefield Park. Riders must be at least 14 years old unless the rider is experienced. The weight limit is 240 pounds. Trail rides must be paid for in advance with a credit card. See www.beaverhollowfarm.com for more information.

Level Green Riding School at 3350 John Tree Hill Rd. in Powhatan offers hour-long, guided, English-style trail rides in 200 acres of woods and fields. Inexperienced riders spend the first 15 minutes in the ring getting acclimated before heading out onto the trail. Riders must weigh less than 200 pounds. Call (804) 794-8463 or see www.levelgreenriding.com for more information.

During squirrel, deer, and turkey seasons, a remote section of 8,000-acre Pocahontas State Park that's closed to other day users opens for public hunting. In addition, every December the entire park closes to all users except 50 hunters a day, chosen by lottery, who are allowed to hunt to thin the deer herd. Five thousand acres of the wooded park are divided into 25 zones with two hunters maximum in each zone, so there's room to roam just 20 miles from Richmond.

ℹ To appreciate the hunting heritage of our region in a whole new light, not to mention the tradition and honor of Virginia's Indian tribes, go to the Executive Mansion in Capitol Square the week before Thanksgiving to see the yearly ceremonial tax tribute to the governor of Virginia by two Virginia tribes, the Pamunkey and the Mattaponi. Lately, the traditional offering is of deer and turkeys.

POWHATAN WILDLIFE MANAGEMENT AREA

The 4,462-acre public area 3 miles west of Powhatan Courthouse off US 60 once was several farms. Crisscrossed by streams and ponds, woods and fields, it now provides a variety of hunting experiences during several hunting seasons. There's the possibility of bear, deer, and turkey during the fall big-game season, small game in the migratory game-bird season, and then furbearers in the trapping season. Beavers, woodcocks, and wood ducks like the swampy areas, and quail, rabbits, and squirrels have their favorite habitats, too.

i Richmond Roller Derby Demons (www.richmondderbydemons.org), founded in 2006, sports women's teams, a men's team, and a co-ed team. They travel and compete as part of the Old School Derby Association. The Demon's home rink is Roller Dome at 4902 Williamsburg Rd. in the East End. Practices are every Monday and Thursday evening. Newcomers are welcome, and rookies get special attention the first and third week of every month.

MOUNTAIN BIKING

RICHMOND AREA MID-ATLANTIC OFF-ROAD ENTHUSIASTS (MORE)

www.richmond-more.org

If you've used the multiuse trails in the James River Park System or the trails in Forest Hill Park, Larus Park, and many other places in the region, thank the members of Richmond MORE (or sometimes RA MORE). They love building (and biking) multiuse trails and educating people about environmentally and socially responsible mountain biking. Richmond's trails rack up the accolades because

of their dedication and hard work. Their Web site is full of links to great mountain-biking sites near and far and opportunities to get involved and make some tracks. See more about mountain biking in the "Parks" chapter.

RUNNING

Running has gotten a lot of attention in the "Parks" chapters since Richmond has been named by *Trail Runner* magazine one of the best trail-running towns in the country. It's also come up in the "Annual Events" chapter since the **Monument Avenue 10K** is so popular (see more below). The **SunTrust Richmond Marathon** has been named a "must run" marathon by editors of *Runners' World*. Every month brings another race coming around the bend, some of them taking advantage of the strengths of our interesting urban terrain. But running isn't necessarily about racing, so here are resources you need to get out there and run.

i Training teams have become a popular way to train for the marathon and shorter road races. Saturday or Sunday group runs help both novices and advanced runners get it in gear, whatever gear that might be. Go to www.richmondmarathon.com or www.sportsbackers.org for information about fees and registration.

Richmond Road Runners Club is your first stop for information about running. Go to www.rrrc.org for route suggestions, training tips, group runs, and if you're so inclined, links to upcoming races. Consider volunteering at races; the more help the club gets, the more races it can run. To get the right equipment for all of Richmond's races, run in to **RoadRunner** in Carytown, **Three Sports**

Ukrop's Monument Avenue 10K

On the verge of becoming the 25th largest race in the world, this race runs so smoothly that even with 37,000 other people running the same morning, you will love every minute, once you find a parking space.

With many contestants taking part in a costume contest, it just might be your only chance to outrun a tornado, as I recently did. Actual professionals run this more seriously, but it's beloved for the community feel, the sense of accomplishment, the togetherness, and the Richmondness of running along Monument Avenue in the spring. Take note of Arthur Ashe's statue as you head back towards the finish. He wrote the book *A Hard Road to Glory*, and around mile 4, you'll likely agree. Check out www.sportsbackers.org for more information.

in two West End locations, or **Runner Bill's** in Midlothian, the area's premier stores for runners and triathletes. For exceptional service, good advice, info about upcoming races, and shoes that actually fit, you can't go wrong at any of these shops.

VOLLEYBALL

RICHMOND VOLLEYBALL CLUB
2921 Byrdhill Rd.
(804) 358-3000
www.rvc.net
At RVC's new 73,000-square-foot digs in Henrico County, its 2,500 members can take part in league play year-round in comfort on 12 regulation volleyball courts. Sand and grass outdoor courts add to the volleyball vibe. Players of all skill levels are welcome— juniors and adults. The place is a flurry of athletic and social activity, as more than 200 teams participate in evening recreational leagues Sun through Fri. Junior teams are also an important part of RVC's mission, and the program is growing.

SPECTATOR SPORTS

In terms of professional sports, Richmond is not a big-market sports town. There, I've said it. Yes, we do score NASCAR doubleheaders two weekends a year at Richmond International Raceway that bring in celebrity drivers like Tony Stewart, Jeff Gordon, and Dale Earnhardt Jr., but the only time the NBA comes to town is when the Washington Wizards hold their training camp at VCU's Siegel Center. Still, between championship-caliber collegiate athletics, minor league baseball, professional soccer, arena football, and nationally recognized road races and extreme sports, Richmond offers a varied menu for the sports enthusiast.

The University of Richmond's success on the football field—claiming the Football Championship Subdivision title in 2008—and on the basketball court, with the men's hoops program ranked in the top 25 in 2010, has energized the faithful. VCU men's basketball program has a raucous following that packs the house during the season, making opponents wilt under the pressure. VCU and UR often get postseason bids, and since Richmond is the site of the Colonial Athletic Association's tournament, with an automatic bid to the NCAA tourney on the line, March Madness means something here.

Through the efforts of former Olympic kayaker Jon Lugbill, Sports Backers, a non-profit sports commission, has brought Richmond into the big time with several sporting events, some recurring, like the Monument Avenue 10K and SunTrust Richmond Marathon, and some, like the World Duathlon Championship, that we hosted for three years. Our unique urban landscape of trails, white water, and boulders makes Richmond a logical choice for extreme sports, as the Xterra folks have known for a decade.

AUTO RACING

RICHMOND INTERNATIONAL RACEWAY
600 E. Laburnum Ave.
(866) 455-RACE
www.rir.com

Two weekends a year in May and Sept, Richmond International Raceway (RIR) is the center of the NASCAR universe when the country's premier short track hosts a Nationwide Series race Fri night and a nationally televised Sprint Cup race under the lights on Sat. The top drivers, including past winners Jimmie Johnson, Kyle Busch, Dale Earnhardt Jr., and local favorite, Denny Hamlin, take on the challenges of RIR's ¾-mile, D-shaped oval track in front of as many as 112,000 rabid racing fans who come from all over the East Coast to cheer them on. The nationally televised Sat night races, the Crown Royal Presents 400 in May, and the One Last Race to Make the Chase in Sept are the main events and can be more difficult to get good tickets to—especially the latter, which really is the last chance for drivers to garner enough points to make it into the field of 12 drivers continuing in the Chase for the Sprint Cup. By this point in the long racing season, the feuds and squabbles between drivers have heated up, so there's as much drama as driving in this race.

Whichever race fans attend, they'll be amazed at the track's latest upgrade—a 153-foot-tall, four-sided video tower with LED video screens that are 38 feet by 24 feet each. No matter where fans are, they won't miss a second of the action. And beneath the gargantuan video screens are four enormous leaderboards, so fans will have up-to-the-second information regarding lap times, points standings, and running order in plain view.

i On Sprint Cup race days, consider parking your car at one of two satellite parking areas—park at the Showplace in Mechanicsville for $5 or at the Richmond Coliseum lot on North 7th Street for $6. Free shuttles will get you to RIR and back once the race is over.

SOUTHSIDE SPEEDWAY
12800 Genito Rd.
(804) 744-2700
www.southsidespeedway.com
The track that gave NASCAR racer Denny Hamlin his start, Southside Speedway is still a destination on Fri nights from Apr to Sept for race fans who watch stock cars race the ¹/₃-mile, oval, semi-banked, asphalt short track. The track fills up its 5,500-seat capacity when Hamlin's foundation puts on the Denny Hamlin Short Track Showdown, bringing in big guns like Kyle Busch to race and to thrill the crowd.

Since 1959, stock-car racing has been going around in ovals here, and now most Fri nights at the Speedway, racing takes place in several divisions—Modified and Champ Karts, Street Stocks, Grand Stocks, Late Model, and U-Car, a novice division. You'll get some 15- and 16-year-old drivers out here hoping to break out and become the next Hamlin, as well as veterans in their 30s and 40s. One driver started racing in his 60s—the oldest rookie ever? Adult tickets range from $8 to $12. It's $5 for kids ages 6 through 11. Kids age 5 and under are free.

i If you're tired of cars going around and around, check out Richmond Dragway near RIR. From March through October, the pedal meets the metal and the rubber meets the road. Children age 12 and under get free admission with a paying adult, and parking is free, too. Admission is $10 on Friday and $12 on Saturday, though special events are higher. You must pay cash at the track, and there is no ATM there. Call (804) 737-1193 or go to www.richmonddragway.com for more information.

BASEBALL

RICHMOND FLYING SQUIRRELS
The Diamond
3001 N. Blvd.
(804) 359-FUNN (3866)
www.squirrelsbaseball.com
Richmond's new minor league baseball team, the AA Richmond Flying Squirrels, took the field at the 9,560-seat Diamond on North Side for its inaugural 2010 season. Affiliated with the San Francisco Giants for the 2010 season, the Flying Squirrels squared off against minor league affiliates of the Red Sox, Phillies, Tigers, Nationals, Orioles, Mets,

Pirates, Indians, Twins, and Blue Jays. Who knows how the season went, but we won the goofiest name contest. At any rate, fans go "nuts" from Apr into Sept, egged on by the mascot, Nutzy. Family-friendly wackiness in between innings is the rule here. Expect lots of antics—a salute to Hush Puppies, for instance—and constant giveaways. The 2010 season featured fireworks after 13 games. If that isn't entertaining enough, the HCA Kids' Zone includes inflatables and games just outside the 2,800-square-foot team store, the Squirrels Nest. Food, such as Squirrelly Fries and other typical ballpark delicacies, including beer, is available, mostly in the $2 to $6 range. Individual game tickets are $6 to $10. Squirrel Tail Kids Club offers special deals and access for children 14 and under, including autograph sessions with players and a free ticket to many Sun games. Parking at the Diamond will set you back $3.

COLLEGE SPORTS

UNIVERSITY OF RICHMOND
(877) SPIDER-1
www.richmondspiders.com

Fielding 19 NCAA Division I athletic teams means the University of Richmond always competes against somebody somewhere. The 2010 football season marks the first time that the Spiders will play their football games on campus at the brand-new $25 million, 8,700-seat Robins Stadium, leaving City Stadium near Carytown behind for the more handsome West End digs. It's likely the stands will fill up fast at this smaller, classy-looking, brick-detailed stadium, as the team, under new head coach Latrell Scott, hopes to build on its recent successes. It will be hard to beat the 2008 season that culminated with the team winning the 2008

Football Championship Subdivision (and running back Tim Hightower being drafted by the NFL's Arizona Cardinals), but the Spiders will try. Richmond competes in the Colonial Athletic Association in football, so games against William & Mary and James Madison draw crowds of loyal alums for and against, with the requisite tailgating, bragging, and boasting. Season tickets cost $150, and single game tickets go on sale Aug 1.

The 9,071-seat Robins Center is the home court of University of Richmond Spiders men's basketball, who, under head coach Chris Mooney, compete in the Atlantic 10 conference. The team lost the A-10 championship in 2010 to Temple University, but received a No. 7 seed in the NCAA tournament. Nationally ranked as high as No. 23 in 2010, the Spiders expect to be a contender for years to come. Tickets for home games cost from $10 to $20, and kids age 12 and under get in free with a paying adult. For more information call the Robins Center Ticket Office at (877) SPIDER-1. The women's basketball team hasn't had quite as much success, but they often rate postseason play. During the regular season, tickets are $5 for every home game, so it's a bargain for its devoted fans. There's plenty of free parking around the Robins Center.

> **i** University of Richmond and VCU have club ice hockey teams whose home ice is at the South Side Ice Zone rink. If you'd like to see intercollegiate games, sometimes tournaments with teams from several universities, the games are open to the public and free. Check out the calendar at www.richmond icezone.com.

VIRGINIA COMMONWEALTH UNIVERSITY

Verizon Wireless Arena at
Stuart C. Siegel Center
1200 W. Broad St.
(804) 828-RAMS
www.vcuathletics.com

With 16 men's and women's intercollegiate teams competing in the NCAA, something sporty is almost always going on here. Winning more than 30 conference championships in just 30 years competing in Division I, VCU brings seriously talented student-athletes to town. Though soccer, baseball, and other sports draw fans, basketball is the big sport on campus here. The VCU Rams play in the Colonial Athletic Association and have thrilled fans over the years with classic March Madness in the NCAA tournament. In 2007 there was the memorable run when point guard Eric Maynor (now playing for the NBA's Oklahoma Thunder), sunk a last-second shot to propel the basketball team past Duke University in the first round of the tournament. The Rams then took the Pittsburgh Panthers to overtime in the second round, but unfortunately were outscored. In 2009 there was a heartbreaking one-point loss to UCLA in the first round. I'm almost over it.

During the regular season, the team takes to the court at Verizon Wireless Arena in the Stuart C. Siegel Center, with 7,500 screaming fans right there with them. With three CAA tournament championships, three NCAA bids, and three NIT appearances since 2004, fans expect March Madness every year. Under new coach Shaka Smart, the Rams aim to return to the top of the CAA.

The VCU women's basketball team usually plays in the postseason as well and competes every year in the CAA tournament. Single-game tickets are usually available at the Siegel Center box office, and parking in nearby garages costs $5.

VIRGINIA UNION UNIVERSITY

(804) 342-1484
www.vuusports.com

The Panthers, members of the Central Intercollegiate Athletic Association (CIAA), play football at Hovey Field on Lombardy Street. For more than 30 years, the annual Gold Bowl Classic in October has been a big draw for football fans. Tickets are between $7 and $15, with an extra $5 for parking.

The basketball program at VUU has strong traditions, not surprising for a school that has won the CIAA championship 20 times and the Division II national championship as well. NBA stars Charles Oakley and Ben Wallace were stars at VUU first. The team plays on campus at the 2,500-seat Barco-Stevens Hall, and more often than not gets a berth in the NCAA Division II tournament. Tickets are between $7 and $10.

COMPETITIONS

XTERRA EAST CHAMPIONSHIP-RICHMOND

Brown's Island
Tredegar St.
www.xterraplanet.com

If you like to see people take things to the extreme, head downtown to Brown's Island and Belle Isle when the Xterra multisport games come to Richmond every June. Since 1999, Richmond has been one of the favorite courses of Xterra athletes who, coming from more than 35 states and countries, love the urban features mixed with the man-made and natural obstacles in the James River and on surrounding trails. Athletes taking part in the off-road triathlon Xterra East Championship shoot for a slot in the Xterra World

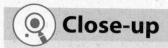

Close-up

CAA Men's Basketball Tournament

March Madness comes to Richmond the first weekend in March, when the CAA men's basketball tournament arrives at the Richmond Coliseum. The **Colonial Athletic Association** is headquartered in Richmond and has held its end-of-season men's basketball tournament here for 21 years. So every year VCU gets a home-court advantage of sorts with students and fans packing the coliseum, just down the street from campus, in black and gold.

Though more than 40,000 fans gather here to watch four days of basketball, it's a relatively easy event to attend. The Richmond Marriott and Hilton Garden Inn Richmond Downtown are within easy walking distance, and there's plenty of parking available if you aren't staying around the corner. Of course, the culmination of the tournament is the nationally televised championship game that determines which team gets the CAA's automatic bid to the 68-team NCAA tournament field. As a mid-major conference, the CAA has rarely had a team receive an at-large bid, even though the conference has produced its share of hoops hoopla, including 11th-seed George Mason University's Cinderella story into the Final Four in 2006 and VCU's recent first-round victories and close defeats. In 2010 CAA tournament champion Old Dominion upset higher seed University of Notre Dame in the first round of the NCAA tourney to underscore the conference's competitiveness. If you attend the CAA tournament, you can say you knew the next Cinderella way back when.

Championship in Hawaii. Other races geared towards locals are offered during the weekend, but if you're perfectly happy to stand on the sidelines, here's your chance to see the pros plunge into the rocky James River for a 1,000-meter swim, then bike 30 kilometers on the twisty trails of the James River Park System and Forest Hill Park, and finally, lace up their running shoes for a 10K sure to bust whatever quads they have left.

With nearly 1,000 athletes giving everything they've got on land and in the water, they deserve some crazy spectators. It's easy to find a spot to watch since the entire course is open to the public. So as long as you don't get in the way, you can catch action at various points on Brown's Island and Belle Isle and in Forest Hill Park. Since Brown's Island is the start, finish, and transition area, you'll see how the athletes suffer and how the race progresses while you relax, listen to music, and eat and drink in comfort. If you'd rather see the mountain biking in all of its gnarly glory, head to Forest Hill Park on the South Side of town to see why the Xterra athletes love Richmond's technical trails so much. Belle Isle offers a good vantage point for the swim and the run, as the race crosses the (usually) dry bed of rocks from the South Side to Belle Isle before runners race across the Pedestrian Bridge to the finish line. I'm tired just writing about it.

HORSE RACING

COLONIAL DOWNS
10515 Colonial Downs Parkway
(804) 966-RACE
www.colonialdowns.com

Colonial Downs, Virginia's only pari-mutuel horse racetrack, is about 30 miles from Richmond, just off I-64 in New Kent County. Odds are good that you'll enjoy the racing and atmosphere here whether you choose to bet or not. The 14-year-old track offers both Thoroughbred- and harness-racing seasons, with the former running from late May into July and the latter running from Sept into Nov. Thoroughbred racing takes place Sat through Wed during the season. Most of the Thoroughbred races are run on the Secretariat Turf Course, the widest grass surface of any track in North America. In the U.S. only Belmont's track is larger than Colonial Downs' 1¼-mile dirt track. Such a track means harness horses trot 1 mile and encounter only one turn, a unique configuration.

The track hosts the annual spectacle of the Strawberry Hill Races, recently moved to May to coincide with the running of the Preakness, and the Virginia Derby in July. Surely you can set aside two minutes in the middle of July to cheer on thoroughbred racing's top 3-year-old turf horses as they pound along 1¼ miles in the $600,000 Virginia Derby. The race, the second of four legs in the Jacobs Investment Grand Slam of Grass, attracts racing's finest in search of that $5 million prize. Colonial Downs' 127,000-square-foot grandstand, 95 wagering stations, and the topflight competition draw more than 9,000 fans to the derby. Virginia Derby winners have gone on to win the Breeder's Cup several times, so these horses can fly. General admission to the derby starts at $5, with additional fees for parking.

Otherwise general admission to the track is $2, which includes grandstand seating. You can upgrade to box seats or get into the Jockey Club for $8 more. If you have more than four in your party, advance reservations are recommended for the Jockey Club, which has a TV at every table so you don't miss a race. Various special events are scheduled, including live music, poker tournaments, microbrew sampling, and Racing to the Stars & Stripes—a triple threat of racing, a concert, and fireworks. See more about Strawberry Hills in the "Annual Events" chapter.

i A relative newcomer to Richmond's sporting scene is the Rockett's Landing Sprints, 1,000-meter sprints hosted by the Virginia Boat Club in June at Rockett's Landing. The James River near downtown becomes a festive scene while 20 different races shove off, showcasing men's and women's crew teams from novice to masters, both fours and eights from all over the region. See www.virginiaboatclub.org for details.

ROAD RACES

UKROP'S MONUMENT AVENUE 10K
(804) 285-9495
www.sportsbackers.org

Even with more than 37,000 people running (and walking) this race, named by *USA Today* one of the 10 best road races in the U.S., and the 26th biggest in the world, it's still fairly easy to watch the action and be a part of it. Since the course is out and back, with just a little twist, it's easy—with a little hoofing it—for spectators to see the early stages of the race on West Broad Street and head south towards Franklin Street, where it ends. If you stake out a spot near the starting line and start clapping, your hands will hurt long before the thousands of participants cruise by in the wave starts that stretch over 1½

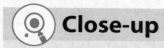

Close-up

Arena Football

Richmond has seen arena football teams come and go, so it's hard to know what to make of the 2010 arrival of two indoor football teams at once. Both the **Richmond Raiders** and the **Richmond Revolution** play March to June seasons, the Raiders in the 13-team American Indoor Football Association and the Revolution in the 25-team Indoor Football League. Both teams have local ownership and started the 2010 season strong, but only time will tell if both live to play a second season.

Though the teams would seem to be mirror images, playing on 50-yard fields with padded boards and fielding eight players at a time in similar formations, there are differences. The Raiders play in the cavernous **Richmond Coliseum,** which should make the kicking game more of a factor, and the team has tailgates in **Festival Park** just outside the Coliseum before the seven home games. Single-game tickets are $10 to $30 and can be purchased through Ticketmaster or at the Richmond Coliseum box office. Call (804) 859-0825 or go to www.richmondraidersprofootball.com for more information.

The Revolution's current home is the 4,000-seat **Arthur Ashe Center** on North Boulevard. The plan is for the Revolution to move to a new facility in the works at **SportsQuest** in Chesterfield County. This team features some local players, including guys that played at Virginia Tech, University of Richmond, and Virginia State University, and they take the field against teams from Chicago, Maryland, Michigan, and elsewhere. Season tickets start at $99 for the seven-game home stand, while single-game tickets are $10 to $25. Call (804) 595-8437 or go to www.richmond revolution.com for the latest information.

hours. Runners need encouragement farther down the road, so think about setting up spectator shop ¼ to ½ mile west of the start and finish, where the crowds aren't so tight. There are live bands every mile of tree-lined Monument Avenue, and in the past, four party stops have pumped up the enthusiasm along Monument Avenue by providing music, drinks, and even sign-making materials for unprepared spectators.

Even if you're not cheering on anyone in particular, there is plenty of good people-watching here. The *Richmond Times-Dispatch* Dress Up & Run Contest brings out the crazies—runners dressed in antebellum attire or bathrobes, Indiana Jones being chased by a giant boulder, a squirrel chasing a nut, and other quirky combinations—in an entertaining attempt to win cash prizes.

It can be hard to remember amid all the silliness that there is an actual race with actual pros from around the world competing for serious cash prizes. Watching the top talent race the 6.2 miles in approximately 28 minutes is humbling and impressive. For added intrigue, Dash for the Cash gives one lucky racer a head start against the top contenders to see if the pressure of $2,500 on the line helps or hurts. When all is said and run, the postrace party in Monroe Park is a bit of a zoo. Don't tell your friends to meet you on the steps of the cathedral after the race—36,999 other racers told their families the same thing. Sports Backers' Web site has all the details on navigating street closings and where to find parking garages and lots if you don't find on-street parking.

SUNTRUST RICHMOND MARATHON
www.richmondmarathon.com

The marathon, held in mid-Nov, attracts enthusiastic crowds along most of the 26.2-mile course that winds its way through several of Richmond's prettiest neighborhoods. Street closings make it a challenge to rush from start to middle to finish if you are supporting a particular runner, but with a good map and information, it's possible, and so appreciated. Besides the official NBC-12 Party Zones that feature music, giveaways, and spirited support at River Road just before the Huguenot Bridge, in Westover Hills near the halfway point, and in North Side near mile 20, there are 26.2 opportunities along the route for spectators to get involved. The start and finish areas downtown are where lots of the action happens, because there are three other races—a kids' run, a half marathon, and an 8K—so somebody is either coming or going nearly all the time. Since there are only so many people crazy enough to run a marathon, the numbers at the finish line aren't overwhelming, and it's not hard to reconnect with friends and family.

SOCCER

RICHMOND KICKERS
City Stadium
3201 Maplewood Ave
(804) 644-5425
www.richmondkickers.com

The Kickers play in the United Soccer League Second Division (USL-2) and bring a gutsy brand of soccer to the 9,000-seat City Stadium near Carytown in Richmond. Always competitive, the team has reached postseason play in 15 of 17 seasons, including playing in the title game five of the past eight years and winning the USL-2 championship in 2006. Some Kickers players go on to Major League Soccer (MLS) teams, and some former MLS players play for a spell here. Because the Kickers organization is involved with the Richmond Kickers Youth Soccer Club, young fans flock to see their heroes (and sometimes coaches) play on the pitch. Concessions are available at the stadium, and parking is free and easy. Single-game tickets are $10 for adults and $5 for youth, but season passes make attending multiple games even more affordable.

ANNUAL EVENTS

Richmond loves a festival and any excuse to get out and have a good time, so there are hundreds of events that keep coming back year after year. Of course, only a portion of what happens annually is listed in this chapter, but have confidence that there are multiple annual events in the area that can tempt and engage every one of your senses on just about every weekend. See the colorful city and the art displayed at the numerous art shows. Taste and smell the flavors of the world at the region's food, wine, and beer festivals. Feel your feet pound the pavement or the mud splatter all over your skin in one of our extreme and extremely fun sporting events. Give your eardrums a workout at the many music festivals (and of course, at NASCAR races).

Under the influence of Sports Backers, a nonprofit sports commission that plans and executes sporting events to build community and generate sports tourism, Richmond is becoming a participatory sports mecca, and many of these events, like the SunTrust Richmond Marathon and Ukrop's Monument Avenue 10K, are nationally known sporting events that draw thousands of runners and spectators to town. More events are added every year. Some, like the Anthem Stride Through Time 10K walk, a history and healthy-living combo, are particularly suited to Richmond's wealth of historic buildings.

The ever-increasing ethnic and cultural diversity of our region makes itself known every time you turn around to breathe in the aromas of another enticing food festival coming round the bend. If you try a new one every year, you'll gain insight, appreciation, and a few pounds. Some festivals and events are small, bare-bones affairs run mostly by volunteers. Others (like the Richmond Folk Festival) are huge, complex affairs run mostly by volunteers. Pitch in when you can, and you'll find yourself richly rewarded.

OVERVIEW

This chapter is organized chronologically. Some events move around from venue to venue; some move from month to month if they're associated with Easter, for instance. If an event starts in November and goes till January, it is listed under November. Prices are based on 2010 listings. Most events are wheelchair accessible, but call to confirm, as venues change and special arrangements may need to be made.

JANUARY

FREEDOM CLASSIC FESTIVAL
Richmond Coliseum
601 E. Leigh St.
(804) 644-8515
www.freedomclassic.com
Every Martin Luther King Jr. weekend, the feature of this festival is a basketball rivalry between historically black colleges and

universities Virginia Union University and Virginia State University. Besides the exciting athletics, a rollicking drum line and gospel music electrify the crowd on hand at the Coliseum. At halftime, there's a performance by a headliner artist, and after the game there's a party for the over-21 crowd that moves around from year to year, so check the Web site for details. Tickets to the Freedom Classic event are $15 to $20 and can be purchased at the Coliseum box office or at www.ticketmaster.com.

i If you need a road race to jumpstart your New Year's resolution, check out www.rrrc.org, the Web site of the Richmond Road Runners Club. You'll find information about the Monacan New Year's Day 10K and the Frostbite 15K that's later in January. Plus there are lots of training tips, route suggestions, running groups to join, and upcoming races to put on your calendar so you'll run happily all year long.

FEBRUARY

MAYMONT FLOWER AND GARDEN SHOW
Greater Richmond Convention Center
403 N. 3rd St.
(800) 332-3976
www.macevents.com
Spring comes early to the Convention Center for four days in Feb, just in time. Creativity blooms with seminars led by experts in garden design, interior design, and horticulture, and, of course, the display gardens that go from the whimsical to the wow. The idea is to bring nature front and center, whether you like to get your hands dirty or just appreciate floral fabrics and garden statuary. Of course, there's a marketplace where you can grab

the latest tools, rare and interesting plants and bulbs, and much more. Tickets are $10, with discounts for seniors and youths ages 12 to 17. Children under 11 are admitted free, and half-price tickets for everyone else are available after 5 p.m.

i The James River Park System offers guided walks along the Richmond Slave Trail on Saturdays in February in honor of Black History Month. Wear comfortable walking shoes and warm clothing, because you will be outside for an hour or more as you trace the steps of those who came here unwillingly. A $5 donation is requested and preregistration at (804) 646-8911 is required. See more about the Slave Trail in the "Commemorating the Civil War and Emancipation" chapter.

VIRGINIA WINE EXPO
Greater Richmond Convention Center
403 N. 3rd St.
www.virginiawineexpo.com
Fri through Sun in the dead of winter, the mid-Atlantic's premier wine and food event warms the cockles of wine enthusiasts' hearts and palates. Featuring more than 40 Virginia wineries from every region of the state, the expo features the awarding of the Governor's Cup, and then it's time to raise a glass all weekend long to see if you agree. Top Richmond restaurants provide food, chefs demonstrate what they do best, and there are special events and areas devoted to cheeses, chocolates, and anything else that goes well with fine wine. Wine is available by the taste, bottle, and to go. Tickets, available for purchase at the door or at the Web site, range from $15 for non-tasters

and some seminars to $35 for a walking-around ticket, to $75 for a special Fri event that includes extra-special vintages and chef specialties.

MARCH

CAA MEN'S BASKETBALL TOURNAMENT
Richmond Coliseum
601 E. Leigh St
(800) 745-3000
www.caasports.com
March Madness comes to downtown Richmond Fri through Mon the first weekend in March, when the local favorite, the VCU Rams, face off against their Colonial Athletic Association rivals, including William & Mary, Northeastern, and Old Dominion. The event at the Richmond Coliseum features four days of defense and dunks to settle once and for all which team gets a coveted spot in the NCAA tournament bracket. Tourney-long tickets are available and are a good deal if you have the time to take in several games. Depending on what teams make runs through the tournament, single-session tickets can be difficult to come by or abundantly available. Parking is available at several lots and decks around the Coliseum. Go to www.richmondcoliseum.net for more parking information.

CHURCH HILL IRISH FESTIVAL
213 N. 25th St.
www.churchhillirishfestival.com
The weekend right after St. Patrick's Day, St. Patrick's Church, a church built by Irish immigrants in the 1850s, celebrates the big guy by throwing a weekend street party. Here's your chance to sample Irish lasagna or the more predictable fish-and-chips. Traditional Irish music and Guinness and Harp will flow,

Irish dancers will step their stuff, and dozens of Irish vendors will hawk their wares. A $2 donation is collected at the gate. Proceeds benefit church restoration and several worthy neighborhood causes. Please leave your pets at home.

APRIL

UKROP'S MONUMENT AVENUE 10K
(804) 285-9495
www.sportsbackers.org
Since its inception, this race has been known as the Ukrop's Monument Avenue 10K, but even though the Richmond grocer sold itself to a multinational corporation in 2010, the name remains, presented by Martin's, Ukrop's successor. We all knew the race would go on; it was too big to fail. Held on a Sat in late Mar or early Apr, it's one of the 10 largest running races in the country, with more than 35,000 people running or walking it in 2010. But don't let the size scare you away. It's so well run, as evidenced by *USA Today* naming it one of the best races in the country, you'll have room to spread your elbows. Running on Monument Avenue gives you plenty of homes to drool over, and the many bands along the route keep you moving. The post-race party in Monroe Park is jammed. See more about the race in the "Spectator Sports" chapter.

EASTER ON PARADE
Monument Avenue, between Davis and Allen Streets
(804) 788-6466
www.venturerichmond.com
Of course, Easter can fall in March or April, but no matter what, there will be Richmonders flocking to Monument Avenue in the afternoon to show off their carefully (and crazily) crafted Easter bonnets. There is method to

the madness—a bonnet contest rewards the wacky. Some dogs wear bonnets, too, for a contest of their own, or are otherwise decked out in Easter finery, so there's plenty to gawk at while you stroll along the avenue, wishing you had friends who invited you to the brunches that spill out onto the porches. Even without connections, it's easy to have a good time, watching Jonathan Austin, the juggling fiend, do his zany stuff, eating food from vendors, and enjoying one of Richmond's very Richmond things to do.

i The Virginia Center for Architecture, at the corner of Monument and Davis Avenues, is open Easter Sunday and doesn't charge admission that day. It's a great place to take refuge from the Easter on Parade crowds, learn a thing or two about architecture and design, let the kids run around in the large, grassy backyard, and avail yourself of the bathrooms.

FAMILY EASTER AT MAYMONT
1700 Hampton St.
(804) 358-7166
www.maymont.org
On the Sat before Easter, hop on over to the Carriage House lawn near Maymont's Hampton Street entrance for a day full of crafts, music, and fun, including photos with the Easter Bunny. An egg hunt for kids ages 2 through 10 with prizes, bonnet making, storytelling, inflatables, and carriage rides make this the place to be. Admission is free, but some activities do require cash.

HISTORIC GARDEN WEEK
Locations vary
(804) 644-7776
www.vagardenweek.org

This is a classic Virginia-wide, weeklong event, sponsored by the Garden Club of Virginia, with a strong Richmond area component that varies every year. What doesn't change is that throngs of people want to see the five or six guaranteed-to-be-lovely homes and gardens that are open each touring day. Inside, you'll see contemporary art collections and antiques galore. Outside, you'll wander through walled gardens, cottage gardens, perennial gardens, and more. Each year the roster of historic and picture-perfect homes and neighborhoods changes, but Richmond is always well represented, as well as James River Plantations and the Ashland and Petersburg areas on different days of the week.

For the Richmond homes, one-day tickets are $40 the day of the tour and $35 purchased in advance. Children's one-day tickets cost $20 for ages 6 through 12 and are free for those age 5 and under. Online ticket sales are available, but if you wait until the day of the tour, bring cash or check. Tickets are available at each tour location and cost $20 for a single-site admission. Proceeds go to improving important and historic Virginia gardens. Wear walking shoes, and please do not wear spike-heeled shoes, since they might damage old floors.

HERBS GALORE & MORE!
1700 Hampton St.
(804) 358-7166
www.maymont.org
Held the last Sat in April on Maymont's Carriage House lawn, this event features gardening gurus expounding on the joys of herbs. Demonstrations are offered for free, but there are fees for classes, and preregistration is recommended. Wandering about and ogling is free as well, but it would be hard to

resist the more than 50 plant and craft vendors offering herbs, herbal products, heirloom plants, delicious fresh food, and more.

MAY

ARTS IN THE PARK
The Carillon at Byrd Park
0 S. Blvd.
www.richmondartsinthepark.com
This granddaddy of outdoor juried art shows in Richmond, sponsored by the Carillon Civic Association, takes over a large swath of Byrd Park around the Carillon on the first weekend in May. More than 450 artists come from all over the country to display their wares for the art lovers and the aimless walkers just looking for eye candy. All work here is made by the artists—furniture, paintings, jewelry, pottery, weaving, and more. How convenient that the event is the weekend before Mother's Day. Parking in the area is tight, so either walk in from a nearby neighborhood or park at City Stadium lots on Maplewood Avenue and Freeman Road and take the free shuttle. Parking for those needing special assistance is available near the event. Please leave your pets at home.

NASCAR
Richmond International Raceway
600 E. Laburnum Ave.
(866) 455-RACE
www.rir.com
You can find more on this in the "Spectator Sports" chapter, but suffice it to say, this is a massively popular event, drawing thousands of fans from around the country to Richmond for race week. Racing is on Fri and Sat, with the 250 NASCAR Nationwide Series and the 400 NASCAR Sprint Cup Series, but

tailgating starts much earlier in the week. Hotels in the area fill up during race week, so make your reservations early and expect traffic jams on Laburnum Avenue, especially on Fri and Sat.

ASIAN AMERICAN CELEBRATION
Greater Richmond Convention Center
403 N. 3rd St.
(804) 245-4974
www.aasocv.org
For more than a dozen years, the diverse Asian American Society of Central Virginia has produced a colorful festival, celebrating and sharing the many cultures that are their heritage. One Sat event is hardly enough to showcase the fascinating array of music, dance, art, and cuisine from more than a dozen Asian cultures, including China, Thailand, Vietnam, the Philippines, Korea, Pakistan, Bangladesh, India, and Japan, but it's worth the overstimulation. Savoring the vast and varied Asian cuisine alone could keep you enthralled from lunch to dinner, but there are art displays and traditional music, too. Dancers, many of them young children adorably attired in beautiful traditional dress, carry on the traditions of their cultures in exciting performances. It's elegant, authentic, educational, and free, though you will want to have cash on hand for the delights of the ethnic food.

STRAWBERRY HILL RACES
Colonial Downs
10515 Colonial Downs Parkway,
**   New Kent County**
(804) 994-2900
www.strawberryhillraces.com
Is it about the five steeplechase races or is it about one big party? That's for you

to decide. Moved to May in 2010 to coincide with the running of the Preakness, this longtime event with origins in the late 19th century announces itself every year with horse-drawn carriage rides through Richmond a few days before the race. Then the frenzy moves out to New Kent County. The fields where the tailgating goes on can be messy, but that doesn't stop some people from dressing to the nines. Tickets must be bought in advance, and admission is vehicle-based, so plan ahead with your friends. A car, loaded with as many people as will legally fit, costs $125 well in advance or $195 the day of the event, but payment is at Richmond Raceway Complex on the day of the race, not at Colonial Downs. It's a quirky system. To avoid a traffic hassle, many people use the shuttle system that runs from Richmond Raceway Complex, which costs $40 per person in advance and $60 the day of the races.

DOMINION RIVERROCK
Brown's Island
S. 5th and Tredegar Streets
(804) 285-9495
www.sportsbackers.org
This river festival, staged on and around Brown's Island, is an unofficial kickoff to summer fun held mid-May, with events on Fri and Sat for the entire family. If flying dogs, acrobatic bikers, muddy people, and music to groove to are up your alley, then you don't want to miss this. Riverrock is the sort of festival that encourages audience participation, with children's activities that include tree climbing and opportunities for older folk to try paddling, flyfishing, and rafting for a fee. There's even a photography contest. Other activities include mountain biking, kayaking, and the infamous James River Scramble—a 10K run with scrapes, bruises, and wet feet

for no extra charge. Food and drink are abundant on Brown's Island. A free concert and party run late into the night on Fri. Performances continue all day Sat. Proceeds go to the James River Fund to help maintain the health of both the James River Park System and the James River.

LEBANESE FOOD FESTIVAL
St. Anthony's Maronite Church
4611 Sadler Rd.
(804) 270-7234
www.stanthonymaronitechurch.org
For more than 25 years, this parish-produced festival has put pounds of cumin, coriander, and other aromatic spices to good use in the Far West End. This event, running from Fri to Sun on the weekend after Mother's Day, focuses on the savory foods of the Middle East. Some—hummus, tabouli, falafel, and roasted lamb—you might be familiar with, and others you'll want to get to know, like *shawarma*, sliced strips of beef or chicken marinated in pungent Middle Eastern spices and cooked over an open flame. Boxed lunches stuffed with four or five Lebanese treats are a bargain at $8. There are shady spots under the outdoor pavilion, or bring a blanket to spread out a picnic under the trees or eat sit-down dinners in the air-conditioned church hall. All that shelter helps when it rains, too. Music and folk dancing will keep you entertained while you sample the cuisine. You might even join in. Both admission and parking are free.

JUNE

RICHMOND GREEK FESTIVAL
30 Malvern Ave.
(804) 358-5996
www.greekfestival.com
Always the first weekend after Memorial Day

weekend, this festival, held Thurs through Sun at Saints Constantine and Helen Greek Orthodox Cathedral, isn't just about the food and wine, but try telling that to everyone in Richmond who heads there precisely because the souvlaki and baklava are not to be missed. Greek wine is available for purchase, by the glass or bottle. Greek music, dancing, and vendors entertain in the agora. Tours of the cathedral edify and educate.

i If you crave the food but can't commit to the festival, a drive-through line is open 11 a.m. to dusk each day. Print out an order form from www.greekfestival.com before you go. Chicken and pork souvlaki, gyros, moussaka, salads, and desserts are available. A $14 meal includes the entree and green beans, pilaf, *tiropita,* spanakopita, and dolmades. The entrance is at Cary Street and Antrim Avenue. Festival helpers will take your order and deliver your food to your car.

ANTHEM STRIDE THROUGH TIME
500 Tredegar St.
(804) 285-9495
www.sportsbackers.org
This 10K is designed for walkers, not runners, and the pace is perfect for taking in a changing menu of historic sites in downtown Richmond. Costumed interpreters roam the streets, musicians play, and registered participants gain admittance to more than 20 historic sites along the way for tours and occasional performances. It's a wonderful introduction to the sights and sites of downtown. Just don't tarry too long; there is a four-hour course limit. The event's start and finish are at the American Civil War Center,

so don't be surprised if you hear cannon fire signal the start. Walk-up registration is $30 for adults and $20 for those under 18. Save up to $10 a person by registering before May 1. Parking is available at the nearby Federal Reserve parking deck for $5.

BROAD APPETIT
100–300 blocks of West Broad Street
www.broadappetit.com
On the first Sun in June, it's one-stop shopping for a variety of signature Richmond viddles at this 3-block-long food festival on Broad Street, between Monroe and Adams Streets. It's free to wander about, but no doubt the sumptuous (shrimp and grits) and the strange (kangaroo, anyone?) will tempt you to fork over $2 to $5 for samples of what more than 60 of Richmond's finest restaurants offer. Some of it is even healthy! More than 15,000 people converge throughout the day to sample, savor, and see regional growers and cooking demonstrations. Proceeds benefit the Central Virginia Foodbank and Meals on Wheels.

JUNETEENTH, A FREEDOM CELEBRATION
Manchester Docks
Maury Street to Brander Street
(804) 644-3900
www.efsinc.org
The Elegba Folklore Society sponsors this celebration of African-American history and culture, the origins of which can be traced to Texas because Texans didn't learn about the Emancipation Proclamation until June 19, 1865, more than two years after President Lincoln issued it.

In addition to music, dancing, and historical reenactments from afternoon to evening, the moving torch-lit nighttime walk along the Richmond Slave Trail commemo-rates the sacrifices and suffering so many endured and illuminates how far we have come as a country and city. See more about the Slave Trail in the "Commemorating the Civil War and Emancipation" chapter.

JULY

FOURTH OF JULY AT THE CARILLON
Byrd Park
0 S. Blvd.
(804) 646-3355
The patriotic concert starts at 5 p.m., but you'll need to get to Dogwood Dell and the lawn around the Carillon earlier to stake out your blanket and chairs if you want to have a spot to sit down. Listen to the Caril-lon bells being played by Larry Robinson and then more patriotic music played by the Richmond Concert Band, with the big finish of the *War of 1812 Overture*, cannons included. Then lie back and watch the fire-works explode right over your head. Food is available for purchase.

ASHLAND FOURTH OF JULY
  CELEBRATION
500 S. Center St.
(804) 798-2728
www.hanoverarts.org
Ashland really is the center of the universe on the Fourth of July if you live in central Virginia and want to see a parade. Its classic parade along the railroad tracks is the sort of event that if you do live there, you (or your dog) are likely participating in it and if you don't, you'll want to move there so you can. Dogs and people are decked out in red, white, and blue whether they're in the parade or not, and the whole town is a picnic and party zone. Everyone's favorite synchronized (or not) lawn-chair precision

brigade puts on a show, costumed Liberty Ladies waltz by, the Basset Hound Brigade moseys along, kids scoot by on their decked-out scooters, and Uncle Sam might even ride by on a unicycle. It really is as all-American as apple pie since there is an apple-pie bak-ing contest as part of the festivities. People picnic, buy food from Boy Scouts, listen to the Hanover Concert Band, and play old-fashioned games, just like you should on the Fourth.

i The Diamond will be the place for postgame fireworks when the Fly-ing Squirrels are in town on the Fourth. If you don't have tickets to the game, drive over to Scott's Addition, near the stadium, and pull over any place that has an open vista toward the Diamond. Just hope the game doesn't go into extra innings and delay the big bangs, but at least you won't get caught in traffic when the rockets' red glare fades away.

HANOVER TOMATO FESTIVAL
8996 Pole Green Park Lane
(804) 779-7948
www.co.hanover.va.us/parksrec
Tomato is king at Pole Green Park in mid-July during this one-day celebration of the tasti-est thing ever to grow in Hanover County, the world-renowned Hanover tomato. All day long more than 40,000 jam the park to eat, buy, and brag about tomatoes. Whether you prefer your tomatoes green or red, in salsas, salads, or sandwiches, you will have no trouble satisfying your hunger with all the food available, for a fee, of course. There are contests to enter, including one for kids age 12 and under, the Best Dressed Tomato competition with all supplies provided.

Other children's activities include the usual suspects—face painting, rides, and animal exhibits. Musical performances from bluegrass to patriotic tunes add to the county-fair flavor, and there is no admission charge to the festival. Parking is free as well, but expect heavy traffic in the area.

AUGUST

CARYTOWN WATERMELON FESTIVAL
2800-3500 W. Cary St.
(804) 422-CARY (2279)
www.carytownrva.org
More than 115,000 people, 2,500 watermelons, scores of restaurants and hip shops, and no admission fee add up to the biggest one-day festival in Virginia, and it's conveniently located right here in Carytown on the second Sun of Aug. More than six stages offer every kind of musical entertainment you'd want to hear, more than 80 performers in all, and while you're sauntering from one to the next, take a stroll through the spray tent to cool off a bit.

Everywhere you turn, bowls of fresh sliced watermelon are for sale, with all proceeds going to the Shriners' Children's Hospital. It's always a hot day—and watermelon helps everyone stay hydrated. Don't worry, this is Carytown, so there are scads of restaurants offering other treats to eat and drink, and of course, other food vendors are spread all along Cary Street. The children's area in Cary Court has inflatables, rides, and too much fun. Pets are welcome as long as you clean up after them. The festival takes over Cary Street from Nansemond to Sheppard Streets, so traffic has to detour. Consider parking in the City Stadium lots on Maplewood Avenue and Freeman Road and walking over.

CHESTERFIELD COUNTY FAIR
Chesterfield County Fairgrounds
10300 Courthouse Rd.
(804) 768-0148
www.chesterfieldcountyfair.org
For one week from Aug into Sept, the fairgrounds earn their name, and the trappings of a county fair are everywhere. It's a great warm-up for the state fair and not as overwhelming. If you are in the mood for a hot dog–eating contest, a petting zoo, and classic midway rides, you'll like it here. If you want to hear live music from R & B to doo-wop, see puppet shows and the Miss Chesterfield Pageant, and view competitions for angel food cake, cucumbers, and photography, then this is the place to mosey around.

SEPTEMBER

NASCAR
Richmond International Raceway
600 E. Laburnum Ave.
(866) 455-RACE
www.rir.com
The racing season has heated up by the time everyone converges at RIR for the last race before the Chase for the Sprint Cup begins. The main event on Fri is the 250 NASCAR Nationwide Series and on Sat is the Chevy Rock and Roll 400. Only 12 drivers move on, so the race for the points is intense. See the "Spectator Sports" chapter for more information. Thousands of fans converge on RIR, so no matter how fast the cars zoom around inside the track, the caution flag is always flying on the neighboring roads during Race Week.

¿QUÉ PASA? FESTIVAL
Science Museum of Virginia
2500 W. Broad St.
(804) 378-4099
www.quepasafestival.com

For a fun and food-filled day of Hispanic culture timed to coincide with Hispanic Heritage Month, don't miss this festival that's designed to get you moving. With Zumba, salsa, and tango dancing demos and lots of audience participation, you'll burn some of the calories from all the food served up. Bands play throughout the day, and there are performances, storytelling, and a themed piñata contest open to local high school students. Admission and parking are free, but you'll want to have some money for the food and the Latin market.

43RD STREET FESTIVAL
1412 W. 43rd St.
(804) 233-1758
www.43rdstgallery.com
On a Sat in mid- to late Sept, the streets around the 43rd Street Gallery near Forest Hill Park are taken over by musicians, artists, and people who like having a good time. Always a benefit for Freedom House, the festival has a great neighborhood feel and showcases 75 local and regional artists who do cool things that I wish I could do. It's a great place to bring children, as it isn't too overwhelming and there are artsy and fun kids' activities. Food is available for purchase, as are all sorts of photography, pottery, jewelry, and much more, all lovingly crafted. Admission and parking are free.

PUBLICK DAYS AT HENRICUS
Henricus Historical Park
251 Henricus Park Rd.
Chesterfield County
(804) 748-1613
www.henricus.org
In mid-Sept, it's time to go back to the 1611 founding of Henricus, the second permanent English settlement in America, to see how things were done back then. See reenactments of military and civilian activities, learn about Virginia Indians, and try your hand at 17th-century games and crafts. In 2010 and 2011, the historical park is celebrating the 400th anniversary of Henricus's founding, and many special events are planned. Admission is free on Publick Days, though there is a fee otherwise.

STATE FAIR OF VIRGINIA
Meadow Event Park
13111 Dawn Blvd., Doswell
www.statefair.com
After its 2009 move up I-95 to Meadow Event Park, 20 miles north of Richmond near Kings Dominion, the state fair has hit its stride. You will need to, too, as you roam about the 360 acres loaded with what every state fair must have—fried food and the excuse to eat it. The grounds, attractive and rolling, spread out on both sides of VA 30 (connected by an underground tunnel, so crossing traffic isn't a problem). Since 1854, some version of this extravaganza has been taking place in Virginia, and at its new home, the state fair has classy new digs to celebrate Virginia's agricultural heritage.

The fair is open 147 hours over 11 days, and there's enough going on to keep every one of those hours occupied. Walk-around admission tickets include concerts at three stages; livestock exhibits; the produce, baked goods, quilts, and more vying for ribbons; and more than 5,000 farm animals. My favorite is the "Best Use of Duct Tape" exhibit—I saw a prom dress and tux one year. For an additional fee, the typical carnival rides for kids and adults zoom around on the midway, and of course there's food and shopping.

For music lovers, three stages feature music and dancing and shows, from big names to country cloggers. At Festival Stage, big-time artists such as Percy Sledge perform to crowds seated on the lawn. Some bring their own blankets or chairs, while others rent chairs for $5. Check the daily schedule before you arrive to make sure you don't miss the lumberjacks, magicians, balloon stunts, racing pigs, rodeos, or whatever out-of-the-ordinary shows are on your must-see list.

If you don't have any livestock or blueberry buckle recipe worth sharing, consider competing in contests as varied as demolition derby, fiddle or banjo, and even karaoke. Life is just more fun at the fair. Tickets are available at the gate or online. Walk-around passes cost more on weekends, but there's always a discount after 5 p.m. Passes for the entire 11-day run are a deal if you make multiple trips. Single-ride tickets or wristbands for rides are extra. Rides cost from two to six tickets, so look for the many deals that pop up in advance of the fair. Check out the Web site for tips and details. Parking costs $5 a vehicle and can be paid in cash only.

CHICKAHOMINY FALL FESTIVAL AND POW-WOW
Chickahominy Tribal Grounds
8200 Lott Cary Rd.
www.chickahominytribe.org
One of the Virginia tribes that met the English in 1607, the Chickahominy open their Charles City County Tribal Grounds to the public one weekend in Sept to celebrate and share their culture in the oldest-running traditional powwow in the Commonwealth. Surrounded by Native American dancers, musicians, drummers, and singers, you'll feel a part of history and help ensure it's not forgotten. You'll learn about the traditional

crafts and skills that they have passed down for generations. Food is available for sale, and there is no fee for parking or admission.

FESTIVAL OF INDIA
Greater Richmond Convention Center
403 N. 3rd St.
www.thefestivalofindia.org
This two-day, free event sponsored by the Hindu Center of Virginia draws 20,000 people to downtown for a well-choreographed extravaganza of music and dance from many Indian traditions—Bollywood, flower dance, Punjabi folk, classical—and more. It's nonstop beauty, artistry, and flow, and dance competitions add to the excitement. Then there's the smorgasbord of food, fabric, and fun, with a dozen food vendors and a children's area.

OCTOBER

2ND STREET FESTIVAL
2nd Street in Jackson Ward
(804) 788-6466
www.venturerichmond.com
This festival, always on the first full weekend of Oct, is all about bringing back the glory days to Jackson Ward. The rip-roaring music on several stages pays tribute to the days when the Deuce was the center of African-American life in Richmond and a who's who of black Americans—Duke Ellington, Cab Calloway, and Ella Fitzgerald, among others—would draw crowds to 2nd Street for the best in entertainment. Today the gospel, soul, jazz, R & B, and dance and community performers draw 50,000 people to Jackson Ward for a big party. Admission is free, but food and the marketplace require cash. Please leave your pets at home.

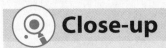

Close-up

Richmond Folk Festival

2nd to 7th Streets downtown along the river
(804) 788-6466
www.richmondfolkfestival.org

Put on your dancing shoes and your walking shoes, too, for the biggest and best festival in Richmond, an outgrowth of the National Folk Festival, which had its three-year run in Richmond from 2005 to 2007. As a part of the deal for hosting the National Folk Festival, Richmond had to agree that it would continue a folk festival on its own, and has it ever. Most of the 185,000 attendees didn't notice a change once Richmond organizers and generous sponsors took over the proceedings in 2008. From rollicking, fast-paced klezmer music, to Mongolian throat singing, to banjo-picking, to gospel, to Japanese drumming, to Mexican pole dancers (not what you think, but oh so cool) playing a flute at the top of a 90-foot-tall pole, to Cajun, to Delta blues, and more, every year the Folk Festival makes Richmond proud. It's staged right along the river, from 2nd Street down to the grounds of the historic Tredegar site and across to Brown's Island, so it brings the best of music to the best venue in town.

It's a perfect setting to soak in the history and heritage of Virginia. Peruse the schedule beforehand so you can plan your attack. Most performers play more than once, and they move about from stage to stage. Previous performers have included Dobro expert Jerry Douglas, go-go band Trouble Funk, and the Sophia Bilides Trio, but don't be swayed by name only. Some of the most enjoyable and intriguing acts have been little-known performers. If you still think folk music is a few old guys playing guitars (which can be plenty fun to listen to, too), then you need to expand your horizons. Folk is about all the folk who've been making music in different ways all over the world. It's about the common need every culture has to make a joyful (and sometimes mournful) noise and the fascinatingly different ways so many people manage to make music. In addition to the music, there are dance performances, storytelling, and crafts demonstrations, not to mention a heritage market and several sites offering cuisine from around the world.

The food is much better than most festival fare. Check out the Irish nachos at Sine's booth or find Croaker's Spot so you can grab yourself a fish boat for instant satisfaction. The festival is free, and parking is available in lots, decks, and on streets surrounding the area. Be prepared to do a lot of walking. Free shuttles run from outlying parking areas if you don't want to worry about parking. See the Web site for details.

ITALIAN STREET FESTIVAL
Richmond Raceway Complex
600 E. Laburnum Ave.
(804) 741-3606
www.richmonditalianfestival.com

On Sat and Sun of Columbus Day weekend, the sights and hunger-inducing smells of Italy take over the Horticultural Gardens at the Richmond Raceway Complex. Just as in an Italian village, there are no problems here that can't be fixed by good food and wine, warm conversation, and stirring music. You'll hear accordion players and see Renaissance dancers performing. And eat! Several local Italian food vendors are set up to serve their best—pizzas, calzones, and herb-infused dishes—and there is wine-tasting, of course. All proceeds go to local charities.

MEADOW HIGHLAND GAMES & CELTIC FESTIVAL
Meadow Event Park
13111 Dawn Blvd.
www.meadowceltic.com
Up near Kings Dominion, off I-95 in Doswell, beware of large men grunting, groaning, and throwing stuff as they compete in what's called "heavy athletics," heaving cabers, stones, hammers, and other old-school heavy things for glory and prizes, all in the name of Celtic heritage the weekend before Halloween. Other competitions are more refined, as dancers, fiddlers, drummers, pipers, and harpists give their best for the crowd. Get your jig on. During the two-day festival, there are performances by both traditional and Celtic rock bands. Authentic food, drink, and shopping at the well-stocked Celtic market, with over 70 vendors, are also available. Parking is free, and dogs on leashes (nonretractable) with a current rabies tag may attend for $5. It costs people a wee bit more. Advance tickets cost $14 for one day. At the gate it will be $19.

NOVEMBER

GENWORTH FOUNDATION'S HOLIDAY VILLAGE
Children's Museum of Richmond–Central
2626 W. Broad St.
www.c-mor.org
A kid-size neighborhood of Fan district–inspired houses helps illuminate holiday

celebrations from around the world: Hanukah, Eid, Lunar New Year, Diwali, Christmas, and Kwanzaa. Through hands-on activities, children can learn about customs and traditions all over the world and in their own neighborhood. This is the place to find Richmond's Legendary Santa, too, along with the Snow Queen and other characters. The holiday village is free to the public, and is located just off the lobby of the Children's Museum of Richmond.

SUNTRUST RICHMOND MARATHON
Starts at 7th and E. Broad Streets
(804) 285-9495
www.richmondmarathon.com
Known as "America's friendliest marathon," this event has sufficiently impressed *Runner's World* magazine so that its editors not only feature it as a "must-do" race, but are set to run it two years in a row as a part of their Runner's World Challenge. If you aren't familiar with the course, free bus tours of it are offered the day before. On race day, besides the usual water and sports-drink stops, at miles 17 and 23 you'll get junk food—gummies, Coca-Cola, and cookies—to give you that extra burst.

The race, a Boston qualifier, starts and ends downtown, with a downhill finish, but in between you'll tour several of Richmond's lovely neighborhoods and get to run along the river for a refreshing flat spell before the toughest hill at mile 10. If the full 26.2-mile run is a little much, a half marathon was resurrected in 2009. An 8K and kids' run round out the field. There's more about this race in the "Spectator Sports" chapter.

CRAFT + DESIGN SHOW
Science Museum of Richmond
2500 W. Broad St.
(804) 353-0094
www.visarts.org

This juried craft show, sponsored by the Visual Arts Center of Richmond but held in the Science Museum of Virginia the weekend before Thanksgiving is an excellent place to start your holiday shopping for those on your list who appreciate finely wrought handcrafted objects. In recent years, the show has taken over the museum's rotunda, a work of art in itself, to display the work of more than 70 artists whose work in fiber, wood, paper, clay, glass, mixed media, and jewelry ranges from the stunning to the sublime. It's $15 for a two-day pass or $10 to $12 daily.

GARDENFEST OF LIGHTS
Lewis Ginter Botanical Garden
1800 Lakeside Ave.
(804) 262-9887
www.lewisginter.org
From the Fri after Thanksgiving into Jan, the 40-acre garden lights up with more than 500,000 lights that decorate larger-than-life spiders, flowers, and butterflies, with a unicorn or train thrown in for good measure. The overall effect is magical. A winter's walk along the illuminated paths between the visitor center, the train and art exhibits in the Education and Library Complex, and the nice and warm Conservatory pack a lot into a small area. Walking down towards the Children's Garden unearths more bright delights. If you'd like to combine the winter wonderland with dinner in the Robins Tea House during the holidays, make reservations in advance (as early as Oct 1).

DECEMBER

GRAND ILLUMINATION
James Center
1051 E. Cary St.
(804) 344-3232
www.thejamescenter.com

With the flip of a switch the holiday season begins, and more than a dozen downtown buildings outlined in a million lights jump out in the sky. Around the James Center, lighted reindeer and a beautiful Christmas tree bring a sparkle to everyone's eye. It can be jammed at the James Center, since there's constant free musical entertainment and all the food and merchandise vendors are hawking their sparkly holiday items, so follow the high school band down Cary Street towards the other activities that are part of Celebrate/Illuminate, the larger holiday celebration. Parking is available for $3 at the parking deck on the corner of 10th and Canal Streets after 4 p.m.

i If you're already downtown for the Grand Illumination, try to squeeze in the Capitol Tree Lighting Ceremony at 5:30 p.m. Or stick around afterwards for tours of the Governor's Mansion. Venture Richmond sponsors Celebrate/Illuminate throughout downtown in conjunction with the Grand Illumination. There are children's activities at Main Street Station, holiday items (and food) at the 17th Street Farmers' Market, carriage rides, and canal boat rides. Canal rides are $2 and carriage rides are free, so expect lines.

DOMINION HOLIDAY PARADE
Starts at 2500 W. Broad Street and ends at 7th and Broad Streets
(804) 788-6478
www.richmondchristmasparade.org
This parade has a new name since the parade has passed by Ukrop's, and the long-time Richmond grocer who cosponsored this event, is no more. What hasn't changed is that on the first Sat in Dec, 100,000 people

line the 2-mile route along Broad Street from the Science Museum to 7th Street downtown. Every year enormous balloons float up above the crowd, marching bands strut their stuff, holiday-themed floats roll past, and Santa waves to all. There is no cost to attend, though you'll want to bring money for snacks and trinkets to fortify (or bribe) the little ones while they wait.

COURT END CHRISTMAS
Various locations downtown
(804) 649-0711
www.richmondhistorycenter.com
This Sunday-only event is a fantastic way to see many of Richmond's historical treasures all dolled up for Christmas, and it's free. It's one of the few times that Monumental Church is open for tours, for instance. Shuttles run regularly between sites (including the Church Hill Historic House Tour), but walking or hailing a carriage ride outside the old Wickham House seems more in keeping with the spirit of the times. The Valentine Richmond History Center has children's activities, and the rest of the museum is open for leisurely learning about Richmond's history. An abbreviated, first-floor-only tour of the Wickham House is a must-do, though

it will whet your appetite to return another day to see the whole thing. You'll feel like you walked in upon a party at John Marshall's home, since colonial dancers cavort in costume in the parlor, and there are sweets to be eaten downstairs. The Capitol, VCU, and the Museum of the Confederacy join in the festivities as well with music and exhibits, as do other venues from year to year.

CAPITAL CITY KWANZAA
3000 Mechanicsville Turnpike
(804) 644-3900
www.efsinc.org
This celebration of the seven principles of Kwanzaa, sponsored by the Elegba Folklore Society, is held at the Showplace and opens with a drum call, processional, and candle-lighting ceremony. Throughout the event, listen to inspirational speakers, learn about African culture and history, and sway to the sounds of R & B, reggae, hip-hop, soul, and African dance and music. Children can focus on craft making, adults can take part in workshops, and everyone can shop for African-inspired artwork and house furnishings and eat at the African market. Children under 12 are free, and it's $5 to $6 for everyone else. Free parking is available.

KIDSTUFF

Whether the children in your lives want to be inside or out, Richmond is an easy sell as a kid-friendly destination. This chapter brings together the classic childhood experiences of Richmond, such as Maymont, with some unexpected directions, as in up—climbing trees with Riverside Outfitters. The chapter is divided into themed lists: Animal Adventures, Massive Machinery, Fit and Fun, etc., and is not geographically arranged. Sure, there are lists of skating rinks and sports centers here, but I don't waste words on what's pretty standard and self-explanatory. The Richmond area has city experiences such as museums and theater, but we also have old-timey country fun like berry picking and animal interactions.

Besides what's listed below, there are so many beautiful parks in and around Richmond where kids love to roam the paths, all but one of which is free, and some get their due in the "Parks" chapter. And don't forget that beautiful river out there that gets a chapter of its own, too. The "Recreation" and "Annual Events" chapters also have good tips for family-friendly activities and events. And of course, the "Museums" and "Attractions" chapters feature many entertaining options as well.

Price Code

The price code is based on the cost of a single admission.

$.....................under $6
$$ ....$6 to $10
$$$ ....over $10

ANIMAL ADVENTURES

MEADOW FARM MUSEUM   **FREE**
3400 Mountain Rd.
(804) 501-2130

This is a family-friendly oasis in the hubbub of the suburbs, with horses, pigs, chickens, cows, and sheep to visit. It's a wonderful place to get a hands-on look at farm life just before the Civil War. Through most of the year and during special events, costumed volunteers give tours of the Sheppard house, set up as if it is still 1860. During the spring Sheep to Shawl event, blacksmithing and sheepshearing go on. Volunteers help visitors do the tasks of yesteryear—spinning wool, weaving, washing clothes the old-fashioned way—and the harvest festival adds other autumnal activities like sorghum pressing and cider making to the mix. Kids can try their hands at old-timey games as well. Crump Park, with a fun playground and picnic shelters, is just around the bend, so today's children can participate in 21st-century playing, too. From Jan to early Mar, the museum is open weekends only. Otherwise, hours are Tues through Sun from noon to 4 p.m. Admission is free.

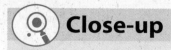

Close-up

Maymont   Free–$

Various locations
(804) 358-7166
www.maymont.org

The notable thing about Maymont is that it has so much going on, it could appear in just about every category in this chapter. Maymont is a favorite of families because it offers so much for free, though donations are accepted and appreciated. Please note that if you're not a Maymont member, there is a charge to explore the **Nature Center** and to take a tram ride. I wouldn't advise anyone, even the most energetic, to try to see all of Maymont in one day. This write-up will focus on animal action at Maymont, but see the "Attractions" chapter for more-detailed information about the house and gardens, which are also well loved by children and adults.

Depending on how much walking you are in the mood for, parking is available at three different entrances. The **Children's Barn**, at Spottswood Road and Shirley Lane, is the best starting point if the barn, farmyard animals, and bear and raptor habitats are on your list. Just remember that the barn is closed on Mon. The **Nature Center,** at 2201 Shields Lake Dr., is where you can see the wettest animals, as in fish, turtles, and otters, in their aquariums, and the Hampton Street entrance, at 1700 Hampton St., is the shortest route to the **Dooley Mansion and Carriage House** *and* the Italian and Japanese Gardens.

Barn Days, on weekends in the spring, are especially crowded, with people vying to see newborn animals. Seeing babies act their age never gets old and appeals to people of all ages. Peacocks, rabbits, pigs, goats, donkeys, ducks, and geese round out the barnyard and nearby fields. Walking farther, you can spot a bull, sika deer, elk, and wily bobcats and foxes. Down the hill is the aviary, and round the bend you'll come upon the bear habitat, which has a pond and steep hill where the bears romp or laze. Take a detour into **Raptor Valley** to get up close and almost personal with a variety of hawks,

---

METRO RICHMOND ZOO $$–$$$
8300 Beaver Bridge Rd.
(804) 739-5666
www.metrorichmondzoo.com

This 50-acre, privately run zoo keeps growing and adding animals and interactive activities for visitors. It's not just about looking through cages here. With a couple of kiddie rides like a jungle carousel, which will cost you $2 for a ride, and the $3-a-pop Safari Sky Ride, this has a bit of the county-fair feel to it, but with more exotic animals. Along the paved paths that are wheelchair- and stroller-friendly, you'll see cheetahs, spider monkeys, zebras, orangutans, apes, waterbucks, Bengal tigers, and 140 more species. You can take a 15-minute train safari through the "savanna" for $3 more per person, but you'll get unbelievably close to 18 different species of animals. The highlight for many visitors is feeding a giraffe here—that's one slimy tongue! I prefer to watch the penguins being fed, thank you very much. If you like the adorable budgies, buy a feeding stick for $1 and you'll have the colorful birds eating right out of your hands. If you're inclined to come back more than twice

owls, and bald eagles. Keep in mind that birds at Maymont are those that couldn't survive in the wild after some injury, but they still are impressive.

Continuing around the bear habitat and past the Cactus Garden, you will eventually come to the **Japanese Garden,** a favorite of children with its waterfall and rocks, picturesque bridges, bamboo forest (with a path through here and there), and a pond with stepping stones and big, colorful carp. In season, gorgeous azaleas are in bloom. Clambering up the stairs will get you new views of the Japanese Garden and deliver you to the Italian Garden, another fun place to explore, especially the acoustical intrigue of the gazebo. Upwards to the west of the Dooley Mansion stand wonderful old cedars that beg to be climbed. There's abundant open space to run around if anyone has any energy left. The Dooley Mansion does offer tours that cater to children, for a fee. For the price of walking down the road, the carriage collection is available for viewing. Bathrooms are nearby, which can help the cause. Paths lead down and up to the Nature Center or back over to the Children's Barn.

The Nature Center's big claim to fame are the 13 tanks brimming with all manner of fish, turtles, and everyone's favorite, river otters, all creatures that live in the same river we live near, drink, and bathe in (after it's been treated, of course.). Ponder that with your little one. It's such a treat to be able to watch the critters here at eye level for as long as you'd like.

On weekends, younger children (and their parents) will appreciate the myriad activities available for them in the **Discovery Room**—plush animal toys and a stick-on felt board with a changeable river, land, and sky. It's all hands-on in this room. Puzzles, games, do-it-yourself puppet show—the sky's the limit here. It will be hard to drag your child out, but the promise of spying real otters or huge turtles might just do the trick. If you like the dark, head into the Nocturnal Gallery to learn who makes what sound, but shhh! The spring peepers, barred owls, flying squirrels, and crickets want to have their say.

a year, it pays to buy the annual pass. Kids under age two are admitted free.

ℹ️ Bring quarters to use in the food-vending machines at the Children's Barn—not for yourself, but for the animals. Feeding the goats is one of the highlights of any trip—or watching others get slimed if you or your child is not so inclined. But don't feed them anything other than what Maymont provides. We don't want any goat tummy aches.

ARTISTIC ADVENTURES

CARPENTER SCIENCE THEATRE $
Science Museum of Virginia
2500 W. Broad St.
(804) 864-1400
www.smv.org

Not where you would expect a theater to be hiding, on the third floor of the Science Museum of Virginia, but this company does a great job of using theater and storytelling to bring scientists and scientific and historical concepts to life in one-act plays for elementary- and middle-school children.

Compelling performances have included *North Star Light: Pathways to Freedom,* about the Underground Railroad, and the more whimsical *Shakespeare and Galileo,* an imaginary meeting between the two great minds that combines wit and wonder. You can attend a play without paying admission to the museum or combine both experiences.

i The Virginia Museum of Fine Arts offers Young @ Art many Wednesday and Thursday mornings, for children ages two through five (accompanied by an adult) to explore art through stories, hands-on fun, and movement. The themes change month to month, but the learning continues. Pay $5 for the child (VMFA members $4), and adults participate for free, but preregistration is required. Call (804) 340-1405 or check out www.vmfa.state .va.us to register.

RICHMOND FOLK FESTIVAL   FREE
2nd Street to 5th Street to Brown's Island
www.richmondfolkfestival.org
Richmond's favorite festival isn't an adult-only affair. Besides special children's activities designed to introduce them to music from many cultures, interactive art activities take place during the day. But that's almost superfluous because kids just love hearing the music and dancing along to it.

Upon entering the festival off 2nd Street, the first stage is a perfect one to park with young children—less walking, proximity to food and drink vendors, and a great big hill that you can lounge on or roll down, depending on the age range of your group. Flat areas for dancing and spinning and all-around socializing make it perfect for families with children. Don't forget the sunscreen, though, if you're there during the day.

Other venues throughout the festival are worth visiting, depending on the musical lineup; just remember that if you walk down the hill, you're going to have to climb back up. Stamina is key. Bring cash for food and drink. Find more about the Folk Festival in the "Annual Events" chapter. It's free to listen, though donations are appreciated and necessary to keep it coming back every year.

i The Visual Arts Center of Richmond offers a deal that can't be beat. For several Saturdays in the fall and winter, children ages 5 through 15 with an accompanying adult can participate in Side by Side Saturdays from 10 a.m. to noon and try out exciting art activities each time. Stained glass, knitting, metalsmithing, and wood turning are just some of the possibilities. There are always five or six options. Did I mention these sessions are free? Visit www .visarts.org/youth-classes-programs/ side-by-side-saturdays to register.

THEATRE IV $$$
114 W. Broad St.
(804) 282-2620
www.theatreivrichmond.org
Whether you're looking for a little culture or a little fun, or both, Theatre IV's plays will likely fill the bill. Staged primarily at the beautiful Empire Theatre downtown, the shows for those age three and older offer Broadway on Broad for families, from fairytale retellings like *Jack and the Beanstalk,* to the historical, like the award-winning *Buffalo Soldier,* to the classic Rodgers and Hammerstein gem, *The Sound of Music.* For the stagestruck, Theatre IV offers an overnight option where budding thespians see a show and take part in stage-related activities—makeup, costuming,

Sports Centers and Laser Tag

The places below are more alike than different, though some have go-karts and some focus more on the miniature golf and batting cages. $$–$$$

Bogey's Sports Park: 1675 Ashland Rd., (804) 784-1544, www.bogeys sportspark.com

Ironbridge Sports Park: 11400 Iron Bridge Rd., Chester, (804) 748-7770, www.ironbridgesportspark.com

G-Force Karts: 4245 Carolina Ave., Building B, (804) 228-0188, www .gforcekarts.com

Laser Quest Richmond: 889 Research Rd., Midlothian, (804) 378-0400, www.laserquest.com

LASERTRON Laser Tag Arena at Skate Nation PLUS, 4350 Pouncey Tract Rd., Glen Allen, (804) 364-1477, www.skatenationplus.com

Oasis Sports Park: 15300 Cosby Rd., Chesterfield, (804) 739-6833, www .oasissportspark.com

Patterson Sports Park: 12586 Patterson Ave., (804) 784-4544, www.pat tersonsportspark.com

Putt Putt Fun Center: 7901 Midlothian Turnpike, (804) 272-4373, www .myputtputt.com

Rockwood Golf Park: 10239 Hull Street Rd., Midlothian, (804) 276-3765, www.rockwoodgolf.com

Windy Hill Sports Complex: 16500 Midlothian Turnpike, Midlothian, (804) 794-0010, www.windyhillsports.com

stage combat, and acting—and then get to spend the night in the historic theater.

FIT AND FUN

Baseball

**RICHMOND FLYING
SQUIRRELS** $$–$$$
3001 N. Blvd.
(804) 359-FUNN
www.squirrelsbaseball.com

It's perfectly legitimate for your kids to go nuts at Richmond's minor league baseball team's games, played at the Diamond, just off I-95. The emphasis is on family fun and entertainment, with the nutso new mascot, Nutzy, leading the way. Special salutes to the marshmallow and hush puppies give you an idea of the wackiness level here, and 13 fireworks shows after games in the 2010 season sound like kid heaven. See more about the team in the "Spectator Sports" chapter.

Climbing

PEAK EXPERIENCES $$–$$$
11421 Polo Circle
(804) 897-6800
www.peakexperiences.com
There are several ways to introduce your child to rock climbing with expert instruction. Peak Experiences offers a summer Base Camp for children ages five through seven, which will give them the chance to climb the walls without driving you crazy. Any time of the year, the Climber's Sampler is a great way to get three climbs in with an expert staff belayer working the ropes. Children ages 8 through 12 can sign up for Cliffhanger, a program with a monthly fee that meets two hours a week and offers instruction in climbing and belaying and occasionally gets the kids climbing out on Belle Isle and at the Manchester Climbing Wall. If you are unsure that your child is up for this, the first session of each month features a one-hour free guest pass. Call in advance to nab one of those.

Additional programs with more high adventure are offered for older children and teens. Of course, all climbers need to fill out a waiver, and in the case of those under age 18, a parent or legal guardian must sign off as well. Equipment rental is available here, plus there's a well-stocked store if your climber gets serious enough to warrant purchase of the gear.

RIVERSIDE OUTFITTERS $$$
6836 Old Westham Parkway
(804) 560-0068
www.riversideoutfitters.net
For an out-of-this-world adventure right here in the city, get in touch with Riverside Outfitters, the only place for miles around that offers recreational tree climbing for kids age five and up. With certified arborists and redundant controls, safety is all taken care of as your child ascends into the trees and zooms down along a zip line. It's too much fun. Birthday parties are especially popular for kids, either in the James River Park System or perhaps even in your backyard. For extra adventure, sign your child up Outdoor Adventure Kamp. Full- or half-day camps are available for children ages 6 through 12, as is a teen camp that teaches climbing, rappelling, orienteering, and includes a whitewater rafting trip.

> **i** For a fun spin on a traditional playground, swing by Mary Munford Elementary School at 211 Westmoreland St. in Richmond when school isn't in session. Your child will love something there, whether it's the wooden bridges or car or tower or house with Wizard of Oz cutouts, the mock ship, or the xylophonesque instruments. In an adjacent fenced area, there are tire swings, traditional swings, and other equipment perfect for spinning, climbing, bouncing, and jumping. There isn't much shade, so come prepared.

Ice-skating

RICHMOND ICE ZONE $$–$$$
636 Johnston Willis Dr.
(804) 378-7465
www.richmondicezone.com

SKATENATION PLUS $$–$$$
4350 Pouncey Tract Rd.
(804) 364-1477
www.skatenationplus.com
Richmond has two public ice rinks, one in the Far West End and one on the South Side. They are partners in ice, but the Far West End one offers a climbing wall and laser tag and

Off to the Races

Admission/registration for the races below is $$–$$$.

The **Anthem Moonlight Ride** is a summertime bike ride at night in the city. Yes, you heard right. Kids age eight and older can ride their own bikes with adult supervision, and parents with bike seats or trailers can bring younger ones along the 8- or 17-mile bike ride through the streets of Richmond. A goody bag includes a blinky light. Of course, helmets and front and back lights are required.

The **Columbia Mini Muddy Buddy** is held at Pocahontas State Park in May for kids ages 4 through 13 to get down and dirty. There is a short obstacle course and the infamous mud pit at the end. Parents must accompany any children ages four through six through the mud pit.

A **Kids' Miler,** associated with the Monument Avenue 10K, will likely have a new name in 2011. It's for kids ages 5 through 12 and goes in waves grouped by age before the 10K begins. A parent may run with a child age eight and younger; the finish line is the same as for the 10K.

The **Mud Guppy** is a fun race that's part of Sports Backers' Henricus Dauber Dash scheduled in Aug. The Mud Guppy run is a 1-mile course with a muddy outcome for participants ages 8 through 14.

The **Richmond Times-Dispatch Kids Run** is held the evening before the annual SunTrust Richmond Marathon. Kids ages 5 through 12 run a 1-mile course that starts at the Diamond. They'll snag a commemorative medal and a T-shirt for the effort. Walk-up registration is available the day of the race.

other extras. Both rinks have packed schedules, with figure-skating and speed-skating lessons, hockey leagues, and other fun activities planned, so check their calendars online before heading over. Skate rentals and lessons are available at both rinks. A growing speed-skating program at Richmond Ice Zone is attracting attention due to world class coaches. Try speed skating for a month for free to see if it's the sport for you or your child.

The name isn't quite right anymore, as the only pick-your-own fruit this farm offers are pumpkins in the fall. Prepicked local berries are available in May. It's a nice ride out in the country to get there, and a side trip to Patrick Henry's Scotchtown could fit in nicely. See about that in the "Attractions" chapter. At the farm, the autumnal activities include free hayrides out to fields and more fun in Pumpkin Playland, including winding your way through a maze for $3. Food such as burgers, hot dogs, fries, and doughnuts are all part of the charm.

FUN ON THE FARM

ASHLAND BERRY FARM $
12607 Old Ridge Rd.
(804) 227-3601
www.ashlandberryfarm.com

CHESTERFIELD BERRY FARM $$–$$$
26002 Pear Orchard Rd.
(804) 739-3831
www.chesterfieldberryfarm.com

This farm, in the Moseley section of Chesterfield County, has transformed itself from a basic pick-your-own place to a mini–county fair during spring through fall, with a price to match. There is an admission fee for adults and children, with a super pass available on the weekends for a train ride and all sorts of over-the-top entertainment. Children age two and under are free.

Picking strawberries can be as simple as picking up your basket, catching a hayride to the strawberry fields, and getting to work. If you teach your children well, perhaps your basket will fill up with red and ripe strawberries as opposed to green and white ones some little hands prefer. You pay by the pound, so make sure you can eat what you pick.

Back at the starting point, there are animal and play areas, a train ride, and more that your little ones might be entitled to, depending on which admission package you choose. No matter, pony rides and some other attractions cost extra, as do the various homemade treats like barbecue and strawberry milk shakes. Picnic tables offer a spot to sit down and relax, but you might not want to stay too long; portable toilets are the only facilities available.

Once the weather turns to fall, pumpkins are the star attractions, so the hayrides head to the pumpkin patch. But there's much more to do than look for a great pumpkin, including an eight-acre corn maze, pig races, duck races, and more autumnal trimmings than you knew there could be.

DODD'S ACRES FARM
4077 Market Rd.
(804) 781-0180
This is the same farm that supplies local grocery stores with produce, but if you want to cut out the middleman, head there yourself for strawberry picking Mon through Sun in season. Hours vary, so be sure to call. The price here depends on how much you feel like picking.

LEWIS GINTER BOTANICAL
GARDEN $$
1800 Lakeside Ave.
(804) 262-9887
www.lewisginter.org
Though children love to roam all the paths here, the specially designed Children's Garden will particularly captivate them and perhaps turn their thumbs green. Find more about the garden's other features in the "Attractions" chapter. The Children's Garden has several sections, all perfectly scaled to younger folks. There's a farm garden with beds where kids can help plant, cultivate, and pick fruits and vegetables, which are then donated to the Central Virginia Foodbank. At the International Village there are several play structures inspired by African, Latin American, Asian, and Native American cultures, and children can take part in building a bamboo structure, Everyone's House. Other sections include a Bird and Butterfly Meadow with paths and bridges, and a garden with weird and whimsical plants that will be sure to spark some interest in the botanical world. One of the favorite sections, the grand and wheelchair-accessible Tree House, sits at one end of the lake and is the sort of magical place every child should have the chance to play in. To get the most out of your stay in the garden, be sure to take advantage of the learning stations sprinkled throughout the garden and the many special programs offered to make each visit active and engaging.

On Tues, June through Aug, the garden is open until 9 p.m., and Families after Five is a great way to take in the pleasures of the Children's Garden when the heat of the summer has dissipated. Water Play, which is open when the air temperature is above 70 degrees in the late spring and summer, goes until 8:30 p.m. every Tues. Bathing suits are the appropriate attire and splashing is encouraged. Plus, a rotating program of kid-friendly activities involving bugs, dirt, garden art, and other engaging good times is offered.

Everything the garden offers for children helps to connect them with nature and underscore their part in nurturing a healthy planet and community. And yes, there are shady spots, among them the Leafy Overlook, and plenty of benches that allow everyone to take a breather and enjoy the vistas that are visible everywhere you look. Food is available at the Garden Cafe back at the visitor center. Of course in winter the big highlight is the GardenFest of Lights, which brightens up every inch of the gardens with half a million twinkling lights. The Conservatory always has special themed displays for children, and it's guaranteed to be warm in there. See more on that in the "Annual Events" chapter.

i Make your holiday reservations starting October 1 for Christmas Teas at the Jefferson Hotel (call 804-788-8000) and Santa Brunches at Lewis Ginter Botanical Garden (804-262-9887) in December. They will sell out!

SWIFT CREEK BERRY FARM
17210 Genito Rd.
(804) 739-2037

In the summer, blueberries are the center of attention at this farm in Chesterfield County. It offers darned good blueberries, and that seems to be enough to entice families here every summer. Buckets are available, and the high bushes usually spread down low enough for young children to nab enough and do their best *Blueberries for Sal* impression: "plink, plank…." As long as you can convince the child in question to pick blue and purply berries, I guarantee they taste so much tastier than the ones you buy at the store. If you can manage it, it's better to pick your berries in the early morning or in the evening, as there isn't much shade in the fields. Please call to hear about picking conditions and hours, and arrive, at the latest, 30 minutes before closing time. Plants and farm-fresh veggies are also available for purchase. During picking season they are open Mon through Sat. The price you pay is dependent on how serious a bunch of pickers you brought along.

i If your child is obsessed with fire engines and the like, have lunch or brunch at the Halligan Bar and Grill at 3 N. 17th St. near the farmers' market. Its claim to fame is an actual flaming red fire engine inside that kids can get up close to, and all sorts of firefighting equipment on the walls and ceiling. The pendant lights over the counter are firefighter helmets, and the crew dresses like firefighters might at the station. Besides the razzle-dazzle, the food—burgers, barbecue, sandwiches, wraps, and piled-high brunch fare—will satisfy a houseful of firefighters and everybody else.

MASSIVE MACHINERY

FIELD DAY OF THE PAST $$
1741 Ashland Rd.
(804) 741-8468
www.fielddayofthepast.net

Field Day of the Past, Goochland County's September event, is more fun than you can shake a stave at, and is free for children under age 13. Kids will think they've stumbled into *Mike Mulligan and His Steam Shovel*, with old-timey equipment hissing and grumbling, a cotton mill, stave mill, steam sawmill, and antique vehicles everywhere. Pig races, tractor races, and carnival rides offer more fun than the 21st century usually does.

KINGS DOMINION $$$
16000 Theme Park Way
(804) 876-5000
www.kingsdominion.com

For those kids who can't get enough roller-coaster rides, perhaps a day here will cure them. With 15 coasters, including the new Intimidator 305, which hits speeds in excess of 92 mph, I wouldn't bother buying lunch here, because somebody's going to lose it. For those not quite so adventurous, there are plenty of nostalgic rides like the log flume, old-timey cars, and a carousel. For the youngest children, Planet Snoopy just opened near the park entrance. Here the Peanuts gang will be on hand to say hi as youngsters tackle the tamest rides in the park. Kings Dominion's water park gets its due under Water World below.

VIRGINIA AVIATION MUSEUM $$
5701 Huntsman Rd.
(804) 236-3622
www.vam.smv.org

With aircraft inside and out, the Virginia Aviation Museum, a partner of the Science Museum of Virginia, aims to tell the story of flight along with the science of flight. The museum, well placed near Richmond International Airport, offers a good spot to watch the planes come in and take off. It's a museum where looking up pays dividends. See reproductions of Wright brothers' gliders, biplanes from the 1920s and '30s, Admiral Richard E. Byrd's *Stars and Stripes,* the first American research plane to fly over Antarctica, and military aircraft from World War I all the way up until the late 20th century. Most children are drawn to the yellow *Piper Cub,* a full-size aircraft that they can climb inside of and work the controls. In addition, the Kids Ready Room allows for role-playing. Outside, imagine you are flying in the enormous SR-71 Blackbird, the U.S. Air Force high-altitude reconnaissance jet that hits Mach 3 and faster, and flies higher than 80,000 feet. Gulp. Glad it's standing still here.

TRAIN TIME

For kids (and adults) who have a thing for trains, Richmond has some unique attractions. For an hour or two devoted to seeing real trains in the city, head to **Bottom's Up Pizza** in Shockoe Bottom for pizza and train watching out on the deck. From there, it's a short walk to the famed **Triple Crossing,** where three train tracks cross the same spot on different levels, the world's first and the only one in the country. Then head over to historic **Main Street Station,** and if you've timed your visit right, go out onto the second-floor balcony when an Amtrak train is either arriving or departing (check schedules at www.amtrak.com but expect delays), because you will be at eye level with the train coming or going around the bend. Freight trains chug through, too, on the western set of tracks.

OLD DOMINION RAILWAY MUSEUM $
102 Hull St.
(804) 233-6237
www.odcnrhs.org/

Visit the newly renovated and expanded Old Dominion Railway Museum in the Southern Railway Station that operated passenger service from 1914 to 1957. Using artifacts accumulated over the years, the museum will re-create a stationmaster's office with telegraph equipment and a waiting room, and tell the story of what working on the railroad was like. In the old, enormous brick-and-beamed freight room, there are plans to set up a huge HO-scale model railroad. Outside, it's "all aboard" the kid-size locomotive and big caboose. Other railroad artifacts, eventually including a Pullman sleeping car, are on display near the 1831 birthplace of Virginia railroad operations. Due to open summer of 2010, the museum is open to the public on Sat and Sun. After your visit, zip nearby to Legend Brewery for lunch on the deck and more potential train spotting.

MUSEUM MARVELS

AGECROFT HALL $–$$
4305 Sulgrave Rd.
www.agecrofthall.com
It's easy to feel transported to another century at Agecroft Hall, but it's the building itself that was transported, all the way from England and the 15th century. Children often think of Agecroft as a castle or a fortress, and the heavy gates and armor displayed here in this Tudor estate incongruously placed on the banks of the James River only add to the vibe. Besides a guided tour of the house, the grounds are perfect for roaming children. And in the summer, a picnic on the grounds before a performance of the Richmond Shakespeare Festival's offerings is a picture-perfect way to introduce older children to the Bard. Children age six and under are admitted free to Agecroft.

CHILDREN'S MUSEUM OF RICHMOND-CENTRAL $$
2626 W. Broad St.
(804) 474-CMOR
www.c-mor.org
The Children's Museum, also known as CMoR (their mascot, Seymour, is a dinosaur), is a bright and busy place, especially for children up to age eight. From Labor Day to Memorial Day, the Museum is open Tues through Sun, though it does open on Mon on major school holidays like Martin Luther King Jr. Day. In the summer, the museum is open every day.

An easy and affordable way to try out the museum occurs during Target $1 nights, held several evenings a year. That's $1 a person for two and a half hours of block building, water playing, fossil digging, make-believing, cave dwelling, and more. The museum features so many separate sections, it would be hard to hit them all in one visit, but the good news is that playtime is crucial for children's development and happiness, and the museum's offerings are sure to entice any child to join in the fun.

Even before you walk in the door, the reverberating discs near the entrance provide a clue to what's in store— noise (well, honestly, yes), along with playfulness and whimsy. Opportunities for role-playing abound in the Town Square, with the popular TV station that kids can operate, a garage, market, cafe, bank, school, and mini emergency room with an ambulance stationed right there. For the ultimate in make-believe, the Playhouse has a perfectly sized stage and audience area, complete with props and costumes.

Budding artists can wield more than paintbrushes in the museum's amazing art studio. Museum helpers are available, as are sinks for hand washing. Kids can let their masterpieces dry on a rack while they explore the rest of the museum and take them home when they are ready.

The Great Outdoors exhibit highlights the James River and the woods and rocks of our area with a climbing area that overlooks a beaver dam. Those who like to get down on their knees can go under the beaver dam and through tunnels, too. The classic Children's Museum cave is still a great place to play hide-and-seek, and it's bright enough in there that no one will get spooked. If the weather suits, real outdoor play is possible, with hula hoops, a sand area, tricycles, musical instruments for a joyful noise, and a playhouse. In the warmer months, don't be surprised to see and feel squirts of water here and there outside to cool things off.

i Head to the Lora Robins Gallery of Design from Nature on the University of Richmond campus to see some of the more than 100,000 objects that range from Jurassic dinosaur fossils to gems, shells, and minerals. A must-see is the crowd-pleasing and spooky Fluorescent Rocks from the Permanent Collection, where a flip of the light switch transforms hundreds of seemingly dull rocks into glowing greens, reds, purples, and yellows. The gallery is closed Mondays and during some school breaks, so call (804) 289-8276 to check. Admission is free.

For the tiniest tots, the Little Farm is a gated, scaled-down, comfy section for them to crawl through and toddle about. There's a nursing room just off this area, so that's handy for breast-feeding moms seeking privacy.

There's a separate outdoor area for these little ones to enjoy outside without being overwhelmed by the bigger kids, and there's a shady spot for adults and children to sit.

CHILDREN'S MUSEUM OF RICHMOND–SHORT PUMP $$
2200 Old Brick Rd.
www.c-mor.org/short-pump

This Far West End satellite of the more centrally located CMoR opened in June 2010 in a 15,000-square-foot section of West Broad Village. The museum features themed areas that use children's literature as the imaginative starting point for kids ages one through eight, including exhibits titled The Enchanted Castle, Pirates' Cove, The Magic Bean Stalk Climber, Whale of a Tale Water Play, and more.

i The castle-like Virginia Center for Architecture offers special children's programs several times a year. It turns out that the story of the *Three Little Pigs* is a great introduction to the concept of building materials. Check out www.virginiaarchitecture.org for more details and see more information in the "Museums" chapter.

SCIENCE MUSEUM OF VIRGINIA $$–$$$
2500 W. Broad St.
(804) 864-1400
www.smv.org

On your way into or out of the Science Museum of Virginia it's likely you'll be mesmerized by at least one of the giant "kugels," granite globes floating on water that make up the *Mary Morton Parsons Earth-Moon Sculpture*. Somehow their rotation is as effortless looking as a pro spinning a basket-ball on a finger, but the larger Earth sphere weighs 29 tons, so I wouldn't recommend spinning that. The relative Earth-to-moon size and distance is to scale. It's all mind-boggling, which is the point. For those with children who have an interest in the sciences, and perhaps even more for those with children who think they don't, this place can turn on some lightbulbs.

In the grand rotunda, there are nods to the buliding's former glory days as Broad Street Station. See how many train references you can find as you make your way through the museum. Of course, the 96-foot, 10-inch Foucalt pendulum takes center stage in the 10-story rotunda. The basement houses Science Unplugged, a large area of interactive, kid-size exhibits that employ several senses. No tasting, please. Kids can build an arch (and knock it down), make huge bubbles and loud noises, and crank some electricity, all without realizing they are learning scientific concepts.

Upstairs are demonstration areas and more interactive displays on space, the human body, optical illusions, and the environment. If your timing is perfect, you might be able to see rats play basketball as they train for their own version of March Madness. Another fun event is the annual egg-drop contest, where students vie to have their cushioned egg survive the drop through the stairwell intact. I feel sorry for whoever cleans up the mess, but it's still fun. If your schedule and pocketbook permit, the IMAX Dome and planetarium shows are entertaining and educational, and often heart-stopping depending on the destination.

WATER WORLD
Water Parks

COBBLESTONES SPLASH ZONE
WATER PARK $$–$$$
13131 Overhill Lake Lane
(804) 798-6819
www.cobblestonespark.com

Splashing and swimming in the 38,000-square-foot pool or zooming down the waterslides are the main attractions here. The Python slide can send you rocketing at 60 mph down into the pool. Don't worry—other, tamer slides are nearby. If you'd rather not swim, or need a break, there's a sandy beach with picnic tables, umbrellas, and beach volleyball courts, not to mention areas for basketball and softball. Something you don't see every day are the goofy floating tricycles; Aqua Cycles are available for rent on the seven-acre lake. A snack bar is on-site, but you are allowed to bring in your own food, which can help make the day more affordable.

HADAD'S LAKE $$$
7900 Osborne Turnpike
(804) 795-2659
www.hadadslake.com

With three large pools, a baby pool, a fishing lake, miniature golf, volleyball and basketball courts, and much more, your family could find plenty to occupy them here. With some parts of the pool as deep as 16 feet, everyone must either pass a swim test or wear a life jacket. Bring yours from home in case they run out of their stash. Activities not usually allowed in pools, including jumping off a rope swing and water trampoline, guarantee more squeals per splash than in a typical pool. Fishing on their small lake is also allowed, but you'll have to bring your own bait and tackle.

ℹ️ For dozens of outdoorsy events and opportunities—too many to list here—get your hands on the yearly James River Days brochure that is chock-full of paddles, treasure hunts, snorkeling expeditions, fishing activities, and so much more to engage children and the whole family in appreciation of the James River's riches. The complete calendar of events is available online at www.jamesriveradvisorycouncil.com.

WATERWORKS AT KINGS DOMINION $$$
16000 Theme Park Way
(804) 876-5000
www.kingsdominion.com

I'm not sure even the ocean can compete with the 20 acres of slides, rides, and wet wonderland that is part of the larger amusement park. Little kids and their parents can frolic around the Surf City Splash House, with slides, a swinging bridge, and more, or at Lil Barefoot Beach. Those who like the wild rides can zip down the numerous twisty and tall waterslides, and the Zoom Flume lets families ride a raft together. Not every ride or activity here is appropriate for all children, so you'll want to check the Web site before you pack the bathing suits.

Whitewater Rafting

RIVER CITY RAFTING $$$
100 Stockton St.
(804) 232-RAFT
www.rivercityraft.com

RIVERSIDE OUTFITTERS $$$
6836 Old Westham Rd.
(804) 560-0068
www.riversideoutfitters.net

Two companies will float you down the James, strings and life jackets attached. Riverside Outfitters offers an Upper River trip that works for families with children as young as eight who weigh at least 50 pounds. It takes two to three hours and explores the river from beneath the Pony Pasture rapids to Reedy Creek, avoiding the largest rapids downtown. River City Rafting ask that your child be nine for its Class I and II rapids trip. RCR offers guided tubing trips for children age nine and up. Both companies agree that children 12 and up who are at least 90 pounds and know how to swim can do the trip that goes through the rollercoaster-like Hollywood Rapids, but that's the parents' call.

ANTIQUES AND COLLECTIBLES

Let's get one thing clear; I am not an antiques expert. The strict definition of an antique is anything 100 years old or older. Adding the word collectibles is the clue that you shouldn't hold me to that 100-year rule, though certainly some stores in this chapter do adhere to that definition religiously.

The Richmond region is home to more antiques stores than you can shake an antique saber at. I honestly don't know how they all manage, but for some, it is by banding together under one roof at an antiques mall. Several notable ones are listed below. Of course, there are just too many antiques and decorative arts and collectible stores in the Richmond area to list them all here, and what some people consider antiques shopping, other people consider merely treasure hunting. You'll find some thrift and consignment stores that might have some antiques but are weighted more towards the collectibles in the "Shopping" chapter.

If the thought of browsing around antiques stores puts you into a coma, consider two related yet quite different activities. Stop by a fast-paced antiques auction at one of the auction houses listed below. There's plenty of action there, so it might change your mind about antiques. Or check out the architectural salvage yards in Richmond. They are full of building materials and house and building parts that nobody makes quite the same way anymore. In each category—Antique Dealers, Malls, Shows, Auctions, and Salvage Yards—the listings start in Richmond and head west, north, and east before crossing the river to the South Side.

ANTIQUES DEALERS

Downtown

BRADLEY'S ANTIQUES
101 E. Main St.
(804) 644-7305
Mr. Bradley has been in the antiques business for 65 years, high-end all the way, so you should expect to see only the finest furniture and artwork when you step in his shop. Covet the 18th- and 19th-century furniture—Queen Anne, Chippendale, Victorian—or check out his silver collection or the 18th- and 19th-century paintings. It's just a couple of blocks from the Jefferson Hotel, behind the Richmond Public Library. Bradley's is open by appointment only, but it's worth making the call.

Carytown

SHEPPARD STREET ANTIQUES
103 S. Sheppard St.
(804) 355-7454
www.sheppardstreetantiques.com

There's a definite botanical vibe in an English-country-garden sort of way here, but with some more modern touches mixed in. Buying trips to England help keep this whimsical Carytown shop floor-to-ceiling full, and looking closely here brings rewards for your home and garden. You'll browse amidst 19th-century furniture, decorative accessories, antique linens, silver, and lamps. Garden accessories, antique and otherwise, are available year-round, but the owner pulls out all the stops on garden ornaments in the spring. If the store isn't on Sheppard Street when you go, don't fret; it has likely moved within Carytown to Cary Street, but details weren't firm at deadline.

i Four local antiques experts, including the owners of Stanley Antiques, Savenkov Gallery, and Sheppard Street Antiques, collaborate on occasional itinerant antique sales that pop up twice a year in otherwise vacant storefronts around Richmond. Go to www.theperfectnestantiques.com to see when the next sale will be.

The Fan

THREE SWALLOWS
1839 W. Broad St.
(804) 622-7760
If you are in the mood for something exotic, wander into Three Swallows and be surrounded by Asian furniture and accessories. Eighty percent of what's here is Chinese, though there are objects from Mongolia and Tibet as well. Not everything is antique here, but what is, you won't find anywhere else around town. Take the Chinese altar table, the rosewood Chinese cabinet with ox-bone inlay, the baskets, the carved water bucket with a swan handle, painted screens, the

jade carvings, or the statuary. The store is closed on Sun and Mon.

i If you're in the Fan on the hunt for fine antiques, you might swing by Bill Adams Antiques at 1423 W. Main St. to see if the shop is open. He doesn't keep regular hours anymore, but the shop is full of classic period furniture and true antiques. Call (804) 355-0254.

West End

ELEPHANT'S TOE ANTIQUES
5808 Grove Ave.
(804) 282-5550
This shop specializes in pieces as unique as its name. Much of the American, English, French, and German furniture dates from the turn of the century to the 1920s, though there are some items from the 19th century, and even earlier if the owner just had to have it. With a selection of chandeliers, mirrors, and sideboards—mostly antique, but some reproduction—this shop outfits many a dining room and entryway, down to the finishing touches of urns and other decorative accessories.

KIM FAISON ANTIQUES
5605 Grove Ave.
(804) 282-3736
www.kimfaisonantiques.com
The fastest way to get to Europe from Richmond is to head to Kim Faison's shop. You travel across the pond just by walking in the door. The owner takes several buying trips a year to Europe, looking primarily for 17th-, 18th-, and 19th-century English, French, northern European, and Scandinavian antiques. The painted Swedish furniture is amazing, and her collection of Delft

pottery is among the best in the country. The furniture and accessories are all antique; you won't find reproductions or any mid-century modern here. The shop is open Mon through Sat, and don't worry if you don't have a truck with you; they routinely deliver pieces to Florida and Connecticut.

STANLEY ANTIQUES AND FINE ART
5612 Grove Ave.
(804) 288-2011
www.stanleyfinearts.com
Located in the Libbie and Grove shopping area in the West End, this shop carries 18th- and 19th-century furniture, art, and accessories from England, France, Japan, China, and elsewhere, as well as letting mid-century modern pieces in the door. The owner has a background in art history and conservation, which accounts for her wide-ranging collection of antiques and fine art.

North Side

BELLEVUE ANTIQUES
4034 MacArthur Ave.
(804) 262-7002
This 1,000-square-foot shop in the cute retail area on MacArthur Avenue in North Side is owned by the owner and manager at Antique Village in Hanover County. Stop in here when you're shopping at Once Upon a Vine, a nearby wine shop. Bellevue offers a general line of merchandise with some actual antique furniture, but here you're more likely to find more pottery, jadeite, toys, and advertising. The shop is open Thurs through Sat.

ROBIN'S NEST ANTIQUES AND COLLECTIBLES
6925 Lakeside Ave.
(804) 553-1061

This Lakeside shop offers an affordable mix of antiques and collectibles, including sterling silver, mainly flatware, postcards, and linens. Some of the furniture is primitive, some country, and some is from the 19th and early 20th century. In business for 15 years, the store is closed on Sun.

Hanover County
Glen Allen

CLASS AND TRASH
11088 Washington Hwy.
(804) 798-0567
www.classandtrash.com
You have to love a place confident enough to sport this jaunty name, and I really appreciate truth in advertising. Within the 6,000 square feet inside, you'll find all sorts of furniture, more vintage than antique, and you'll find architectural pieces, too, including stained-glass windows and lots of shabby chic. It is a huge mix and a lot of fun, with the large outdoor area filled with garden furniture and statuary. It's open seven days a week.

Mechanicsville

LAUREL MEADOW ANTIQUES & REPRODUCTIONS
8348 Lee-Davis Rd.
(804) 559-2400
www.laurelmeadow.com
Housed in Laurel Meadow, a circa-1800 home that is registered as a Virginia Historic Landmark and is also on the National Register of Historic Places, this business deals in both 18th- and 19th-century antiques and reproductions, with the emphasis on reproductions. Still, the English and American antique tables, chairs, case pieces, and accessories are worth a look. The Windsor

chair once owned by General Henry Knox has sold, but maybe you'll bond with the 1730 William & Mary blanket chest from the Shenandoah Valley. They are open by appointment or on most weekends, but be sure to call first.

Hanover Courthouse

TWO FROGS ON A BIKE
13262 Hanover Courthouse Rd.
(804) 537-5213
As quirky as its name, this shop, on US 301 in an old general store built around 1900, has all sorts of treasures for those willing to wander out to Hanover Courthouse. Here you'll find furniture from 1900 to 1940, early clocks, vintage toys, and glassware. They've been in business 20 years, so they know what their customers want. The shop is closed on Tues.

Doswell

SQUASHAPENNY JUNCTION
10570 Doswell Rd.
(804) 876-3083
This out-of-the-way old general store, not far from railroad tracks or Kings Dominion, looks exactly like what an antiques store of a certain style should look like, with white siding and a porch overflowing with who knows what—a rowboat, old signs, you name it. You won't find anything new or any reproductions here, but you will find more than enough merchandise dating from 1880 to 1960, all of it nostalgic, some of it just plain wacky. The main room overpowers you with old store advertising, signs, counters and equipment that lived their previous lives in another general store, gas station, barbershop, or a factory. The Mystery Room has old medical equipment mixed in with the religious and soulful, and then there's a folky room with hordes of folk

art. Time your visit well, as the store is open only Sat through Mon. The owner is traveling those other days, as far as 12 hours away, getting more cool stuff.

Chesterfield County

Bon Air

WILD ORCHID ANTIQUES
2624 Buford Rd.
(804) 267-1788
Now no one is saying that everything in here is antique, but the pieces that are, are exceptional, and everything else is beautiful as well. If you're lucky, the turn-of-the-century English oak gateleg table will still be here when you visit, but on any visit you might come across some interesting early to mid-20th-century pieces or even a barometer from 1800 to 1840. This store's niche is completely refurbished European chandeliers, mostly Spanish from the 1940s but a couple Florentine ones as well. There might be 20 of them glistening at any time. The store is open seven days a week.

Midlothian

GATES ANTIQUES, LTD.
12700 Old Buckingham Rd.
www.gatesantiques.com
Tucked up on a hill in a residential neighborhood, it's easy to zip past this sprawling complex that looks like someplace you'd want to live. A family-run and -owned business since 1961, the Gates specialize in American and British furniture, from 1650 to 1890, with a little bit into the 20th century. Of course there will be other items from other places, such as a gorgeous 19th-century porcelain bowl from China. Four buildings are loaded with prime antiques. The main building has furniture and accessories arranged as if in a

home and is the only one with heat and air-conditioning, so be prepared if you want to see everything they have. This family clearly loves the antiques business and wants to educate its customers every chance they get. To that end, they've made an educational DVD series, written a book, and they hold antiques classes periodically so people will know what they are looking at when they shop. As much as is visible on the Web site, that's still just scratching the surface. And speaking of scratches, they've just started selling the best furniture polish on the planet, Gates Red Oil furniture polish. The secret is there's no silicone in it, because silicone will ruin any finish out there.

SAVENKOV GALLERY
628 Scotter Hills Court
(617) 283-5050
www.savenkovgallery.com
Specializing in Biedermeier, Empire, and Neoclassical antiques, this husband-and-wife team moved their high-end antiques business from Boston to Richmond recently. Their stunning collection also includes Art Deco from 1920 to 1930. Once their European buying trips turn up gems, the furniture is refurbished by craftsmen at their workshop near Prague. The owners, who are members of the Antiques Council, open the gallery by appointment only.

Powhatan County

BOB BLEVINS ANTIQUES
4171 Old Buckingham Rd.
(804) 598-4830
In the antiques business since 1994, Bob Blevins has a full antiques restoration shop that's been going strong for 30 years. His 1,500-square-foot retail space has furniture from 1690 into the 20th century. Most of the furniture is American, but there are some fine English chests and a revolving bookcase made in Dover in 1920. Besides the furniture, you'll have plenty of glasswork to look over. The shop is open Mon through Sat.

TYE'S ANTIQUES
4050 Anderson Hwy.
(804) 598-1220
www.tyesantiques.com
This family-run business features 1,800 square feet of Victorian, Empire, primitive, and country antique furniture, along with pieces of more recent vintage. At least 70 percent of the contents of the place is furniture, most of it antique, including some mid-19th-century pieces. The owners like the old styles but carry items that appeal to all sorts of customers, including plenty of glassware and collectibles. Along with the retail trade, they operate a furniture restoration business and can handle the lost arts of caning chairs. They are open Mon through Sat, and on Sun by appointment only.

ANTIQUES MALLS
Richmond

Stratford Hills

FOREST HILL ANTIQUE MARKET
6800 Forest Hill Ave.
(804) 320-7344
Over the years, this market has grown and changed names, but it's still tucked in the Stratford Hills Shopping Center on Forest Hill Avenue. More than 20 dealers stock a little bit of everything here, including china, porcelain, silver, jewelry, and collectibles. As far as furniture goes, you might find some 19th-century pieces, but more often 20th-century, including one booth of mid-century modern pieces. The market is open seven days a week.

Henrico County/West End

WEST END ANTIQUES MALL
2004 Staples Mill Rd.
(804) 359-1600
www.westendantiquemall.com
Get your game face on before you decide to tackle the two buildings full of 250 booths in what *Richmond Magazine* readers always say is the best antiques mall around. That's 53,000 square feet of antiques and collectibles just off West Broad Street in the Crossroads Shopping Center. It's mind-boggling. Of course, the quality and array of goods varies from vendor to vendor, but in all this space, it would seem you could find the (fill in the blank here) of your dreams. Local delivery is available, and they offer a 72-hour return policy for a full refund. They are open seven days a week.

WILLOW PLACE ANTIQUES GALLERY
5446 W. Broad St.
(804) 288-6301
With 20 booths of high-end antiques, including old wallpaper and 18th- and 19th-century furniture from Europe and Japan, you won't be disappointed by the quality of merchandise here. Richmond arts maven Pam Reynolds shops here on occasion, and her porcelain collection is legendary, so that's telling you something.

Hanover County

Mechanicsville

ANTIQUE VILLAGE
10203 Chamberlayne Rd.
(804) 746-8914
www.antiquevillageva.com
Amongst the 50 dealers here in the 10,000-square-foot space that is central Virginia's oldest antiques mall, open since 1971, 50 percent of them sell antique furniture. That should give you enough to choose from. There are other serious dealers here, such as the Civil War Room, which handles an astounding array of both Union and Confederate relics, including uniform parts, documents, and weapons. There is plenty of almost anything else you can think of, from folk art to Fiestaware, too. The village is closed on Wed.

COLD HARBOR ANTIQUE MALL
8147 Mechanicsville Bypass
(804) 427-7555
Open seven days a week in the Windmill Shopping Center in Hanover County, this place has made a name for itself since opening in 2005. With more than 70 dealers showing their wares, you'll need some serious time to take it all in. Certainly, some of what's here is more in the collectible category, and I don't know what to say about the Stephen King book I saw, but there is no shortage of dealers here with antique furniture, fine art, and vintage jewelry.

THROUGH THE GARDEN GATE ANTIQUES
10351 Chamberlayne Rd.
(804) 746-5778
Over 60 dealers jam this 20,000-square-foot place that's attached to the sweet and feminine Through the Garden Gate gift shop. Men roll their eyes at the gift shop but can handle the antiques area. It stocks perhaps 70 percent antiques to 30 percent home decor. The owner hits up one to two auctions a week from as far afield as Maryland and Pennsylvania, besides estate sales and auctions in Virginia. They are open seven days a week.

THE VILLAGE SHOPPES
8007A Mechanicsville Turnpike
(804) 746-7337

This antique mall hides out in an old Southern States building and shouldn't be confused with Antique Village, but it is. Twenty dealers share space here, and you'll find a mix of merchandise that includes furniture, some from the 19th century, glassware, American pottery, art glass, currency, coins, stamps, clocks, and toys. They pride themselves on personal service and swear they give customers a half million reasons to shop in Mechanicsville.

Chesterfield County

Midlothian

MIDLOTHIAN ANTIQUES CENTER
13591 Midlothian Turnpike
(804) 897-4913
Again, the term antiques is applied loosely here, in this expansive place with over 100 dealers, but it's a popular place to go treasure hunting for furniture, glass, china, coins, and even dolls. It's quite a mix of merchandise. In the village of Midlothian, it's open seven days a week.

SIXTY WEST ANTIQUE MALL
8004 Midlothian Turnpike
(804) 560-5557
This building showcases the wares of 85 dealers seven days a week. Though there is an emphasis on reproductions and home decor, you will find some 19th-century furniture in here, along with porcelain, china, glasswork, and original oil paintings.

ANTIQUES SHOWS

RICHMOND ACADEMY OF MEDICINE
ALLIANCE BENEFIT ANTIQUES AND
FINE ARTS SHOW
www.ramaf.org

If you haven't found the piece of your dreams at local shops, make sure to hit up this annual event, held at the Science Museum of Virginia in Feb. This charity fund-raiser has been bringing the country's finest antiques dealers to Richmond for almost 50 years. The quality is extremely high, and so is the fun quotient. Three dozen exhibitors from the mid-Atlantic, South, Northeast, and even Michigan and Ohio, bring their wares, and proceeds from ticket sales go to local charities that improve the health of Richmond's citizens. A weekend (Fri through Sun) pass for the show is $15.

Henrico County/East End

RICHMOND ANTIQUES SPECTACULAR
The Showplace
3000 Mechanicsville Turnpike
(804) 769-8866
www.renaissancepromotions.net
This show, held four times a year, brings 175 dealers from all over. Each show features a specialty within the larger show, such as antique tools, garden, Civil War, and antiquarian books, but every show will have a mix of antique maps, toys, furniture, and much more.

ANTIQUES EXTRAVAGANZA
The Showplace
3000 Mechanicsville Turnpike
(336) 924-4359
www.antextofnc.com
This three-day antiques and old collectibles show has been coming to the Showplace in Mechanicsville twice a year since 1985, bringing as many as 150 high-quality dealers to town from up and down the East Coast. Buyers come from throughout the mid-Atlantic to browse and buy American and European furniture and decorative accessories, including silver, linens, pottery, period clothing, and much more. A weekend pass is $7 or $6 for one day. Parking is free.

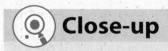

Close-up

Architectural Salvage

Perfectly suited for a green lifestyle, salvage places are the ideal fit in Richmond, since the historic housing stock provides beautiful materials when some owners update and renovate. For owners who want to restore their homes to their original grandeur or need to match the porch railing, the door style, or lighting fixtures, the salvage yards are the places to go.

NORTH SIDE

Paul's Place
1009 Overbrook Rd.
(804) 228-9999
www.paulsplaceonline.com
Founded in 2008, Paul Ferramosca has acquired an astounding collection of house parts for you to reuse and repurpose. The possibilities are endless. It would be a full-time job to go through his warehouse; just looking online can eat up your day, but the old railings, corbels, lighting, and building materials, including heart of pine flooring, have such character, it's tempting to want to give them a good home again.

EAST END

S. B. Cox Salvage
5200 Hatcher St.
(804) 222-3500
Old school, perhaps because they just demolished an old school, this place is in a scruffy, out-of-the-way part of town east of downtown. It is worth a look simply because they are in the demolition business and therefore get first dibs on some very interesting material. Some of what you'll find here is raw building materials—brick, stone, etc.—but if you want a claw-foot bathtub or other plumbing fixtures or need several doors for your 500-room mansion, you will have plenty to choose from. They are open Mon through Sat.

SOUTH SIDE/MANCHESTER

Caravati's
104 E. 2nd St.
(804) 232-4175
www.caravatis.com
This is the granddaddy of architectural salvage joints in Richmond, in the same family since 1939. For the remodeler and do-it-yourself person, walking around here is like being a kid in a candy store—more expensive than most candy stores, but still. It is hard to walk through their massive, 40,000-square-foot warehouse and not covet the many things I don't need that are displayed or stacked or piled here—staircases, ironwork, barn doors, old fireplace mantels, and old wood flooring and beams. Their stained-glass comes from all over the U.S. and England. I can't wander through here without thinking that my husband needs to make cool furniture out of the doors and shutters and everything else that's here. He has a different reaction—he sneezes. Then it's time to go outside and check out their extensive holdings out there. Caravati's is open Mon through Sat. Make sure you plan on spending at least an hour here.

ANTIQUES AUCTIONS

Richmond

MOTLEY'S AUCTION
4402 W. Broad St.
(804) 355-2100
www.antiques.motleys.com

What started in a Chester dairy barn in 1967 is now an auction company with an international reach. Preview day is usually the day before the irregularly scheduled auctions. Motley's has auctions for real estate, autos, and industrial items, besides antiques, but they know more than the difference between a Ford and a Chevy. Their research over the years has identified a set of four Gothic Revival chairs by Philadelphia cabinetmaker Crawford Riddell and an important late-18th-century Valley of Virginia corner cupboard. A typical auction, if one is ever typical, includes jewelry, coins, and furniture. In 2010 a standing-room-only crowd bid on surplus state items, including chandeliers that had hung in the State Capitol. Depending on the auction, bids are accepted online, in person, by telephone, or by absentee bids.

Hanover County

GRINDSTAFF AUCTIONS
8073 Mechanicsville Turnpike
(804) 730-0756
www.grindstaffauctions.com

This auction house holds antiques and collectibles auctions frequently throughout the year and throughout the area—50 auctions in all if you count their on-site estate auctions that often include antiques. The antiques auctions are generally held on the weekend, usually with a preview the same day. Depending on the day, you might get the chance at furniture from the 19th century, coins, jewelry, fine porcelain, and folk and fine art.

i Antiques expert and Richmond writer, the late Emyl Jenkins, wrote widely praised nonfiction antiques books such as *Emyl Jenkin's Appraisal Book* before she turned to fiction. Her first novel, *Stealing with Style,* follows antiques appraiser Sterling Glass as she unravels a mystery. The *New York Times* called it a "highly entertaining tale of thieving, mystery and fraud . . . . Delightful." She followed it with another Sterling Glass mystery, *The Big Steal.* Perhaps the books will make your visits to antique stores that much more intriguing.

Chesterfield County

ALEXANDER'S
9131 Midlothian Turnpike
(804) 674-4206
www.alexandersantiques.com

Perhaps I should have put this place in the nightlife chapter, because their famous Thurs auctions start at 6:30 p.m. and go typically until 1 a.m. and sometimes until 4 a.m. Preview the 700 items up for bid the day of the auction, starting at 9 a.m., and if you can't be there during the auction, you can leave a bid with one of their agents, who will bid on your behalf up to your limit. It's an archaic yet well-oiled machine that never fails to entertain. Not everything being auctioned off is an antique, but it's typical to find such pieces as a 19th-century Chippendale chest on chest or a leaded-glass dressing screen up for grabs. Thank goodness food is available for purchase, so nobody will faint from hunger.

SHOPPING

Richmond's array of stores includes many of the chains you encounter just about anywhere in the U.S. of A.—Target, Gap, Whole Foods, and on and on. Throughout the region there are several malls and strips filled with the expected, but the big players are two high-end malls—the larger, two-level Short Pump Town Center, and Stony Point Fashion Park. The former is stacked with Nordstrom, Macy's, Crate & Barrel, Pottery Barn, and dozens of other national retailers along with some local stores. Just south of the river, Stony Point Fashion Park features Saks, Dillard's, Anthropologie, Restoration Hardware, and more of the usual suspects. Both malls tried to re-create the old-fashioned outdoor shopping feel that Richmond already has in spades, or at least in Carytown, Shockoe Slip, Libbie and Grove, and Lakeside.

Richmond's shopping districts have their own organic feel that draws shoppers in for the realness vibe as much as for the good goods, not to mention that the food and ambience are far superior to any mall food court. Shockoe Slip and Shockoe Bottom have an urban chic about them, with cobblestones and small brick-faced shops intermixed with larger stores in old warehouses. North Side has an interesting little shopping area on MacArthur Avenue, and the Lakeside section is a destination for thrift and gifts. The shops on the avenues of Libbie and Grove have an appeal beyond their West End addresses. But just one word sums up Richmond's most fun and funky shopping destination: *Carytown*. This 1-mile stretch of shops, restaurants, and other businesses along West Cary Street between Thompson and Boulevard was named the South's ninth-best shopping neighborhood by *Southern Living* in December 2008. Take that, big malls!

OVERVIEW

This chapter doesn't come close to naming all the worthwhile shopping destinations in and around town—it couldn't possibly. What follows is a sampling of stores in categories in which Richmond excels. Not all the gems are in jewelry stores, but if you browse the shopping districts named above, you'll find many more. FYI, the "A River Runs Through It" and "Recreation" chapters contain most of the sporting-goods store information.

BOOKSTORES
Shockoe Slip

FOUNTAIN BOOKSTORE
1312 E. Cary St.
(804) 788-1594
www.fountainbookstore.com
Tucked snugly into Shockoe Slip, this charming, small, independent bookstore is what bookstores are supposed to be like—warm, friendly, and full of good books. The staff here makes fabulous recommendations and

will help you find what you want even if you don't know what that is. The site of many literary events and author signings, the shop is open seven days a week. Park on the street or in the Virginia Street parking deck on level 5. It's free until 3 p.m. on weekends.

The Fan

BLACK SWAN BOOKS
2601 W. Main St.
(804) 353-9476
www.blackswanbooks.com
Black Swan Books rates as perhaps the classiest used-book store in Richmond because it's interested in rare, out-of-print, leatherbound, and antiquarian tomes. Here you'll find some beautiful books—classic literature, art, Civil War, and more, including a selection of children's books, too. Black Swan is open Tues through Sun and on Mon by appointment.

Carytown & Museum District

CHOP SUEY BOOKS
2913 W. Cary St.
(804) 422-8066
www.chopsueybooks.com
This place has a friendly, hipster vibe courtesy of the community-minded crowd that runs this mostly used-book shop with 45,000 volumes on two floors in Carytown. Though it probably doesn't have the latest best seller, it offers a strong selection of literature; photography, art, and design books; and graphic novels. The store's contents are in great shape—no musty books allowed. Thoughtful staff will order anything in print for you and give you a 10 percent discount if they didn't have it in stock when you wanted it. Chop Suey features 800 hand-picked new titles in stock, ones you likely wouldn't come

across at those predictable chains. Check the Web site for literary events and readings.

NARNIA CHILDREN'S BOOKS
3100 Kensington Ave.
(804) 353-5675
This adorable shop packs the best of classic and contemporary literature into its Museum District spot. With close to 1,500 titles to choose from, you will be impressed by the staff's expertise at matching book to child. The little bookstore that could, Narnia brings several nationally known authors, such as Tomie dePaola, to Richmond every year for literacy promotion and special events. Gift wrapping is complimentary, and there's a parking lot behind the store. E-mail narniabks@aol.com for more information. The store is closed on Sun.

Near West End

BOOK PEOPLE
536 Granite Ave.
(804) 288-4346
www.bookpeoplerichmond.com
This is an old-fashioned bookstore with 20,000 new and used books jammed into an old house just off Patterson Avenue. Among other treasures, you'll find foreign-language books and a good mystery selection. These book people take your book search seriously—if it's out there, out of print or not, they will do their best to find it for you. Lots of book signings and monthly book swaps add to the community feel.

North Side

CARYTOWN BOOKS
4021 MacArthur Ave.
(804) 261-7710

The name is a vestige of all the years in Carytown, but this small, independent bookstore has been in North Side the last five of its 80 years in business. Cassandra is the resident book kitty. For bookworms, there are 6,000 new and used books, cards, and gift bags.

COMICS & COLLECTIBLES

The Fan

VELOCITY COMICS
904 W. Broad St.
(804) 225-7323
www.velocitycomics.com
Bringing comics to serious and silly fans since 2003, Velocity Comics offers great fun and great deals near Virginia Commonwealth University. Look out for sudden "sneak attack sales" that chop 25 percent off everything in the store for two hours.

South Side/Westover Hills

STORIES
5067 Forest Hill Ave.
(804) 231-4213
www.storiescomics.com
You need to know two things about this store, in business since 1982: Its motto is "If it's weird, we probably have it." And it has an inventory of more than one million comics, so go get what you want, including Manga, graphic novels, posters, and action figures. A second location is at 9040 W. Broad St. in the West End (804-270-4216).

West End

DAVE'S COMICS AND CARDS
7019 Three Chopt Rd.
(804) 282-1211
Nestled in the hallway of the Village Shopping Center for years, Dave's has an impressive comic book collection from A (*Adventures of Spiderman*) to X (*X-Men*) and just about everything else in between, from the golden age of comics to tomorrow, somehow. The 1700-square-foot shop has a toy department, too.

GARDEN SHOPS

Bon Air

**SNEED'S NURSERY AND
GARDEN CENTER**
8756 Huguenot Rd.
(804) 320-7798
www.sneedsnursery.com
Sneed's offers a relaxed shopping experience. Its size is manageable, yet you can still find a varied selection of annuals, perennials, shrubs, and trees. The unexpected gem here is in the small, well-stocked gift cottage. It's the perfect place to find something interesting for the gardener in your life, but it also has a quirky selection of home decor and unusual holiday decorations.

Far West End

STRANGE'S GARDEN CENTER
12111 W. Broad St.
(804) 360-2800
www.strangesgardencenter.com
If you want to plant it, Strange's has it. There's a full selection of vegetables, herbs, perennials, annuals, shrubs, and trees here. Walk around; you can steal ideas for your garden and browse among the selection of statuary, fountains, and birdbaths. Indoors you'll find houseplants including orchids, bonsai, cacti, and more. A second location is at 3313 Mechanicsville Pike in Mechanicsville (804-321-2200).

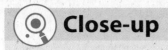 # Close-up

Farmers' Markets

For years the only farmers' market in town was downtown at 17th Street, but now—almost year-round—there are markets sprouting up all over.

There's been a public market here at the **17th Street Farmers' Market** in Shockoe Bottom (www.richmondgov.com/farmersmarket or 804-646-0477), in one form or another since 1779. Offering differently themed market days Thurs through Sun from Apr into Dec, this market features good breads, produce, plants, herbal products, jewelry, and much more. There's free parking on-street or in a nearby lot. The market is also the site of special events such as Shamrock the Block and the Shockoe Tomato Festival.

Tuesday afternoons, consider stopping by the **Byrd House Market** in the Fan, www.byrdhousemarket.blogspot.com, a community-minded effort in conjunction with nearby William Byrd House. It's a feel-good market, stocked with classic area vendors. Its winter version, the **Renegade Market,** keeps the goods coming Oct through May. Also on Tuesday afternoons, May through Oct, is the **North of the James Market** (www.themarketumbrella.com) hidden inside Bryan Park in North Side. If you need a farmers' market fix on Wednesday, try the **Lakeside Farmers' Market** (804-262-6593), which runs May through Nov, Wednesday morning and evening and Saturday mornings as well. Find it at 6110 Lakeside Ave. under its new pavilion, which looks that an old train depot. The other Wednesday/Saturday combo is the **West End Farmers' Market** (www.westendfarmersmarket.com) at the corner of Gayton Road and Ridgefield Parkway from May through Oct.

On Saturday mornings during May through Oct, the **Ashland Farmers' Market** (www.town.ashland.va.us) joins the crowd, as does **Goochland Farmers' Market** (www.centerforruralculture.org), near so many of the farms that produce the goods. From bison to herbs to wine, you'll find everything for your next meal here, including woven place mats from a fiber artist. Luckily for the Near West End, there's the **Saturday Market** at St. Stephen's Episcopal Church (www.saintstephensrichmond .net). Find farm-fresh eggs, pork, beef, plants, herbs, fruit, veggies, goat's milk products, handmade jewelry, and chocolate. Folks on both sides of the river love the **South of the James Market** in Forest Hill Park (www.themarketumbrella.com). From May to Dec, it's a great gathering spot even if you don't buy anything. There are fresh veggies and fruits in season, delicious baked goods, poultry, meats, art, music, and coffee.

Finally, **Farm to Family** (www.farmtofamilyonline.com) is a mobile mini farmer's market housed in a brightly painted school bus that brings organic Virginia food from the farm to your neighborhood. You can't—and don't want to— miss this bus. Farm to Family hauls in organic eggs, yogurt, butter, oyster mushrooms, cheese, sweet potatoes, grass-fed meats, and more. Facebook and Twitter keep everyone up to date about current stops.

i Sandy's Plants in Mechanicsville, (804) 746-7092 or www.sandys-plants.com, is a working farm that sells most of its thousands of perennials to garden centers in the mid-Atlantic. Plants are available for purchase, but familiarize yourself with the offerings on the Web site first and get a map once you arrive. Retail customers can explore in golf carts. Just looking at the display gardens alone is worth a visit.

Midlothian

CROSS CREEK NURSERY
501 Courthouse Rd.
(804) 794-9760
www.crosscreeknursery.com
This 10-acre nursery has beautiful display areas for roaming about—over bridges, by ponds, under pergolas, and beside a waterfall. Make a list of what you want to copy. They grow 60 percent of what they sell, so the prices—especially on shrubs—are competitive with the big chains. The greenhouse is full of indoor plants and whatever's in season, from poinsettias to geraniums.

THE GREAT BIG GREENHOUSE AND MEADOWS FARMS NURSERY
2051 Huguenot Rd.
(804) 320-1317
www.greatbiggreenhouse.com
Whether you have a large plot or a couple of pots to fill, you'll be impressed with the greenhouse's 3½ acres of trees, shrubs, and the mind-boggling array of perennials and annuals. It's a winter's treat to walk through the greenhouse, as the warmth and blossoms convince you spring will return. There's a silks department for dried or silk arrangements, and a strong selection of indoor and outdoor pots, seasonal decor, and furniture.

The greenhouse offers a farmers' market on Thurs.

GIFTS
Downtown

QUIRK GALLERY
311 W. Broad St.
(804) 644-5450
www.quirkgallery.com
Discover handcrafted jewelry, clever artwork, adorable yet offbeat stuffed animals for children, and much more here. If you're looking for a gift that's out of the ordinary, you're bound to find it here. The store is closed on Sun.

VISUAL ART STUDIO
208 W. Broad St.
(804) 644-1368
www.visualartstudio.org
Besides the large-scale paintings and artwork for sale here, you'll find nicely priced pottery, glass, jewelry, small works of art, and prints sure to please the artsy person on your list. The shop is closed on Sun and Mon.

Carytown

FOR THE LOVE OF CHOCOLATE
3136 W. Cary St.
(804) 359-5645
Before you set foot in this shop in the Cary Court Shopping Center, make sure you have either willpower or money. This chocolate and candy shop is jammed with fine chocolate, including Lake Champlain and Leonidas Belgian brands, and Gifford's caramels. For truffle fiends, Nancy's are out of this world—but made in Virginia. The selection also includes fine chocolate from Europe, South America, and beyond. For bakers, there are racks of ingredients you've never heard of

but suddenly need. And for the proverbial kid in the candy store, there's a large section devoted to sugary sweets of yore.

MONGREL
2924 W. Cary St.
(804) 342-1272
www.mongrelonline.com
This store caters to "all breeds of humans," as they say. The ethos is cool and sophisticated in the home-decor area of the shop, pet-friendly in another section, and sometimes practical-minded in cards, stationery, and accent items. But part of the point here are the items that have a bit of an attitude—snarky and funny. The store is always rated at the top by *Richmond Magazine* readers, as the best place to buy a gift.

Near West End

GEARHART'S FINE CHOCOLATES
306B Libbie Ave.
(804) 282-1822
www.gearhartschocolates.com
Chocolatier Magazine ranked Gearhart's among its favorite "20 artisan chocolatiers," in its 20th-anniversary issue. One sniff of the store and you'll understand why. Perhaps you'd like TAJ, bittersweet chocolate ganache flavored with candied ginger, cardamom, and rose and then dipped in dark chocolate. Remember, you're here to buy a gift for someone else! The shop is closed on Sun.

SHOPPES AT 5807
5807 Patterson Ave.
(804) 288-5807
www.shop5807.com
With two dozen shops within, there's an eclectic mix of items from the cutesy, to the practical, to the pewter. Each little shop is jam-packed, displaying apparel, home decor, gifts, handcrafted pieces, or accessories. Layer upon layer of goods fill the space, so it pays to look closely. The store is closed on Sun.

Far West End

APPALACHIAN SPRING
11800 W. Broad St.
(804) 364-9700
www.appalachianspring.com
This artful store, recognizable to those from the Washington, D.C., area, brings an enormous and appealing collection of American handicrafts to Short Pump Town Center. The work is often achingly beautiful and includes jewelry; useful items for the home such as candlesticks, clocks, and pottery; and the sweetest birdhouses you'll ever see.

TWEED
11743 W. Broad St.
(804) 249-3900
www.tweedathome.com
This cheery store is for those who like their gifts and home decor on the preppy side. You'll find plenty of pink and green and silver baubles here. Don't let the owner's promise of "ferocious customer service" scare you. They just want you to love what you buy. Monogramming and engraving are specialties, so you could monogram a fleur-de-lis wine cooler or personalize a hot-pink laundry bag.

North Side

EMBELLISH
5105 Lakeside Ave.
(804) 622-7770
www.embellish-yourhome.com
This adorable shop has been a Lakeside attention-getter since 2006. It's stocked

with whimsical garden ornaments, unusual lamps, unique home decor, handcrafted jewelry, and art for your home or someone else's. The shop is closed on Mon.

South Side

43RD STREET GALLERY
1412 W. 43rd St.
(804) 233-1758
www.43rdstgallery.com
Robin Cage's pottery studio as well as a shop, this small gallery displays and sells beautiful and practical pottery by a variety of artists, as well as handcrafted furniture, jewelry, and more. It's the perfect place to buy a wedding or birthday gift. It's usually closed on Sun.

Midlothian

GATHER
920 Mount Hermon Rd.
(804) 379-0441
www.shopgather.com
When you're in the mood for a drive in the country, come here. Gather might just make your day if you're looking for home decor, cute T-shirts, and something you didn't quite expect but just have to have.

i If you've been here before and are surprised not to see Ukrop's, Richmond's homegrown grocer, it's because the beloved chain was sold to an international company in 2010. The stores that remain are now Martin's. The entire area heaved a sigh of relief when it was learned that Ukrop's will continue its prepared foods business and supply Martin's (and perhaps other grocers) with, among other *very* Richmond items, Dot's White House Rolls, fried chicken, and other foods locals can't live without.

JEWELRY
Shockoe Slip

DRANSFIELD JEWELERS
1308 E. Cary St.
(804) 643-0171
www.dransfieldjewelers.com
Since 1991, this intimate shop has offered beautiful gemstones, gold, silver, platinum, pearl, and diamond pieces, but what sets this store apart is its commitment to custom-designed jewelry for customers. Whether it's an entirely new piece or a reworked heirloom or gem that you'd like incorporated into something new, Dransfield's three in-house designer goldsmiths will work with you to create a wearable work of art. The shop offers free parking validation at the 14th and Cary Streets lot or the deck at 12th and Canal Streets.

Carytown

JAY SHARPE
3405 W. Cary St.
(804) 353-4733
www.jaysharpe.com
One of the reasons Carytown is cool is because Jay Sharpe's jewelry shop has been here since 1999. His sleek and luxurious custom designs are worn by celebs such as Queen Latifah and Lauryn Hill, and he'll gladly give you the same star treatment. The shop is open Tues through Sat.

KAY ADAMS
3439 W. Cary St.
(804) 254-2000
www.kayadams.com
Putting vintage bits and pieces to work in extraordinary necklaces, Kay Adams designs and crafts unique jewelry that cannot be duplicated. Her shop window, which shares

space with the Anthill Antiques shop she owns with her mother, gives you an idea of the exuberance of her work. Her collections include Juice, Pop, Posh, and Toc, but the names don't begin to describe the possibilities here—a necklace of cameos, or one of vintage watch parts. Seeing is believing— and might involve buying.

Near West End

CARRERAS JEWELERS
121 Libbie Ave.
(804) 282-7018
www.carrerasjewelers.com
Newly renovated, Carreras is the classic Richmond go-to store for fine jewelry, in the classic West End. Whether you're looking for extravagant designer pieces, engagement rings, or gifts from Salisbury Pewter or Reed & Barton, you'll find plenty to choose from here. Its estate jewelry collection sets it apart from other destinations. With exquisite pieces from the Victorian, Art Nouveau, Edwardian, Art Deco, and Retro periods, there's something to dazzle you here.

JACK KREUTER JEWELERS
6231 River Rd.
(804) 288-3900
www.shopriverroad.com
In the comfortable setting of River Road Shopping Center, this store features beautiful objects to adorn your person—including Virginia's largest collection of Hidalgo—and your home, such as Waterford's colorful, modern Evolution collection. Specializing in gemstones, the passionate and friendly staff prides itself on people-to-people service, so expect to enjoy your shopping experience here. The store is closed on Sun.

COCOANUT JEWELRY
1601 Willow Lawn Dr., No. 247
(804) 282-1335
In the Willow Lawn Shopping Center, this store's vibe is more contemporary and funky than traditional jewelry stores. The shop carries work from 300 artists, with prices that range from $10 to $10,000. Besides jewelry, the extensive gift selection includes handcrafted pottery, clocks, frames, and more. Some higher-end work is limited edition or one of a kind. A staff jeweler creates custom work and handles repairs. A second location is at 11800 W. Broad St., No. 2116, in the Short Pump Town Center (804-360-9634).

Far West End

PENELOPE
11533 W. Broad St.
(804) 364-4630
www.penelope-jewelry.com
Specializing in sterling silver jewelry at reasonable prices, with some women's clothing and accessories thrown in, Penelope carries styles ranging from the basic to the bohemian. It's a popular spot for costume jewelry, too. Closed on Sun. A second and third location are at 9972 Brook Rd. on the North Side (804-266-7300) and 1229 Sycamore Sq. in Midlothian (804-794-1674).

Midlothian

VERA'S FINE JEWELERS
16701 Midlothian Turnpike
(804) 794-5671
www.verasfinejewelers.com

In 2009 *Richmond Magazine* readers voted Vera's the best place to find a unique engagement ring. If you can't find what you want within the 27 jewelry cases in the three-showroom shop, the two master jewelers on-site will be happy to custom design a piece for you. The store is closed on Sun.

KIDS' CLOTHING
Near West End

RATTLE AND ROLL
5003 Huguenot Rd.
(804) 282-0141
www.rattleroll.com
This whimsical specialty store in River Road II Shopping Center has a large selection of clothing for newborns to kids' size 6X—from bathing suits to smocked dresses—but it's much more than a children's clothing store, with high-end furniture, decor, and baby gifts and toys for little ones.

West End

BUTTONS & BOWS
1517 N. Parham Rd.
(804) 285-0482
www.buttonsandbowskids.com
This very Richmond, 4,800-square-foot traditional children's clothing and toy store has dress-up clothes for real-life events and for fun. Besides special-occasion clothes, it's also a place to find more casual clothes, rainwear, dance wear, and a wide selection of shoes, including 110 styles and colors of shoes for girls and 35 styles and colors for boys. The store also carries toys, room accessories, and baby gifts.

Bon Air

MILBY'S JUST KIDS
3016 Stony Point Rd.
(804) 330-8158
This shop, in the courtyard of Stony Point Shopping Center, has been dressing up Richmond's children for 50 years, with a classic selection of clothing that grandmothers will swoon over. Though there's playwear and bathing suits here, the specialty is clothing for those more formal occasions—christenings, portraits, weddings, and cotillion. The shop is closed on Sun.

MEN'S CLOTHING
Near West End

BEECROFT & BULL
5029 Huguenot Rd.
(804) 783-0633
www.beecroftandbull.com
For those who want to "dress better than they have to," this Virginia men's clothier offers the goods to look good. Clothing lines from AG Denim to Zanella feature everything from shorts to suits. Custom clothing is also available for the discerning shopper. The store is closed on Sun.

PETER-BLAIR
5718 Grove Ave.
(804) 288-8123
www.peterblair.com
You are in the West End, so it makes sense that you'll find classic, conservative clothing here, though the owners throw in a twist—and a special emphasis on colorful and distinctive men's ties, bow and regular. You can even have ties custom designed here if you want to up the creativity a notch or two.

Far West End

FRANCO'S
11800 W. Broad St., Suite 1168
Short Pump Town Center
(804) 364-9400
www.francos.com
Dressing gentlemen of Richmond for more than 35 years, Franco Ambrogi's stores offer exceptional service along with the finest in men's fashions. You'll find Hugo Boss, Ermenegildo Zegna, and Robert Talbott here, among many other lines. From Bill's Khakis and Lacoste for casual wear to Hickey Freeman and Hart, Schaffner & Marx tuxedos, Franco's outfits men for any occasion. A second location is at 5321 Lakeside Ave. on the North Side (804-264-2994).

SHOES

Near West End

RICHEY & CO.
5015 Huguenot Rd.
(804) 282-7463
www.richeyco.com
Whether you're looking for shoes to turn heads or make tracks outside, Richey & Co. has hundreds of styles from the brands you trust. If your footwear focus is comfort first, let the certified pedorthists on staff fit you in the right shoe. In-house orthopedic technicians fabricate foot orthoses and can make adjustments to shoes, so foot pain is a thing of the past.

THE SHOE BOX
401 Libbie Ave.
(804) 288-2303
www.libbiegrove.com
On "the avenues" in Richmond's West End, this boutique carries high-end women's shoes in a refined setting. Several of its lines, such as Sigerson Morrison and Miu Miu, are available in Richmond only at the Shoe Box. Jewelry and accessories complete the look. It's closed on Sun.

Far West End

SAXON SHOES
11800 W. Broad St., No. 2750
(804) 285-3473
www.saxonshoes.com
This two-level store in Short Pump Town Center is evidence of a local institution that's made it big, as in 27,000 square feet of big, with enough shoes to fit a lot of feet. Saxon's, the largest full-service shoe store in Virginia, carries more than 200 well-known brands of shoes and accessories for men, women, and children. Whether you're looking for something trendy or traditional—as long as your foot is between a lady's size 4 to 14, extra slim to extra wide, or men's 6 to 18, narrow to extra-extra wide—you'll likely find something suitable here. And don't forget to head to the Backroom, where shoes are marked down 25 to 70 percent. No wonder it's nicknamed the Lucky Lady room.

i The area is home to several chain sporting-goods stores, including Bass Pro Shops, REI, Dick's Sporting Goods, and Gander Mountain Sports. See the yellow pages for locations. For local sporting goods stores, Disco Sports, Dixie Sports, and Strictly Soccer have great selections of your favorite team's colors.

TOYS

Carytown

WORLD OF MIRTH
3005 W. Cary St.
(804) 353-8991
www.worldofmirth.com
Playful and surprising, this store has been amusing its customers with toys and what-nots for all ages since 1993. It's kitschy and cool, and determined that kids shouldn't be the only ones to have fun. You'll find some expected brands of toys here, but the emphasis is on the unexpected. Books, baby toys, games, and costumes add to the fun quotient, as do all the goofy and irreverent merchandise aimed at adults with plenty of kid left in them—an assortment of buttons, magnets, hipster T-shirts, accessories, and the all-important bacon bandages.

West End

THE TOY CENTER
5811 Patterson Ave.
(804) 288-4475
This classic shop features toys that don't usually need batteries or need to be recharged. You'll find puzzles, games, dress-up clothes, outdoorsy equipment, dolls, stuffed animals, craft kits, and more. The shop still has a section devoted to model trains, so there might be some older "kids" shopping here as well.

TOYS THAT TEACH
Gayton Crossing Shopping Center
1342 Gaskins Rd.
(804) 741-5611
www.toysthatteachonline.com
For 23 years this specialty toy store has made it easy on parents, aunts, uncles, and grandparents when they need thoughtful

gifts that will last. Sure, there are plastic play-things here, but this shop's toys, trains sets, dolls, puzzles, craft kits, science experiments, and costumes are more likely to make a lasting impression. Gift wrapping is free. A second location is in the Stony Point Shopping Center at 3038 Stony Point Rd. in Bon Air (804-272-2391).

i When looking for toys and gifts for children, don't forget the gift shops of the Children's Museum of Richmond and the Science Museum of Virginia. Both are well stocked with mind-boggling and fun toys.

VINTAGE, THRIFT, AND RESALE

The Fan

EXILE
935 W. Grace St.
(804) 358-3348
It's all about adventure here because the goods—new and vintage jeans, screen-printed T-shirts, and shoes and accessories for men and women—are packed in. Edgy accessories and vintage housewares add to the mix. Not surprisingly, college students love it here.

HALCYON-VINTAGE CLOTHING
117 N. Robinson St.
(804) 358-1311
For 25 years this has been a go-to spot for high-quality vintage clothing (for men, too) and jewelry. With its classic advertising on the side of the building, you can't miss it, nor should you. The hat wall, the cowboy shirts, the dresses, and jewels are begging to be given a second chance at a cool life. Halcyon has great men's clothing, too.

Carytown

BYEGONES VINTAGE CLOTHING
2916 W. Cary St.
(804) 353-1919
Known far and wide as a destination for true vintage clothing and accessories, Byegones' window display is worth the trip even if you're not in the market for its beautiful offerings for men and women. Well organized and well stocked, Byegones has been outfitting folks in vintage hats, tuxedos, jewelry, shoes, and dresses since 1979.

East End

THE LOVE OF JESUS THRIFT STORE
5158 Nine Mile Rd.
(804) 737-9493
www.lojts.com
Here, folks stroll the aisles to find rocking vintage jackets, hip, urban dress shoes, and the best selection of '50s, '60s, and '70s dishware anywhere in the city. The subliminal spiritual messages are free. A second location is at 5503 Midlothian Turnpike on the South Side (804-230-4144).

North Side

BOOKS, BIKES, AND BEYOND
302 W. Brookland Park Blvd.
(804) 592-4591
www.booksonwheels.com
The colorfully painted brick wall is a clue you've come to the right place. Though the used books, bikes, housewares, and clothing are good and the prices better, all proceeds from thrift sales here go toward a nonprofit organization that the store owner cofounded, Books on Wheels, which delivers free books and bike repair to at-risk kids around Richmond and beyond. The shop is open Tues through Sat.

CONSIGNMENT CONNECTION
5517 Lakeside Ave.
(804) 261-3600
People I know go crazy for this place, which is always full of furniture, glassware, china, and shoppers in Lakeside. Sometimes it's hard to see the dining room furniture for the crystal and china displayed in and around. But new merchandise comes in as fast as shoppers head out the door with their purchases.

DIVERSITY THRIFT
1407 Sherwood Ave.
(804) 353-8890
www.diversitythrift.org
Within this store's 15,000 square feet you'll find five rooms of furniture for home and office. There's a music room, kitchenware room, sports room, art, collectibles, and roughly 50 racks of clothing. It's a treasure trove if you're willing to put in the time. Located in the Gay Community Center of Richmond, it's open Wed through Sun.

MCADOOS'
6921 Lakeside Ave.
(804) 262-9021
www.mcadoosvintagethriftand
    collectibles.com
Don't let the small storefront deceive you—McAdoos' features five rooms filled with a little bit of everything—small furniture, cookware, dishes, crystal, glassware, music, linens, vintage board games, women's clothing, jewelry, books, and ceramics. It's closed on Sun.

WOMEN'S CLOTHING

Carytown

ANNETTE DEAN
3325 W. Cary St.
(804) 359-8240
www.annettedean.com

I'm not saying that fans of this 2,000-square-foot classic women's-wear shop, which is housed in what looks like a temple, worship fashion, but once you see the gorgeous pieces from several American designers on the hangers, pulled together into outfits, you won't blame them if they do. It's closed on Sun.

GLASS BOAT

3226 W. Cary St.
(804) 358-5596
www.glassboat.com

Mixing fine furniture with the clothes you should wear while lounging on it might seem an unlikely pairing, but Glass Boat aims to dress you and your home with one-stop shopping. Browse through brand-name clothing that's sure to turn heads, and switch gears to flounce around on a sofa. Take a peek at their funky jewelry, too.

NEED SUPPLY CO.

3010 W. Cary St.
(804) 355-5880
www.needsupply.com

You either belong here or you don't. Considered by some young women to be the best (read: most expensive) place to buy cool jeans, Need carries hip designer clothing and shoes for men and women—exactly what some young folk think they need to look fabulous.

i If you can't find on-street parking in Carytown, there are two free parking garages around the corner from West Cary Street, one on Crenshaw Avenue and one on Colonial Avenue.

THE PHOENIX

3039 W. Cary St.
(804) 354-0711
www.thephoenixrichmond.com

This recently renovated specialty shop offers beautiful clothing in a relaxed setting. From the dressed down to the dressed up, The Phoenix brings global fashions with a sense of style to Carytown. It's strong in the basics, too, with the best-fitting slacks and tops ever. Jewelry and shoes offer the finishing touches, and the wonderful staff excels at personal service. Trust me on that one.

PINK

3158 W. Cary St.
(804) 358-0884
www.pinkstore.com

Trendy designer duds and the most clever display windows in town reside here at the corner of Cary Court Shopping Center. From Marc by Marc Jacobs, to Theory, to Velvet, to Diane von Furstenberg, this store brings the best of NYC., LA, London, and Paris fashion, including shoes, to this two-level store. You might even spot a celebrity here, since Danica Patrick, Angelica Huston, and quite a few others have shopped here.

ROAN

3142 W. Cary St.
(804) 288-3699
www.roanshop.com

Formerly Coplon's in the River Road Shopping Center, Roan was reborn in early 2010 as a Carytown chic spot. You'll know the Roanies when you see them, wearing Stella McCartney or Jason Wu or whatever was just delivered hot off the fashion runways of the world. This is the new home of world-class ready-to-wear clothes, shoes, and accessories.

Near West End

FRANCES KAHN
6229B River Rd.
(804) 288-5246
www.franceskahn.com

In the original River Road Shopping Center, Frances Kahn has been dressing Richmond women in the finest clothing, including designer evening wear, since 1988. New designers' collections are added every season to a roster that includes Armani, Michael Kors, Halston Heritage, and Diane von Furstenberg. Since 2004 the store has made Harper's Bazaar's list as one of the "top tier 100 women's fashion specialty retailers." The shop is closed on Sun.

Far West End

HIGH COTTON
11753 W. Broad St.
(804) 360-0200

Don't let the name fool you—cotton's just one of the fabrics you'll want to get your hands on in this eclectic boutique. You'll be in high cotton among its comfortable skirts, dresses, and tops. The attentive sales staff will gladly help you find the right look, perhaps suggesting a necklace from the store's jewelry selection.

Midlothian

NYFO BOUTIQUE
11400 W. Huguenot Rd.
(804) 794-0777
www.nyfoboutique.com

In the Shoppes at Bellgrade, NYFO is a South Side destination for contemporary women's clothing and classic looks with a fashion-forward twist. The great selection of clothing from such names as Nougat, Theory, and Pure, the jewelry, and the personal service almost guarantee you'll leave happy.

DAY TRIPS

You just got here. Why would you want to leave? Oh, all right, so you have a hankering for the mountains or wine or James River plantations or Williamsburg. I aim to please, so here's some friendly advice on roaming the region beyond Richmond. Just make sure you know the way back. I could have steered you toward Mount Vernon, Alexandria, or D.C., all fabulous destinations, but I didn't want you to get stuck in traffic up there.

Within an hour or two of Richmond are all sorts of worthy destinations whether you're in the mood for outdoor adventure, historic sites, or leisurely wine-tasting. With both the Blue Ridge Parkway and Skyline Drive less than two hours away, it's easy to heed the call of the mountains. Virginia's plantations haven't been around quite as long as the mountains, but the James River plantations east of Richmond have played an important role in the region's history since the 17th century. Williamsburg has staying power, too, as the esteemed College of William & Mary, founded in 1693, can attest. Williamsburg doesn't just cater to the life of the mind though; it caters to 21st-century foodies, too. With more than 150 wineries, Virginia is renowned for its winemaking industry, which has spread across the state. I've highlighted several area wineries, but the sky, or the road, is the only limit.

JAMES RIVER PLANTATIONS

Take a ride in the country to see how the wealthy few lived back in the day. From Richmond, head out VA 5 east into Charles City County for a trip back through the centuries. The first stop is **Shirley Plantation,** the oldest plantation in Virginia and the oldest family-owned business in America—in the Hill-Carter family for 11 generations. Shirley Plantation dates back to 1613, and though it's just 10 miles east of I-295, it's a world away. The spectacular **Great House** was completed in 1738 and is still lived in by Hill-Carter descendants. The guided tour of the house features family artifacts and lore and the famous flying staircase, the only one of its period intact. The self-guided grounds

tour includes outbuildings and sprawling grounds overlooking the James where you're likely to spy bald eagles and other significant birds. The staff birding expert occasionally leads bird walks. In late 2010 a slavery exhibit is scheduled to open in the courtyard kitchen building, an original early-18th-century outbuilding. Tours are available every day except Thanksgiving and Christmas. Call (800) 232-1613 or visit www .shirleyplantation.com for details.

If you have time for another stop, pull into **Berkeley Plantation** (888-466-6018 or www.berkeleyplantation.com), a bit farther east. All of the James River plantations try a bit of one-upmanship—the oldest, the most historic, the one with the oldest bricks, etc., but Berkeley takes the dueling to new heights. It takes on the Pilgrims' claim to the first Thanksgiving. Berkeley (and any child who attends fourth grade in a Virginia school) is adamant that the first Thanksgiving was right here along the James in 1619 because English colonists led by Captain John Woodlief went down on bended knee and said something like, "Thank God we made it," after they came ashore at Berkeley. At any rate, guided tours of the antique-filled 1726 mansion and the small museum with Civil War artifacts tell visitors about the history that has transpired here—four centuries' worth. It's the birthplace of a signer of the Declaration of Independence, a president, and taps, the army's last bugle call at night. Benjamin Harrison IV took Thomas Jefferson's advice on architectural matters when he made some changes to the house. See if you think he did the right thing. The plantation is open every day but Thanksgiving and Christmas.

While you're cruising VA 5, make the pilgrimage out to **Westover** (804-829-2882), built circa 1730 by the founder of Richmond, William Byrd II. You'll see why he wanted to live here rather than amid the hubbub of trading, traffic, and industry. It's a Georgian masterpiece on gorgeous grounds overlooking the James River. The grounds and gardens are open daily from 9 a.m. to 6 p.m. House tours are available during Historic Garden Week and during two special fundraising events, one for the James River Association and another for Westover Church. Admission to the grounds is $2 for adults, even less for children. If you're traveling with a large group, house tours for groups of 12 or more are $12 a person and must be arranged in advance.

Besides the three described above, other plantations, including **Sherwood Forest,** the home of President John Tyler, are also along VA 5 and open to the public, if only for tours of the grounds. See www.jamesriverplantations.org and www.charlescity.org for more information. Consider bringing your bikes to sample a 7-mile completed stretch of the paved Virginia Capital to Capital Trail that goes west from Charles City County Courthouse just past Berkeley and Westover Plantations. Eventually the trail will connect Richmond to Jamestown and Williamsburg for a human-powered and traffic-free cruise. See www.virginiacapitaltrail.org for information and maps.

VIRGINIA WINERIES

A couple of the wineries discussed below are so close to Richmond, you could easily pop in on your way home from the grocery store, but to make the visit more relaxed, I'm assuming you're making a day of winery touring, and also assuming that you have a designated driver who isn't imbibing. There are scores of wineries in Virginia that offer tours and tastings, and you could wear out a set of tires visiting them all. This chapter highlights several that are closest to Richmond. Go to www.virginiawine.org to scout out all the wineries in Virginia and find out about special events.

i Woodland Vineyard (www.woodlandvineyard.com or 804-739-2774) is the smallest farm winery in Virginia, making just 200 cases of wine per year. You can visit this family-run vineyard tucked away near Swift Creek Reservoir for wine tastings, but call first.

James River Cellars (804-550-7516 or www.jamesrivercellars.com) sits along Washington Highway in Hanover County. The name conjures up a scenic winery along the James, but you'll fight only the current of traffic to get to this award-winning, family-run winery, stashed as it is between I-95 and US 1 in Glen Allen. Once you step inside the tasting room and notice the awards, the suburbs recede and the wine is the thing—more than 15 varieties—so there's a lot to learn. It's a pleasant atmosphere, not a bit stuffy, with a knowledgeable, enthusiastic staff that likes to boast about their 2007 Petite Verdot that bested Barboursville in the Governor's Cup. Using their own grapes grown on one acre here and 20 acres in Montpelier, and other Virginia grapes, this winery has produced many an award winner among its 5,000-case annual output. I'm a fan of the chardonel, but the chambourcin is the most popular, as it's great with chocolate. They have a great gift selection as well, besides the wine. Fridays on the Patio, held throughout the year on select Fridays, offer wine tasting, light appetizers, and live music for $14.

Continuing north, you could stop at the award-winning **Lake Anna Winery** (540-895-5085 or www.lawinery.com) for some of the more interesting entertainment combos around. They've figured out a way to combine wine with college basketball's March Madness, employing a big-screen TV, a crackling fire, and winery tours. Other weekends you might hear a zydeco band or stumble upon a Caribbean beach party.

Veering to the southwest, you can mosey over to **Cooper Vineyards** (540-894-5253 or www.coopervineyards.com) in Louisa County. Midway between Richmond and Charlottesville, easily accessible from I-64, this winery is known for its Noche Chocolate,

which has won gold in the Virginia Governor's Cup two years in a row and consistently wins awards beyond Virginia as well.

i The Heart of Virginia Wine Trail is a collaboration between Grayhaven Winery, James River Cellars, Cooper Vineyards, and Lake Anna Winery. Buy a pass for $10 and hit the trail for tastings at all four wineries and a souvenir glass. It doesn't have to be done in a day, and these vineyards often plan special events such as a chili cook-off competition, jingle bell festivities, and other seasonal events that showcase all four wineries together. Check out www.hovawinetrail.com for the latest events.

Coming back along I-64 toward Richmond, just 20 minutes from Short Pump, **Grayhaven Winery** (804-556-3917 or www.grayhavenwinery.com) in Gum Spring is what you get when three generations of one family work together—50 acres of idyllic farmland with ponds, rolling hills, pastureland, and vineyards. This Goochland winery specializes in Old World, small-batch wines and is known for its South African Food and Wine Festival, held the weekend after the Fourth of July every year, which brings in 20 varieties of South African wine. One of Grayhaven's most popular wines is the pinotage, from a grape grown in South Africa and on their farm in Goochland. You might be able to see part of the wine-making process through the window from the classy and comfortable tasting room to the work area. Virginia-made goat cheese and baguettes are available for purchase, along with other goodies and gifts, and picnics are always welcome. It's a family-friendly property with horses, a playground for children, and plenty of room to romp, so this is a place children will enjoy as much as their parents.

New Kent Winery (877-932-8240 or www.newkentwinery.com), east of Richmond off I-64, attracts attention first for its good looks. The surrounding area is still undeveloped, with a polo club and a major housing development on the way, but something worthwhile is developing inside the winery—5,000 cases of seven varieties of wine. Pre–Civil War brick and recycled timber give the building old-time character. Front and back porches add to the visual appeal, with comfortable seating and heaters on the back porch. The beams in the cask room hail from a Shockoe Bottom rail depot., but don't be fooled by the "Richmond VA" stamp on the massive ones in the tasting room; they're actually from an old building in Connecticut and have been turned Virginian with an antique stamp, but it adds to the rustic yet refined ambience. There's an upstairs room for sitting and enjoying the wine if the weather doesn't allow relaxing on the porch. Snacks are for sale, and picnics are always welcome. After a tour and tasting here, if you'd like to enjoy a casual, upscale meal with New Kent Winery's wine, head down the road to **Rose & Crown Restaurant,** serving breakfast, lunch, and dinner in a historic house in New Kent Courthouse Village. Small plates, blue plate specials, sandwiches, and entrees with a contemporary English flair await you. Call (804) 966-1325 or check out www.roseandcrownrestaurant.com.

On the Northern Neck, 90 minutes from Richmond in the quaint town of Irvington, sits **White Fences Vineyard & Winery.** You can't miss it—not so much because of the fences, but the 40-feet-tall corkscrews that mark the entrance. Worth a day trip any time, it's especially noteworthy as the host of the **Irvington Stomp** (804-438-5559), a fun September festival that celebrates the *I Love Lucy* way of wine making—feet first. Take part in grape-stomping competitions, imprint T-shirts with your purply footprint, and stomp your feet to live music, too. If you decide to stay longer, the lovely, waterfront **Tides Inn** (800-843-3746 or www.tidesinn .com), rated the No. 1 resort in Virginia by *Travel & Leisure* in 2009, is a stone's throw away, and White Fences offers accommodations on vineyard property and also operates the romantic **Hope & Glory Inn.**

MOUNTAIN MOOD

When you're in the mood for a mountain vista, drive westward from Richmond along I-64, and it won't be long before you see southern Appalachian mountaintops. There are many great hikes in this neck of the woods, but I've narrowed them to two classic ones that are almost rites of passage around here.

The easier of the two, and doable even with young children, is at **Humpback Rocks** along the Blue Ridge Parkway out past Charlottesville. Atop Afton Mountain, **Skyline Drive** (worthy of a trip any day) takes off north, and the Blue Ridge Parkway starts its 469-mile journey along the crest of the Appalachians. Don't worry, Humpback Rocks (828-298-0398 or www.nps.gov/blri) is only 5 or so miles down the parkway, and there's a parking lot at the trailhead. The hike up Humpback isn't particularly long, but it is very vertical, with stairs and boulders and lots of quad-busting good times. It's only about 40 minutes to the wide-open, rocky overlook at the top that's a lovely spot to tarry if there aren't too many people around, though the drop-offs would no doubt give some people a touch of vertigo. After the trip down, you could amble over to the nearby Mountain Farm exhibit that features several 19th-century Appalachian farm buildings, such as a springhouse and cabin. In the summer, living history demonstrations might be going on. Now that you've worked up an appetite, it's time to head back toward Charlottesville. Assuming you're visiting between mid-Apr and Dec when the orchard is open, take the VA 20 exit south and look for the sign to **Carter Mountain Orchard** (434-977-1833 or www.cartermountainorchard.com). Sure, you could go to **Monticello,** the fascinating home that Thomas Jefferson designed for himself that's on the same road, if your timing doesn't square with the orchard's schedule, but if you're debating which to go to, remember that the orchard has fresh-baked cider donuts, barbecue, and apple-caramel cookies (and peaches and apples to pick in season) and Monticello doesn't. A hike, mountaintop apple picking, and a picnic with peach barbecue sauce—now that's a classic Virginia day trip.

For a more serious and strenuous hike, northwest of Richmond, pack food and water and take the long and winding roads to **Old Rag** in the **Shenandoah National Park** (www.nps.gov/shen). This day trip will wear you out because the hiking can easily take six or more hours, and some of those hours are quite challenging. There are two ways to do it—the cheater's way, where you park near the fire road and come up the Saddle Trail, and the legitimate way, where you park at the official entrance (and pay your fee to the National Park Service) and climb the Ridge Trail. The latter is much more arduous and rewarding. This 8.8-mile hike is for people in good physical condition.

As you ascend 2 miles through the woods on switchbacking trails, it's easy to think this is just a walk in the woods. When you start seeing boulders, the hike becomes a 1.5-mile rock scramble. You're not just hiking anymore. Continuing toward the summit requires fancy footwork and jumping, squeezing, scrambling, huffing and puffing, and eating lots of trail mix. There are several false summits, so it feels like you will never reach the top. Once you do, and look out over the 360-degree view of 300,000 acres of the Shenandoah National Park, you'll be glad your tax dollars protect this. It's a much easier route down if you do the recommended circuit hike. It's an exceptionally popular hike, so parking is problematic. Avoid weekends if you can, and do not park on the surrounding roads.

CULINARY WILLIAMSBURG IS FOR DINERS

Almost everyone knows that **Colonial Williamsburg** (www.history.org) is well worth a visit for its historic sites and living history, but if you have a "been there, done that" attitude toward Williamsburg, think again. You can have a pleasant visit here without putting on a tricornered hat.

Combine the culinary with the collegiate. Wandering about the picturesque campus of the **College of William & Mary,** the second-oldest university in the U.S., seeing the Wren Building, the oldest academic building in the U.S., and taking in the view of the Sunken Gardens might make you envious of the students there now, especially since they'll be fellow alums with Thomas Jefferson, Glenn Close, and Jon Stewart. On Saturday mornings throughout much of the year and Tuesday afternoons in the summer, you won't have to contend with college students as you weave through the stalls at the wonderful **Williamsburg Farmers' Market** in Merchants Square (757-259-3768 or www .williamsburgfarmersmarket.com), so there's more good food for you.

When it's time for lunch, remember that food in the 21st century is far superior to that of the 18th, so bypass the colonial spots and consider a visit to **The Williamsburg Winery** (757-229-0999 www.williamsburgwinery .com), just a short drive away. Its **Gabriel Archer Tavern** is a lovely lunch (and dinner most of the year) spot, and you can try out the wines that *Wine Spectator* gives such high ratings to. If you'd rather not get in the car, stay in Merchants Square and hit up **The Cheese Shop** for sumptuous sandwiches (and cheese, of course), or if you stay long enough for dinner and want fine dining, you can't go wrong at **Berret's** (757-253-1847 or www.berrets.com), the AAA four-diamond **Fat Canary** (757-229-3333 or www .fatcanarywilliamsburg.com), the **Blue Talon** (757-476-2583 or www.bluetalonbistro .com), or **The Trellis** (757-229-8610 or www .thetrellis.com). A less expensive and just as delectable option is to stop by **Pierce's Pitt-Bar-B-Que** (757-565-2955 or www.pierces .com) on the way back to Richmond and fill up with some of the best barbecue in Virginia.

Appendix

LIVING HERE

In this section we feature specific information for residents or those planning to relocate here. Topics include real estate, education, health care, and much more.

RELOCATION

I'm betting it's Richmond's low cost of doing business, laid-back lifestyle, and cool cultural and recreational destinations that led Forbes.com in late 2009 to rank Richmond number 65 on its list of "Best Bang-for-the-Buck Cities." And though the Richmond region has taken its lumps like everywhere else in the U.S. during this recent financial downturn, it's also well positioned for the future. Indeed, Forbes.com also named Richmond one of America's fastest-recovering cities in November 2009, and in a study by Manpower reported in *BusinessWeek* in June 2009, Richmond was the sixth best place in the country to start over.

If the Richmond region's sensible cost of living (slightly above average for the country as a whole, but much lower than Northern Virginia and Washington, D.C., for instance), stress-free commuting, diverse economy, recreational opportunities, and cultural amenities haven't quite persuaded you to make the move, let me try another tack. Within Richmond, you can live in a riverside condo downtown, a converted warehouse loft, a Victorian townhome, on an acre in an established, tree-filled neighborhood, in a charming Arts and Crafts home, or along the river—and every sort of situation in between. Extend your range into the counties and you can reside on a horse farm, or in a home dripping with character in an established neighborhood, a no-maintenance apartment, townhome, or a single-family home in a planned community near shopping.

Because of Virginia's independent-city structure, cities are separate entities from counties, and each locality has its own government, schools, tax rates, etc. Residents take advantage of the region's boundless amenities regardless of lines on a map—living, working, shopping, playing, and eating all over. It's the politicians who haven't always figured out how to get past boundaries and cooperate.

Though home sales and prices did dip here like everywhere else, Richmond real estate never suffered the huge declines that some other areas did in recent years. And things are looking up. The fourth quarter of 2009 showed strong growth in Metro Richmond, with the number of homes sold up 38 percent over the same period in 2008.

RICHMOND

Downtown, Shockoe Slip and Bottom, Tobacco Row

Loft living, gorgeous architecture, and river views are the keys to downtown residential life—oh yeah, and location, location, location. Whether you prefer a contemporary high-rise along the Canal Walk in **Shockoe Slip or Bottom** or the rental loft apartments in the renovated **Tobacco Row** buildings—where one-bedroom apartments are $800 to

$1000 a month and up—or the various condominium projects in cool buildings, you can live downtown for a lot or not. Being close to restaurants, nightlife, and work—if you work near Capitol Square, at VCU Medical Center, or in the financial district—and having such unique living quarters to choose from make this area appealing to young professionals and down-sizing or second-home-buying empty nesters alike. One-bedroom condos start in the low $100,000s and, depending on the location and size, can run all the way to million-dollar penthouses overlooking the river. Cross the Belle Isle Pedestrian Bridge and you're in what *Blue Ridge Outdoors* magazine says is the best urban park in the mid-Atlantic.

Off on its own a bit, **Rockett's Landing** is a large, riverfront development east of Tobacco Row that's a mix of renovated and contemporary buildings that house a variety of stylish living quarters and a riverfront restaurant. You can get a one-bedroom condo here for $190,000 or spend well over $680,000 on a penthouse. Multi-level, luxury townhomes are priced from the mid-$400,000s.

Church Hill

Above downtown sits beautiful **Church Hill**, where the first Old and Historic District was established in 1957 to protect the bounty of 18th-and 19th-century architecture, With great views of the city and river below, many residents here dote on their historic homes—in between stops at the coffee shops, restaurants, and green spaces such as **Libby Hill Park, Chimborazo Park,** and **St. John's Mews.** Three-bedroom, single-family homes, generally older row houses, start in the upper $100,000s and top out near $500,000, with gems running higher. Renters

in renovated buildings such as Nolde Bakery can get a one-bedroom apartment for $895 per month and up. For those in the market to buy, condos run between $133,000 and $259,000. Adjacent Union Hill offers more opportunities for historic preservation around Jefferson Park with its views of the city below.

Jackson Ward and Carver

Proximity to downtown is a draw here, but the beautiful Greek Revival and Queen Anne town houses with gorgeous ironwork and the neighborhood's proud history as a center of African-American heritage are every bit as important. The presence of the **Maggie L. Walker House,** a National Park Service site, and the **Black History Museum and Cultural Center of Virginia** ensures the neighborhood won't forget its roots, no matter how many buildings are turned into condos. Annual festivals ensure traditions continue and restaurants pop up in renovated storefronts. **Carver,** to the west, is a combination of longtime residents in single-family homes and VCU students in condos built with them in mind. Condos range from $119,000 to $289,000. Depending on how much renovation is required, single-family row houses run from the mid-$100s to $350,000.

The Fan and Museum District

The Fan is the home of **VCU's Monroe Park Campus** and, as the largest intact Victorian community in the U.S., boasts beautiful architecture—not all of it on Monument Avenue. The **Museum District** is across Boulevard from the Fan and enjoys proximity to **Carytown** and museums, as well as more lovely architecture. These neighborhoods are among the most popular in the city because, besides their charm and architecture, they offer a lifestyle many people covet—no lawn to mow, but likely a porch to sit on, neighbors to chat with, and great restaurants, shops, and museums within walking distance. And then there's **Monument Avenue,** practically a museum itself, where you'll find the priciest addresses. More typical single-family homes here are in the $200,000 to $600,000 range, with occasional million-dollar-and-up homes. The condo market has tightened, but the available stock runs from the low $100,000s up to $499,000. For renters, there are some renovated, managed apartment buildings where a one-bedroom apartment might be $775 to $950, plus utilities.

Near West End

Home to Agecroft Hall and Virginia House in exclusive Windsor Farms, the **Near West End** has manses for the masses, too. Beautifully landscaped grounds and easy access to downtown, the University of Richmond, and the Country Club of Virginia attract some folks to this side of town, while others appreciate shopping and dining at nearby Libbie and Grove and Carytown, as well as being in the Mary Munford Elementary School district. Not every West End home is a mansion—the area is a mix of high-end homes doing their impression of an English village, and more modest but still charming cottages, bungalows, and brick colonials, mostly pre–World War II. Small ranches start at $200,000, but the English cottages, Tudor Revivals, and other classic architectural styles start in the upper $300,000s and go up past $1 million in **Windsor Farms** and **Hampton Gardens.**

Though mostly an area of single-family homes, luxury condo and townhomes are tucked away in spots. Renters can take advantage of what the area offers near Malvern and Cary Streets for $950 a month for a one-bedroom apartment.

North Side

Arts and Crafts homes, colonials, Tudor Revivals, bungalows, and more are available in this relaxed side of town. Easy access to downtown and Virginia Commonwealth University makes this neighborhood popular with professors and other professionals, while **Bryan Park'**s many amenities and the shopping and restaurants along Lakeside, Bellevue, and MacArthur make this a very appealing area.

Bellevue and **Ginter Park,** old streetcar suburbs with lovely homes built in the early 20th century, are just two of the many charming North Side neighborhoods with mature trees and handsome architecture. Single-family home prices are higher in these sections of North Side—$130,000 for a small place and up past $750,000 for a showplace—than in **Battery Park** and **Highland Park,** where fixer-uppers might start at $79,000. **Ginter Place,** an old hospital renovated into condos, offers another option, from $284,000 and up.

North Side is also home to some popular senior citizens communities—**Imperial Plaza** and **Westminster-Canterbury,** to name just two.

Manchester

Just across the Manchester and 14th Street bridges, **Manchester'**s old warehouses are safe behind the flood wall now, so development continues. As anyone who's walked along the flood wall knows, some of the best views of downtown are in Manchester. An artsy neighborhood getting more

Quirky Places to Hang Your Hat in Richmond

This is not an exhaustive list, but within the city limits, you can live in a former:

Bakery (Nolde)

Box factory (Pohlig Box)

Car dealership (Emrick Flats)

Cleaners (Hamlet)

Dairy (Richmond Dairy)

Department store (Miller & Rhoads)

Firehouse (Engine Co. No. 2)

Icebox (Richmond Cold Storage)

Pie factory (Manchester Pie Factory)

Post office (Manchester)

Stove factory (Southern Stoveworks)

School (Robert E. Lee on Kensington and Fulton Hill)

Tobacco warehouse (Tobacco Row and others)

Virginia ham warehouse (Todd's Virginia Ham)

creative all the time, with Plant Zero, Art-Space, and now Dogtown Dance's renovated performance space, Manchester offers creative living space as well in renovated stove-works, tobacco, and pie factories. Rents vary, but in a recently renovated building, a one-bedroom starts around $700 per month.

Woodland Heights, Westover Hills, Forest Hill

Forest Hill Park, which was an amusement park in streetcar days and amuses people now with its farmers' market, multiuse trails, and zany regatta on its three-acre lake, attracts many residents to these surrounding South Side neighborhoods. Access to VCU and downtown is a breeze, since the Lee and Manchester Bridges are a stone's throw away, as are several entrances to the many-splendored **James River Park System.** Not a tough sell, especially when you see the mix of architectural styles and sizes of the early-20th-century and pre–World War II homes. From Victorian to Cape Cods, brick or wood, the choice is yours. Not all the homes have central air, so that is reflected in the price. The range of single-family homes on the market is $120,000 to $400,000, with the lower-priced homes typically south of Forest Hill Avenue. Some homes have stunning views of the river and are priced accordingly in the upper $400,000s, depending on the size. Apartments off Jahnke Road are available in the $500- to $700-per-month range.

Stratford Hills and Stony Point

Though in the city, these neighborhoods share rolling hills, mature oaks, loblolly pines, and proximity to three sections of the **James River Park System** and **Larus Park.** Homes from the mid-1950s and '60s predominate along these shaded streets—a mix of colonials, ranches, and tri-levels (or split-levels), a popular style of house on the hilly terrain because it uses space efficiently. Single-family homes here generally run from $200,000 to $450,000, though some newer homes and riverfront homes along the James can sell for $1 million or more. Typically, the pricier homes in this area are west of the Huguenot Bridge along Cherokee Road; some even back up to the river and offer powerboat access above Bosher's Dam. **Stratford Hills** and **Stony Point** both have townhomes and apartments, mainly clustered near the Forest Hill Avenue and Stony Point retail areas. Rents at the apartments adjacent to **Stony Point Fashion Park** start in the mid-$900s a month.

COUNTIES

Henrico County

Henrico County is split in two by I-95, and the **West End** and the **East End** are quite different in character. The West End has exploded with growth and has more retail development than you can swipe a credit card at, and it is more densely populated than the rural yet slowly developing East End. County-wide, the median price of single-family homes sold in 2009 was $212,000, but the difference between the areas becomes clear when noting that the price range of homes on the market in the western side of the county is $90,000 to $2.7 million, while in the East End prices start at $29,950 and there's only one home—and it's riverfront—for more than $600,000.

Near West End/West End

Just over the border from the city near Willow Lawn Shopping Center, the Jewish Community Center, and St. Mary's Hospital, **Monument Square** offers housing options ranging from luxury one-story condos that start near $200,000 to multilevel townhomes for $390,000. Neighborhoods adjacent to the **University of Richmond** in the **Near West End** are some of the loveliest around, with rolling hills, classic architecture, and beautifully landscaped yards. So close to all the

city offers, this area appreciates the lower county taxes and handy pockets of retail in several areas. The Tuckahoe school district is sought after, and even smaller homes tend to start around $300,000 and go north, so to speak. You'll find lovely brick and wood-sided single-family houses in wooded neighborhoods spread out along River Road, with the pricier ones often south of River Road.

Far West End/Short Pump/Glen Allen

These areas are a mix of affluent and middle-class neighborhoods, high-end and strip shopping malls, and corporate headquarters and business parks. Many older neighborhoods in the **Godwin High School district** have classic colonial single-family homes from the upper $100,000s into the $400,000s. The **Deep Run district** tends to have more expensive homes, though there are also plenty of townhomes to choose from in **Twin Hickory,** for example.

Trader Joe's, Whole Foods, Crate and Barrel, and Pottery Barn out in **Short Pump** took their sweet time coming to Richmond, but have been embraced wildly by shoppers all over the region. The proximity to consumer goods is popular with those who move here from other metropolitan areas' suburbs, but the amount of retail therapy jammed on both sides of West Broad Street can make you feel like you are anywhere, U.S.A. It's full of the chains that upper-middle class folk desire (and the ones they disdain but still frequent).

If you'd like a smaller lot in a neighborhood of expensive homes, many above a half-million dollars, try **Wyndham,** from townhomes, to large single-family residences, to condos. Condos and townhomes out this way can range from the lower $100,000s to more than $500,000. Rental apartments around Short Pump average from $800 to 950 per month.

Glen Allen spreads north along Staples Mill Road and west to **Innsbrook,** which is an 800-acre office park between West Broad Street and I-295. Innsbrook has the most highly concentrated number of workers in the area outside of downtown, and many of these workers like the convenience of living nearby. Rentals here are less expensive than in Short Pump. It's often hard to tell where Glen Allen stops and Short Pump begins, but you might want to pay attention: *Money Magazine* named Glen Allen one of the "100 Best Places to Live" in the U.S. in Aug 2009.

East End

Apartments and homes here are less expensive than in the West End because of the rural character and lack of retail. Nearby shopping is limited to the **Laburnum Avenue corridor,** though more is coming. Some of the area is scruffy and light industrial due to the airport's East End location. **Sandston** and **Highland Springs** are older areas with longtime residents and not much new building going on. Heading out along the river in **Varina,** quiet neighborhoods that feel a million miles away from the city feature homes that start in the mid-$100,000s. The higher-priced properties are riverfront, have more land, or are townhomes or penthouses in **Rockett's Landing,** a luxury riverfront development that straddles Henrico and Richmond, with prices from $200,000 to almost $1 million. Besides Rockett's Landing, condos and town houses are not plentiful here, but they range from below $100,000 to the low $200,000s. One-bedroom apartments are available for $600 per month and up.

Hanover County

According to Forbes.com in Feb 2010, **Hanover County** ranked as the nation's "10th Best Place to Get Ahead," based on employment and income growth. It traditionally has the lowest unemployment in the region and certainly has appealing home prices and options, whether you want a sprawling horse farm or a neighborhood feel.

Hanover is huge and much of the county still has a rural feel to it. The famous Hanover tomatoes need room to grow. The county has preserved almost 6,000 acres of historic land and open space. It could take you an hour on winding roads to drive from **Beaverdam** in the northwest to **Cold Harbor** in the southeast. For homes sold in 2009, the median price for all Hanover was $246,950.

The homeowner rate here is 87 percent higher than the state average of 68 percent, and rental housing is not as prevalent here as other parts of the region.

Ashland/Western Hanover

With **Randolph-Macon College** in **Ashland** and its quaint yet bustling retail and restaurant district, the area appeals to those wanting a small-town feel just up the road from the big city. Ashland itself has charming, older homes on tree-lined streets. If you like the sound of a train rumbling by, you are in luck because trains roll right through town. It doesn't take long outside of Ashland to be on country roads, so palatial homes on big spreads are available here, including several at more than $1 million, with stables and acreage, and one even near $5 million. Golf-course communities are abundant here. Most single-family homes in the market near Ashland and in the **Kings**

Charter neighborhood are priced in the $200,000 to $400,000 range. Townhomes aren't a big part of the market, but they tend to be clustered near I-295 and range from the mid-$100,000s up into the $300,000s. Apartments in Ashland start at around $600 per month. Remember, some parts of well-regarded Glen Allen are in Hanover County.

Mechanicsville/Eastern Hanover

Mechanicsville gets rated highly according to *Money Magazine*'s "100 Best Places to Live," and most residents would agree. There are enough stores for the basics on US 360, and Courthouse Park, Pole Green Park, and the many preserved battlefield sites give the area plenty of green space. Then there are the good schools and highway access with I-95 and I-295 nearby. If you want lots of land with a ranch house, you can have it here. Or if you like your land topped with a custom luxury home, that's a popular way to go, too. Houses for sale in early 2010 ranged from $119,950 to $2,995,000, but most single-family homes on the market are in the $200,000 to $500,000 range. There are some new townhomes going up, some in age-restricted communities and others in **Pebble Lake** and **Bell Creek.** These range from the upper $100,000s to $300,000. Apartments in this neck of the woods tend to be two-bedroom units and run $750 a month.

Chesterfield County

Chesterfield County, the most populous locality in the region, known for booming development and strong schools, is quite popular, too. In 2009 the median price for single-family homes sold in the entire county was $215,000. The median price of condos sold in 2009 in Chesterfield was $150,000.

Bon Air

Some streets of **Bon Air** look like the twins of Stratford Hills because they were one neighborhood before **Chippenham Parkway** cut through. Victorian-era houses remain from the area's days as a resort for wealthy city dwellers and newer homes add a 20th-century twist on Victorian style. Other homes in the tree-canopied area are a mix of ranches, colonials, and tri-levels, and the price range reflects the variety. Smaller homes can be had for just under $200,000, while $300,000 to $400,000 is typical for the larger ones, though the historic homes can be in the $500,000 ballpark. One-bedroom apartments can be found for about $720 a month.

Chesterfield Courthouse/Southern Chesterfield

Heading down VA 10 east and south of the city gives prospective residents several living options—golf-course communities, newly built neighborhoods with a mix of townhomes and single-family housing, and even lakefront living on Lake Chesdin. Expansive neighborhoods dot the area, and you're never far from **Pocahontas State Park**, a river, a lake, or a reservoir. **Chester** has a village-like feel, and new development is trying to duplicate that. New townhomes start at $120,000, and new single-family homes range from near $200,000 on up. Houses on Lake Chesdin are the priciest—as high as $799,000. Monthly rent for a one-bedroom apartment ranges from $750 to $975.

Midlothian

A sprawling, popular area, **Midlothian** includes established, quiet neighborhoods of single-family homes that back up to woods; gated communities; and scads of planned communities with a mix of housing options—many along Swift Creek Reservoir and US 360— and others sprouting up as a result of the completion of VA 288 and Chesterfield County's unabated growth. Single-family homes in older neighborhoods closer to the city line are priced in the $200,000s to start and head upwards. Home prices jump noticeably—upwards of $500,000— in well-manicured **Salisbury,** with its lake, country club, and large lots, and continue upward in upscale **Founders Bridge** along the Powhatan County line. Many neighborhoods line Robious Road, and some west of Huguenot have access to the James River; Robious Landing Park behind James River High School offers river access for all.

Established neighborhoods near the Village of Midlothian on US 60 take advantage of the retail corridor there, and along US 360 vary from predominantly single-family home subdivisions to the huge Charter Colony area that offers houses, townhomes, and condos near the Midlothian campus of **John Tyler Community College.** The price range of single-family homes on the market now goes from $310,000 to the neighborhood of $2,000,000. One-bedroom rental apartments run the gamut from $750 to $900 per month.

OUTLYING COUNTIES
Goochland County

Goochland County has the highest per-capita personal income in the Richmond metro area at $58,642 and is one of the wealthiest counties in the country, yet not everyone has a fortune to spend on a home. Though rolling horse farms and the $1 million-plus lakefront homes surrounding the 70-acre lake at the luxury development of **Kinloch** skew the picture, starter homes on the market start at in the low $100,000s

and then the sky is the limit, with the most expensive property priced at $2,495,000. The median for homes sold in '09 was $321,000, with neighborhoods of older homes near **Tuckahoe Plantation** and **Goochland Courthouse** providing old-fashioned charm at a more liveable price point.

New Kent County

In the land of **Colonial Downs Race Track,** off I-64 between Richmond and Williamsburg, there remains a lot of land. For those who like large lots in the country within a neighborhood, there are several golf-course communities such as **Brickshire** or **Vinterra** at **New Kent,** which even boasts its own winery and has plans for a polo club. **Patriots Landing** is a planned community with trails, 80 acres of undeveloped land, and lakes. It's a mix of townhomes starting in the low $200,000s and single-family homes from the low $300,000s heading toward $500,000.

Powhatan County

Realtors say "Powhatan is popping," since that's where the land is and the completion of VA 288 makes regional access easier. Homes out here range from $100,000 to more than $2 million, with the median price of county homes sold in 2009 right at $227,396. Known for its rural lifestyle and heritage, though increasingly adding restaurants and stores, **Powhatan** does have five-acre average lot sizes or two-acre minimum requirements in some areas, though some communities, such as **Scottville** at **Powhatan Courthouse,** sport smaller lots because they're designed for active adults who want to walk to the park and library and such.

REAL ESTATE AGENCIES AND RESOURCES

The listings below are meant to be a starting place in the search for your new home, whether it's an apartment, or a horse farm, or something in between. It is absolutely not inclusive, and dozens of other reputable companies and agents would be just as happy to help you find your place here.

The **Richmond Association of Realtors** (www.rarealtors.com or 804-422-5000), the main trade group for Realtors in central Virginia, has many useful articles and tools on its Web site about home-buyer tax credits and links to affordable housing for renters, for instance. Their information is available in English and Spanish. A useful Web site with access to the Central Virginia Multiple Listing Service is **www.homes.richmond.com.**

The Real Estate Book can be found at local stores in the free publication racks, and the same information is available at www .realestatebook.com, which has the advantage of being updated daily. For home rentals, check out **www.homerentals.net** and for apartments, see **www.apartmentpros .com** or call (866) 560-4701. Of course, the *Sunday Richmond Times-Dispatch* has a large real estate section that lists the open houses for the day. Go to www.timesdispatch .com to search real estate listings online.

CHAMBER RELOCATION
3212 Skipwith Rd., Suite 110
(804) 564-7823
www.chamberrelocation.com
Ollie Chambers runs this five-to-eight-person relocation business out of a larger 40-person US Realty office. Her relocation services are designed to build relationships so the agents can understand how best to help the client's situation. Agents will work with trailing spouses and educate clients about the school options if the client has school-age children. In one case, when a family's son wasn't happy about moving and Ollie heard he played the guitar, she gave him a gift certificate to Guitar Works. The company has developed a niche helping seniors relocate. They break down the overwhelming process into smaller pieces, doing as much for the customers as anyone could want, including decluttering. With a diverse staff, some of whom are bilingual in French, Italian, and Spanish, you'll get a great sense of how to make the area your home after you've spoken with them.

COLDWELL BANKER JOHNSON AND THOMAS REALTORS
504 Libbie Ave.
(804) 288-4163
www.wesellrichmond.com
This agency impresses the minute you dive into its Web site. It's almost one-stop shopping because besides the typical real estate information, it links to a vast array of useful sites, including schools, media, and cultural institutions. So with just a few clicks of the mouse, you get a feel of the place you'll soon call home. Fifteen trained agents work with those relocating from out of the area and they have the listening skills and energy to walk newcomers through the life-changing process. In business for 35 years, this outfit knows the entire region well. Some agents speak Spanish, and translators are available for other languages.

HOMETOWN REALTY
(804) 565-3606
www.hometownrealtyservices.com
With offices all around the city, this agency would be a good fit for those who already

know they want to be in Hanover, Henrico, Goochland, and New Kent Counties, though they certainly are happy to find people the right city spot, too. The Web site's blog is a great way for those outside of Richmond to get a peek at what's going on here. This group will work hard to set you up with an agent you can relate to. Perhaps the most forward-thinking gadget on the site is the agent finder by language. Need an agent who speaks Chinese? Click here. They have one, as well as one who speaks Hindi, Urdu, and Spanish.

LONG AND FOSTER RELOCATION
2800 Buford Rd.
(804) 272-2800
www.longandfoster.com
This company's 12 relocation counselors will ask you simple yet illuminating questions when you start the stressful moving process: "What are you leaving? What are you looking for? How much of a commute do you want?" Once they get answers, they put lifestyle options on the table, from a planned community to a downtown loft. Some people come to town having been told by their sister-in-law that they *must* live in such and such neighborhood, or you *can't* live south of the river. That's hogwash, and this outfit knows it.

Since the relocation counselors aren't actually selling you real estate, they listen to your needs and share with you the many possibilities within this region. Then they hook you up with a selling agent who will work as part of the team. They love the challenge of doing a mass relocation when a new company comes to town, presenting Richmond in all its glory, but are just as excited to work with individual newcomers. They pride themselves on listening to

each client, and not parking the next 20 people who walk in the door in the same "in" neighborhood. After the last big corporate move they handled, they ran the zip codes to see where the hundreds of newcomers had landed. They were sprinkled all over the region, proof positive that this operation doesn't try to fit a square peg into a round hole. Long and Foster has many agents who are bilingual.

NAPIER REALTORS ERA
14361 Sommerville Court
(800) 966-7669
www.napierera.com
Though the relocation department is run out of the Midlothian office, Napier ERA has three other area locations, in Powhatan, Glen Allen, and in Colonial Heights for the Petersburg region. Whether it's working with corporations or individuals, the relocation department prides itself on matching agents with clients for customer satisfaction. Everybody wants a good neighborhood. These experts will help you figure out where in the region yours is. Out of the 150-plus agents in all of the offices, a few are bilingual in Spanish, French, and Russian.

PRUDENTIAL SLATER JAMES RIVER
REALTORS
2737 McRae Rd.
(800) 500-0028
www.prurichmond.com
This firm's relocation section has three counselors dedicated to helping you get where you want to go. If you've ever driven around with the wrong Realtor, you know you don't want that to happen again, so this group listens to your story and works to match you with the most qualified and compatible of their relocation-certified agents, and

the counselors continue to be part of the process through your entire move. Some of their 75 to 80 agents speak Spanish, Korean, and Vietnamese.

SMALL AND ASSOCIATES REAL ESTATE
114 N. Meadow St.
(804) 353-1250
www.smallrealestate.com

In business since 1982, this agency has seven agents who know and love the ins and outs of Richmond's neighborhoods north and south of the river, including North Side, Jackson Ward, Church Hill, the Fan, Woodland Heights, and Westover Hills. They enjoy nothing more than welcoming out-of-towners and showing off the architecturally and culturally vibrant neighborhoods in the city. Of course, they handle real estate all over the area as well, but Chris Small has noticed more 50-somethings, tired of driving in the suburbs and a bit bored out there, moving back to the city for the fun. They also can hook you up with great rental property—apartments and houses. Two agents speak Spanish, and one, Anne Thomas Soffee, is an acclaimed memoirist as well (*Snake Hips: Bellydancing and How I Found True Love*), so I'm betting she'll tell better stories while you're riding around Richmond with her than the typical Realtor schtick.

INFORMATION FOR NEWCOMERS

Auto Insurance

Virginia law requires that the minimum insurance coverage for a registered vehicle must cover $25,000 for bodily injury or death of one person, $50,000 for bodily injury or death of two or more people, and $20,000 for property damage. If you do not purchase auto insurance, you must pay a $500 uninsured motor vehicle fee, which doesn't provide insurance coverage but does allow you to register and operate your vehicle in Virginia for one year. You face stiff fines, suspensions, and penalties for failure to carry the minimum liability insurance or pay the Uninsured Motor Vehicle (UMV) fee.

Pet Licenses

All applications must be accompanied by a copy of a current rabies certificate.

Richmond: $10 annually for dogs and cats; renew by Jan 1; www.richmondgov.com/animalcontrol; (804) 646-5573

Chesterfield: $7 annually for dogs only, discounted to $5 for neutered dogs; www.chesterfield.gov; (804) 748-1683

Hanover: $6 annually dogs only; www.co.hanover.va.us; (804) 365-6485

Henrico: $10 annually dogs only; www.co.henrico.va.us; (804) 501-4678

i The Richmond SPCA has a multitude of useful information for pet owners on its Web site, www.richmondspca.org. Click on Pet-friendly Places to find apartment communities, senior communities, and even an art gallery and a restaurant that allow pets. Assorted stores in the high-end Stony Point Fashion Park allow dogs, too. Check for the dog icon in the store window.

Vehicle Registration

Before registering your vehicle in Virginia, you must title it here, within 30 days of moving to the state. Registering the vehicle and getting new license plates must also be done within the same 30-day period. To obtain a Virginia title, fill out the title application, available online (www.dmv.state.va.us/webdoc/forms/index.asp) and bring it to a DMV Customer Service Center along with proof of your new Virginia address, your registration and title from your previous state, and proof of purchase price if you bought the vehicle within the past year. You will also need to pay the $10 titling fee and either $35 or the 3 percent motor vehicle sales-and-use tax that is based on the vehicle's sales price, whichever is greater.

DMV issues you two plates per vehicle, two decals showing the expiration date of your registration, and your registration. Motorcycles get one plate.

The registration fee is based on the gross weight of your vehicle, the type of license plate you choose, and whether you choose to register your vehicle for one or two years.

Vehicle Inspection

Once your vehicle is registered, get a vehicle inspection as soon as possible. There is no grace period. Vehicles registered in Virginia must pass an annual safety inspection and display a valid safety inspection sticker on the front windshield. Driving without an inspection sticker can lead to hefty tickets and fines. Many service and gas stations in Virginia are licensed to complete state inspections, as are new car dealerships. The annual inspection costs $16. To learn more about the vehicle inspection program, contact the Virginia State Police at www.vsp.virginia.gov or call (804) 743-2217.

Driver's Licenses

The Commonwealth of Virginia requires that new resident drivers obtain a Virginia driver's license within 60 days of moving here. If you are 19 or older and already have a driver's license from out of state, DMV may exchange that for a Virginia license, assuming you meet the identity, legal presence, residency, Social Security, and driver education requirements, but you will be required to pass the vision screening and surrender your old license. Licenses are valid for eight years and cost $4 per year. Go to **www.dmvnow.com** for a list of what constitutes valid ID documents. You may fill out the paperwork ahead of time, downloading the application from DMV's Web site.

Moving within Virginia is easier in regards to your driver's license, as you may update your address by purchasing a new license online or in person, if you must. Virginia residents have 30 days from the date of their move to notify DMV of an address change. New driver's licenses are issued through the mail, so make sure you keep your address updated accurately. Driver's licenses will not be forwarded by the U.S. Postal Service.

DMV Locations

Customer Service Centers are open Mon through Fri from 8 a.m. to 5 p.m. and on Sat from 8 a.m. to noon, but call first to make sure the hours haven't changed. There are two kinds of DMV locations, the full-service ones listed here and the DMV select offices that are run by approved partners. Vehicle transactions can be handled at DMV select offices, but driver's licenses and learner's permits cannot. Check out the DMV's Web site for more information and to see if there's a DMV select office near you.

VIRGINIA DEPARTMENT OF MOTOR VEHICLES
www.dmv.state.va.us
Customer Service Centers,
(804) 497-7100

RICHMOND
2300 W. Broad St.

HENRICO/NORTH SIDE
9015 Brook Rd.

HENRICO/EAST END
5517 S. Laburnum Ave.

HENRICO/WEST END
9237 Quioccasin Rd.

CHESTERFIELD
610 Johnston-Willis Dr.

CHESTER
12100 Branders Creek Rd

Religious Institutions

Some of Richmond's religious institutions have been here for hundreds of years, others just a decade or less. With more than 1,000 religious organizations and places of worship, there is more diversity in the region than ever before. We are, after all, where Jefferson penned the Virginia Statute of Religious Freedom.

Those new to the community looking to connect with a synagogue might contact the **Weinstein Jewish Community Center** (www.weinsteinjcc.org, 804-285-6500) for assistance in finding the right fit. Buddhists of all stripes might be interested in the multidenominational **Ekoji Buddhist Sangha** (www.ekojirichmond.org, 804-355-6657). The expanding **Hindu Center of Virginia** can be reached at (804) 346-9954 or www.hinducenterofvirginia.org. The **Islamic Center of Virginia** (www.icva1.com, 804-320-7333) lists all of the regional mosques for Muslim newcomers. Some folks might be interested in the ecumenical fellowship of **Richmond Hill** (www.richmondhillva.org, 804-783-7903) on, poetically enough, Church Hill. There are far too many Christian denominations around town to list, but you will find hundreds of churches and other houses of worship in the yellow pages.

Voter Registration

If you are already at the DMV dealing with your driver's license and vehicle registrations, apply to register to vote or change your voter registration name or address at the same time, as long as you are over 18 and a U.S. citizen. Just answer the citizenship and voter registration questions on the driver's license application and you'll be given a voter registration form to complete.

Otherwise, you may download a voter registration application from the **Virginia State Board of Elections** Web site at www.sbe.virginia.gov and send your voter registration application in by mail, but you must provide a copy of identification that shows your name and current Virginia address. See the State Board of Education Web site for the list of approved documents. Contact your local registrar or call (800) 552-9745 for more information.

EDUCATION AND CHILD CARE

The Standards of Learning (SOL) is Virginia's approach to measuring academic progress in public schools. SOLs have been determined for every grade level, and testing in English, math, science, and history starts in grade 3 and continues into high school. The combined counties now have more citizens living in poverty than the city does, and the challenge of educating kids from difficult circumstances is a task undertaken by all of the local school systems. Each of the four largest localities has at least one technical center for high school students interested in career pathways right out of high school.

To enroll your child in a Virginia public school, you must have your child's original birth certificate, Social Security number, immunization records, and proof of residency for the locality where you are registering your child.

PUBLIC SCHOOLS

RICHMOND PUBLIC SCHOOLS
(804) 780-7710
www.richmond.k12.va.us
RPS serves more than 24,000 students in 45 schools, 44 of which have achieved full accreditation under the Virginia Standards of Learning program. Every elementary school offers instruction in foreign languages. International Baccalaureate programs are in place in middle and high schools, and dual enrollment and Advanced Placement (AP) classes are offered in high schools. Besides comprehensive high schools, eighth-graders can apply to several other schools as well. Open High partners with J. Sargeant Reynolds Community College and Virginia Commonwealth University to offer students accelerated learning, Community High features a college-preparatory curriculum and enrichment programs designed to ensure college success for disadvantaged students, and Franklin Military Academy was the first public military high school in the U.S. The Governor's Career and Technical Education Academy for science, technology, engineering, and math just opened at Richmond Technical Center, offering students other career paths. Approximately one third of graduating seniors earned advanced diplomas.

J. E. B. Stuart Elementary and Open High School have been named national Blue Ribbon Schools of Excellence, and Bellevue and Fairfield Court elementary schools received Governor's Awards for Educational Excellence in 2010. Fourteen schools earned the state Board of Education's Excellence Awards in 2009. Though the drop-out rate is the highest in the area, the on-time graduation rate for students is improving.

HENRICO COUNTY PUBLIC SCHOOLS
3820 Nine Mile Rd.
(804) 652-3600
www.henrico.k12.va.us

Enrolling nearly 50,000 students in 71 schools, Henrico County Public Schools are known for their emphasis on technology in the classroom. Partnering with Apple and Dell, the school system loans laptops to high school and middle school students and staff through the Teaching and Learning Initiative. Elementary school classrooms have access to laptops as well. With nine specialty centers in areas such as leadership, world languages, and information technology, International Baccalaureate programs at three middle schools and two high schools, and two technical centers, Henrico makes opportunities available. In addition, four high schools offer JROTC programs. Known for its top-notch music education, Henrico has been named, ten years in a row, one of the "Best Communities for Music Education." Thirteen Henrico schools earned the 2010 Governor's Award for Educational Excellence and twelve have earned the Department of Education's national Blue Ribbon designation. Sixty-six out of a possible 67 schools were fully accredited in 2009. Honors, AP, and dual-enrollment classes are offered in high school, and 84 county teachers are National Board certified. With 1604 graduates earning advanced diplomas, 82 percent of all Henrico County 2009 high school graduates planned to continue their education.

HANOVER COUNTY PUBLIC SCHOOLS
200 Berkley St., Ashland
(804) 365-4500
www.hcps.us
Serving nearly 20,000 students from prekindergarten through high school, the Hanover County Public School system employs approximately 1,500 classroom teachers in 25 schools, including an alternative education center and a trade and technology

center. In 2009, for the eighth year in a row, 100 percent of Hanover public schools earned full accreditation. Awarded ten National Blue Ribbon School Awards by the U.S. Department of Education since 1996, the district offers International Baccalaureate diploma, Advanced Placement courses, and dual-enrollment classes for secondary students. The district's students have the highest average SAT scores in the region. More than half of 2009 graduates earned an advanced diploma. Eight Hanover schools received Governor's Awards for Educational Excellence in 2010, and the entire school system and seven schools received Board of Education Excellence Awards in 2010.

CHESTERFIELD COUNTY PUBLIC SCHOOLS
(804) 748-1405
www.chesterfield.k12.va.us
Serving more than 58,000 students in 64 schools, Chesterfield County is the largest school division in the Richmond region and among the 100 largest in the country. CCPS is the largest division in Virginia to have every school fully accredited in 2008 and 2009. With 78 National Board–certified teachers and almost 2,000 teachers with master's degrees, the school system hires and develops talented educators, and it shows. The Milken Family Foundation has bestowed National Educator Awards, accompanied by $25,000, on three county teachers. Four schools—James River High, Clover Hill Elementary, Grange Hall Elementary, and Robious Elementary—are national Blue Ribbon Schools. Twelve schools earned the 2010 Governor's Award of Educational Excellence.

Students entering high school in Chesterfield County can apply to programs as diverse as Spanish immersion,

Regional Governor's Schools

Eighth-graders from the Richmond region are eligible to apply, depending on what locality they live in, to one or both of the public, full-time regional Governor's Schools in the area: **Maggie L. Walker Governor's School for Government and International Studies** in Richmond and **Appomattox Regional Governor's School for Arts and Technology** in Petersburg.

Maggie Walker (www.gsgis.k12.va.us or 804-354-6800), conveniently located in the center of Richmond, is considered one of the best high schools in the country. *Newsweek* magazine has named it one of only two of Virginia's "Public Elites." Most of the 712 Maggie Walker students come from the counties of Henrico, Chesterfield, Hanover, and the city of Richmond, but Powhatan, Goochland, New Kent, and other localities send students as well. Besides the traditional college-preparatory curriculum, students choose from 11 foreign languages and take four years of one language and two years of another. Most students take several dual-enrollment and AP classes. One hundred and forty hours of community service are required to graduate, and 70 percent of students play sports, so the school provides a well-rounded, vibrant high school experience. Its graduates attend prestigious schools such as the College of William & Mary, the University of Virginia, Dartmouth, and many more.

Appomattox Regional Governor's School in Petersburg (www.args.k12. va.us or 804-722-0200), draws 350 students from the cities of Richmond and Petersburg and the counties of Chesterfield, Powhatan, and several other localities. Students applying here must submit a portfolio for review and have an audition and interview. Its talented students concentrate in one area, such as dance, technology, musical theater, literary arts, or other programs, while fulfilling challenging college-preparatory high school requirements. Dual-enrollment classes are offered, and the school sends graduates to many excellent schools, including the University of Virginia, Savannah College of Art and Design, and VCU School of the Arts.

pre-engineering, health sciences, the arts, and International Baccalaureate programs, to name just a few. Of the more than 4,000 high school graduates in the class of 2009, more than half earned advanced diplomas, and 83 percent planned to continue their education. In 2009 more than 3,000 students took more than 5,410 Advanced Placement exams.

OUTLYING COUNTIES

GOOCHLAND COUNTY PUBLIC SCHOOLS
2938-I River Rd. West
(804) 556-5316
www.glnd.k12.va.us

This district of 2,568 students has instituted the G21 program, which brings new media and technology into the classrooms at the three elementary schools, one middle school, and one high school. A center for gifted students works with students in grades three through five and six through eight, and Gifted Resource teachers are in the home schools.

More than half of Goochland High's seniors take dual-enrollment classes at nearby J. Sargeant Reynolds Community College, and AP classes are offered as well. Some high school students take part in the Blue Ridge Virtual Governor's School, which emphasizes math, science, and technology. Goochland Elementary has won the Governor's Award for Educational Excellence two years in a row, and the school system as a whole and Byrd and Randolph elementary schools received the state Board of Education's Excellence Award.

i Find more information about Virginia schools at the Virginia Department of Education's Web site, www.doe.virginia.gov. By clicking on Virginia School Report Card, you can find reams of data about particular schools and school divisions.

NEW KENT COUNTY PUBLIC SCHOOLS
11920 New Kent Hwy.
(804) 966-9650
www.nkcps.k12.va.us

With just two elementary schools, one middle school, and one high school, this school district offers instruction from prekindergarten through the secondary level, including vocational, special education, and enrichment programs for gifted students of all ages. All four schools earned full accreditation for 2009 to 2010. New Kent Elementary received the state Board of Education Excellence Award for 2010, and New Kent High School earned the Governor's

Excellence Award. Advanced Placement and dual-enrollment classes are offered for high school students.

POWHATAN COUNTY PUBLIC SCHOOLS
2320 Skaggs Rd.
(804) 598-5700
www.powhatan.k12.va.us

Powhatan County School District has just six schools in it: three elementary schools, a middle school, a junior high school, and a high school. The elementary schools are for prekindergarten through grade four, the middle school handles grades five and six, junior high is seventh and eighth grade, and the high school serves students in grades 9 through 12. Enrichment, including math competitions and robotics, is offered to students. Powhatan Elementary and Powhatan Junior High received the state Board of Education Excellence Award. In a partnership with J. Sargeant Reynolds Community College, dual enrollment classes are offered to high school students. More than half of 2009 high school graduates received advanced diplomas.

PRIVATE SCHOOLS

COLLEGIATE SCHOOL
103 N. Mooreland Rd.
(804) 740-7077
www.collegiate-va.org

Collegiate School is by far the largest private school in the area, with 1,553 students in grades kindergarten through 12. It's a coeducational college-preparatory school for students in Henrico County's West End. Foreign language instruction takes place at every grade level. After-school care is offered for students up to grade seven. Students' SAT scores here are well above Virginia and national averages. In 2008, 88 percent of students who took AP exams scored 3 or higher, and graduates go on to many prestigious colleges. Athletics take place on the main campus as well as at the 182-acre Robins Campus 7 miles away.

ST. CATHERINE'S SCHOOL
6001 Grove Ave.
(804) 288-2804
www.st.catherines.org
This all-girls Episcopal school serves girls from junior kindergarten through high school on its beautiful 16-acre West End campus. Sixty-five percent of the faculty members have advanced degrees, and St. Catherine's is known for its innovative college-preparatory curriculum. It works—in 2009, 90 percent of students taking AP exams earned a 3 or higher, and graduates head to some of the country's finest colleges. Its Upper School offers coeducational classes with nearby St. Christopher's, and the school-wide athletic program includes 45 teams in 15 different sports.

ST. CHRISTOPHER'S SCHOOL
711 St. Christopher's Rd.
(804) 282-3185
www.stchristophers.com
Dedicated to educating the "whole boy," since 1911 St. Christopher's has 950 boys from junior kindergarten through grade 12 on its West End campus. Strong programs in athletics and the arts work in concert with the college-preparatory curriculum. More than half of the 150 faculty members have advanced degrees, and almost 100 percent of graduates go on to four-year colleges. Year-round extended day care is offered for students in junior kindergarten through grade seven for both St. Christopher's and St. Catherine's. Coed classes for high school

students from St. Christopher's and St. Catherine's take place on both campuses.

ST. GERTRUDE HIGH SCHOOL
3215 Stuart Ave.
(804) 358-9114
www.saintgertrude.org
An all-girls independent Catholic high school in the Museum District, St. Gertrude enrolls 283 girls in grades 9 through 12. Since 1922 St. Gertrude has specialized in the way young women learn. Students take advantage of their proximity to the Virginia Museum of Fine Arts, Virginia Historical Society, and the Science Museum of Virginia to enhance the college-preparatory curriculum. Many students take honors and AP classes and compete in 11 varsity sports as well. The average class size is 15, and all that attention pays off—100 percent of the class of 2009 was college bound.

THE STEWARD SCHOOL
11600 Gayton Rd.
(804) 740-3394
www.stewardschool.org
This school teaches 600 students from kindergarten through high school on its 37-acre Far West End campus. In existence since 1972, it recently received a $1 million anonymous donation to increase diversity and endow a scholarship fund. Child-centered education and individualized attention are the keys here. Its college-preparatory curriculum offers honors and AP courses, and after-school care is available.

South of the River

MILLWOOD SCHOOL
15100 Millwood School Lane
www.millwoodschool.org

Offering junior kindergarten through 10th grade, this 79-acre school next to Woodlake in Chesterfield County is in the process of adding one grade of high school per year until it spans junior kindergarten through 12th grade. It is a coed, independent, college-preparatory school with 304 students, though that number will be heading upward with growth. Sports and other activities are offered, as is extended care before and after school.

ST. MICHAEL'S EPISCOPAL SCHOOL
8706 Quaker Lane
(804) 272-3514
www.stmschool.net
This coed, Episcopal school in Bon Air, for students in kindergarten through grade eight, has recently added a separate middle school campus and is a candidate for the International Baccalaureate Middle School Years program. With 371 students, St. Michael's emphasizes involvement, whether through in-school clubs, after-school sports, theatrical performances, or robotics. Spanish instruction begins in the fourth grade. By the time students graduate eighth grade, most are ready for Spanish II in high school.

TRINITY EPISCOPAL SCHOOL
3850 Pittaway Dr.
(804) 272-5864
www.trinityes.org
On 35 acres in a residential neighborhood, Trinity features small classes for its 405 students in grades eight through 12. It's a coed, independent, Episcopal, college-preparatory school that offers individual attention and many options for growth. Trinity was the first Richmond area school to offer the International Baccalaureate program, and its students

have a choice of many of the commonwealth's and country's finest colleges.

ℹ️ For a list of private, independent schools, go to the Virginia Council for Private Education at www.vcpe.org.

CHILD CARE AND PRESCHOOLS

The Virginia Department of Social Services licenses child-care centers and family day-care providers and maintains lists of these facilities. The department also maintains lists of unlicensed facilities, including religious-exempt child day-care centers, voluntarily registered home day care, and certified preschools. To learn about licensing requirements for child care and to search the database for all child-care facilities in the area, go to the Department of Social Services' Web site at www.dss.virginia.gov/family/cc/index.html.

RAINBOW STATION
(804) 747-5900
www.rainbowstation.org
With four facilities around town, in Hanover County, Chesterfield County, and two in Henrico County, Rainbow Station takes care of children from infants through age 14 in a variety of programs. Offering early-education programs through age five at preschool and nursery schools, Rainbow Station's focus then shifts to the Village at Rainbow Station, where school-age kids are supervised before and after school and offered all sorts of activities to meet their changing needs. Each Rainbow Station has an infirmary staffed by a pediatric nurse for mildly sick children, for those days when parents just can't miss work.

TUCKAWAY CHILD DEVELOPMENT AND EARLY EDUCATION CENTERS

2125 Tuckaway Lane
(804) 270-4841
www.tuckaway.cc

This child-focused, family-owned center offers developmentally appropriate, year-round child care for infants, toddlers, and preschoolers, and before- and after-school care for children at six locations in the region—in Carytown, Mechanicsville, Varina, and three facilities in the West End. Each site has somewhat different facilities, but the commitment to individualized attention is evident everywhere. Each location has an on-site chef who prepares healthy, warm, family-style meals for the children. Playgrounds and pools at some locations provide lots of space for fun.

HIGHER EDUCATION

The Richmond region produces nearly 10,000 graduates every year from every kind of college and university imaginable: four-year school, urban university, suburban liberal arts, small-town liberal arts, law school, seminary, Historically Black College and University (HBCU), public and private, art school, engineering school, law school, and community college—in the city, suburbs, and country. As if that's not enough, continuing education is available from some of the best names in the business, and education and technical schools are in abundance.

COLLEGES & UNIVERSITIES

Richmond

UNIVERSITY OF RICHMOND
28 Westhampton Way
(804) 289-8000
www.richmond.edu

Many people, even some Virginians, assume that the liberal arts University of Richmond is a public university like the University of Virginia or William & Mary, but though plenty of aspiring students have all three schools on their wish lists, Richmond is actually a quite selective private university, founded in 1830 and ensconced at this idyllic Near West End campus since 1914. Its list of accolades goes on and on, but suffice it to say that UR ranked 30th among liberal arts colleges in the country for 2010, according to *U.S. News & World Report,* and its business school ranked 15th in the nation, according to *BusinessWeek.*

The University of Richmond's 350-acre campus is what a liberal arts college should look like—rolling wooded hills, quads surrounded by grand brick, Collegiate Gothic–style buildings (several designed by Ralph Adams Cram, the architect responsible for much of Princeton and West Point), and the library overlooking a lake. Even the new on-campus Robins Stadium continues the classy architectural theme. It's almost cruel to expect the 4,250 students to do work here, but work they do, choosing among 60 majors in UR's five schools: the School of Arts and Sciences, Jepson School of Leadership, Robins School of Business, Richmond School of Law, and the School of Continuing Studies.

With an undergraduate population of 2,767 and a full-time faculty of 350, the student to faculty ratio is eight to one, and the average class size is 16, so students know their teachers and vice versa. Since 2005, several students have studied assiduously enough to merit Fulbright, Truman, Rhodes, Marshall, and several other prestigious scholarships.

Richmond's latest push emphasizes student engagement in the university, community, and the world—246 student organizations, 14 fraternities and sororities, and 19 Division I sports make getting involved on campus easy as pi. The Bonner

Center for Civic Engagement, which assists students with internships and volunteer opportunities—including a recent Habitat for Humanity house-building project—and the new UR Downtown Campus, which offers pro bono legal help, increase the connections between campus and city. As far as engaging the world goes, 8 percent of undergraduates are international students, and in 2007, *Newsweek* named Richmond the "Hottest School for International Studies," perhaps because UR students have 75 programs in 30 countries to choose from. And choose they did—58 percent of the class of 2008 studied abroad. That's before the Carole Weinstein International Center opened on campus in 2010.

The university practices the engagement it preaches by bringing the best of the performing arts to Richmond every year through its Modlin Center for the Arts. Find more on that in the "Performing Arts" chapter. As a sponsor of First Fridays Art Walk and now with a downtown presence at UR Downtown, UR will be even more involved in cultural and community issues. Richmond students interact with local, national, and international leaders from a variety of fields on campus in conjunction with the multidisciplinary Jepson Leadership School, the only one of its kind in the country. Leland Melvin, NASA astronaut and University of Richmond alumnus, has served as leader-in-residence, and former governor of Virginia, former mayor of Richmond, and current chairman of the Democratic National Committee, Tim Kaine, teaches at UR.

UR offers need-blind admissions and awards such hefty need-based financial aid that it regularly makes the lists of great-value private schools. Richmond is committed to enrolling students from all backgrounds, so admitted Virginia students whose family income is under $40,000 receive full scholarships.

The Spiders compete in the Division I Atlantic 10 Conference for most sports. In football, they are members of the CAA conference and compete in the Football Championship Subdivision. In fact, UR competes so well, in 2008 the football team was the national champion.

VIRGINIA COMMONWEALTH UNIVERSITY
(804) 828-0100
www.vcu.edu

The largest university in Virginia, at 32,000 students and 1,900 full-time instructional faculty members, VCU has come a long way from its commuter-school roots. One faculty member, John B. Fenn, shared the Nobel Prize for Chemistry in 2002. One student, Caressa Cameron, a junior broadcast journalism major, won the Miss America title in 2010. And one school, VCU School of the Arts, recently ranked in *U.S. News and World Report* as No. 1 among public arts and design graduate schools in the country, and fourth among all graduate arts and design schools in the country.

This vibrant, diverse, and bustling urban university resulted from the 1968 merger of the Medical College of Virginia with Richmond Professional Institute, and has grown by leaps and bounds since, tripling the student body and adding 30 acres in the city. It's an academic powerhouse, offering bachelor's degrees in 60 areas, master's in 67, doctorates in 40, and professional and certificate programs in 43. A major research institution, VCU ranks among the top 100 in the U.S. for sponsored research. *U.S. New & World Report* ranks 28 graduate and professional programs at VCU among the nation's best graduate schools, including the No. 1 nurse anesthesia program and the No. 1 sculpture program.

The 21,000-plus undergrads spend most of their time on the 90-acre Monroe Park campus in the Fan. In a mix of architecture from the charming and historic, to mid-century mistakes, to brand-new, state-of-the art buildings, the campus houses schools of the arts, business, education, engineering, government and public affairs, humanities and sciences, mass communications, social work, world studies, and life sciences. The 52-acre, downtown Medical College of Virginia campus isn't exactly a slouch. It contains the schools of dentistry, medicine, public health, nursing, pharmacy, and allied health.

From its commuter-school beginnings, VCU has transformed itself into a school where 65 percent of freshmen live on campus. With a student population that's 60 percent female and 40 percent nonwhite, and with more than 1,500 international students, VCU is one of the most diverse student bodies in the country. Its international education programs include having a satellite school of design at VCU Qatar.

Interdisciplinary education is the word at VCU these days. The engineering school was developed to tap into the strengths of the life sciences at VCU, so there's an emphasis on biomedical engineering. The new business school building adjacent to an additional engineering building was built expressly for collaboration, and the Da Vinci Center connects the art students with the business and engineering types. Leonardo would be proud.

The Rams compete in 16 sports in Division I in the CAA conference, and do quite well, winding up in postseason play in men's and women's basketball, baseball, golf, men's soccer, and men's and women's tennis. See more about VCU in the "Area Overview" chapter.

i You can't buy them, but VCU's Cabell Library Special Collections has an amazing Comic Arts Collection that consists of more than 30,000 comic books in an overall collection of 100,000 comics-related items. Check it out Monday through Friday. See www.library.vcu .edu/jbc/speccol for the details.

VIRGINIA UNION UNIVERSITY
1500 N. Lombardy St.
(804) 257-5600
www.vuu.edu

This North Side, historically black, private Baptist university traces its beginnings to a school for freed slaves set up after the Civil War. The school moved to the site of what had been Lumpkin's Jail, a slave jail downtown, and then other sites before settling on its current location in the late 19th century. VUU has grown and prospered, graduating countless alumni who have broken ground for African Americans all over the nation, including Samuel Gravely Jr., the first African-American admiral in the U.S. Navy, Dr. Jean Louise Harris, the first African-American graduate of the Medical College of Virginia, and L. Douglas Wilder—for whom the library is named—the first elected African-American governor in the U.S. VUU's proud history includes students staging a sit-in at downtown lunch counters in 1960 to protest unequal treatment and welcoming then–presidential candidate Barack Obama to campus for a rally during the run-up to the 2008 presidential election.

Dotted with more than two dozen buildings in a mix of Romanesque Revival granite and brick the campus includes the Belgian Friendship Building with its beautiful sculptural relief and the landmark Vann Tower, both originally part of the Belgian Exhibition at the 1939 New York World's Fair.

The 1,200 undergraduate students pursue bachelor's degrees in the schools of business; humanities and social sciences; education, psychology, interdisciplinary studies; and mathematics, science, and technology. Three hundred graduate students work toward master's degrees and doctorates at the Samuel DeWitt Proctor School of Theology, which is part of the Richmond Theological Consortium.

Ashland

RANDOLPH-MACON COLLEGE
(804) 752-7200
www.rmc.edu

Randolph-Macon College, founded in 1830 by the Methodists, is an independent, private college of 1,175 students, tucked onto 110 acres in the picture-perfect town of Ashland. Just 15 miles north of Richmond, the college has a charm not often found in a suburban setting. Three of its brick campus buildings are on the National Register of Historic Places, but it's more than just a pretty place; it's had a chapter of Phi Beta Kappa since 1923.

Right from the start, making connections is emphasized with the First Year Experience, a program that helps freshmen see the interrelations among the disciplines they'll be studying. The average class size is 15, with a student-faculty ratio of 11 to 1, so even with all these statistics, no one is a number here. The academic program offers 29 majors and numerous minors, and the four-one-four semester schedule allows for a monthlong January term that's perfect for internships, study abroad, or an in-depth class.

More than 60 student organizations provide plenty of chances to live a well-rounded, connected life at the college, and 15 teams compete for the Yellow Jackets in Division III athletics.

Chesterfield County

VIRGINIA STATE UNIVERSITY
1 Hayden Dr.
(804) 524-5000
www.vsu.edu

On the edge of our region in the Ettrick area of Chesterfield County, along the Appomattox River adjacent to Petersburg, is one of two land-grant institutions in Virginia, Virginia State University. Founded in 1882, it was the first fully state-supported, four-year institution of higher education for blacks in the U.S., and its proud heritage now includes being named by *U.S. News & World Report* in 2008 and 2009 the top public master's-level Historically Black College and University (HBCU) in the country.

Approximately 5,000 students choose from among the schools of liberal arts and education; engineering; science and technology; business; agriculture; and graduate studies, research, and outreach. Fifty majors are offered on the 236-acre main campus, which features more than four dozen buildings, including 15 dormitories and a 416-acre agricultural research facility. In 2006 VSU inaugurated the Low Income Families With Talented Students (LIFTS) financial-aid program, the first of its kind among HBCUs. LIFTS meets 100 percent of a qualifying student's financial need with a mix of scholarships, grants, and loans.

Jazz great Billy Taylor is a VSU alum, and the school's drum line, the Trojan Explosion, performed at the White House in 2010, likely the first drum line in White House history.

The university competes in the CIAA conference in Division II. Its men's basketball team regularly wins the CIAA championship, and the Lady Trojans were a No. 7 seed in the 2010 NCAA Division II tournament.

COMMUNITY COLLEGES

Community colleges do double duty for the community—offering quality college education for the first two years at half the price of a public university and acting as an economic engine by training local workers in the latest technologies so the region stays competitive.

Continuing Education

Mary Baldwin College in Richmond
(800) 822-2460 or (804) 282-9111
www.mbc.edu/adult

University of Virginia Richmond Center
(804) 662-7464
www.scps.virginia.edu/richmond

Virginia Tech Richmond Center
(804) 662-7288
www.vto.vt.edu and www.richmondvt.edu

---

i An agreement between Virginia's community colleges and more than 20 of Virginia's finest four-year colleges and universities makes a four-year college degree more affordable for students. A student who graduates from a Virginia community college with an associate's degree, a minimum grade-point average, and other requirements is eligible for guaranteed admission to four-year public and private universities in the commonwealth. See www.vccs.edu for more details about the transfer program.

JOHN TYLER COMMUNITY COLLEGE
Chester Campus
13101 Jefferson Davis Hwy.
(804) 796-4000
www.jtcc.edu
Serving 12,608 students at last count, and growing every year, JTCC is one of the five largest community colleges in Virginia. Students take freshman- and sophomore-level classes or study within 60 career-related and technical programs. With an average class size of 19, it's a comfortable entry into

college academics. Eighty-one percent of JTCC students attend part time, and students often transfer to colleges such as James Madison University, VCU, University of Virginia, University of Richmond, and the College of William & Mary. The Midlothian Campus is located at 800 Charter Colony Parkway.

J. SARGEANT REYNOLDS COMMUNITY COLLEGE
Downtown Campus
700 E. Jackson St.
(804) 371-3000
www.reynolds.edu
Offering programs in downtown Richmond, suburban Henrico County, in the country out in Goochland County, and through distance learning, J. Sarge, as it is affectionately known, has grown in just 38 years into the third-largest community college in Virginia. It serves 19,500 students taking for-credit courses, and 15,500 students take classes as part of the Workforce Alliance program. The array of classes and programs is astounding, with a liberal arts curriculum suitable for students to transfer to a four-year school,

occupational and technical courses, horticultural, equine management, mechanics, business, engineering, and so much more. The Parham Road Campus is located at 1651 E. Parham Rd., and the Western Campus is on VA 6 in Goochland.

SEMINARIES

BAPTIST THEOLOGICAL SEMINARY AT RICHMOND
3400 Brook Rd.
(804) 355-8135
www.btsr.edu
Founded in 1991, Baptist Theological Seminary offers master's of divinity and doctoral programs in ministry as well as continuing education to students at its North Side campus and online. Along with a master's of divinity, some students pursue another degree in pastoral counseling or social work in conjunction with VCU. As evidence of its ecumenical leanings, the seminary shares Morton Library at Union Theological Seminary and Presbyterian School of Christian Education.

i Noncredit lifelong-learning courses are available for adults at the Shepherd's Center of Richmond (www.richmondshepcntr.org or 804-355-7282), VCU's Commonwealth Society (www.outreach.vcu.edu), and at UR's Osher Lifelong Learning Institute (www.scs.richmond.edu/osher or 804-287-6608).

UNION THEOLOGICAL SEMINARY AND PRESBYTERIAN SCHOOL OF CHRISTIAN EDUCATION
3401 Brook Rd.
(800) 229-2990
www.union-psce.edu
With roots that go back to 1812, these two venerable institutions officially joined forces in 1997 after working alongside each other educating ministers and lay people for most of the 20th century. The seminary's name is due to change to Union Presbyterian Seminary soon. Though most of the more than 300 students pursuing graduate degrees on the Ginter Park school's historic 56-acre campus are Presbyterian, students and faculty from many denominations are represented here. A recent guest lecturer spoke on "A Buddhist View on the Art of Dying," as part of an annual series devoted to religious understanding and interfaith dialogue. The beautiful, quaint campus is anchored by the beautiful Morton Library, a noted theological library.

HEALTH CARE

People come from all over Virginia—even out of state—to get medical care in Richmond. With its cutting-edge practitioners and facilities, Virginia Commonwealth University Medical Center, the only academic medical center in central Virginia, is the big player in the area, with 500,000 outpatient visits, 30,000 admissions, more than 18,000 surgeries, and 80,000 people treated in the emergency room annually. As a teaching institution with medical, nursing, dental, pharmacy, and allied health schools, the medical center, which includes Medical College of Virginia (MCV) hospitals, produces highly trained health professionals schooled in the latest techniques each year, many of whom stay in the area when they graduate and work out of the area's other hospitals, so excellent medical care is readily available. (The MCV/VCU monikers can be confusing; though a part of Virginia Commonwealth University, the MCV name keeps alive the proud tradition of the Medical College of Virginia that was founded here in 1838.)

For health care, downtown isn't the only game in town. Besides VCU Medical Center, Richmond area hospitals are part of either Bon Secours Richmond Health System or Health Corporation of America Virginia Health System (HCA). The area has several comprehensive, award-winning hospitals and three Level III Trauma Centers, as well as rehabilitation and children's specialty hospitals. Chesterfield, Henrico, and Hanover Counties all have hospitals within their boundaries, but people head in all directions to see doctors and practitioners they like. The private hospitals in the area keep growing, adding space and features, and gaining accolades. Just as VCU Medical Center can, the HCA Virginia and Bon Secours hospitals all over the region can trot out impressive awards, pioneering physicians, talented staff, and state-of-the-art facilities, too.

OVERVIEW

Four of the eleven hospitals below—Retreat, Parham Doctors', Community, and the VA— do not provide a labor and delivery ward, but that still gives pregnant women seven great options for in-hospital childbirth. The hospitals that deliver babies offer a variety of birthing options for new mothers, from maternal/fetal specialists to midwives and doulas. All of the area hospitals seem to be in a constant state of renovation to keep up with the latest medical technologies. Paperless records are the trend in hospitals here, as is valet parking, believe it or not.

The referral list near the end of the chapter is just a starting place; ask friends, neighbors, and coworkers for their go-to list of providers. And though I hope you never need to use the emergency numbers listed at the end, better safe than sorry.

HEALTH DEPARTMENTS

All of the area's health departments strive to promote health and wellness amongst their citizens by providing preventive health care—including immunizations for the H1N1 virus, for instance—by leading public-health initiatives against sexually transmitted diseases and teen pregnancy, and by educating citizens about environmental hazards such as lead paint or mosquito-borne illnesses and communicable diseases. In addition, health departments are involved in emergency preparedness for the community. Many localities have more than one location where services are offered. Check out www.vdh.virginia.gov/lhd to find all the information about the services offered in your locality.

City of Richmond

CLINICAL SERVICES HOME
401 E. Main St.
(804) 482-5500

County Health Departments

CHESTERFIELD HEALTH DEPARTMENT
9501 Lucy Corr Circle
(804) 748-1691

GOOCHLAND HEALTH DEPARTMENT
1800 Sandyhook Rd.
(804) 556-5343

HANOVER HEALTH DEPARTMENT
12312 Washington Hwy., Ashland
(804) 365-4313, (800) 464-5506

EAST HENRICO HEALTH DEPARTMENT
Glen Echo Building
3810 Nine Mile Rd., Henrico
(804) 652-3190

WEST HENRICO HEALTH DEPARTMENT
8600 Dixon Powers Dr., Henrico
(804) 501-4651
www.vdh.virginia.gov/lhd

NEW KENT HEALTH DEPARTMENT
12025 Courthouse Circle, New Kent
(804) 966-9640

POWHATAN HEALTH DEPARTMENT
3908 Old Buckingham Rd, Suite. No. 1
Powhatan
(804) 598-5680

HOSPITALS

BON SECOURS MEMORIAL REGIONAL MEDICAL CENTER
8260 Atlee Rd.
(804) 764-6000
www.bonsecours.com
This 225-bed Hanover County hospital opened in 1998 and has received numerous accolades for its clinical excellence, cardiac care, and stroke treatment, among many other gold stars. HealthGrades recognized the hospital as among the top 5 percent in the U.S. for women's health, awarding it a 2009/2010 Women's Health Excellence Award. Its nursing care is acknowledged as excellent by the Magnet rating from the American Nurses Credentialing Center. Physicians use the da Vinci Surgical System for minimally invasive procedures. Like all Bon Secours hospitals here, Memorial Regional has a no-wait care policy in its emergency room.

BON SECOURS RICHMOND COMMUNITY HOSPITAL
1500 N. 28th St.
(804) 225-1700
www.bonsecours.com

Richmond Community has been providing care to city and East End residents for more than 100 years. Recently renovated, this Church Hill hospital now offers state-of-the-art hospital beds in its 104 private and semiprivate rooms, including a dedicated 36-bed unit for acute psychiatric and detox stabilization. This hospital does not have labor and delivery. It has a no-wait care policy in its emergency room, which offers 24-hour emergency psychiatric evaluation.

BON SECOURS ST. FRANCIS MEDICAL CENTER
13710 St. Francis Blvd.
(804) 594-7300
www.bonsecours.com
This may be the only hospital in the area whose interior design leaves an impression—wow, that's a two-story waterfall in the lobby! With 130 rooms and growing, this newest hospital in the region, built in 2005, serves patients south of the James River, near the intersection of VA 288 and the Powhite Parkway. The 60,000-square-foot Bon Secours Cancer Institute at St. Francis is a freestanding facility that offers medical and radiation oncology as well as support services and thoughtful extras for both patients and families. The emergency room has 21 private bays for patients and a no-wait care policy.

BON SECOURS ST. MARY'S HOSPITAL
5801 Bremo Rd.
(804) 285-2011
www.bonsecours.com
Part of Bon Secours Richmond Health System, St. Mary's has been serving Richmond-area patients since 1966 in its West End location just off Monument Avenue in Henrico County. With 391 private and semiprivate

rooms, this hospital has received many accolades, including being named one of the 2009 Thompson Reuters top 100 hospitals for cardiac care. Its Heart Institute at Reynolds Crossing recently opened, and St. Mary's is a Bariatric Surgery Center of Excellence as well as a Primary Stroke Center. It achieved Magnet Recognition status from the American Nurses Credentialing Center, which recognizes nursing excellence.

i Virginia Blood Services (VBS) provides a reliable blood supply to all of central Virginia's hospitals. To keep up with the need, VBS has four blood-donation locations in the area where you can donate with an appointment: 2825 Emerywood Parkway in the Near West End; 4040-A Cox Rd. in the Far West End; 9200 Arboretum Parkway, Suite 102, in Chesterfield County; and 12212 Bermuda Crossing Lane in Chester. Since operating days and hours vary, call (800) 989-GIFT for details and to make appointments or check out www.vablood.org for more information.

CJW MEDICAL CENTER/CHIPPENHAM HOSPITAL CAMPUS
7101 Jahnke Rd.
(804) 320-3911
www.cjwmedical.com
Known for its cutting-edge Levinson Heart Hospital, Chippenham is one campus of HCA Virginia Health System's CJW Medical Center. The 466-room hospital has a Trauma Level III designation and just opened a Wound Healing Center in 2010 with two hyperbaric oxygen therapy chambers for treatment. It also offers Tucker Psychiatric Pavilion and a pediatric-specific ER as part of its full service emergency room.

CJW MEDICAL CENTER/JOHNSTON-WILLIS HOSPITAL CAMPUS

1401 Johnston-Willis Dr.
(804) 330-2000
www.cjwmedical.com

Part of HCA Virginia Health System's CJW Medical Center, the well-regarded, 292-room Johnston-Willis Hospital is just off Midlothian Turnpike in Chesterfield County. The hospital, a Primary Stroke Center, is also known for its Neuroscience and Gamma Knife Center. Since 1980 the Thomas Johns Cancer Hospital, on the Johnston-Willis campus, has provided the latest in oncology services to patients, and since 2009 its inpatient and outpatient care have been combined in a new building designed to make cancer care as convenient and comfortable as possible. Special services include a Cancer Recovery Exercise Program. Also in the building is the Foot and Hand Spa, the city's only medical spa that focuses on hands and feet.

HENRICO DOCTORS' HOSPITAL

1602 Skipwith Rd.
(804) 289-4500
www.henricodoctors.com

This 340-bed hospital is undergoing a $100 million expansion that will remake several departments, including the Emergency Department, Ambulatory Surgery Center, and Cancer Specialty Clinics. Parham Doctors' Hospital and Retreat Doctors' Hospital are considered (by their PR department anyway) to be campuses of Henrico Doctors' Hospital, which has been providing high-quality care to area patients for three dozen years.

PARHAM DOCTORS' HOSPITAL

7700 E. Parham Rd.
(804) 747-5600
www.henricodoctors.com

Another part of the HCA Virginia Health System, this facility is home to an Express ER for minor injuries and illnesses as a part of its full-service emergency room. Its recently opened Orthopaedic Hospital features a Joint and Spine Center that combines the latest technology with hotel-like amenities to ease the stress of surgery. It does not offer inpatient obstetrics care.

RETREAT DOCTORS' HOSPITAL

2621 Grove Ave.
(804) 254-5100
www.henricodoctors.com

The oldest hospital in Richmond, this Fan facility is considered a campus of Henrico Doctors' Hospital and is part of the HCA Virginia Health System. All of its 227 rooms are private, and it has a full-service emergency room. Same-day appointments are available for outpatient diagnostic imaging, but you'll have to have your baby somewhere else; there is no obstetrics ward here.

HUNTER H. MCGUIRE VETERANS AFFAIRS MEDICAL CENTER

1201 Broad Rock Blvd.
(804) 675-5000
www.richmond.va.gov

Serving veterans since 1946, McGuire is a 409-bed teaching and research hospital on Richmond's South Side. It provides medical and surgical care for more than 200,000 veterans from central and southern Virginia and parts of North Carolina. One of only four poly-trauma rehabilitation centers in the U.S., McGuire opened its transitional rehab center in 2010, especially important for veterans of Iraq and Afghanistan. Telephone care is available 24/7 for veterans at (804) 784-8381.

VIRGINIA COMMONWEALTH
UNIVERSITY MEDICAL CENTER
1250 E. Marshall St.
(804) 828-9000
www.vcuhealth.org

One of the leading academic medical centers in the country and the only Level 1 Trauma Center in central Virginia, this busy complex (its emergency room treats 80,000 patients a year) includes the 779-bed MCV hospitals, the Ambulatory Care Center, Massey Cancer Center, numerous outpatient clinics downtown and at suburban locations, and the health sciences schools of VCU, with the country's top-ranked nurse anesthesia program. Singled out by *U.S. News & World Report* in its "America's Best Hospitals" listings for 2007–2009, VCU has recently opened the only Critical Care Hospital in Virginia. It features state-of-the-art intensive-care units to treat the most seriously ill and injured patients. The medical center's 600 physician-faculty group, MCV Physicians, includes nationally and internationally respected leaders in health care and provides top-notch care in more than 200 specialty areas. One such area is the nationally recognized VCU Pauley Heart Center, a pioneer in "the bridge to transplant" implantable total artificial heart, which gives hope to otherwise terminal patients and extends their lives while they wait for a suitable donor heart to become available.

The Medical Center's nursing care was recognized as a Magnet site by the American Nurses Credentialing Center (ANCC). VCU is especially acclaimed for burn care, organ transplants, stroke care, head and spinal-cord trauma, and cancer care. VCU's renowned Massey Cancer Center, a National Cancer Institute–designated cancer center, even has a healing rooftop garden for patients, families, and staff.

VCU's largest satellite location at 9000 Stony Point Parkway in Stony Point (804-628-2374) offers outpatients easy access to much of the same high-caliber medical care and treatment as its downtown facilities. Stony Point is the home of VCU's Women's Health Center (a nationally recognized model), a branch of the Massey Cancer Center, and many more specialists and therapies, bringing VCU's innovative, proactive, and caring approach to a suburban location with free parking. Hanover County also is home to a satellite facility of Massey.

VCU's Hospital Hospitality House

The Hospital Hospitality House is a "home away from home" for families of patients in VCU Medical Center. Just 3 blocks away from VCU in a renovated hotel, HHH provides comfortable setting where guests can accommodate their own schedules. Rooms include a private bathroom and a fully stocked kitchen and pantry, Volunteers provide all the touches of home for out-of-towners, those outpatients and their families receiving continuing treatment, and same-day surgery patients. Guests must be 14 or older to stay and are asked to contribute what they can toward the cost of the room. Check out www.hhhrichmond.org or call (804) 828-6901 for more information.

Emergency Phone Numbers

Adult Protective Services Hotline
(888) 832-3858

Animal Control (City of Richmond)
(804) 646-5573

Chesterfield County 24-hour Crisis Line
(804) 748-6356

Child Protective Services Hotline
(800) 552-7096

Richmond Behavioral Health Authority Crisis Hotline (mental health)
(804) 819-4100 (City of Richmond)

YWCA Crisis and Counseling
(804) 643-0888 Richmond Hotline
(804) 796-3066 Chesterfield Hotline

Family Violence and Sexual Assault Hotline
(800) 838-8238

National Domestic Violence Hotline
(800) 799-SAFE

National Sexual Assault Hotline
(800) 656-4673

Poison Control Hotline
(800) 222-1222

Police/Ambulance
911 (emergency)
(804) 646-5100 (City of Richmond non-emergency)
(804) 205-3912

ROSMY 24/7 Youth Support Line (for sexual-minority youth and their parents)
(888) 644-4390

Runaway Hotline
(800) 621-4000

Suicide Prevention
(800) SUICIDE (784-2433)

SPECIALTY MEDICAL CENTERS

CHILDREN'S HOSPITAL OF RICHMOND
2924 Brook Rd.
(804) 228-5818
www.chrichmond.org

Children's Hospital, Pediatric Specialty Services joined VCU Health System in 2010 to become Children's Hospital of Richmond, a multispecialty pediatric hospital that provides specialized care and therapeutic services on an inpatient, outpatient, and day-patient basis. Helping children for more than 90 years, the core focus of the hospital is now five-pronged: a pediatric therapy program, pediatric dental program, transitional care unit for children and young adults, a children's feeding program for those whose medical condition affects their growth, and the multispecialty clinics for chronic illnesses such as cerebral palsy, muscular dystrophy, and spina bifida. The hospital also runs four therapy centers in Central Virginia, including one in Chesterfield County and one in Henrico County.

HEALTHSOUTH REHABILITATION HOSPITAL OF VIRGINIA
5700 Fitzhugh Ave.
(804) 673-4434
www.healthsouthrichmond.com

This 40-bed acute-care hospital that treats orthopedic, neurological, pulmonary, and other conditions has private and semiprivate rooms in the West End near both St. Mary's and Henrico Doctors' Hospitals. It provides physical, occupational, and speech-language therapies for patients on the mend on an inpatient or outpatient basis. Health-South has several other area clinics and rehab centers throughout the region. Check their Web site for more details.

SHELTERING ARMS PHYSICAL REHABILITATION, INPATIENT AND OUTPATIENT CENTERS
(877) 56-REHAB
www.shelteringarms.com
Whether patients are recovering from joint replacement surgery, learning to live with amputations or multiple sclerosis, or coming back from a stroke, Sheltering Arms has both inpatient and outpatient treatment available. Inpatient care is either at their site on the Memorial Regional Hospital or on the St. Francis campus. A full range of outpatient treatment, rehab, and wellness is available at several sites throughout the area. See the Web site for details and locations.

REFERRAL SERVICES

BON SECOURS PHYSICIAN LOCATOR
(804) 359-WELL
www.bonsecours.com

HCA HOSPITAL REFERRAL (HENRICO, RETREAT, CJW)
(804) 320-DOCS
www.cjwmedical.com

VIRGINIA COMMONWEALTH UNIVERSITY MEDICAL CENTER PHYSICIAN REFERRAL SERVICE
(804) 628-2374
www.vcuhealth.org/physicians

VIRGINIA LEAGUE FOR PLANNED PARENTHOOD
201 N. Hamilton St., Richmond
(804) 355-4358

INDEX